# TOTTENHAM HOTSPUR
## Player by Player

TO SIGNED

IVAN PONTING
with TOM MORGAN

KNOW!
THE SCORE

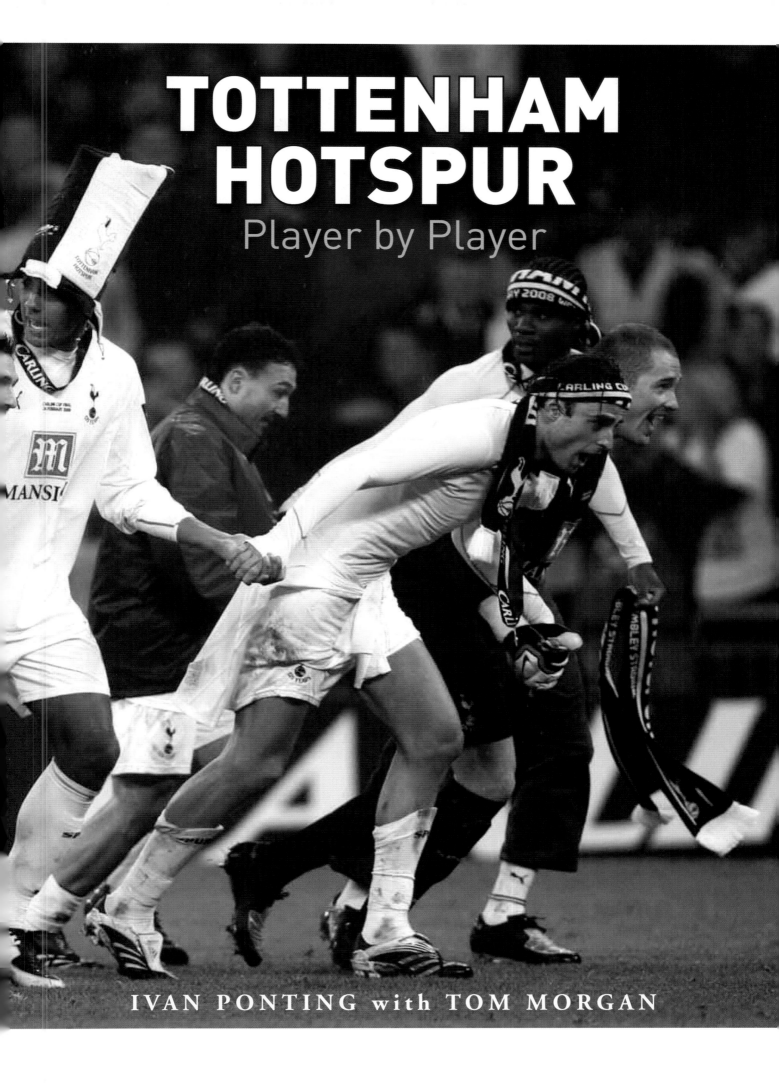

# TOTTENHAM HOTSPUR
## Player by Player

IVAN PONTING with TOM MORGAN

# DEDICATION

This book is dedicated to Glyn Church, an ancient chum who cheered Spurs to the double in 1961, and to Les Gold, another good friend with Tottenham in his heart.

# ACKNOWLEDGMENTS

The authors would like to thank the following: Andy Cowie of Colorsport, who supplied nearly all the pictures; designer Trevor Hartley; Nigel Dando; Quita Morgan; Les Gold; Nick Manning; John Matthews; Francis McInally; Tom Hodson; Charlotte Dunlavey; Colin Calderwood; Ian Russell; Tom Buchan; Tom Cunningham; publishers Simon Lowe and Tony Lyons. For earlier contributions: Steve Perryman, Dave Mackay, Cliff Jones, Alan Mullery, Pat Jennings, Peter Taylor, Charles Richards, Geoff Simms; Bob Goodwin, author of the splendid *Tottenham Hotspur: The Complete Record*. Finally, as ever, Pat, Rosie and Joe Ponting.

# ILLUSTRATIONS

First published in 1993 by Guinness
Second edition published by Hamlyn in 1998


Published in 2008 by Know The Score Books


Design by Trevor Hartley
Printed & Bound In Poland
www.polskabook.co.uk

ISBN 978-1-84818-301-8

# INTRODUCTION

It is time for the cockerel to crow again. That was the final line of the introduction to the second edition of this book, written ten years ago. Sadly, over the course of the subsequent decade, a periodically jaded rooster managed only a few brave but intermittent squawks which tended to peter out in strangled discord and disappointment. But eventually, under the shabbily treated Martin Jol, there issued the beginnings of a healthier, more melodious, altogether more vibrant note. Now, with the shrewd and ambitious Juande Ramos at the Tottenham helm, the long-suffering White Hart Lane legions have genuine reason to believe that a proud, full-throated chorus is building, and that it is set to echo around the football world. Spurs haven't quite reached Glory Glory Hallelujah territory yet, but at least they are on the march again, with a place among the Premier League elite firmly in their sights. What more appropriate juncture, then, to embark on the third incarnation of *Tottenham Hotspur Player By Player*?

The book has expanded in two directions. Last time I attempted to do justice, in words and pictures, to every man who had kicked a ball for Spurs in senior competition between 1958, when the great Bill Nicholson accepted the managerial reins, and 1998, when Christian Gross held sway. Now the story is extended to 2008 by taking in another decade's worth of stars and lesser lights, but also we make a trip into the north Londoners' hallowed past to encompass Arthur Rowe's ground-breaking push-and-run maestros, who bestrode the English game so majestically in the early 1950s.

In addition, there is another new dimension in the form of an entry on every footballer to wear the Tottenham shirt in Football League and FA Cup matches since the club was formed, together with concise profiles of some of the old-time heroes, the likes of Arthur Grimsdell, Jimmy Seed, Fanny Walden and Jimmy Dimmock.

Although the book has evolved and mushroomed in scope since its inception, still the core of it concerns the period since 1958, my original kick-off point, which holds a double significance for me, one part obvious, the other part personal. Most important is the Nicholson connection, but also it coincided with the onset of my own addiction to the game, which consumed me in early boyhood and has never loosened its hold. Since those far-off days I have been an avid spectator at grounds all over the country, and the evidence of my own eyes has been a central pillar of *Player By Player*. Also I have drawn extensively on the reminiscences of former Tottenham footballers – Steve Perryman was particularly helpful and illuminating – and of some of the most knowledgeable and opinionated supporters it has been my pleasure to meet.

A word of welcome is appropriate here for my new co-author, Tom Morgan, a gifted young journalist and a lifelong Spurs fanatic who offers a fresh and lively take on the new generation of players, while exhibiting a sensitive feel for the rich White Hart Lane tradition which has built up steadily over more than a century.

Then there are the statistics. Alongside our profiles of the footballers we offer the basic facts of games played, with substitute appearances in brackets, and goals scored. The Tottenham figures refer to all senior matches for the club (a breakdown for each competition begins on page 300) but under the heading of 'Other Clubs' the appearances and goals are for League games only. The dates in large type refer to the seasons in which the player appeared in the first team, not when he joined or left the club. Under 'Honours' we have included only those gained at Tottenham, except in the cases of individual awards and international caps, the figures for which cover each man's career to date. Transfer fees are unofficial, being those favoured in the press. All statistics are complete to 21 May 2008.

As to the club's future, it looks brighter than for many a long year. Guided by an enterprising and imaginative manager who is also a proven winner, and with a new-look team gilded by exciting signings such as the Croatian prodigy Luka Modric, Spurs are ready for a realistic tilt at breaking the monopoly of the so-called 'big four'. If the dream comes true, and the cockerel does indeed crow once more from the top of the pile, I hope there will be a fourth edition of *Tottenham Hotspur Player By Player* to chronicle the triumph. Here's to that happy day!

**Ivan Ponting**,
Chewton Mendip,
*August 2008*

# CONTENTS

## PLAYER BY PLAYER

The Early Years .............. 18
The New Dawn ............ 28

THE MANAGERS
Clive Allen ..................... 16
Jimmy Anderson ........... 31
Ossie Ardiles ................ 12
Keith Burkinshaw ......... 10
Gerry Francis ................ 13
George Graham.............. 14
Christian Gross ............. 13
Trevor Hartley.............. 11
Glenn Hoddle ............... 14
Chris Hughton ............. 13
Martin Jol ..................... 16
Doug Livermore ............ 12
Terry Neill................... 10
Bill Nicholson ................ 8
Steve Perryman............. 12
David Pleat ................... 11
Juande Ramos .............. 17
Arthur Rowe ................. 30
Jacques Santini ............. 15
Peter Shreeves.............. 10
Terry Venables.............. 11

THE PLAYERS
Milenko Acimovic........ 248
Milija Aleksic .............. 128
Clive Allen .................. 160
Les Allen ...................... 72
Paul Allen.................... 170
Rory Allen.................... 230
Darren Anderton........ 206
Steve Archibald ........... 138
Ossie Ardiles ............... 136
Chris Armstrong ......... 220
Gerry Armstrong......... 127
Benoit Assou-Ekotto .... 279
Thimothee Atouba....... 259

Dean Austin ................. 188
Espen Baardsen ........... 214
Eddie Baily................... 36
Peter Baker .................. 54
Gareth Bale ................. 289
Andy Barcham ........... 267
Nick Barmby .............. 195
Lee Barnard................ 267
Ken Barton .................. 84
Phil Beal...................... 108
Stuart Beavon ............. 146
Les Bennett ................. 38
Darren Bent ................ 294
Dimitar Berbatov ........ 290
Gudni Bergsson ........... 182
Nicola Berti ................ 230
Danny Blanchflower ...... 48
Jon Blondel ................. 266
Kevin-Prince Boateng... 295
Dennis Bond ................ 90
Andy Booth ................ 242
Mark Bowen .............. 156
Robert Brace ............... 147
Garry Brady ............... 231
Alan Brazil ................. 145
Garry Brooke ............. 149
Johnny Brooks ............. 47
Noel Brotherston ........ 146
Bill Brown .................... 64
Laurie Brown .............. 82
Michael Brown............ 255
Roy Brown .................. 85
Ron Burgess ................ 32
Guy Butters................ 173
Goran Bunjevcevic ....... 245

Colin Calderwood........ 216
Sol Campbell .............. 218
Stephen Carr .............. 212
Michael Carrick .......... 272

Darren Caskey ............ 196
Radek Cerny ............... 279
John Chiedozie............ 152
Pascal Chimbonda........ 288
Martin Chivers ............. 98
Nico Claesen ............... 162
Jamie Clapham ........... 232
Harry Clarke ............... 39
Ray Clarke ................... 85
Eddie Clayton ............... 77
Ray Clemence ............. 154
Stephen Clemence........ 228
Shaun Close ............... 147
Ralph Coates............... 116
Allan Cockram ............ 147
Jimmy Collins.............. 84
John Collins ................. 85
Peter Collins ................. 96
Alfie Conn ................. 121
Richard Cooke ............ 148
Pat Corbett ................. 147
Ian Crook.................... 156
Garth Crooks .............. 140
Ian Culverhouse .......... 147
Jason Cundy................ 186

Barry Daines ............... 127
Stephane Dalmat.......... 249
Calum Davenport ........ 274
Edgar Davids............... 282
Simon Davies .............. 241
Sean Davis .................. 263
Michael Dawson ......... 276
Kevin Dearden ............ 233
Jermain Defoe ............. 264
Dorian Dervite............ 267
Ally Dick..................... 148
Mike Dillon ................. 97
Jimmy Dimmock .......... 27
Ted Ditchburn .............. 42

Billy Dodge.................... 84
Gary Doherty.............. 240
Jose Dominguez .......... 228
Jason Dozzell.............. 194
Ilie Dumitrescu ........... 200
Len Duquemin............. 35
John Duncan............... 119
Dave Dunmore ............ 46
Gordon Durie ............. 193
Terry Dyson ................. 74

Justin Edinburgh......... 189
Erik Edman ................ 258
Mike England .............. 102
Matthew Etherington... 240
Ray Evans.................... 101

Chris Fairclough.......... 167
Mark Falco.................. 132
Neale Fenn ................. 231
Terry Fenwick ............. 172
Les Ferdinand............. 224
Ruel Fox..................... 208
Steffen Freund ............ 236

Tony Galvin ................ 143
Anthony Gardner........ 250
Peter Garland ............. 232
Paul Gascoigne .......... 174
Hossam Ghaly............. 287
Terry Gibson .............. 145
Gilberto ..................... 299
Alan Gilzean................ 94
David Ginola .............. 226
John Gorman .............. 122
Richard Gough ........... 157
Mark Gower................ 266
Andy Gray ................. 186
Phil Gray.................... 232
Jimmy Greaves ............. 78
Arthur Grimsdell........... 26
Chris Gunter............... 296

Ken Hancock ................ 85
Tommy Harmer............ 52
Mike Hazard .............. 142
Ian Hendon................. 232
John Hendry .............. 182
Ron Henry................... 62
Danny Hill ................. 231
Johnny Hills ............... 50
Glenn Hoddle ............. 158
Steve Hodge ............... 163
Lee Hodges ................ 233
Phil Holder ................ 100

John Hollowbread .......... 76
Jimmy Holmes ............. 122
Mel Hopkins ................. 51
Scott Houghton ........... 177
David Howells ............. 210
Roger Hoy ..................... 85
Tom Huddlestone ........ 292
Chris Hughton............. 131
Alan Hutton................. 298

Philip Ifil..................... 267
Jim Iley ........................ 50
Jeff Ireland ................... 84
Steffen Iversen ............. 221

Johnnie Jackson........... 254
Jermaine Jenas............. 280
David Jenkins............... 90
Pat Jennings ................ 110
Neil Johnson ................ 82
Chris Jones.................. 120
Cliff Jones ................... 68

Younes Kaboul ............. 287
Frederic Kanoute.......... 253
Robbie Keane.............. 256
Andy Keeley................. 146
Kasey Keller ................ 246
Stephen Kelly .............. 262
Mark Kendall .............. 126
David Kerslake............. 199
Ledley King.................. 260
Joe Kinnear ................. 86
Jurgen Klinsmann ........ 204
Cyril Knowles .............. 92
Paul Konchesky ........... 249
Willem Korsten............ 242

John Lacy.................... 133
Colin Lee ................... 126
Terry Lee...................... 85
Lee Young-Pyo ............ 278
Aaron Lennon ............. 284
Oyvind Leonhardsen.... 234
David Leworthy .......... 147
Gary Lineker............... 178
Roy Low ...................... 84

Gary Mabbutt............. 180
Mbulelo Mabizela ....... 254
Don McAllister ........... 123
David McDonald ........ 233
Dave McEwen............. 266
Chris McGrath............ 118
Dave Mackay ............... 66
Ged McMahon ........... 196
Neil McNab ................ 125
Paul McVeigh ............. 233
Paul Mahorn ............... 233
Steed Malbranque ........ 293
Tony Marchi ................ 59
Dean Marney ............... 249

Giorgio Mazzon ........... 146
Les Medley.................. 38
Terry Medwin ............... 58
Pedro Mendes .............. 263
Johnny Metgod ........... 162
Mido......................... 271
Paul Miller ................. 130
Bobby Mimms ............. 163
Jeff Minton ................. 232
Ian Moores.................. 118
Paul Moncur ............... 177
Paul Moran ................. 177
Roger Morgan.............. 91
Alan Mullery................. 88
Danny Murphy ........... 275

Nayim ....................... 176
Terry Naylor............... 112
Jimmy Neighbour ........ 105
Stuart Nethercott ......... 196
Noureddine Naybet..... 258
Bill Nicholson .............. 39
Allan Nielsen................ 223
Roger Nilsen ............... 266
Maurice Norman .......... 60

Jamie O'Hara ............... 296
Gary O'Reilly.............. 149
Keith Osgood.............. 113
Tim O'Shea ................ 147

Noe Pamarot ............... 259
Tony Parks .................. 152
Jimmy Pearce .............. 104
Chris Perry.................. 235
Steve Perryman ........... 134
Martin Peters............... 106
John Piercy.................. 266
Ron Piper .................... 84
Steve Pitt...................... 85
Andy Polston............... 232
John Polston................ 173
Gica Popescu............... 201
Derek Possee ................ 80
Helder Postiga ............. 248
Gus Poyet................... 247
John Pratt................... 114

Paul Price ................... 144
Alf Ramsey................... 34
Grzegorz Rasiak ........... 270
Sergei Rebrov .............. 243
Jamie Redknapp........... 252
Andy Reid ................. 275
Dean Richards.............. 251
Rohan Ricketts............. 255
George Robb................ 44
Graham Roberts........... 150
Jimmy Robertson .......... 83
Martin Robinson........... 146
Paul Robinson.............. 268
Steve Robinson............. 233
Mark Robson .............. 232
Ricardo Rocha............. 287
Ronny Rosenthal.......... 198
Wayne Routledge ......... 270
Neil Ruddock.............. 190
Hugh Ryden................. 46

Moussa Saib ................ 229
Vinny Samways............ 166
Frank Saul .................... 81
John Scales ................. 229
Kevin Scott ................. 199
Steve Sedgley .............. 183
Jimmy Seed.................. 26
Hans Segers................ 266
Fred Sharpe ................. 84
Teddy Sheringham ....... 202
Tim Sherwood ............. 239
Andy Sinton................. 209
Jamie Slabber .............. 266
Steve Slade ................. 233

Bobby Smith ................. 56
Gordon Smith............. 144
Ian Smith ................... 146
John Smith ................... 76
Graeme Souness ......... 100
Peter Southey ............. 146
Paul Stalteri ............... 274
Brian Statham ............. 167
Micky Stead ............... 126
Gary Stevens ............. 168
Paul Stewart ............... 184
Mark Stimson ............. 232
Alfie Stokes ................. 45
Neil Sullivan ............... 244

Adel Taarabt ............... 295
Teemu Tainio ............. 283
Mauricio Taricco ......... 237
Peter Taylor ............... 124
Ben Thatcher ............. 244
Alton Thelwell ........... 242
Danny Thomas ........... 153
Mitchell Thomas......... 169
Erik Thorstvedt .......... 197
Kazuyuki Toda ........... 267
Paolo Tramezzani......... 234
Andy Turner ............... 198
David Tuttle............... 182

Pat Van Den Hauwe..... 187
Ramon Vega ............... 222
Terry Venables............. 87
Ricky Villa ................. 129

Chris Waddle ............. 164
Fanny Walden .............. 27
Steve Walford ............. 146
Ian Walker................. 217
Paul Walsh ................. 192
Sonny Walters ............. 38
Tony Want ................... 97
Kevin Watson.............. 233
Simon Webster............ 147
Keith Weller ............... 80
John White ................... 70
Clive Wilson ............... 215
Jonathan Woodgate...... 297
Roy Woolcott............... 85
Len Worley .................. 84

Mark Yeates................. 267
Terry Yorath ............... 128
Luke Young................. 238
Willie Young ............... 121

Bobby Zamora ........... 248
Christian Ziege ........... 245
Reto Ziegler ............... 262
Didier Zokora ............. 286

STATISTICS
Players' Records........... 300

# BILL NICHOLSON

## MANAGER October 1958 → September 1974

Desptite the avalanche of glib superlatives with which sporting heroes tend to be engulfed, genuine and universally acknowledged greatness remains as properly rare in football as in any other sphere of life. But there can be no doubt that Bill Nicholson attained it with Tottenham Hotspur in 1960/61.

He was the architect of a team as exhilarating, as balanced, as downright beautiful as any British combination in living memory, a glorious fusion of sumptuous skill and explosive athleticism which became the first in the 20th century to win the coveted League and FA Cup double.

Yet in scaling that lofty pinnacle relatively early in his managerial career, the gruff, deep-thinking, inscrutable Yorkshireman had condemned himself to perpetual frustration in his never-ending quest for soccer perfection.

The names of the class of '61 read like a sacred litany to Spurs fans of that era: Brown; Baker, Henry; Blanchflower, Norman, Mackay; Jones, White, Smith, Allen and Dyson. By no means all of them were 'great' players individually; indeed, of the 11, only wing-halves Danny Blanchflower and Dave Mackay, winger Cliff Jones and inside-forward John White merit anything approaching such an accolade.

But Nicholson's achievement lay in blending disparate talents into a magnificent whole. An impeccable judge of character and ability, he bought brilliantly, got the best out of players already at his disposal and coached imaginatively. The chemistry was right and the rest followed, often sublimely.

The glitter and gloss of White Hart Lane were far removed from Nicholson's beginnings, between the wars in Scarborough, as the second youngest of a hansom cab driver's nine children. Growing up during the Depression, he became so used to austerity that it was to remain integral to his way of life even when he was earning the wages of a top manager.

Indeed, while his star players would inhabit lavish homes in the north London commuter belt, Nicholson didn't move from a modest end-of-terrace house close to Tottenham's ground, though that was due only partly to his simple tastes and lack of ostentation. The most pressing reason was his utter dedication to his work, which was so near that he could – and usually did – burn the midnight oil disposing of routine matters neglected during the day's tracksuit toil.

Having completed an eminent playing career as a Spurs wing-half (see page 39) Nicholson joined the coaching staff in 1954, stepped up to become assistant to manager Jimmy Anderson three years later, then took the top job in October 1958. His reign got under way with an astonishing 10-4 home victory over Everton, but Bill's head was not for turning. He realised there was much work to be done on a flawed team and suffered early setbacks as Spurs flirted with relegation that season, eventually scraping narrowly to safety.

Before long, though, he got it right, extracting the absolute best from Blanchflower – as romantic and loquacious as Nicholson was dour and taciturn – and the rest as he pieced together that most lovely of sides. A stern realist, he was ever a grudging dispenser of praise, and it grated on some observers that even in the hour of his most memorable triumph, when defeat of Leicester City at Wembley in 1961 secured football's most famous double, he appeared unable to relax and enjoy the moment.

Instead he bemoaned the fact that, in a disappointing match marred by injury to Leicester's Len Chalmers, his Spurs had not shown the world how well they could *really* play.

That summer he strengthened his side by the acquisition of Jimmy Greaves from AC Milan and in 1961/62 Tottenham retained the FA Cup, reached the semi-final of the European Cup before losing narrowly and controversially to Benfica, and finished third in the title race. In 1962/63 they were First Division runners-up and, more momentously still, became the first British club to lift a European trophy, the Cup Winners' Cup.

Yet that milestone 5-1 annihilation of Atletico Madrid in Rotterdam proved to be a valedictory triumph. The team broke up, as even the best must do, and the manager set about rebuilding.

He did so ably, maintaining the Tottenham tradition for attractive football and backing his judgement with a series of big-money signings; but alas, having scaled Olympian heights with his first creation, the only way was down.

True, with victories in the FA Cup (1967), the League Cup (1971 and 1973) and the UEFA Cup (1972) Spurs were hardly on short rations compared with most other clubs, but Nicholson never again presided over a Championship triumph and his teams resembled mere mortals compared with what had gone before.

Inevitably, in view of his perfectionist's outlook, he became increasingly dissatisfied, a situation which defeat in the 1974 UEFA Cup Final did nothing to relieve. Still, few people imagined that the energetic 55-year-old was on the verge of quitting the job with which he had become

synonymous, yet in September 1974, after a run of dismal results, he did just that.

In truth, Bill was reacting not merely to current circumstances at White Hart Lane, but to what he considered were disturbing trends in football. He despised the onset of functional modern modes of play, was out of tune with the new, precocious breed of player, was disenchanted at the creeping commercialisation of his beloved game and sickened by widespread hooliganism.

Though the board and players tried to get him to change his mind, in the end Nicholson's departure was handled clumsily. Upset that he couldn't choose his successor – he wanted Blanchflower – he took a brief rest (during which he was awarded an OBE) before spending a year as an adviser to West Ham United.

Happily, 'Bill Nick' was back at the Lane in 1975, having been requested to return as a consultant by new boss Keith Burkinshaw. He continued to fill that role under successive managers until 1991, after which he became club president until his death in 2004.

# TERRY NEILL

## MANAGER: September 1974 → June 1976

Managing Spurs is a demanding proposition in any circumstances; for Terry Neill in the autumn of 1974 it was a task of particularly awesome magnitude. Though he arrived at the Lane fresh from guiding the fortunes of Hull City, and had been player-boss of Northern Ireland, he had spent the bulk of his career as an Arsenal player. Thus, in the fans' eyes, he was a Highbury man to the core, a stigma which he never overcame.

Articulate, bubbly and easy-going, Neill offered a striking contrast in style to his illustrious predecessor. However, at 32 he found himself in charge of footballers of his own generation, some of whom had achieved far more than he, and the Irishman found it difficult to command universal respect. Having taken over a side in decline, and unable to compete at the top end of the transfer market – he was thwarted in efforts to sign both Johan Cruyff and Charlie George – he struggled.

Relegation was narrowly avoided in his first season, and though 1975/76 saw an improvement to ninth position in the League and a run to the League Cup semi-final, his relationship with the board deteriorated. That summer he resigned, following a dispute over players' bonuses, and two weeks later Terry Neill was back in his spiritual home as the new manager of Arsenal.

# KEITH BURKINSHAW

## MANAGER: July 1976 → May 1984

Let there be no doubt: Keith Burkinshaw can be proud of his record at White Hart Lane. After stepping up from the position of coach under Terry Neill to inherit a lacklustre side, he couldn't prevent Spurs dropping into Division Two at the end of his first term in charge, but the board, to their enormous credit, retained faith in the honest, downbeat Yorkshireman.

Promotion in 1977/78 justified that decision, then the bold acquisition of Argentinians Ossie Ardiles and Ricky Villa caught the imagination of the soccer world and raised the curtain on one of the most stirring periods in Tottenham's post-war history. Other high-quality performers were acquired as Burkinshaw assembled an attractive squad which, though never consistent enough to take the Championship, was to lift the FA Cup in 1981 and 1982 and the UEFA Cup in 1984.

However, he became unhappy with boardroom politics and announced during 1983/84 that he would resign at season's end, thus departing on the wings of European triumph. Essentially a player's man, despite a much-publicised tiff with Steve Archibald, he had earned widespread respect in the game, and went on to coach in the Middle East before becoming Ardiles' number-two at West Bromwich Albion.

# PETER SHREEVES

## MANAGER: June 1984 → May 1986
## & July 1991 → May 1992

Peter Shreeves remains the most underrated manager in Spurs' modern history. Quiet, uncharismatic and an almost shadowy figure in the public eye, he tends to be brushed aside as a twice-sacked failure, yet that is far too harsh for a final judgement.

After contributing hugely to Tottenham's early-1980s success as coach under Keith Burkinshaw, Shreeves landed the top job in 1984/85 and that term led the club's most (only) meaningful title challenge since the prime of Bill Nicholson. Indeed, but for injuries in the spring the Championship pennant might have been fluttering over White Hart Lane, and Shreeves would have been placed on a pedestal. Instead there followed a disappointing campaign, and though he remained in high esteem among the players, who approved of his emphasis on skill and imaginative training routines, he was axed.

After coaching stints elsewhere, he had another chance in 1991/92, when Terry Venables opted to concentrate on business affairs. Not surprisingly with the club still reeling from recent turmoil, the side slumped and, as cynics had predicted, Peter Shreeves it was who paid the price. True, some of his selections mystified the fans; possibly he was 'too nice'; but Spurs knew their man well when they appointed him, and it's hard to see his second coming as anything other than a hiding to nothing.

# DAVID PLEAT

MANAGER: May 1986 → October 1987
CARETAKER MANAGER: September 1998 → October 1998,
March 2001 → April 2001, September 2003 → May 2004

David Pleat, it seemed, was on the right track. In his first season at White Hart Lane, the former Luton boss lifted Tottenham to third place in the First Division (admittedly they never looked likely to win it), and took them to the FA Cup Final and a League Cup semi-final, both of which they lost after holding the upper hand.

He had bought boldly (notably new club captain Richard Gough), boosted the confidence and performance of Chris Waddle, demonstrated tactical flair – the five-man midfield that so ably supported prolific goal-scorer Clive Allen was but one example of his innovative thinking – and, a factor not to be underestimated, he picked well-balanced sides that made sense to the supporters. Many believed Pleat was the man to make Spurs great again; sadly their theory was never to be tested. That summer he was the subject of lurid newspaper allegations about his private life, but appeared to have survived them, and Spurs made a promising start to 1987/88. Then a second wave of scandal in the autumn proved too much and Pleat resigned, later serving Leicester unsuccessfully before returning to Luton.

When he had gone Spurs nosedived, begging the question: were they already on the verge of decline or did his departure precipitate the slide? In January 1998, after a stint at Sheffield Wednesday, Pleat rejoined Tottenham as director of football and found himself holding the reins as caretaker boss three times before he departed in July 2005 – for a month when Christian Gross was sacked, for two weeks after the dismissal of George Graham, and for most of 2003/04 after Glenn Hoddle was shown the door. Each time he was a safe pair of hands in testing circumstances.

# TREVOR HARTLEY

CARETAKER MANAGER: October 1987 → November 1987

When David Pleat departed, first-team affairs were placed briefly in the hands of assistant boss Trevor Hartley, who was helped by coach Doug Livermore. It was a difficult time at the Lane with the team in poor heart, and results were dreadful. Then came Terry Venables.

# TERRY VENABLES

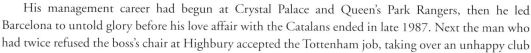

MANAGER: December 1987 → May 1991
CHIEF EXECUTIVE: May 1991 → June 1993

Terry Venables remains a unique figure in British football. An inspiringly innovative coach who became a successful manager, he went on to sink his life savings – and then some – into the club he had loved since childhood, claiming as his reward the total top-to-bottom control he had craved for so long. How sad that it should all terminate in tears.

His management career had begun at Crystal Palace and Queen's Park Rangers, then he led Barcelona to untold glory before his love affair with the Catalans ended in late 1987. Next the man who had twice refused the boss's chair at Highbury accepted the Tottenham job, taking over an unhappy club heading for the foot of the old First Division. Venables led Spurs to a mid-table finish, then invested boldly for the future, buying Paul Gascoigne and Paul Stewart. Now his side looked attractive but as Chris Waddle was sold and Gary Lineker bought against a background of mounting cash problems, it was amazing that he was able to juggle his attention between business and football.

The irrepressible Venables deserved monumental credit for the FA Cup triumph of 1991, and the combination of courage and acumen he displayed under intense pressure during the club takeover that same year is a source of pure wonder. Invariably approachable and chirpily streetwise, he was adept at handling the media and it was a tribute to that Cockney nous that he never received a truly savage press mauling, no matter how low Tottenham's fortunes dipped.

Having taken a season off from coaching in 1991/92, he climbed back into his tracksuit thereafter to considerable effect. His ambitions to run the club off the pitch as well as on it were challenged by chairman Alan Sugar in the summer of 1993, a confrontation that ended with his summer sacking as chief executive. Ahead lay an exciting spell in charge of England, a horribly tangled tale of business misadventure and further enterprising work with other teams, notably Middlesbrough. Whatever else, Terry Venables was never dull.

# DOUG LIVERMORE
. . . . . . . . . . . . . . . . . . . . . .
### CHIEF COACH: May 1992 → June 1993

It would have been an unreasonably demanding Tottenham fan who did not own himself more than satisfied with Doug Livermore's single season in charge of team affairs. After a sticky opening as new players settled in, his side entertained royally, at time looking the equal of any in the land, and with so many youngsters involved the future seemed buoyant.

He did not shoulder responsibility alone, working in harness with his assistant, former Liverpool team-mate Ray Clemence, and chief executive Terry Venables, still very much active as a coach. With two such media-friendly colleagues, Livermore – whose lububrious features belied a typically keen Scouse wit – was content to adopt a relatively low public profile, but supporters perceived him as a sound, wise man, and certainly his selections met with wider approval than those of Messrs Venables and Shreeves before him.

A former assistant boss of Wales and a coach for several clubs, Livermore arrived at the Lane to run the reserves in 1984. There was a fleeting stint at the first-team helm along with another coach, Trevor Hartley, in Autumn 1987, then he became assistant manager in 1989 and chief coach in 1992. Eighth place in the Premier League and an FA Cup semi-final represented a splendid start, but one on which he was destined not to build.

When Ossie Ardiles was drafted in by Alan Sugar, Livermore became a coach with the added duties of chief scout, a role he relinquished with little delay to return to Anfield as assistant manager to his old friend, Roy Evans.

# OSSIE ARDILES
. . . . . . . . . . . . . . . . . . . . . .
### MANAGER: June 1993 → November 1994

The idea was sublime and, sadly, even a little ridiculous in the hard-nosed world of the Premiership. But for a short time Ossie Ardiles purveyed a beautiful if impossible dream, a romantic brand of cavalier football which was sumptuously entertaining in all its attacking splendour, but ultimately doomed as defensively disastrous. The Ardiles appointment in the summer of 1993 was hailed as a massive PR coup for Alan Sugar. Though he had failed ominously at Newcastle, the little Argentinian had forged commendable management credentials at Swindon and West Bromwich and, given the huge fund of goodwill established during his playing days at the Lane, he seemed the right man for the club.

His first campaign began brightly enough before the long-term loss through injury of Gary Mabbutt and Teddy Sheringham unhinged his plans. Then a crippling midwinter sequence of defeats turned many fans against him and presaged a relegation battle which was safely negotiated only after dropping several of his own widely-questioned signings in favour of Venables men.

All that was put to one side when 1994/95 began with Spurs under the cloud of a 12-point deduction for financial irregularities (by stages commuted to a fine) though the gloom was lifted by a succession of exotic buys and the creation of the 'Famous Five' forward line of Darren Anderton, Nick Barmby, Jurgen Klinsmann, Sheringham and Ilie Dumitrescu.

Several swaggering wins were greeted with euphoria, but the side was as anaemic in defence as it was red-blooded going forward and the inevitable collapse to mid-table anonymity, with the fear of worse to follow, brought about Ardiles' sacking in November.

A mild, personable fellow who perhaps lacked the fire to lift a struggling team, Ossie bore the pressure with grace and stoicism before leaving White Hart Lane with a wistful smile. His transfer record had been undeniably bold (Klinsmann's acquisition was a masterstroke), though generally poor, and his tactics were wildly idealistic.

But for all he had done wrong, there was much he did right, certainly for those who subscribe to Danny Blanchflower's philosophy that football was not all about winning, it was about glory . . .

# STEVE PERRYMAN
. . . . . . . . . . . . . . . . . . . . . .
### CARETAKER MANAGER: November 1994

Steve Perryman's fate – being sacked as one of the first acts of new boss Gerry Francis – saddened all those who had believed that the former White Hart Lane stalwart might make an ideal Spurs manager himself. Of course, it was natural enough that Francis would not want to work with the man who had been number-two in the Ardiles regime, but it seemed a shame that Perryman's fusion of enthusiasm and experience, warmth and strength of character, should be lost to the club.

Some blamed him for the defensive frailties of Ossie's team, but that was unfair as policy matters rested with the Argentinian, and Steve had shown himself to be an adept organiser at both Brentford and Watford. In different circumstances, who knows?

# GERRY FRANCIS

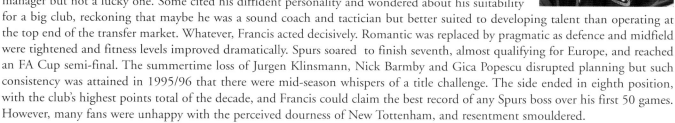

## MANAGER: November 1994 → November 1997

Gerry Francis was an inspired choice to succeed Ossie Ardiles and extract Tottenham from the immediate mire, as he proved by transforming their fortunes in the winter and spring of 1994/95. In the medium term, too, he could hardly be faulted, guiding his charges to third spot in the Premiership during January 1996 and fuelling rational expectations of tangible future success. But was he the man to build on that solid base and restore to Spurs the eminence and style demanded by long-suffering fans? It seems that he was not.

The former England captain arrived from Queen's Park Rangers with the reputation of a capable manager but not a lucky one. Some cited his diffident personality and wondered about his suitability for a big club, reckoning that maybe he was a sound coach and tactician but better suited to developing talent than operating at the top end of the transfer market. Whatever, Francis acted decisively. Romantic was replaced by pragmatic as defence and midfield were tightened and fitness levels improved dramatically. Spurs soared to finish seventh, almost qualifying for Europe, and reached an FA Cup semi-final. The summertime loss of Jurgen Klinsmann, Nick Barmby and Gica Popescu disrupted planning but such consistency was attained in 1995/96 that there were mid-season whispers of a title challenge. The side ended in eighth position, with the club's highest points total of the decade, and Francis could claim the best record of any Spurs boss over his first 50 games. However, many fans were unhappy with the perceived dourness of New Tottenham, and resentment smouldered.

The 1996/97 campaign was effectively shattered by a chronic, never-ending injury crisis, though it must be said that the manager's constant moaning about it grated painfully. A tenth-place finish, followed by aching mediocrity in early 1997/98, eroded his popularity still further until, in November, he duly fell on his sword.

Some believed he was wrong to bow to pressure by investing in flair towards the end of his tenure and that he should have followed his instincts and opted for tightness. But the majority, while sympathetic to injury problems and understanding that cash was not available for top transfer targets, were critical of his overall approach and reckoned, perhaps cruelly, that he was simply too staid for Tottenham. In the end, Alan Sugar was sorry to see Gerry Francis go, but most Spurs fans were not.

# CHRIS HUGHTON

## CARETAKER MANAGER: November 1997

Following the resignation of Gerry Francis, Christian Gross was appointed swiftly as his replacement, but Chris Hughton took charge for one Premiership game, a 1-0 home defeat by Crystal Palace. After that the genial Irishman, who had played nearly 400 senior games for Spurs before becoming a coach at White Hart Lane, was installed as Gross's assistant, going on to serve four more Spurs bosses in that role.

# CHRISTIAN GROSS

## CHIEF COACH: November 1997 → August 1998

With calmness under constant fire and a dignified resolve which never slipped, Christian Gross led Spurs to safety in 1997/98. In the end there wasn't a lot to spare, and there were moments of nerve-shredding anxiety along the way, but he achieved his immediate aim and was entitled to feel hard done by when he was axed only three games into the following campaign.

On arrival to inherit a club in strife, he announced that he would demand discipline as well as ability and he was as good as his word. He wasn't afraid to upset senior players – even Jurgen Klinsmann, whom he brought back to be a leader – but he made the squad fitter and more resilient, making sure that when the springtime pinch came, his men were up for the battle. Studious and seemingly austere, nevertheless he extracted the best from the free spirit that was David Ginola, something neither Kenny Dalglish nor Gerry Francis could manage on such a consistent basis.

Twice a title-winner with Zurich Grasshoppers in his Swiss homeland, Gross seemingly had earned the chance to build steadily towards the English equivalent. Yet even as the season ended in escape from relegation, there were mutterings that he might be replaced by a famous name, and so it proved as George Graham was drafted in.

True, he appeared to obsessed with bar charts and spreadsheets in the build-up to matches, and he was never taken to the hearts of the White Hart Lane faithful, the majority of whom felt he sacrificed style in favour of more prosaic qualities.

Duly, after being the butt of constant criticism, his profile sank so low it was widely assumed he was stuck somewhere in the London Underground, unable to get out with the ticket he had famously brandished on his arrival.

Gross, who concluded his brief tenure as he had started it, with a hard-fought win at Everton, resurfaced in club management in July 1999 with Basel, where he would enjoy the most successful period of his career. Hordes of his old critics would wince with incredulity as the Swiss minnows beat Juventus and knocked Liverpool out of the Champions League in 2002, suggesting that he might have achieved considerably more in north London, given an even break.

# GEORGE GRAHAM

## MANAGER: October 1998 → March 2001

If Tottenham fans truly craved success, they would, initially at least, have to swallow their pride. That was the unspoken message the men in suits delivered by recruiting George Graham, possibly the most unlikely Spurs bedfellow imaginable. For everything the Londoners purveyed about fantasy, glamour and style, the former Arsenal manager could counter with pragmatism, dourness and expediency. For Graham, who had arrived at White Hart Lane after leaving a promising young Leeds squad, reputations meant nothing, results meant everything.

Despite the inevitable protests, Graham and Spurs were united from the start on at least one front. They both desperately desired revenge over Arsenal, the dominating local power which had cast such a looming shadow over the Lane in recent years. Graham, who had been lionised at Highbury after delivering heady and consistent success to the club during the late 1980s and early '90s, had felt cheated by his sacking over a transfer scandal. There could hardly be a better way to level the scores than by leading a Spurs side to trophies.

His mission got off to an ideal start. Graham, as he always does, made the defence a priority. Then, with a stiff backbone established, he went to work on his more exuberant talents. Contrary to the prediction that David Ginola would be cheese to Graham's chalk, the French play-maker initially flourished under his new manager, as the pair inspired the club to their first silverware in eight years. The Spurs team that lifted that 1999 League Cup was a typical George Graham outfit. They weren't pretty against Leicester on that tense Wembley afternoon but, crucially, they won.

But Tottenham were to encounter serial difficulties in the following campaign. Several expensive signings – including the £11 million Ukrainian Sergei Rebrov – were misfiring and, after the team exited all the knockout competitions over the period of a few painful weeks, it became apparent that the majority of fans hadn't accepted Graham into their hearts. The manager – or Mr Graham as he preferred to be addressed – did himself few favours with an abrasive attitude to his players and the press, but still it came as something of a shock when the new board dismissed him just a few days before a mouthwatering FA Cup tie against . . . Arsenal. An outburst to the media over the availability of transfer funds was given as the cause. More likely was the fact that Tottenham and Graham were fundamentally made of different stuff – and neither was prepared to change their ways.

# GLENN HODDLE

## MANAGER: March 2001 → September 2003

The 'Hod is God' graffiti had disappeared over the two decades since it was first scrawled on streets in north London, but Spurs fans needed little convincing that they had witnessed a second coming in the spring of 2001. The appointment of Glenn Hoddle was perhaps the easiest decision the Tottenham board of directors ever made. Who better, they thought, to bring glory back to the club than a man already adored within N17?

In George Graham, Hoddle had replaced a man with little appreciation for the club's traditional passing game. Hoddle, on the other hand, had been one of its finest purveyors. The committed Christian had said that bossing Spurs was his dream, and he had proved himself already as a manager of impressive tactical acumen. His former charges – Swindon, Chelsea, England and, latterly, Southampton – were always impressively well drilled and reasonably effective.

Initially Spurs responded positively to the clarity of his vision for attractive, expansive football. But while his popularity was slow to fade on the terraces and in the stands, problems appeared in the dressing room at a very early stage.

Just a few games into his reign, Hoddle reportedly ignored the advice of senior professionals who called for defensive reinforcements after Tottenham surrendered a 3-0 advantage over Manchester United to lose 5-3 to the reigning champions at White Hart Lane. Instead he tinkered with his existing squad and, in fairness, results improved over the ensuing months.

Spurs progressed to the 2002 League Cup Final, only to be beaten by Blackburn, and Hoddle won a manager of the month award as his team climbed to the top of the Premiership table early in the subsequent campaign.

But criticism of his man-management ability was growing louder. On leaving the club, Tim Sherwood said: 'No one at Tottenham would shed a single tear if Glenn Hoddle was sacked tomorrow. The dressing room is not together and there is no team spirit.' It seemed that Hoddle had a habit of rubbing people up the wrong way and with the players turning against him, so did the results.

After he signed three strikers in the summer of 2003 when what he really needed was a holding midfielder, his fortunes nosedived rapidly. A defeat against Southampton, the club he had left in acrimonious circumstances two years earlier, sealed his fate. Perhaps the dressing room welcomed the board's decision to dismiss him but the fans, who still remembered the halcyon days of his playing prime, sung Hoddle's name with affection in the weeks that followed. That, at least, was a crumb of comfort for the man with the broken dream.

# JACQUES SANTINI

MANAGER: June 2004 → November 2004

Jacques Santini, it seemed, didn't bother to read his job description. The outgoing manager of France, the man who ended Tottenham's eight-month wait for a head coach – a period in which David Pleat had held the fort – had barely unpacked his bags at White Hart Lane before he started arguing over transfer policy with Frank Arnesen, the club's sporting director.

Santini, a stoutly authoritarian figure who spoke little English, certainly had an impact on the team in his 13 games in charge; unfortunately it was not quite what the fans had in mind. After a string of narrow wins at the start of his tenure, Spurs became nothing less than a chore to watch.

The new manager was cramming his team with defenders, invariably erring on the side of caution. Despite an array of creative talent at his disposal, Tottenham's attackers were starved of service.

Supporters were bemused that despite this obvious problem, Santini, who had done well in club football across the English Channel, continued to overlook the gifted schemer Michael Carrick, a recent arrival from West Ham. The fact was that it had not been Santini's decision to bring the midfielder to the club, and he told Carrick so in no uncertain terms.

Finally, with off-field disharmony clearly overshadowing performances, Santini fell on his sword. Later he admitted that his difficulties with Arnesen, whose footballing philosophy was diametrically opposed to his own, were central to his decision. He returned to coach in France where he appeared to be more content. Perhaps his exit from White Hart Lane was in everybody's interests.

# MARTIN JOL

## MANAGER: November 2004 → October 2007

It took an earthily likeable Dutchman to restore Tottenham Hotspur's old-fashioned values. From the moment Martin Jol assumed full control of team affairs, White Hart Lane became the theatre of glorious possibilities it always used to be. Team line-ups that were rigid, cautious and staid were replaced by starting elevens crammed with players intent on passing the ball and using their brains. Jol, and his equally personable assistant Chris Hughton, transformed Spurs from farce to force – and then, through no fault of their own, they led them back to frustration.

Soon after the new boss had taken charge, initially in a caretaker capacity, after the troubled reign of Jacques Santini, choruses of 'I love Martin Jol, Martin Jol loves me' were echoing around the ground. Jol, with his chubby features and wry sense of humour, had restored a fun factor to the club. The players were enjoying training again, the performances improved and, inevitably, so did the results.

Jol's biggest initial tactical triumph was a very simple one. Whereas Santini had ignored Michael Carrick in favour of a hard-tackling central midfield, Jol knew he had a gem waiting on the sidelines. The former West Ham general was installed as play-maker and the change in Tottenham's output was dramatic. Soon they embarked on a sequence of five straight Premiership wins, which secured for Jol a manager of the month award.

If his impressive record was a surprise then it shouldn't have been because the new man – whom Spurs had been lucky enough to recruit as assistant to Santini – was held in vast esteem throughout the European game, so much so that he had been linked with the number-two roles at both Manchester United and Ajax.

The north Londoners prospered under Jol as they had never done since the Premiership was launched in 1992. A management style based on honesty, fairness and good player relations combined brilliantly with the club's improved acumen in the transfer market. Only a sickness bug which afflicted many of his players on the last day of 2005/06 prevented Jol from guiding the club into the European Cup for the first time in more than 40 years.

That was such a cruel blow for a young side which had never been out of the top six and had led Arsenal into the final weeks of the season. Still, a UEFA Cup run and another fifth-placed finish in the following season, which had included a first League triumph over Chelsea since 1990, appeared to suggest that Spurs were at last ready to mix it with the best of them.

But, sadly, Jol became a victim of his own success. The club spent heavily in the summer of 2007 but when the new-look team made a woeful start to the new campaign, he was singled out for damaging blame by the directors. Soon rumours circulated that Juande Ramos had been approached, and the haunted-looking Jol became a dead man walking. Now it seemed that his characteristic fighting spirit had disappeared into the same black hole of despair occupied by his under-performing defence.

After his dismissal many fans, enraged by such savage treatment of the man who had given them new hope, still chanted his name. With one of the best managerial records in Tottenham's modern history, Martin Jol could count himself as unfortunate, indeed.

# CLIVE ALLEN

## CARETAKER MANAGER: October 2007

After ably guiding Tottenham's reserve team, Clive Allen, who served the club so prolifically as a goal-scorer, took charge of a 2-1 defeat at Blackburn while Juande Ramos – the club's incoming head coach – watched from the stands.

# JUANDE RAMOS

## MANAGER: October 2007 →

It would be encroaching on dangerous territory to start comparing Tottenham's latest custodian to the late, great Bill Nicholson. Yet Juande Ramos, the brooding Spaniard who flew into London on a private jet to take up the reins at White Hart Lane, was soon to reveal plenty in common with the blunt Yorkshireman. Ramos, like Nicholson before him, is a strict disciplinarian and a man who believes in attending to every minute detail of his assignment, a man who will leave no stone unturned in pursuit of his goal. Of course, he has a long road to travel before he can think realistically of emulating the legendary 'Bill Nick'. But he has already achieved something which eluded the double-winning boss – a trophy in his first season.

That League Cup triumph over Chelsea – and the blood-quickening semi-final thrashing of Arsenal which preceded it – stand bold both for the instant glory they brought to a success-starved institution and as evidence of quietly raging long-term ambition. Crucially, putting a trophy in the White Hart Lane cabinet bought time for the new manager.

Juande Ramos inherited a team sprinkled with an aura of under-achievement, one which had somehow slipped into the relegation places. But his toughest task wasn't ensuring that Tottenham beat the drop in his first campaign. It was in persuading the fans, who were still in love with his harshly dismissed predecessor, that he was the man who could take the team to the next level.

Perhaps Ramos felt a touch of *deja vu* in his first few months in north London. He had arrived at his previous club, Sevilla, to be confronted by a doubting crowd who had been taken to unforeseen heights by their former manager, Joaquin Caparros. Within weeks he had converted the Andalusian masses as his brand of skilful, breakneck-speed football launched the start of the club's most trophy-laden era, an achievement which offers heady grounds for optimism in N17.

However, we must not be carried away. Other than the Wembley victory, Tottenham endured mixed fortunes during the new man's first term. An initial unbeaten run was soon ended, and a 4-1 reverse against Newcastle sparked a mass walk-out at the Lane. But Ramos, who brought with him Gus Poyet as his assistant and translator, suggested that a major change in personnel beckoned, and a radically altered side was expected to start the next campaign. He was promised that the cash needed to break into the Premiership's top four was in place and his movements in the January 2008 transfer window suggested an intent to spread his net wide.

The new recruits from Scotland, Wales, England and Brazil, together with the sitting incumbents, were left in no doubt that their fitness was of paramount importance. Ramos, a stern character who initially spoke little English, is said to have told at least half the squad to lose weight. Gone was the ketchup and mayonnaise in the club canteen, and the players, who weren't even allowed their favourite juices, were ordered to put in extra hours on the training field.

Maybe there was grumbling, but the stamina the new slimline Spurs showed as Chelsea flagged in the final minutes of extra time at Wembley suggested the rigorous Ramos regime was already proving its worth. For losing the pounds, the players were paid back handsomely; as for the fans, they are praying it was merely a first instalment.

# THE EARLY YEARS

Though fans who began following Spurs in the Glory Glory Hallelujah era of Bill Nicholson's all-conquering side might find it difficult to credit, the north Londoners were comparatively late starters in the business of collecting silverware. In fact, when they garnered their first major trophy, the FA Cup in 1901, they were members of the Southern League, and a further seven seasons passed before they were elected to the senior competition.

Once in, they were promoted at the end of their opening campaign, but then struggled among the elite and were relegated in 1915. After the Great War Spurs were a more buoyant force, with the scintillating likes of Arthur Grimsdell, Jimmy Seed and Jimmy Dimmock in their pomp, and the Second Division Championship was secured in 1919/20, then the FA Cup a year later.

There followed a lengthy period of mediocrity during which they twice slid back to the second tier, and it was not until after the Second World War that the Lilywhites' star began to rise again.

Here is a list of the men who represented Tottenham Hotspur at senior level between 1908/09, the club's first term in the Football League – this category includes a handful of individuals who also competed in earlier Southern League campaigns – and 1939/40, the latter season being abandoned after three matches when Hitler invaded Poland. The records refer to appearances and goals in the Football League, the FA Cup and the FA Charity Shield.

NOTE: Players who appeared on both sides of the Second World War are to be found in The New Dawn, which begins on page 28.

*Spurs were a non-League club when they won the FA Cup for the first time, in 1901. Left to right, back row: C Taylor (assistant secretary), Harry Erentz, George Clawley, Sandy Tait, W Johnson (trainer). Middle row: John Cameron (player-manager), Tom Morris, Ted Hughes, John Leonard Jones (captain), John Kirwan. Front row: Tom Smith, Sandy Brown, David Copeland.*

**STAN ALEXANDER** 1936/37
Inside-forward or winger: 9 games, 1 goal

**JOE ALLEN** 1932/33
Inside-forward: 1 game, 1 goal

**WALLY ALSFORD** 1930/31 → 1936/37
Half-back: 90 games, 0 goals

**JIMMY ARCHIBALD**
1919/20 → 1921/22
Wing-half: 25 games, 1 goal

**JIMMY ARMSTRONG**
1927/28 → 1929/30
Forward: 33 games, 5 goals

**PERCY AUSTIN** 1927/28
Centre-forward: 1 game, 0 goals

**JIMMY BANKS** 1913/14 → 1922/23
Winger or inside-forward: 80 games,
10 goals

**BILL BANN** 1925/26 → 1928/29
Full-back: 12 games, 0 goals

**FRED BARNETT** 1922/23 → 1928/29
Outside-right: 16 games, 1 goal

**JIMMY BAUCHOP** 1913/14
Inside-forward: 10 games, 6 goals

**SAM BELL** 1934/35 → 1936/37
Inside-forward: 16 games, 6 goals

**WALTER BELLAMY** 1926/27 → 1934/35
Winger: 73 games, 9 goals

**FRANK BENTLEY** 1909/10 → 1911/12
Half-back: 41 games, 0 goals

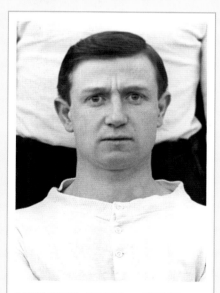

**BERT BLISS** 1911/12 → 1922/23
Inside-forward: 217 games, 105 goals

There wasn't much of the prolific
little Black Country-born marksman
but defenders took him lightly at
their peril. His career was filleted by
the First World War, but he was still
potent after the conflict, earning a
Second Division title medal and his
sole England cap.

**EDDIE BIRNIE** 1910/11
Half-back: 4 games, 1 goal

**JOHN BLAIR** 1926/27 → 1927/28
Inside-forward: 29 games, 15 goals

**HERBERT BLAKE** 1921/22 → 1923/24
Goalkeeper: 56 games, 0 goals

**JIM BLYTH** 1936/37
Centre-half: 11 games, 0 goals

**LEN BOLAN** 1933/34 → 1934/35
Outside-right: 10 games, 3 goals

**FRED BOREHAM** 1908/09 –1909/10
Goalkeeper: 20 games, 0 goals

**ERNIE BOWERING** 1911/12
Half-back: 7 games, 0 goals

**GEORGE BOWLER** 1913/14
Half-back: 3 games, 0 goals

**JIMMY BRAIN** 1931/32 → 1934/35
Centre-or inside-forward: 47 games,
10 goals

**CHARLIE BRITTAN** 1911/12 → 1912/13
Full-back: 42 games, 0 goals

**JOCK BRITTON** 1925/26 → 1927/28
Goalkeeper: 40 games, 0 goals

**SAMMY BROOKS** 1922/23 → 1923/24
Outside-left: 10 games, 1 goal

**JOE BROUGH** 1908/09
Half-back: 2 games, 0 goals

**BOB BROWN** 1919/20 → 1923/24
Full-back: 46 games, 0 goals

**DAVID BROWN** 1910/11
Centre-forward: 1 game, 0 goals

**IVOR BROWN** 1909/10 → 1910/11
Centre-forward: 12 games, 0 goals

**JIMMY BROWN** 1936/37
Inside-forward: 4 games, 0 goals

**WALTER BULL** 1904/05 → 1908/09
Half-back: 27 games, 1 goal

**ED BULLING** 1910/11
Full-back: 2 games, 0 goals

**ARCHIE BURGON** 1934/35
Winger: 4 games, 0 goals

**OLLIE BURTON** 1907/08 → 1909/10
Defender: 42 games, 0 goals

**JIMMY CANTRELL** 1910/11 → 1922/23
Centre-forward: 176 games, 85 goals

Like Jimmy Greaves half a lifetime
later, Cantrell favoured finesse over
brute strength, being sparklingly adept
at passing the ball into the net. After
helping to lift the Second Division crown
in 1920 and the FA Cup in 1921, he
became, at 40, the oldest Spur to play
League football.

**TOMMY CLAY** 1913/14 → 1928/29
Full-back: 353 games, 24 goals

The cool, intelligent Midlander was
a model of consistency and class,
making up for a lack of pace by an
acute positional sense. An England
international and a penalty expert, he
skippered Spurs during the 1919/20
Second Division title campaign and
was an FA Cup winner in 1921.

**TOMMY CABLE** 1928/29 → 1931/32
Centre-half: 44 games, 0 goals

**BILL CARTWRIGHT** 1913/14
Full-back: 15 games, 0 goals

**SID CASTLE** 1919/20 → 1920/21
Outside-right: 5 games, 0 goals

**FRED CHANNELL** 1933/34 → 1935/36
Full-back: 109 games, 1 goal

**JIMMY CHIPPERFIELD** 1919/20
Forward: 15 games, 6 goals

**TOM COLLINS** 1910/11 → 1914/15
Full-back: 122 games, 1 goal

**DAVIE COLQUHOUN**
1931/32 → 1934/35
Wing-half: 87 games, 2 goals

**BILLY COOK** 1929/30 → 1930/31
Inside-forward: 67 games, 24 goals

**ERNIE COQUET** 1908/09 → 1910/11
Full-back: 84 games, 1 goal

**ARTHUR CROMPTON**
1928/29 → 1929/30
Outside-right: 15 games, 3 goals

**ELLIS CROMPTON** 1910/11 → 1911/12
Centre-forward: 10 games, 0 goals

**SID CROWL** 1913/14
Winger: 1 game, 0 goals

**JOHN CURTIS** 1908/09 → 1912/13
Outside-right: 89 games, 5 goals

**JABEZ DARNELL** 1906/07 → 1914/15
Half-back: 161 games, 3 goals

**WILLIE DAVIES** 1929/30 → 1932/33
Outside-right: 115 games, 19 goals

**ALF DAY** 1933/34 → 1935/36
Half-back: 14 games, 0 goals

**JIMMY DIMMOCK** 1919/20 → 1930/31
Outside-left: 440 games, 112 goals
*See profile on page 27*

**FRANK DRABBLE** 1909/10
Goalkeeper: 1 game, 0 goals

**ANDY DUNCAN** 1934/35 → 1938/39
Inside-forward: 103 games, 26 goals

**JOHN EADON** 1914/15
Goalkeeper: 5 games, 0 goals

**BILL EDRICH** 1935/36 → 1936/37
Winger: 20 games, 4 goals

**JACK ELKES** 1922/23 → 1928/29
Inside-forward or centre-half: 201 games, 51 goals

**BERT ELKIN** 1909/10 → 1910/11
Full-back: 28 games, 0 goals

**JIMMY ELLIOTT** 1911/12 → 1919/20
Centre-forward or half-back: 13 games, 4 goals

**ALBERT EVANS** 1927/28 → 1928/29
Centre-forward: 5 games, 0 goals

**TOM EVANS** 1929/30 → 1936/37
Half-back: 101 games, 4 goals

**WILLIE EVANS** 1931/32 → 1936/37
Winger: 195 games, 86 goals

**BILL FELTON** 1931/32 → 1933/34
Full-back: 75 games, 1 goal

**JIM FLEMING** 1913/14 → 1914/15
Centre-forward: 19 games, 3 goals

**TOM FORMAN** 1910/11 → 1911/12
Winger: 8 games, 1 goal

**MATT FORSTER** 1920/21 → 1929/30
Full-back: 244 games, 0 goals

**JAMES FULLWOOD** 1934/35 → 1937/38
Full-back: 35 games, 1 goal

**RANDOLPH GALLOWAY** 1928/29
Centre-forward: 3 games, 2 goals

**GEORGE GEMMELL** 1913/14
Centre-forward: 1 game, 0 goals

**JACK GIBBONS** 1937/38
Centre-forward: 33 games, 18 goals

**GEORGE GOLDSMITH** 1934/35
Full-back: 1 game, 0 goals

**BERT GOODMAN** 1919/20
Full-back: 17 games, 1 goal

**ALBERT GOSNELL** 1910/11
Outside-left: 7 games, 0 goals

**GEORGE GREENFIELD**
1931/32 → 1934/35
Inside-forward: 31 games, 11 goals

**FRANK GRICE** 1935/36 → 1938/39
55 games, 1 goal

**ARTHUR GRIMSDELL**
1911/12 → 1928/29
Wing-half: 362 games, 27 goals
*See profile on page 26*

**ALAN HALL** 1933/34
Centre-forward: 2 games, 0 goals

**ALMER HALL** 1934/35 → 1935/36
Inside-forward: 21 games, 3 goals

**JACK HALL** 1936/37 → 1938/39
Goalkeeper: 58 games, 0 goals

**WILLIE HALL** 1932/33 → 1939/40
Inside-forward: 224 games, 29 goals

**CHARLIE HANDLEY**
1921/22 → 1928/29
Forward: 131 games, 35 goals

**HARRY HARGREAVES**
1923/24 → 1925/26
Inside-forward: 34 games, 7 goals

**TED HARPER** 1928/29 → 1931/32
Centre-forward: 67 games, 63 goals

**WILLIAM HARRIS** 1909/10
Full-back: 7 games, 0 goals

**FRANK HARTLEY**
1922/23 & 1927/28 → 1929/30
Inside-forward: 7 games, 1 goal

**FOSTER HEDLEY** 1933/34 → 1934/35
Outside-left: 5 games, 1 goal

**SID HELLIWELL** 1927/28 → 1928/29
Centre-half: 9 games, 0 goals

**EDWIN HEROD** 1928/29 → 1930/31
Full-back: 59 games, 0 goals

**BOB HEWITSON** 1908/09
Goalkeeper: 34 games, 0 goals

**BILL HINTON** 1924/25 → 1925/26
Goalkeeper: 64 games, 0 goals

**ARTHUR HITCHINS**
1937/38 → 1939/40
Centre-half: 44 games, 1 goal

**BERT HODGKINSON**
1930/31 → 1931/32
Full-back: 58 games, 0 goals

**PERCY HOOPER** 1934/35 → 1939/40
Goalkeeper: 112 games, 0 goals

**LES HOWE** 1930/31 → 1938/39
Utility: 182 games, 28 goals

**PERCY HUMPHREYS**
1909/10 → 1911/12
Forward: 50 games, 29 goals

**DOUG HUNT** 1934/35 → 1936/37
Centre-forward: 19 games, 6 goals

---

**GEORGE HUNT** (right)
1930/31 → 1936/37
Centre-forward: 198 games, 138 goals

A vigorous and immensely prolific Yorkshireman, dubbed 'The Chesterfield Tough' after signing from the Spireites. Naturally rumbustious but skilful to boot, he netted 33 times when Spurs rose to the top flight in 1933 and was the club's all-time top scorer until overhauled by Bobby Smith. Capped three times by England.

---

**ALEX HUNTER** 1920/21 → 1921/22
Goalkeeper: 27 games, 0 goals

**JOHN ILLINGWORTH**
1929/30 → 1934/35
Full-back: 12 games, 0 goals

**BILL JACQUES** 1914/15 → 1922/23
Goalkeeper: 139 games, 0 goals

**GEORGE JEFFREY** 1937/38
Inside-forward: 1 game, 1 goal

**CHARLIE JONES** 1934/35 → 1935/36
Centre-half: 18 games, 0 goals

**GORDON JONES** 1912/13
Utility: 7 games, 0 goals

**JOHN 'TINY' JOYCE**
1909/10 → 1914/15
Goalkeeper: 81 games, 1 goal

**BILL KAINE** 1925/26
Goalkeeper: 12 games, 0 goals

**JIMMY KENNEDY** 1909/10 → 1911/12
Half-back: 13 games, 1 goal

**ARTHUR KERRY** 1909/10
Winger: 1 game, 0 goals

**ARTHUR KING** 1913/14
Goalkeeper: 20 games, 0 goals

**EDDIE KING** 1934/35
Full-back: 1 game, 0 goals

**JOHN KNIGHT** 1928/29
Centre-half: 1 game, 0 goals

**BILL LANE** 1924/25 → 1926/27
Centre-forward: 29 games, 9 goals

**TOM LESLIE** 1908/09 → 1910/11
Half-back: 12 games, 0 goals

**DAVID LEVENE** 1932/33 → 1934/35
Half-back: 10 games, 0 goals

**ED LIGHTFOOT** 1911/12 → 1914/15
Half-back: 66 games, 2 goals

**ALEX LINDSAY** 1919/20 → 1929/30
Half-back or forward: 236 games,
50 goals

**HUGH LORIMER** 1919/20 → 1921/22
Winger: 5 games, 0 goals

**ARTHUR 'DARKIE' LOWDELL**
1927/28 → 1929/30
Half-back: 90 games, 0 goals

**HARRY LOWE** 1914/15 → 1926/27
Half-back: 72 games, 0 goals

**TOMMY LUNN** 1909/10 → 1912/13
Goalkeeper: 91 games, 0 goals

**ARCHIE LYLE** 1909/10
Inside-forward: 1 game, 0 goals

**BERT LYONS** 1930/31 → 1931/32
Full-back: 57 games, 3 goals

**JIMMY McCORMICK**
1932/33 → 1938/39
Outside-left: 150 games, 28 goals

**BOB MacDONALD** 1919/20 → 1924/25
Full-back: 126 games, 0 goals

**DOUG McFARLANE**
1908/09 → 1909/10
Centre-forward: 21 games, 2 goals

**BOB McTAVISH** 1910/11
Inside-forward: 12 games, 3 goals

**JOHN McTAVISH** 1910/11 → 1911/12
Outside-right: 40 games, 0 goals

**GEORGE MADDISON**
1922/23 → 1923/24
Goalkeeper: 41 games, 0 goals

**HARRY MARSHALL** 1931/32
Inside-forward: 1 game, 0 goals

**TOM MASON** 1911/12
Inside-forward: 7 games, 1 goal

**FRED MASSEY** 1908/09
1 game, 0 goals

**TOM MEADS** 1929/30 → 1934/35
Half-back: 189 games, 6 goals

**JOE MEEK** 1935/36 → 1938/39
Inside-forward: 51 games, 16 goals

**CECIL POYNTON**

1923/24 → 1932/33
Full-back: 158 games, 3 goals

Best remembered at White Hart Lane as a faithful trainer and physio, roles which took him to more than half a century of service to Tottenham and encompassed the glorious Nicholson years. As a player he was converted from wing-half to full-back, but never quite cemented a long-term berth.

**ALF MESSER** 1930/31 → 1931/32
Centre-half: 52 games, 2 goals

**BERT MIDDLEMISS** 1908/09 → 1919/20
Outside-left: 262 games, 54 goals

**LES MILLER** 1936/37 → 1938/39
Outside-left: 65 games, 26 goals

**BILLY MINTER** 1908/09 → 1919/20
Inside-forward: 263 games, 101 goals

**JACK MORAN** 1931/32
Full-back: 12 games, 0 goals

**TOM MORRIS** 1899/1900 → 1911/12
Half-back: 101 games, 3 goals

**JOHN MORRISON** 1932/33 → 1939/40
Centre-forward: 155 games, 104 goals

**JAMES MORTON** 1908/09
Centre-forward: 2 games, 0 goals

**ERNIE NEWMAN** 1909/10 → 1913/14
Forward: 32 games, 6 goals

**JOE NICHOLLS** 1926/27 → 1935/36
Goalkeeper: 129 games, 0 goals

**EUGENE 'TAFFY' O'CALLAGHAN** 1926/27 → 1934/35
Inside-forward: 263 games, 98 goals

**WILLIAM OLIVER** 1913/14
Outside-left: 2 games, 0 goals

**FRANK OSBORNE** 1923/24 → 1930/31
Forward: 219 games, 82 goals

**JOHN PEARSON** 1914/15 → 1922/23
Full-back: 50 games, 0 goals

**ERNIE PHYPERS** 1934/35 → 1936/37
Half-back: 33 games, 0 goals

**CHARLIE RANCE** 1910/11 → 1920/21
Centre-half: 110 games, 1 goal

**JACK REDDISH** 1929/30 → 1931/32
Left-back: 7 games, 0 goals

**JOCK RICHARDSON** 1926/27 → 1928/29
Full-back: 41 games, 0 goals

**BERT RINGROSE** 1936/37
Full-back: 10 games, 0 goals

**TOM ROBERTS** 1928/29
Centre-forward: 4 games, 2 goals

**TOMMY ROE** 1925/26 → 1926/27
Forward: 6 games, 4 goals

**JIMMY ROSS** 1922/23 → 1923/24
Full-back: 7 games, 0 goals

**ARTHUR ROWE** 1931/32 → 1937/38
Centre-half: 201 games, 0 goals
*See profile on page ??*

**DICK ROWLEY** 1929/30 → 1931/32
Forward: 24 games, 10 goals

**BILLY SAGE** 1919/20 → 1925/26
Half-back: 13 games, 0 goals

**ARTHUR SANDERS** 1926/27 → 1927/28
Centre-forward: 13 games, 7 goals

**FRED SARGENT** 1933/34 → 1939/40
Outside-right: 112 games, 33 goals

**JOE SCOTT** 1928/29 → 1930/31
Outside-left: 18 games, 4 goals

**MAX SEEBURG** 1908/09
Forward: 1 game, 0 goals

**JIMMY SEED** 1919/20 → 1926/27
Inside-forward: 256 games, 77 goals
*See profile on page 26*

**BUCHANAN SHARP** 1922/23 → 1924/25
Inside-forward: 3 games, 0 goals

**JIMMY SKINNER** 1919/20 → 1925/26
Half-back: 93 games, 3 goals

**HARRY SKITT** 1924/25 → 1930/31
Half-back: 230 games, 0 goals

**JIMMY SMAILES** 1930/31 → 1931/32
Outside-left: 16 games, 3 goals

**JIMMY SMITH** 1925/26 → 1926/27
Goalkeeper: 31 games, 0 goals

**JIMMY SMY** 1928/29 → 1930/31
Inside-forward: 17 games, 6 goals

**HARRY SPARROW** 1913/14 → 1914/15
Centre-forward: 19 games, 7 goals

**ISAAC SPELMAN** 1937/38 → 1938/39
Half-back: 32 games, 2 goals

**CYRIL SPIERS** 1927/28 → 1931/32
Goalkeeper: 169 games, 0 goals

**BERT SPROSTON** 1938/39
Full-back: 9 games. 0 goals

**ALEX STEEL** 1909/10
Half-back: 1 game, 0 goals

**BOBBY STEEL** 1908/09 → 1914/15
Inside-forward and centre-half: 246 games, 46 goals

**DANNY STEEL** 1907/08 → 1911/12
Centre-half: 141 games, 3 goals

**JOHN TATE** 1912/13 → 1913/14
Goalkeeper: 4 games, 0 goals

**WALTER TATTERSALL** 1911/12 → 1914/15
Winger: 47 games, 5 goals

**ALLAN TAYLOR** 1931/32 → 1935/36
Goalkeeper: 69 games, 0 goals

**ANDY THOMPSON** 1920/21 → 1930/31
Forward: 166 games, 21 goals

**ALBERT TOMKIN** 1938/39 → 1939/40
Winger: 4 games, 0 goals

**JIMMY TOWNLEY** 1927/28
Inside-forward: 3 games, 2 goals

**DANIEL TULL** 1909/10 → 1910/11
Centre-forward: 10 games, 2 goals

**SOLOMON UPTON** 1912/13
Winger: 2 games, 0 goals

**FANNY WALDEN** 1912/13 → 1923/24
Winger: 236 games, 25 goals
*See profile on page 27*

**BERT SMITH** 1919/20 → 1928/29
Half-back: 321 games, 10 goals

Though tending to be outshone by fellow wing-half Arthur Grimsdell, Smith was a fearsomely solid performer, his diligence at the back allowing his more adventurous comrade the freedom to attack. His honours included two England caps and medals for winning the Second Division title and the FA Cup.

**CHARLIE WALTERS**  1919/20 → 1925/26
Centre-half: 118 games, 0 goals

**JOE WALTON**  1904/05 → 1908/09
Outside-right: 42 games, 6 goals

**FRED WEBSTER**  1911/12 → 1914/15
Full-back: 86 games, 0 goals

**FINDLAY WEIR**  1912/13 → 1914/15
Half-back: 101 games, 2 goals

**BILL WHATLEY**  1932/33 → 1938/39
Full-back: 254 games, 2 goals

**SID WHITE**  1923/24 → 1925/26
Half-back: 22 games, 0 goals

**HARRY WILDING**  1928/29
Centre-half: 12 games, 1 goal

**FRED WILKES**  1908/09 → 1911/12
Full-back: 60 games, 0 goals

**CHARLIE WILSON**  1919/20 → 1922/23
Centre-forward: 62 games, 33 goals

**CHARLIE WOODRUFF**
1908/09 → 1909/10
Winger: 10 games, 1 goal

**ALEX YOUNG**  1911/12
Centre-forward: 5 games, 3 goals

**CHRIS YOUNG**  1912/13
Centre-forward: 4 games, 0 goals

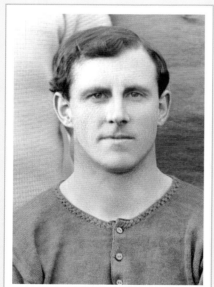

**VIVIAN J WOODWARD**
1902/03 → 1908/09
Centre-forward: 50 games, 23 goals

Willowy, stylish Woodoward was a
gentleman footballer, an amateur
who captained his country to two
Olympic golds and also netted
29 times while collecting 23 full
England caps. Spurs' top scorer as
they gained promotion to the top
flight in 1908/09, he served also as a
club director.

*The classy combination which lifted Tottenham's second FA Cup, in 1921. Left to right, back row: Billy Minter (trainer), Bert Smith, Tommy Clay, Alex Hunter, Arthur Grimsdell (captain), Charlie Walters, Bob MacDonald. Front row: Jimmy Banks, Jimmy Seed, Jimmy Cantrell, Bert Bliss, Jimmy Dimmock.*

# ARTHUR GRIMSDELL

## 1911/12 → 1928/29

It is said that there was no footballer in the land with a more ferocious enthusiasm for the game than Arthur Grimsdell. But while his boundless energy and passion for the cause were remarkable, they did not begin to encompass the breadth of his overall contribution.

Grimsdell was a supremely efficient craftsman, an attacking left-half whose dynamic surges into enemy territory were underpinned by exceptional all-round ability. His ball control was assured, his passing imaginative, his tactical intelligence acute, and his shooting both powerful and accurate enough to account for 14 goals as the Second Division crown was claimed in 1919/20. Though never happier than when marauding forward, he was a terrific defender, too, endlessly determined and flinty in the tackle.

In addition, he possessed that indefinable quality which marks out natural leaders, and he proved an ideal choice to succeed the admirable Tommy Clay as skipper, lifting aloft the FA Cup at the end of his first full season in the role and generally stamping his authority on the team. Clearly he was the Ron Burgess or Dave Mackay of his day.

Grimsdell, who also captained England in his last three internationals, had been a free-scoring centre-forward as a schoolboy, but he moved to centre-half during an amateur stint with Watford, then completed his transition to the midfield engine room not long after his arrival at the Lane as an 18-year-old in March 1912. In October 1925 he broke his leg horribly, missing nearly two seasons, and was never quite the same irresistible force again.

**ARTHUR GRIMSDELL**
BORN: Watford, Hertfordshire, 23 March 1894.
HONOURS: FA Cup 20/1. Second Division Championship 19/20. 6 England caps (20-23).
OTHER CLUBS: Clapton Orient 29/30 (11, 0).
MANAGER: Clapton Orient (29-30).
DIED: Watford, 12 March 1963.

GAMES 362
GOALS 27

# JIMMY SEED

## 1919/20 → 1926/27

Jimmy Seed was one of the canniest signings in Tottenham's history, but his subsequent exit represented a transfer gaffe of colossal proportions.

Before arriving at White Hart Lane, the former miner from the north-east had surmised that he had no future in the professional game, having been ditched by Sunderland in the belief that he would never fully recover from being gassed in the First World War trenches. However, the thoughtful, deep-lying inside-forward recuperated successfully in South Wales with Mid-Rhondda, who then allowed him to leave for a mere £350.

Now he emerged as a shrewd and subtle midfield prompter, his smooth technique and sharp intelligence matched by impressive stamina which made nonsense of the Rokerites' earlier fears. A natural organiser who masterminded Spurs' response to confusing changes in the offside law and who knew when to hang back to facilitate Arthur Grimsdell's frequent forward sorties, Seed was rewarded by England recognition and an FA Cup winner's medal in 1921.

Bizarrely, the immense influence he had wielded did not secure his long-term tenure in north London, and following an injury he was released to join Sheffield Wednesday in August 1927, Spurs manager Billy Minter preferring the younger Taffy O'Callaghan as his principal play-maker. That proved a disastrous decision as Seed became captain of the Owls, inspiring them to avoid relegation – and Tottenham went down instead. Then, to further underline the folly of his sale, the former Spur led Wednesday to two successive League titles.

**JAMES MARSHALL SEED**
BORN: Blackhill, County Durham, 25 March 1895.
HONOURS: FA Cup 20/1. 5 England caps (21-25).
OTHER CLUBS: Sheffield Wednesday 27/8-30/1 (134, 32).
MANAGER: Clapton Orient (31-33); Charlton Athletic (33-56); Bristol City (caretaker 58); Millwall (58-59).
DIED: Farnborough, Kent, 16 July 1966.

GAMES 256
GOALS 77

# FANNY WALDEN

## 1912/13 → 1923/24

To the uninitiated, Spurs right winger Fanny Walden cut an odd, even comical figure as he lined up to face his opponents at the start of a game. But invariably, once the first whistle had sounded, his would-be markers and rival supporters alike discovered rapidly enough that the diminutive Midlander was to be taken very seriously indeed.

Walden stood a mere 5ft 2ins – at least, after a haircut, as he liked to joke – but he was wirily resilient, a dazzling dribbler and often virtually uncontrollable. For instance, how could a hulking 6ft-plus full-back hope to shoulder-barge such an elusive sprite, who sometimes gave the illusion of dashing between defenders' legs as he tiptoed through a crowded penalty box.

Astonishingly, during his Southern League days with Northampton Town he was known to play at centre-forward, though soon he was converted to a flankman for whom Tottenham readily parted with £1,700 to sign in April 1913. Striking up a compelling partnership with inside-right Jimmy Seed, Walden excelled as Spurs rose from the Second Division as champions in 1919/20, but injury forced him to miss out on the following term's FA Cup Final triumph.

Fanny, whose two England outings were separated by the First World War, returned to the Cobblers, his home-town club and by then a member of the Football League, in 1926. A gifted all-round sportsman, he played county cricket for Northamptonshire, compiling more than 7,000 first-class runs and completing a century of wickets. Later he became an umpire, officiating in 11 Test matches in the late 1930s.

**FREDERICK INGRAM WALDEN**
BORN       Wellingborough, Northamptonshire, 1 March 1888.
HONOURS:   Second Division Championship 19/20. 2 England caps (14-22).
OTHER CLUBS:   Northampton Town 26/7 (20, 1).
DIED:      Northampton, 3 May 1949.

GAMES 236
GOALS 25

---

# JIMMY DIMMOCK

## 1919/20 → 1930/31

Jimmy Dimmock was a swashbuckling entertainer, an individualist who lit up the left flank of Tottenham's attack for more than a decade with his sorcery and speed, and if his occasional over-elaboration could be infuriating, he more than paid his way in goals.

Blessed with beautiful balance, the solidly built north Londoner was a thoroughbred with no notion of how to play the game dully. Dimmock's way was to fly past his marker, then climax his dash with a shot or a cross, both of which he was capable of dispatching expertly with either foot. The records suggest that just such a scenario proved decisive in the 1-0 1921 FA Cup Final triumph over Wolverhampton Wanderers, but more detailed research reveals that Jimmy was a remarkably fortunate match-winner that day at a swamp-like Stamford Bridge.

Attempting to dance over the quagmire, he took full advantage of two lucky bounces to leave opponents in his wake, then netted with a 15-yard cross-shot which deceived Wolves 'keeper Noel George as it skidded in the mud.

Dimmock joined Spurs as amateur from Edmonton Ramblers in 1916, spurning Arsenal to turn professional at White Hart Lane three years later. At first he was principally a provider, but around the middle 1920s he started scoring more heavily – his best tally was 20 in 1926/27 – and had Tottenham been a more successful side, then surely he would have accumulated more than three full caps. As it was Jimmy Dimmock had one international claim to fame, being the first player born in the 20th century to play for England.

**JAMES HENRY DIMMOCK**
BORN:      Edmonton, London, 5 December 1900.
HONOURS:   FA Cup 20/1. Second Division Championship 19/20. 3 England caps (21-26).
OTHER CLUBS:   Thames 31/2 (37, 12); Clapton Orient 32/3 (18, 3).
DIED:      Enfield, London, 23 December 1972.

GAMES 440
GOALS 112

# THE NEW DAWN

When peace brought a return to something approaching normality in 1945, first-class football resumed and was more popular than ever with the sports-minded public, which had been substantially starved of mass entertainment for the six harrowing years of conflict.

The first manager entrusted with guiding Spurs' fortunes was Joe Hulme, famous as a goal-scoring winger in Arsenal's serially triumphant team of the 1930s. He deserved immense credit for assembling almost the entire side which would attain such heady heights under his successor, Arthur Rowe, but he was unable to lead them out of the Second Division and was sacked in the spring of 1949.

In came Rowe and not only did Spurs lift the divisional crown at his first attempt, they followed it up with the League title in 1950/51. However, as key players aged the standard was not maintained, the over-stressed manager became ill and he resigned in July 1955.

There followed three and a bit seasons of reconstruction presided over, diligently and with more enterprise than sometimes he is credited with, by Arthur's former assistant, Jimmy Anderson. When he, too, fell prey to pressure and poor health, stepping down in October 1958, it was the cue for the coronation of Bill Nicholson and the beginning of a grand new order.

Listed here are the footballers – some distinguished, some not – who sported the cockerel on their chests between season 1945/46 and the outset of the Nicholson era. The records cover appearances and goals in the Football League, FA Cup and FA Charity Shield.

**CHRIS ADAMS** 1951/52 → 1952/53
Forward: 6 games, 1 goal

**BILL ADAMS** 1945/46
Full-back or winger: 1 game, 0 goals

**EDDIE BAILY** 1946/47 → 1955/56
Inside-forward: 326 games, 69 goals
*See profile on page 36*

**LES BENNETT** 1946/47 → 1954/55
Inside-forward: 295 games, 119 goals
*See profile on page 38*

**TOMMY BING** 1957/58
Winger: 1 game, 0 goals

**COLIN BRITTAN** 1950/51 → 58
Wing-half: 45 games, 1 goal

**RON BURGESS** 1938/39 → 1953/54
Wing-half: 328 games, 16 goals
*See profile on page 32*

**JACK CHISHOLM** 1947/48
Centre-half: 2 games, 0 goals

**HARRY CLARKE** 1948/49 → 1956/57
Centre-half: 323 games, 4 goals
*See profile on page 39*

**BOBBY COOK** 1949/50
Outside-right: 3 games, 0 goals

**FREDDIE COX** 1938/39 → 1948/49
Winger: 105 games, 17 goals

**LES DICKER** 1952/53
Outside-left: 10 games, 2 goals

**RONNIE DIX** 1939/40 → 1947/48
Inside-forward: 43 games, 5 goals

**DICKIE DOWSETT** 1954/55
Outside-left: 1 game, 1 goal

**MICKY DULIN** 1955/56 → 1957/58
Winger: 11 games, 2 goals

**LEN DUQUEMIN** 1947/48 → 1956/57
Centre-forward: 308 games, 134 goals
*See profile on page 35*

**BRIAN FARLEY** 1951/52
Centre-half: 1 game, 0 goals

**KEN FLINT** 1947/48
Outside-left: 5 games, 1 goal

**GEORGE FOREMAN** 1946/47
Centre-forward: 38 games, 14 goals

**LEN GARWOOD** 1948/49
Half-back: 2 games, 0 goals

**JOHNNY GAVIN** 1954/55 → 1955/56
Winger: 34 games, 16 goals

**EDDIE GIBBINS** 1952/53
Centre-half: 4 games, 0 goals

**HARRY GILBERG** 1946/47
Forward: 3 games, 0 goals

**VIC GROVES** 1952/53 → 1953/54
Forward: 4 games, 3 goals

**ALAN GRUBB** 1952/53
Outside-right: 2 games, 0 goals

**ALBERT HALL** 1935/36 → 1946/47
Forward: 45 games, 11 goals

**ROY HOLLIS** 1952/53
Centre-forward: 4 games, 3 goals

**ARCHIE HUGHES** 1945/46 → 1947/48
Goalkeeper: 4 games, 0 goals

**GEORGE HUTCHINSON** 1953/54
Outside-right: 5 games, 1 goal

**ERNIE JONES** 1946/47 → 1948/49
Winger: 57 games, 14 goals

**JOHNNY JORDAN** 1947/48
Inside-forward: 27 games, 13 goals

**LEON JOSEPH** 1946/47
Winger: 1 game, 0 goals

**DEREK KING** 1951/52 → 1954/55
Centre-half: 19 games, 0 goals

**GEORGE LUDFORD**
1936/37 → 1949/50
Forward or half-back: 83 games, 8 goals

**VIC BUCKINGHAM**
1935/36 → 1948/49
Defender: 234 games, 1 goal

A cultured performer, Buckingham rose through Tottenham's junior ranks, making the journey from centre-half to wing-half to full-back. Probably most suited to the midfield role, he was bright and adventurous but no match for Burgess or Nicholson. Later he became a flamboyant manager, notably with West Bromwich Albion.

**PETER MURPHY**
1950/51 → 1951/52
Inside-forward: 39 games, 15 goals

A north-easterner raised in the Midlands, ex-bricklayer 'Spud' was an unassuming but energetic fellow who packed a venomous shot and contributed nine goals to the 1950/51 title triumph after arriving from Coventry. He never quite claimed a regular place and soon moved to Birmingham City, with whom he excelled.

**COLIN LYMAN** 1937/38 → 1945/46
Winger: 55 games, 11 goals

**SID McCLELLAN** 1950/51 → 1955/56
Forward: 70 games, 32 goals

**LES MEDLEY** 1945/46 → 1952/53
Outside-left: 165 games, 46 goals
*See profile on page 38*

**BILL NICHOLSON** 1938/39 → 1954/55
Wing-half: 345 games, 6 goals
*See profile on page 39*

**ALED OWEN** 1953/54
Winger: 1 game, 0 goals

**ALBERT PAGE** 1936/37 → 1945/46
Centre-half: 57 games, 0 goals

**ALF RAMSEY** 1949/50 → 1954/55
Full-back: 250 games, 24 goals
*See profile on page 34*

**RON REYNOLDS**
1953/54 → 1957/58
Goalkeeper: 95 games, 0 goals

There were interludes when the former Aldershot custodian displaced Ted Ditchburn between Tottenham's posts on merit, but fundamentally he was never quite in the England man's class. Still, Reynolds was a proficient all-rounder who might have secured a regular place at other clubs.

**BILLY REES** 1949/50
Inside-forward: 13 games, 3 goals

**HARRY ROBSHAW** 1951/52
Half-back: 1 game, 0 goals

**CHARLIE RUNDLE** 1946/47 → 1948/49
Centre-forward: 29 games, 12 goals

**JIMMY SCARTH** 1949/50 → 1951/52
Winger: 7 games, 3 goals

**GEORGE SKINNER** 1946/47
Inside-forward: 1 game, 0 goals

**LES STEVENS** 1946/47 → 1948/49
Outside-left: 59 games, 5 goals

**SID TICKRIDGE** 1946/47 → 1950/51
Full-back: 101 games, 0 goals

**CYRIL TOULOUSE** 1948/49
Centre-half: 2 games, 0 goals

**CYRIL TRAILOR** 1946/47 → 1947/48
Half-back: 12 games, 0 goals

**DENNIS UPHILL** 1950/51 → 1952/53
Inside-forward: 6 games, 2 goals

**ERNIE WALLEY** 1955/56 → 1957/58
Half-back: 5 games, 0 goals

**SONNY WALTERS** 1946/47 → 1955/56
Outside-right: 234 games, 71 goals
*See profile on page 38*

**RALPH WARD** 1935/36 → 1945/46
Full-back: 135 games, 11 goals

**RALPH WETTON** 1951/52 → 1954/55
Half-back: 46 games, 0 goals

**CHARLIE WHITCHURCH** 1946/47
Winger: 8 games, 2 goals

**ROY WHITE** 1945/46
Half-back: 2 games, 0 goals

**BOB WILKIE** 1956/57
Winger: 1 game, 0 goals

**ALAN WOODS** 1954/55
Half-back: 6 games, 0 goals

**HORACE WOODWARD**
1946/47 → 1948/49
Centre-half: 67 games, 1 goal

**ALEX WRIGHT** 1950/51
Centre-forward: 2 games, 1 goal

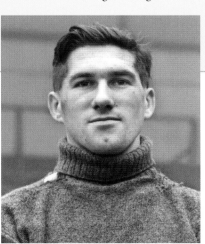

**ARTHUR WILLIS**
1945/46 → 1953/54
Full-back: 161 games, 1 goal

A Yorkshireman and a former miner, Willis was quick, neat and alert, a thoughtful performer who earned his sole England cap after playing his part in the title glory of 1950/51. He spent much time in the reserves as manager Arthur Rowe could not really decide on Willis or Charlie Withers as Alf Ramsey's full-back partner.

**CHARLIE WITHERS**
1947/48 → 1955/56
Full-back: 165 games, 2 goals

Local boy Withers was pacy and powerful, flinty in the challenge, quick to recover if he was beaten and renowned for the perfect timing of his sliding tackles. He missed only two games as Spurs topped the Second Division in 1949/50, but an injury cleared the way for Arthur Willis during the subsequent top-flight Championship campaign.

# ARTHUR ROWE

PLAYER: 1931/32 → 1937/38
MANAGER: May 1949 → July 1955

Arthur Rowe transformed Tottenham Hotspur and, beyond that, was one of the major influences on the whole of British soccer in the years immediately after the Second World War.

The clue to his success at White Hart Lane – which peaked with winning the Second and First Division titles in consecutive campaigns, 1949/50 and 1950/51 – could be found in his philosophy while captaining Spurs during the 1930s. Although

nominally a centre-half, the once-capped England international was never a mere stopper, employing a more constructive, thoughtful approach than the majority of his contemporaries.

When injuries forced him to quit, Rowe took his expertise to Hungary, a nation which appreciated his emphasis on skill and acute tactical strategy. He was offered the job of managing the Magyars, but his ambition in that direction were frustrated by the war.

Back at the Lane, after a sojourn at Southern League Chelmsford City, he introduced his famous 'push-and-run' method, which involved quickfire wall-passing by all ten outfield players.

# JIMMY ANDERSON

Jimmy Anderson was the faithful retainer who took charge of Spurs between the jewelled reigns of Arthur Rowe and Bill Nicholson. The former White Hart Lane groundstaff boy, trainer and coach inherited a side on the slide, but after a successful relegation fight he transformed them into a title-chasing combination which finished

runners-up in the top tier in 1956/57 and third a year later. But then, with his health failing, Tottenham struggled through the autumn of 1958 and Anderson resigned.

*Left: The pushers and the runners, League Champions of 1950/51.*
*Back row, left to right: Cecil Poynton (trainer), Alf Ramsey, Len Duquemin, Peter Murphy, Ted Ditchburn, Harry Clarke, Les Bennett, Charlie Withers. Front row: Bill Nicholson, Sonny Walters, Arthur Willis, Ron Burgess, Eddie Baily, Les Medley.*

*Below: Arthur Rowe (right) ponders his line-up before a game at White Hart Lane in 1950. Helping with the deliberations is his loyal trainer, Cecil Poynton.*

Using the nucleus of the squad employed by his predecessor, Joe Hulme – his only expedition into the transfer market was to sign full-back Alf Ramsey from Southampton – he brought then-unprecedented glory to the club.

As his health suffered under the strain of maintaining the impetus of his lovely team – he was forced into premature retirement in 1955 – some critics reckoned that he had allowed his players to grow old together, and that remains a matter for debate.

But there is no doubt that Rowe, a man of intelligence and integrity who worked himself into the ground, deserves an exalted place in the annals of his beloved Tottenham.

# RON BURGESS

## 1938/39 → 1953/54

In the case of Ron Burgess, mining's loss was football's immeasurable gain. People who knew him as a boy joked that, with his boundless vitality, immense strength and readiness to toil until he dropped, he might singlehandedly have emptied the South Wales coalfield in which he grew up expecting to spend his working life.

Instead he hewed out a glorious niche as one of the most influential performers in the history of Tottenham Hotspur, emerging as a titanic presence at the heart of the team which took English club football by storm midway through the 20th century.

Burgess was both skipper and midfield inspiration as the north Londoners topped the Second Division table in 1949/50, then lifted the League Championship a year later, and if one man embodied the ethos of visionary manager Arthur Rowe's exhilarating combination, it was the genial, prematurely balding Welshman.

His perpetual motion and irrepressible enthusiasm, melding potently with the wily passing game of inside-forward Eddie Baily, facilitated the side's fluid push-and-run style, which highlighted Rowe's credentials as one of the game's most progressive thinkers.

Not that Burgess was merely a workhorse, his characteristic dynamism and resilience being gilded by comprehensive all-round ability; his ball control was neat, his distribution assured, he was positionally astute, formidable in the air and quick over the ground.

He excelled, too, at international level, missing only two appearances for his country in eight post-war seasons, winning most of his 32 caps as captain. In addition he was the first Welshman to represent the Football League and he played for Great Britain against the Rest of Europe in 1947.

Burgess learned the game on rough pitches next to Rhondda Valley slagheaps, shining initially as a prolific centre-forward. Soon he attracted the attention of Cardiff City, whom he joined as an amateur in his mid-teens, but the Bluebirds' interest cooled and he took a mining job while playing for local side Cwm Villa.

Now a future in the pits appeared inevitable, but after plundering 59 goals in one season he was spotted by Tottenham, who recruited him, again on amateur terms, in 1936.

Initially it seemed likely that Burgess's reprieve from the coalface was only temporary as he failed to make the grade at White Hart Lane, and he was on his way home to South Wales when he stopped off to watch his Spurs contemporaries in a junior game. They were a man short, he stepped in at right-half and performed so impressively that he was offered a place at the club's Northfleet nursery in Kent.

In the new role he progressed rapidly, turning professional in 1938 at the age of 21 and making his senior debut in a Division Two fixture at Norwich in February 1939, only for his momentum to be shattered by the outbreak of war.

During the conflict Burgess served as a physical training instructor in the RAF, but found there was plenty of time for football, turning out for both Tottenham and Wales in unofficial competition as well as guesting for Huddersfield Town, Millwall, Nottingham Forest, Notts County and Reading.

When peace resumed he settled as Tottenham's regular left-half and it was a tribute to his insatiable drive that he emerged as leader of a team which included two men marked out for massive achievements in management – Alf Ramsey was destined to guide England to World Cup triumph in 1966, five years after Bill Nicholson had presided over Spurs becoming the first club that century to lift the League and FA Cup double.

At first Burgess's swashbuckling determination to surge forward, sometimes heedless of defensive duties, was perceived as a weakness, but after Rowe became boss in 1949 the skipper tempered his adventure with a dash of caution, and became even more effective. Indeed, years later the shrewd Nicholson would describe him as the best midfielder the club had ever known, thus outranking the illustrious likes of Danny Blanchflower, Dave Mackay, Glenn Hoddle and Paul Gascoigne.

That's some accolade, but then Burgess, who was in his 38th year when he moved on to Swansea Town in 1954, truly was some player.

| | |
|---|---|
| **WILLIAM ARTHUR RONALD BURGESS** | |
| BORN: | Cwm, Monmouthshire, 9 April 1917. |
| HONOURS: | League Championship 50/1. Second Division Championship 49/50. 32 Wales caps (46-54). |
| OTHER CLUBS: | Swansea Town 54/5-55/6 (46, 1). |
| MANAGER: | Swansea Town (55-58); Watford (59-63). |
| DIED: | Swansea, Glamorgan, 14 February 2005. |

| GAMES | 329 |
|---|---|
| GOALS | 17 |

# ALF RAMSEY

· · · · · · · · · · · · · · · · · · · · · · · · · · · · ·

## 1949/50 → 1954/55

The name of Alf Ramsey is enshrined forever among football's immortals, but more than a decade and a half before he entered history as the only man to guide England to World Cup glory in 1966, the solemn, single-minded son of a Dagenham grocer had already made an indelible mark as a hugely influential figure in one of the most entertaining teams of the 20th century.

In his playing days in Arthur Rowe's breathtaking push-and-run creation, the future Sir Alf was an immaculate right-back, composed, stylish and metronomically consistent. Though never the quickest, he made good that deficit by intelligent positioning, and while he didn't lack bite in his defensive work, it was the precision and shrewdness of his attacking contribution which rendered him remarkable.

Ramsey's perceptive passing was a connoisseur's delight, a productive speciality being raking dispatches to the opponents' near post, enabling Les Bennett to nod dangerously across goal. Alf was a dead-ball expert, too, reliable from the penalty spot and devastatingly accurate with free-kicks.

The complete antithesis of flamboyance, he adopted a meticulously studious approach to his profession which less serious colleagues could find irritating, but his attention to detail often benefited the side, his photographic memory for practically every incident in every game helping him constantly to analyse and to improve.

The Ramsey outlook had always been singular. As a youth blessed with considerable ability, he might have been expected to dream of high attainment on the field; instead, the ambition of which he spoke was to emulate his father as a successful grocer.

He was already an amateur with Portsmouth when Southampton spotted him playing services football and took him to The Dell in 1944 as a stocky, powerful and skilful centre-half cum centre-forward. Converted by his manager Bill Dodgin into a right-back, Ramsey matured rapidly. By 1948 he had played for England but then, surprisingly, was ousted from both club and country teams by Bill Ellerington and the following year joined Tottenham, valued at £21,000 in a player-exchange deal which saw Welsh international winger Ernie Jones travelling in the opposite direction.

Now Ramsey found himself under the aegis of a fellow deep-thinker, Rowe, who was in the process of putting together his famous side, with the expensive newcomer – the only member to cost a substantial fee – seen as the final constituent.

The Tottenham boss proved perfect for Ramsey, educating him in the benefits of short passing which complemented his majestic long-range repertoire, and the full-back emerged as the team's defensive marshal, being dubbed 'The General' as Spurs achieved back-to-back Second and First Division title triumphs.

Though his 32-cap England career, which included 29 successive appearances, ended in 1953, he remained a force at club level, going on to replace the departed Ron Burgess as skipper before losing his place in his middle thirties and moving into management with Ipswich Town.

Sensationally Alf Ramsey led the unfashionable Suffolk club from the Third Division to the League championship. All that remained was to take on the world . . .

---

**ALFRED ERNEST RAMSEY**

| | |
|---|---|
| BORN: | Dagenham, Essex, 22 January 1920. |
| HONOURS: | League Championship 50/1. Second Division Championship 49/50. 32 England caps (48-53). |
| OTHER CLUBS: | Southampton 46/7-48/9 (90, 8). |
| MANAGER: | Ipswich Town (55-63); England (63-74); Birmingham City (caretaker 77-78). |
| DIED: | Ipswich, Suffolk, 28 April 1999. |

GAMES **250**
GOALS **24**

# LEN DUQUEMIN

## 1947/48 → 1956/57

No one who spent time with Len Duquemin was surprised to discover that the squarely-built centre-forward in Tottenham Hotspur's first League Championship-winning team had worked in a monastery before stepping into the hectic world of professional football at White Hart Lane.

The Guernsey-born marksman, a ceaselessly competitive study in perpetual motion on the pitch, was a quiet, gentle, engagingly unassuming fellow away from the action, and somehow it was not difficult to imagine him moving tranquilly among the monks as he tended their garden during the German occupation of the Channel Islands in the Second World War.

Indeed, of his two nicknames, 'Reliable Len' and 'The Duke', the first fitted his character far more neatly, offering due recognition of his unobtrusive but incalculably valuable service to one of the outstanding sides of the era, while the second was no more than a glib abbreviation of his surname.

Duquemin scored heavily and consistently for his solitary Football League club, and despite his lack of extravagant natural ability, he was considered a key man by manager and team-mates as he helped to lift the Second Division title in 1949/50, then the First Division crown in the following campaign.

Arthur Rowe's team won renown for its flowing, quickfire ball manipulation, but there was a need, too, for players who would run ceaselessly when they were not in possession, providing extra passing options for their artistic colleagues; they didn't always get the ball and rarely took the eye, but without them the system would have foundered. One such was Duquemin, whose honest sweat was an important lubricant to the smooth running of Rowe's captivating machine.

Quick, strong and immensely effective in the air, 'Reliable Len' netted on his senior debut in August 1947, and thereafter retained a regular place. At that point Spurs were a tolerably enterprising but unexceptional second-flight outfit, but they were transformed when Rowe replaced Joe Hulme as manager in 1949, sweeping to their divisional championship in his first season with the help of 16 Duquemin goals.

The Channel Islander supplied 14 more on the title trail in 1950/51, including the sole strike of a tense springtime home encounter with Sheffield Wednesday which clinched the domestic game's top prize. In 1951/52 he continued to prosper as Tottenham finished second and enjoyed his most prolific personal season in 1952/53, when he registered 24 senior goals.

When meaningful competition arrived in the shape of York City's David Dunmore in February 1954, he resisted it doggedly, and it was not until 1956, when he was past 30, that finally he was supplanted as first-choice number-nine by future England spearhead Bobby Smith. Two years on, with a typical absence of fuss, Len left to join non-League Bedford Town.

**LEONARD STANLEY DUQUEMIN**
**BORN:** Cobo, Guernsey, 17 July 1924.
**HONOURS:** League Championship 50/1. Second Division Championship 49/50.
**DIED:** London, 20 April 2003.

GAMES **308**
GOALS **134**

# EDDIE BAILY

## 1946/47 → 1955/56

Eddie Baily personified both the quicksilver style and the exuberant soul of the Tottenham Hotspur side which lifted the Second and First Division titles in successive seasons.

A nimble and imaginative inside-forward blessed with assured mastery over a moving ball, the loquacious little Londoner was a gleeful executioner of Arthur Rowe's push-and-run method, exemplifying the manager's catchphrase of 'make it simple, make it quick.'

But it was not only Baily's one-touch wizardry which made him a darling of the White Hart Lane faithful during the first decade after the Second World War. They embraced him, too, for the infectious warmth of his personality – his tendency to cavort with untrammelled joy on scoring a goal or to clutch his head in despair at a missed opportunity was novel in an era when few players were prone to extravagant displays of public emotion.

With his heart on his sleeve, the cockerel on his chest and, frequently, a colourful profanity on his lips, the 5ft 7in midfield general radiated pride in the Tottenham cause, and he was a key constituent of the social cement which bonded the team spirit of Rowe's exhilarating creation.

An outstanding performer as a schoolboy, Baily was snapped up by Spurs as an amateur and sent to develop his game with non-League Finchley, then being used by the north Londoners as a nursery club.

During the war he served with the Royal Scots Fusiliers and although he emerged unscathed from the conflict, news filtered back to White Hart Lane that he was missing in action. Thus his registration was allowed to lapse.

On returning to civvy street, hearing nothing from Tottenham and unaware of the administrative bungle, the disappointed Baily, fresh from excelling for the British Army team on the Rhine, was still determined to forge a career in football and signed amateur forms for Chelsea.

The misunderstanding was revealed only after he dropped into the Spurs ground to meet a friend, after which the Stamford Bridge club, reacting with impeccable honour, released him from his obligation, and in February 1946 he was back at the Lane.

By now in his early twenties, he progressed rapidly, soon turning professional and making his senior debut in January 1947. Manager Joe Hulme did not offer him a regular place until the following autumn, but thereafter he was a fixture in a promising side which didn't take flight fully until Rowe became boss in May 1949.

Under his enlightened guidance Tottenham romped to the Second Divison crown in the next campaign, with Baily a prominent factor. Meshing effectively with the dynamic Ron Burgess, and striking up a productive left-wing partnership with flankman Les Medley, the diminutive play-maker was at the hub of a free-flowing, hugely entertaining unit.

Oozing flair and football intelligence, he was a distributor both perceptive and precise, and the quickness of mind was matched by fleetness of foot, his sudden bursts of acceleration often startling opponents who were expecting a trademark pass.

He was a goal-scorer, too, packing a shot in either foot that was remarkably powerful for such a small fellow, the secret of his high-velocity dispatches being down to exquisite timing rather than brute force.

Indeed, Baily was not a hard man in the physical sense – barnstorming tackles were left mainly to the irrepressible Burgess – but he was a relentless and voluble competitor whose animated imprecations to team-mates were frequently discernible above the roar of the crowd.

He shone ever more brightly as Spurs lifted the League Championship in 1950/51, their first season back in the premier flight, and finished as runners-up to Manchester United in 1951/52.

Over the next few seasons, Baily remained a force, but the team declined into mid-table mediocrity and in January 1956, aged 30, he was sold to Port Vale for £6,000. He extended his playing days with Nottingham Forest and Leyton Orient, eventually returning to the Lane as assistant manager to Bill Nicholson in October 1963 and making a new mark as a high-decibel motivator until the pair of them left in 1974.

In 2008 Eddie Baily, still rightly revered at White Hart Lane, was the last surviving member of Arthur Rowe's beautiful side.

**EDWARD FRANCIS BAILY**

| | |
|---|---|
| BORN: | Clapton, London, 6 August 1925. |
| HONOURS: | League Championship 50/1. Second Division Championship 49/50. 9 England caps (50-52). |
| OTHER CLUBS: | Port Vale 55/6-56/7 (26, 8); Nottingham Forest 56/7-58/9 (68, 14); |
| | Leyton Orient 58/9-59/60 (29, 3). |

| | |
|---|---|
| GAMES | 325 |
| GOALS | 69 |

# LES BENNETT

1946/47 → 1954/55

Lean, loping Les Bennett brought a dash of the unexpected to Arthur Rowe's high-tempo push-and-run marvels. A subtly skilful inside-forward, the beautifully balanced Londoner was wholly capable of joining in with his colleagues' sparkling quickfire passing combinations, but equally he might embark on a sudden bewitching dribble, or change the angle of attack with a sumptuous turn, thus introducing a touch of thrilling variety to Tottenham's exhilarating style.

As the one man in the side likely to put his foot on the ball, Les was criticised sometimes for slowing the game down, but the canny Rowe saw the value of occasional contrast and was more than content with the Bennett contribution, which included a generous helping of goals. Les was an indefatigable worker, too, roaming ceaselessly to all attacking areas, making him a nightmare for markers to pin down and frequently offering a target for ambitious passers such as Alf Ramsey and Eddie Baily.

Arguably he was unlucky never to win a cap – the closest he came was selection as 12th man in the days before substitutes were allowed – but he was operating in an era blessed by a plethora of top-quality inside-men. As it reads, Bennett's record is impressive enough, but having signed for Spurs shortly before the war, he was then deprived of six years of his early prime and did not make his senior debut until he was 28. Given his exceptional ability, it is tempting to reflect on the peaks he might have scaled given an uninterrupted career.

**LESLIE DONALD BENNETT**
BORN: Wood Green, London, 10 January 1918.
HONOURS: League Championship 50/1. Second Division Championship 49/50.
OTHER CLUBS: West Ham United 54/5-55/6 (26, 3).
DIED: 29 April 1999.

| | | |
|---|---|---|
| GAMES | **295** | |
| GOALS | 119 | |

# LES MEDLEY

1945/46 → 1952/53

He tends not to be feted in the history books, but the part played by the livewire little left winger Les Medley in the triumphs of Tottenham Hotspur midway through the 20th century should never be underrated.

The stocky local lad was an ever-present and top-scored with 18 goals as Arthur Rowe's team finished 1949/50 straddling the Second Division pinnacle, then struck 11 more times on the way to the League Championship a season later.

Medley packed power in either foot and sometimes startled much taller defenders by rising above them, having timed his leap perfectly, to head probing dispatches from the likes of Alf Ramsey.

Often he wrong-footed opponents, too, by forsaking the left touchline to pop up where he was least expected, perhaps on the opposite flank, maybe in the centre-forward channel, and his impeccable all-round technique enabled him to capitalise on their momentary disarray.

Though possessed of a beguiling body-swerve and capable of solo runs, the nimble Medley was at his most compelling when working slick passing triangles with Ron Burgess and Eddie Baily, literally pushing and running as prescribed by Rowe.

Medley, who rose through the club's junior ranks but then spent time in Canada before commencing his senior career, accumulated six England caps, all after he had turned 30, and was never on the losing side for his country.

**LESLIE DENNIS MEDLEY**
BORN: Edmonton, London, 3 September 1920.
HONOURS: League Championship 50/1. Second Division Championship 49/50. 6 England caps (50-51).
OTHER CLUBS: Toronto Greenbacks, Ulster United, both Canada, 46-47.
DIED: Ontario, Canada, January 2001.

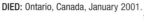

| | | |
|---|---|---|
| GAMES | **165** | |
| GOALS | 46 | |

# SONNY WALTERS

1946/47 → 1955/56

Outside-right Sonny Walters was ideal for the exhilarating give-and-go style imposed by manager Arthur Rowe on his richly entertaining team. He was adept at lightning one-two interchanges with his right-side colleagues Alf Ramsey and Bill Nicholson and could leave markers for dead with bursts of explosive acceleration. But also he was gloriously unselfish, in general not a man to light up contests with lengthy dribbles but magnificently efficient within the system.

The hugely industrious Walters also enabled Ramsey to widen the scope of his own contribution by dropping deep to take safe, short passes from the right-back, who at the time of his arrival from Southampton had been more likely to limit himself to riskier long-distance missives. This new gambit, initiated by the visionary Rowe, benefited Walters, too, as often he found himself in plenty of space due to his own marker's reluctance to track him beyond the halfway line.

The dashing north Londoner, a product of Tottenham's enterprising nursery system which included the top amateur outfit Walthamstow Avenue, made his first-team breakthrough during the war but didn't establish ascendancy over right-wing rival Freddie Cox – who was soon to move on to a trophy-winning stint with Arsenal – until the spring of 1949.

A year later Walters was called up for England 'B', but the enduring excellence of Stanley Matthews and Tom Finney denied him further international advancement.

**WILLIAM EDWARD WALTERS**
BORN: Edmonton, London, 5 September 1924.
HONOURS: League Championship 50/1. Second Division Championship 49/50.
OTHER CLUBS: Aldershot 57/8-58/9 (66, 11).
DIED: Enfield, London, 25 November 1970.

| | | |
|---|---|---|
| GAMES | **234** | |
| GOALS | 71 | |

# HARRY CLARKE

## 1948/49 → 1956/57

Lofty and gangling, engagingly unassuming yet fiercely determined, Harry Clarke was the pillar of defensive strength who gave Arthur Rowe's team of push-and-run entertainers the firm foundation on which to sparkle.

Invariably calm no matter how hectic the action raging around him, he enjoyed an almost uncanny understanding with goalkeeper Ted Ditchburn, each man knowing instinctively when to go for the ball and when to leave it for his comrade. Crucially, too, there tended not to be peaks and troughs in Clarke's performance level; he was dependability personified.

Tremendous in the air and no slouch with the ball at his feet, the towering pivot was left-sided, which was an advantage when facing most right-footed strikers, who tended to dart towards his strongest wing.

Harry helped non-League Lovells Athletic to win the Welsh Cup in 1948, then joined Spurs as a 26-year-old in the following spring. Recognising his quality, Rowe wasn't worried about his lack of high-grade experience, pitching him straight into the senior fray. He didn't miss a match for the next two seasons, in each of which a title was garnered, sometimes playing through painful injuries rather than let the side down.

Clarke, who made his one England appearance in 1954 when he was marginally past his best, netted only four times as a Spur, curiously all in his penultimate campaign, 1955/56. He finished his time at White Hart Lane as a coach, later sampling management with non-League Llanelli and Romford.

**HENRY ALFRED CLARKE**
BORN: Woodford, Essex, 23 February 1923.
HONOURS: League Championship 50/1. Second Division Championship 49/50. 1 England cap (54).
DIED: 16 April 2000.

GAMES **323**
GOALS **4**

# BILL NICHOLSON

## 1938/39 → 1954/55

Bill Nicholson is revered as Tottenham's most successful boss of all time, and rightly so, but it would be a shame if those magnificent managerial achievements were allowed to obscure totally his doughty playing contribution to the wonderful side constructed by the most eminent of his predecessors in the White Hart Lane hot seat, Arthur Rowe.

After brief experience at left-back and centre-half, Nicholson made a permanent switch to right-half soon after the war, and immediately it became obvious that he had found his niche.

The sturdy Yorkshireman was an unspectacular performer, robust, industrious and efficient, his play as unadorned by fripperies as his down-to-earth character and lifestyle. Playing alongside his ebullient skipper, Ron Burgess, and in front of the enterprising Alf Ramsey, Nicholson acted as an endlessly consistent linkman and ball-winner, becoming a crucial component in that fine trophy-winning team team.

Unaccustomed personal glory arrived in May 1951 when, at the age of 32, Bill was called up for his sole full England cap. He celebrated in untypically dramatic manner by scoring with his first kick, a powerful shot from long range, a mere 19 seconds into the action against Portugal at Goodison Park. The lack of further international recognition could be ascribed to a combination of injuries, advancing age and the excellence of Billy Wright.

Come 1954 Nicholson, whose honesty was a byword, told Rowe it was time to replace him in the team, and he accepted an invitation to join the club's coaching staff. That turned out to be an inspired decision for all concerned.

**WILLIAM EDWARD NICHOLSON**
BORN: Scarborough, Yorkshire, 26 January 1919.
HONOURS: League Championship 50/1. Second Division Championship 49/50. 1 England cap (51).
MANAGER: Tottenham Hotspur (58-74).
DIED: Potters Bar, Hertfordshire, 23 October 2004.

GAMES **345**
GOALS **6**

# EXPLANATORY NOTE

Next we move on to what might be termed the modern age of Tottenham Hotspur, beginning in 1958 when the glorious governance of Bill Nicholson commenced, then working gradually through the decades until we reach the present day and the richly promising reign of Juande Ramos.

Here, to set the tone, is a photograph of the greatest team in White Hart Lane history, the League and FA Cup double winners of 1960/61.

Appended to the profiles which follow, starting with Ted Ditchburn on page 42, are statistics covering the Football League and Premiership; the FA Cup; the Football League Cup in all its guises; the European Cup; the European Cup Winners' Cup; the UEFA Cup; and the FA Charity Shield.

*One of the greatest sides of all time, the 1960/61 Tottenham Hotspur League and FA Cup double-winners. Back row, left to right: John White, Ron Henry, Bill Brown, Maurice Norman, Peter Baker, Dave Mackay. Front row: Cliff Jones, Bobby Smith, Danny Blanchflower, Les Allen, Terry Dyson.*

# TED DITCHBURN

## 1946/47 → 1958/59

There must have been moments when the name of Ted Ditchburn made those who followed him between the Tottenham posts feel heartily sick. Even Ditchburn's respected long-term successor, the Scottish star Bill Brown, and the ultimately majestic Pat Jennings in his early, rather faltering days at White Hart Lane, were not immune to unflattering comparisons with the towering Kentish custodian.

For 15 years and more after his retirement, if a cross was dropped or a shot fumbled, there would be dark mutterings, not only from the terraces but also from Spurs insiders, that such a calamity would never have happened in Ditchburn's day. Of course, Ditchburn made mistakes, but they were precious few and to see him line up behind the north Londoners' defence, all lithe muscle and imposing presence, it was easy enough to credit his omnipotence.

The son of a professional boxer, Ditchburn followed his father into the ring and during the mid 1930s he raised money for an early pair of football boots through a series of bouts at Rochester Casino. At that point there were influential voices in the local fight fraternity urging him to make a career out of pugilism, but his heart was set on soccer and, after working in a paper mill, he joined the Tottenham groundstaff in 1937.

After toiling single-mindedly to hone his craft during a stint on loan at non-League Northfleet, he returned to White Hart Lane to sign professional forms in 1939, only for his encouraging momentum to be jolted by the outbreak of war. Service in the RAF afforded plenty of opportunities for football, however, and the big Kentishman represented Spurs in the Football League South, an emergency competition which ran during the conflict and which he helped them to win in 1943/44.

When peace resumed he made his Second Division debut in August 1946, and once in the team, as a succession of reserve 'keepers discovered to their frustration, Ditchburn was damnably difficult to dislodge. He missed only two League games over the next seven seasons, including an unbroken spell of appearances between April 1948 and March 1954. Until eventually overhauled by Jennings, and then Steve Perryman, he held the club record for senior outings (453), an achievement rendered doubly remarkable by the fact that the war had cost him seven years of action.

Ditchburn's longevity owed plenty to superlative athleticism and strength, towards which he strove constantly and with an almost obsessive attention to detail. He was renowned for daring plunges at the feet of lone marauders; indeed, no goalkeeper of his era was more adept at winning one-on-one confrontations with attackers. This knack was due in part to sharp reflexes and a raw courage which verged on foolhardiness, but also was a result of a rigorous training routine which he devised, in which he dived, saved, threw the ball out, then dived again, continuing the sequence over and over again until he was exhausted. Generally assured when plucking crosses from the air and a fierce concentrator whom it was difficult to drag out of position, he was fiery and aggressive, too, ready and willing to withstand fearsome physical challenges from the bustling spearheads of the day.

His kicking was a slight weakness, but there was ample compensation in his close understanding with full-back Alf Ramsey, which involved the goalkeeper launching swift attacks with instant throw-outs. When the thoughtful Ramsey spoke of this then-rare manoeuvre as a tactical advance, the irreverent Ditchburn would grin and maintain that he'd started doing it merely because his kicks were so poor. Whatever its origin, the strategy was perfect for the fluid push-and-run style with which Spurs won their two consecutive titles, of Second and First Division.

As the club quested constantly for honours, Ditchburn was a tower of rock-like stability, though arguably his most memorable display came in less rarefied circumstances, during a Second Division defeat at Newcastle in January 1947. Three days after suffering concussion and severe bruising to his hip, he stood defiant as shots rained in on his goal, no sooner making one stupendous save than another was necessary. In the end he was beaten only once, by Len Shackleton, and at the final whistle some 62,000 Geordies treated the limping hero to one of the most moving ovations ever accorded to a visitor at St James' Park.

Ditchburn's unbending attitude on the pitch was underpinned by a forthright character, which occasionally upset those who were shy of home-truths, but many of his team-mates had cause to be grateful for his willingness to confront authority, and often he was asked to state the players' case in discussions with management.

By the late 1950s, with the team lacking consistency and Ditchburn in his late thirties, he began to lose his place periodically, sharing first-team duties with Ron Reynolds, but he was never heard to complain, always buckling down to fight for the goalkeeping jersey that had been his private preserve for so long. When his top-flight tenure was ended by a broken finger sustained at Chelsea in August 1958, he was the last member of the 1951 Championship side still playing, and his place in White Hart Lane folklore was inviolate.

A tribute to his enduring reputation is that many experts cannot choose between Ditchburn and Jennings as the finest custodian the Lane has known. More telling yet, others – including one Terry Venables – disdain equivocation by naming Ted as the top man. Persuasive advocacy, indeed.

**EDWIN GEORGE DITCHBURN**
**BORN:** Gillingham, Kent, 24 October 1921.
**HONOURS:** League Championship 50/1. Second Division Championship 49/50. 6 England caps (48-56).
**DIED:** Ipswich, Suffolk, 26 December 2005.

| | |
|---|---|
| GAMES | 453 |
| GOALS | 0 |

# GEORGE ROBB

. . . . . . . . . . . . . . . . . . . . . . . . . . . . . . . . .

1951/52 → 1958/59

England amateur international star George Robb had already impressed in guest outings on the Tottenham left wing when Arthur Rowe signed the dashing, dark-haired teacher as a part-time professional from non-League Finchley in June 1953. On his debut, on Christmas Day 1951, he had scored in a 3-0 victory over Charlton Athletic and subsequent appearances had confirmed his talent.

Understandably, Robb never quite matched the deeds of Les Medley, his popular predecessor in the number-11 shirt, but when he left the club in 1958 he could look back on his stay at White Hart Lane with considerable pride.

Playing under three managers in a period of marked under-achievement by Spurs, he had provided service that was at times exhilarating and never less than staunch, and he had won a full England cap into the bargain.

Robb was a strong-running, hard-shooting raider who made up in vigour and aggression what he lacked in Medley-style finesse. In 1953/54, his first full term, he netted 16 times in 37 matches and, following a concerted campaign by the London press, was called up by his country. Unfortunately for the gritty Londoner the opponents on his big day at Wembley were the majestic Hungarian side who, at least for those with eyes to see, nailed emphatically and enduringly the myth of eternal English superiority, handing out a 6-3 mauling and a football lesson.

Though never capped again – the nearest he got was a trio of 'B' internationals – Robb continued to perform reliably at club level, and enjoyed a particularly active FA Cup campaign in 1956. After scoring three times in the early rounds, he was about to push the ball into an empty net for a semi-final equaliser against Manchester City when German goalkeeper Bert Trautmann appeared to grab his legs. Amazingly, no penalty was given and Spurs were out.

Thus when a combination of age, knee injuries and the arrival of the coruscating Cliff Jones signalled his retirement and full-time return to the classroom in 1958, George Robb was left to reflect on a career devoid of medals but certainly not without worth.

| **GEORGE ROBB** | | | |
|---|---|---|---|
| BORN: | Finsbury Park, London, 1 June 1926. | GAMES | **200** |
| HONOURS: | 1 England cap (53). | GOALS | 58 |

# ALFIE STOKES

## 1952/53 → 1958/59

Viewed purely in cold statistics, the Tottenham career of Alfie Stokes remains something of a mystery. Here was a marksman who could occupy any inside-trio position and whose goals-to-games ratio was remarkable – in the region of one strike every match and a half. In addition, he was strong and skilful with a fierce shot and adequate pace. Why, then, was Stokes rarely assured of a regular berth, and why was he allowed to depart for Fulham, ostensibly a giveaway at £10,000, having netted 33 times in his previous 50 League appearances?

The fact was that the well-liked blond local boy, who had signed for Spurs from non-League Clapton in February 1953, was maybe a mite too easy-going to forge a career at the top level. Habitually, it seemed, Stokes' best form would be displayed in the early part of a game, his contribution tending to fade disappointingly as the second half grew old, a circumstance which raised awkward questions concerning fitness and commitment.

There was, however, no doubting the Stokes goal-scoring pedigree, especially when he was prompted by the creative likes of Tommy Harmer and Danny Blanchflower. He hit the target on his debut at Bolton in his first spring as a Spur, netted twice in his only outing for England under-23s in 1955, and on one unforgettable evening at White Hart Lane in September 1957 he cracked five past Birmingham City's England goalkeeper Gil Merrick.

That season Stokes played for the Football League and England 'B' but made no further progress and, languishing increasingly in the shadow of Bobby Smith at Tottenham, he took his talents to Craven Cottage in the summer of 1959. His sojourn with Fulham was brief, however, and after sampling non-League football with Cambridge City, the amiable Alfie completed an ultimately rather anti-climactic career with a short stint at Watford.

**ALFRED FREDERICK STOKES**

| | | |
|---|---|---|
| BORN: | Hackney, London, 3 October 1932. | |
| OTHER CLUBS: | Fulham 59/60 (15, 6); Watford 61/2 (14, 2). | |
| DIED: | 2002. | |

| | |
|---|---|
| GAMES | 69 |
| GOALS | 42 |

# DAVE DUNMORE

## 1953/54 → 1959/60

Dave Dunmore was a dashing centre-forward who flattered to deceive during six years at White Hart Lane. The unassuming north-easterner cost £10,500 from York City a few days before his 20th birthday in February 1954, and was given an early chance to show his mettle. Replacing the faithful Len Duquemin for the local derby at Highbury, he showed enough promise to earn an extended opportunity until season's end.

Building on this foundation, Dunmore started 1954/55 brightly, netting a home hat-trick against Wolves in the second game, and retained his place until 'The Duke' returned in January.

Thereafter his progress was stunted both by National Service and the purchase of Bobby Smith, and never again did he quite convince as the Spurs' spearhead. Big, fast and reasonably skilful, Dunmore, who could also play on the right flank, was at his best running on to a ball played into space, and he could climax his sprint with a dynamic shot.

But too much of his most telling work was performed outside the box and he appeared to lose confidence at close range. This limited his effectiveness and in March 1960 he was exchanged for West Ham's John Smith. Later Dunmore enjoyed the most successful spell of his career with Leyton Orient, top-scoring as the O's won promotion to the First Division in 1962.

**DAVID GERALD IVOR DUNMORE**
BORN: Whitehaven, Cumberland, 8 February 1934.
OTHER CLUBS: Cliftonville, Northern Ireland; York City 51/2-53/4 (48, 25); West Ham United 59/60-60/1 (36, 16); Leyton Orient 60/1-64/5 (147, 55); York City 65/6-66/7 (63, 13).

GAMES 81
GOALS 26

# JOHN RYDEN

## 1955/56 → 1958/59

John Ryden put his heart and soul into playing centre-half for Spurs, but in a time of transition for the north Londoners, he lacked the overall quality to make the position his own.

The blond, angular Scot arrived from Accrington Stanley for £8,400 in November 1955 as one of Jimmy Anderson's first managerial signings. After waiting five months for his debut, he deputised for veteran Harry Clarke at Preston and made an immediate impression by scoring in a 3-3 draw. With Harry's career drawing to an end, Ryden was given his first settled run in mid-1956/57 before making way for the younger and more mountainous Maurice Norman.

Nothing if not a trier – he was fearless in the tackle and combative, if not wholly dominant, in the air – he reclaimed the number-five shirt to kick off 1957/58 and became captain following the departure of Tony Marchi. That term Ryden played his finest football, making 35 League appearances including a lengthy stint at left-half, as Tottenham finished third.

But Norman's game was improving while Ryden's remained constant and a handful of appearances in 1958/59 proved to be his senior swansong. He remained at the Lane until June 1961, when he joined Watford before serving a succession of non-League clubs

**JOHN JOHNSTON RYDEN**
BORN: Dumbarton, Scotland, 18 February 1931.
OTHER CLUBS: Alloa Athletic 51/2-53/4; Accrington Stanley 53/4-55/6 (80, 0); Watford 61/2 (24, 1).

GAMES 68
GOALS 2

# JOHNNY BROOKS

## 1952/53 → 1959/60

Through all their glory years, Spurs boasted few more gifted footballers than one who never helped them to lift an honour. In training, Johnny Brooks displayed freely the most scintillating of skills: he was a brilliant dribbler who could lay defences to waste, he possessed a superb touch with either foot, he was as clean and crisp a kicker of the ball as it is possible to imagine.

Yet so often, when it came to applying his abundant talent to the practical business of winning games, the curly-haired inside-forward failed to deliver. Some crucial ingredient – call it devil, determination or whatever – was missing from the Brooks make-up, and without it he was never going to fulfil completely that vast potential.

Not that Johnny's career was a flop; far from it. After arriving from Reading, his home-town club, in February 1953 in exchange for a £3,000 fee plus the services of Dennis Uphill and Harry Robshaw, he did much to convince Arthur Rowe of his fitness for a key role as that most thoughtful of managers set about major surgery to his beloved 'push-and-run' title-winners.

Brooks, who could scheme and score with equal facility, gave some memorable displays in the mid 1950s, but there was always an underlying, worrying lack of consistency. This was never illustrated more aptly than when in the winter of 1956, during which he was helping Spurs to achieve an eventual runners-up slot in the First Division, he was picked for England, then dropped by his club within a month.

Thus Brooks' frustrating progress continued until December 1959 when Chelsea recruited him for their relegation battle, exchanging his services for those of Les Allen. Having helped to stave off the drop, he didn't linger at Stamford Bridge, seeing out his career in the lower divisions.

He will go down as a player with special abilities but one who, perhaps, never relished life among the muck and bullets of close combat.

Still Brooks, whose son Shaun was to enjoy a long League career with Crystal Palace, Leyton Orient and Bournemouth, retained both his fitness and his appetite for the game long after retirement, and was playing local football beyond his 60th birthday.

**JOHN BROOKS**

BORN: Reading, Berkshire, 23 December 1931.
HONOURS: 3 England caps (56).
OTHER CLUBS: Reading 49/50-52/3 (46, 5); Chelsea 59/60-60/1 (46, 6); Brentford 61/2-63/4 (83, 36); Crystal Palace 63/4 (7, 0).

GAMES **179**
GOALS **51**

# DANNY BLANCHFLOWER

## 1954/55 → 1963/64

Twentieth-century soccer produced no more inspiring, challenging and downright fascinating personality than Danny Blanchflower. A born leader who captained Spurs to their unforgettable triumphs of the early 1960s, the charming but waspishly outspoken Ulsterman was a revolutionary free thinker, an incurable romantic and perhaps the most beguiling talker the game has known. But though he held forth so eloquently, Blanchflower was no mere blarney merchant. Anyone fortunate enough to have caught him at the zenith of his playing powers, between 1957 and 1962, would speak of a magnificently creative right-half who could dictate the tempo of a game like few footballers before or since.

Wirily slim, though minimally endowed with power and pace, Blanchflower was not a spectacular performer, more a subtle, all-pervasive influence possessed of the priceless knack of losing his marker at crucial moments. Having thus seized centre-stage while less thoughtful fellows milled around unproductively, he imposed his presence emphatically, dispensing shrewd first-time passes, both long and short, that could paralyse at a stroke the most meticulously marshalled defence.

Always he wanted the ball and would demand it vociferously; then his poise and grace would be seen at their most vivid, often wherever the combat raged the fiercest and no matter how dire the physical danger.

Such a rare combination of qualities had impressed Tottenham manager Arthur Rowe who, in December 1954, took advantage of Arsenal's apparent attack of cold feet over a mooted £40,000 deal for Blanchflower and signed the artistic 28-year-old from Aston Villa for £30,000, still a British record fee for a half-back.

Having bemused the staid Villa Park regime by suggesting tactical experiments, the Irishman was captivated by Spurs' intricate passing style. What might have matured into a visionary partnership was fractured when ill health forced Rowe's premature retirement, but Blanchflower progressed to the captaincy under new boss Jimmy Anderson, only to be deprived of it in April 1956 after his bold bid to reverse the tide in an FA Cup semi-final against Manchester City by making positional changes on his own initiative had ended in defeat. Ironically, similar enterprise had paid off in earlier matches.

Despite this hiccup, Blanchflower continued to make his presence felt and in 1957/58 he completed what many contemporaries assert was his finest individual season, then led his valiant countrymen to the quarter-finals of the World Cup in Sweden.

Even then, however, the path to glory was not to be unremittingly smooth. Anderson's successor Bill Nicholson, from whom Blanchflower had inherited Spurs' number-four shirt, dropped him the following winter, declaring the Irishman to be invaluable to a good side but a luxury in a poor one, and citing the need for more defensive input. A transfer request was refused before the 33-year-old was reinstalled as captain in March 1959, immediately displaying the majestic form that he was to maintain through the 1960/61 League and FA Cup double campaign and beyond.

Defying the evidence of his birth certificate, Blanchflower was voted Footballer of the Year in 1961 – as he had been in 1958 – and continued to plot his opponents' downfall, both as Britain's canniest midfield general and by taking an increasingly dominant role in training, until suffering severe knee damage against Rangers at Ibrox in a European Cup Winners' Cup encounter in December 1962. Even then he carried on, his cutting distribution destroying OFK Belgrade in the European semi-final and, having been injected with pain-killers, he performed nobly in the final thrashing of Atletico Madrid.

Come 1964, aged 38 and in considerable discomfort, he could no longer stave off the inevitable; the great footballing intellectual, perfectionist and wit, persuasive coaxer of lesser lights, indefatigable champion of players' rights and mortal foe of self-righteous authority, had played his last game.

Later Blanchflower, who was Bill Nicholson's choice to succeed him at the White Hart Lane helm in 1974 – the directors were less keen on such an independent spirit – excelled as a courageous and often controversial journalist and dabbled in management with Northern Ireland and Chelsea before falling tragic prey to a debilitating illness in his sixties. Nothing, though, could erase the name of Danny Blanchflower from any list of the sporting elite; he was the ultimate in soccer culture.

| | |
|---|---|
| **ROBERT DENNIS BLANCHFLOWER** | |
| **BORN:** | Belfast, 10 February 1926. |
| **HONOURS:** | European Cup Winners' Cup 62/3. League Championship 60/1. FA Cup 60/1, 61/2. |
| | 56 Northern Ireland caps (49-62). FWA Footballer of the Year 58, 61. |
| **OTHER CLUBS:** | Glentoran, Northern Ireland, 45/6-48/9; Barnsley 48/9-50/1 (68, 2); |
| | Aston Villa 50/1-54/5 (148, 10). |
| **MANAGER:** | Northern Ireland (76-78); Chelsea (78-79). |
| **DIED:** | Cobham, Surrey, 9 December 1993. |

GAMES 384
GOALS 21

# JOHNNY HILLS

## 1957/58 → 1959/60

In the late 1950s, Peter Baker stood between Johnny Hills and a regular berth in the Tottenham first team. Unfortunately for Hills, like many a wingman of the era he was unable to find a way around the stalwart and more experienced right-back.

Recruited from non-League Gravesend by Arthur Rowe in August 1953, Johnny waited four years for his senior debut, ousting Baker on merit for the second half of the 1957/58 term, in which Spurs recovered from a disappointing start to finish a creditable third.

During this period of grace, the powerful, stockily-built Hills let no one down, tackling hard, keeping his game simple and offering a potent attacking option with his long throw-ins. But there was a question-mark over both his positional play and speed of recovery and, quite simply, he lacked the overall class of his rival.

Thereafter Baker returned, and although Hills remained at the Lane until 1960/61, he didn't get a game as the League and Cup double was won, having fallen behind Ken Barton in the pecking order of deputies.

That summer he joined Bristol Rovers but, sadly, injury brought a premature end to the Eastville career of this cheerful Kentishman, an all-round sportsman who wielded a cricket bat with memorable verve.

**JOHN RAYMOND HILLS**
BORN: Northfleet, Kent, 24 February 1934.
OTHER CLUBS: Bristol Rovers 61/2 (7, 0).

GAMES **32**
GOALS **0**

---

# JIM ILEY

## 1957/58 → 1958/59

Mention the name of Jim Iley to most football fans of a certain age and they will conjure up an image of Newcastle United's bold, bald midfield driving force in the middle and late 1960s. But Tottenham aficionados of the previous decade will recall a fellow with a little more hair who was bought from Sheffield United for £16,000 by manager Jimmy Anderson in August 1957 to replace the temporarily departed Tony Marchi.

In fact, Iley was a splendidly creative wing-half who might have carved a long-term niche at White Hart Lane had he not been paired with Danny Blanchflower. The two smooth-passing prompters offered contributions that were too similar, and they had a disconcerting habit of sallying forward together, thus leaving yawning gaps behind them.

Though there were a few occasions when the Yorkshireman was preferred to Blanchflower, there could be no doubt – with no slight intended to an admirable and popular performer – that the Irishman was the better player, and it was no surprise in August 1959 when Bill Nicholson allowed Jim to join Nottingham Forest, recouping the purchase price in the process. However, it was as a Magpie that Iley's all-round ability and leadership qualities were seen to best advantage before he embarked on a solid managerial career in the lower divisions.

**JAMES ILEY**
BORN: South Kirkby, Yorkshire, 15 December 1935.
OTHER CLUBS: Sheffield United 54/5-57/8 (99, 7); Nottingham Forest 59/60-62/3 (92, 3); Newcastle United 62/3-68/9 (232, 15); Peterborough United 68/9-72/3 (68, 4).
MANAGER: Peterborough United (69-72); Barnsley (73-78); Blackburn Rovers (78); Bury (80-84); Exeter City (84-85).

GAMES **57**
GOALS **1**

# MEL HOPKINS

· · · · · · · · · · · · · · · · · · · · · · · · ·

## 1952/53 → 1963/64

A sickening accident on international duty robbed Mel Hopkins of his Tottenham place as Bill Nicholson's side were on the threshold of greatness. The Welshman's nose was smashed horrifically in a collision with Scotland's Ian St John at Hampden Park in November 1959, leaving Ron Henry to slip into Spurs' left-back berth.

Until then Henry had been no more than an understudy and there had been no question of Hopkins standing down; but the Englishman took his chance so well that he wore the number-three shirt through the 1960/61 League and FA Cup double campaign and half a decade beyond.

It was a cruel cut for Hopkins, who certainly would not have disgraced that great team. While his loping, spidery gait made him seem awkward, that was a deceptive impression from an accomplished all-rounder. Aerially combative and quick, he passed smoothly and those long legs were adept at last-minute saving tackles, even if he didn't exude quite the same aura of impregnability as his successor.

He enjoyed getting forward, too, though the nearest he came to the scoresheet was hitting the bar in his only European encounter, at home to Slovan Bratislava in March 1963.

Hopkins, who grew up in a Rhondda rugby stronghold and as a boy had to form his own team to get a game of soccer, was highly rated by Spurs boss Arthur Rowe, who blooded him as a 17-year-old at Derby in October 1952.

With the redoubtable Arthur Willis and Charlie Withers ageing, he claimed a regular place in 1954/55 and retained it ably until that fateful day at Hampden. His international career flourished, too, the highlight being the 1958 World Cup, Wales bucking the odds to reach the quarter-final in which the left-back gave a faultless display against Garrincha, the revered Brazilian flankman.

After five years in the White Hart Lane shadows, Hopkins followed Bobby Smith to Brighton in October 1964, playing a sterling part in lifting the Fourth Division title in his first term at the Goldstone. That medal was the least he deserved.

| **MELVYN HOPKINS** | | | |
|---|---|---|---|
| **BORN:** | Ystrad, South Wales, 7 November 1934. | | |
| **HONOURS:** | 34 Wales caps (56-63). | **GAMES** | **240** |
| **OTHER CLUBS:** | Brighton 64/5-66/7 (58, 2); Ballymena, Northern Ireland; Bradford Park Avenue 68/9-69/70 (30, 0). | **GOALS** | **0** |

# TOMMY HARMER

## 1951/52 → 1959/60

Tommy Harmer was born too late to be a soccer superstar. Perhaps in the first half of the century, before the clarion calls for strength, speed and stamina were so stridently insistent, this frail but wondrously gifted Tom Thumb of an inside-forward would have been feted as an entertainer supreme. Lamentably for those who delight in audacious sleight of foot, revering artistry while remaining unmoved by mere athleticism, he was granted a comparatively brief tenure as Spurs' premier play-maker.

For sheer wizardry on the ball, Tommy was unrivalled. Shy and nervous in the dressing-room – half a calming cigarette before a game, with the rest saved for half-time, became a Harmer ritual – he was capable of an astonishing transformation if the Muse was with him when he walked on to the pitch. There he became impudent, even insolent at times, tempting the lungers and scythers into his orbit before swaying his puny frame and dancing away with the ball at his feet.

Yet beguiling though his dribbling undoubtedly was, it was matched inspirationally by a passing technique that bordered on the sublime. 'Harmer the Charmer' was a master of backspin, swerve and every variation of trajectory and, better still, could produce his devilish manipulations in the heat of battle.

Indeed, for all that technical mastery, he was never a self-aggrandising trickster, better suited to circus ring than football field; rather he was an instinctive improviser whose subtle wiles were employed faithfully in his team's cause.

So with such prodigious ability, why did the gaunt-featured 5ft 6in Eastender, such a distinctive figure with his jerkily inelegant gait, his voluminous shorts and his mop of black hair crowning a head which appeared fractionally too big for that pipe-cleaner of a frame, not claim a regular first-team slot until he was 28? The answer is not merely his lack of physical stature – which years of special beef-steak diets failed dismally to improve – although certainly that was a major factor, causing him to be relatively ineffective in a significant percentage of matches.

He was handicapped, too, by turning professional in 1948, at a time when Spurs were developing their distinctive push-and-run style. Manager Arthur Rowe, while recognising Harmer's rare talent, reckoned that he interrupted the flow of an otherwise fluid combination, consequently not offering the schemer a senior debut until he was 23 and limiting his opportunities thereafter.

So disenchanted did he become at one point that he asked for a transfer, but the only firm offer came from Cardiff City, located too far from London for the home-loving Harmer, who thus had no choice but to bide his time.

Happily for Harmer, selection policy changed drastically in mid-decade, after veteran midfield general Eddie Baily had departed and Jimmy Anderson succeeded Rowe as boss, and for two seasons Tommy flourished in a delightfully creative midfield partnership with Danny Blanchflower. Together they sparkled as Tottenham finished as First Division runners-up in 1956/57, during which Harmer answered criticism about his lightweight contribution by netting 17 League goals, and came third the following term. As the decade drew towards its close with Bill Nicholson now at the helm, Harmer remained a near-regular, although appearing occasionally as a deep-lying outside-right.

The beginning of the end for the little Londoner was the arrival in October 1959 of John White, though at first the two enchanters played together as twin inside-forwards, then in tandem on the right flank. But the balance was wrong and, understandably in view of his 32 years, it was Harmer who made way.

A £6,000 fee took him to Watford in October 1960 – that old reluctance to stray far from familiar territory led him to reject approaches from higher-ranking but more distant clubs – and later he lent his experience to Tommy Docherty's young braves at Chelsea, scoring the goal that won promotion to the top flight in 1963, before coaching at Stamford Bridge.

Back at White Hart Lane, where he was always held in high affection, fans still recount tales of his uplifting performances, none more remarkable than in the 10-4 annihilation of Everton in 1958, in which legend has it he made nine goals and scored one, though that might be stretching the facts ever so slightly!

Movingly described by Danny Blanchflower as a beloved outcast, he was arguably the right man at the wrong time for Spurs, missing out on the League and FA Cup double and contenting himself philosophically with an England 'B' cap as his sole representative honour. To aficionados of unalloyed skill, it remained anathema that he was never awarded a full cap, his supporters bitterly denouncing what they saw as a disgraceful triumph of functionalism over flair.

Born too late? Maybe, but those who watched him play should guard the memory jealously. The like of Tommy Harmer will not be seen again.

**THOMAS CHARLES HARMER**

| | | |
|---|---|---|
| **BORN:** | Hackney, London, 2 February 1928. | |
| **OTHER CLUBS:** | Watford 60/1-61/2 (63, 6); Chelsea 62/3-63/4 (8, 1). | **GAMES** 222 |
| **DIED:** | London, 25 December 2007. | **GOALS** 51 |

# PETER BAKER

· · · · · · · · · · · · · · · · · · · · · · · · · · · · · · · ·

## 1952/53 → 1964/65

In terms of popular public acclaim, Peter Baker was the poor relation in Tottenham Hotspur's greatest side. Of the other so-called journeymen in the 1960/61 League and FA Cup-winning combination, even his similarly unsung full-back partner and close pal Ron Henry went on to earn the kudos of an England cap, while the only other non-internationals, Les Allen and Terry Dyson, inevitably grabbed more of the limelight as members of a free-scoring forward line. Yet the slightest suggestion that Baker was fortunate to find a place in such star-studded company was rejected emphatically by the only authorities who mattered, his team-mates and manager at White Hart Lane.

In fact, the blond, squarely-built number-two was a consummate professional who performed a crucial and highly specialised function, albeit of the decidedly unspectacular variety, in the double-winning side.

Certainly no verdict on Baker's contribution is valid without due consideration of the telling circumstance that the right-half in front of him was a certain Danny Blanchflower, and though it was undeniably a privilege to be in the presence of such an immense talent, life behind the Irish rover was not always easy. When his adventurous skipper disappeared on his habitual attacking sorties, Baker found himself frequently with two men to mark, and occasionally with an unholy mess that was not of his own making to clear up.

The loyal Londoner was perfectly equipped for the demanding role. Fast and intelligent, composed and reliable, he was not prone to commit himself to rash challenges, electing instead to jockey opponents away from the danger area until cover arrived. When the need arose, however, he could be remorselessly hard in the tackle and was brave too, as he showed when heading the ball off Albert Cheesebrough's boot to deny the Leicester winger an almost certain goal in the 1961 FA Cup Final.

Although not prone to over-elaboration on the ball – Baker's preferred option was the simple push to Blanchflower – occasionally he would catch opponents unawares, unleashing a sudden, penetrating through-pass after appearing to dally tranquilly in possession. Add to that his powers of motivation – he was voluble both on and off the field – and the picture of a splendidly capable competitor is complete.

Indeed there was a time in the early 1950s, after he had arrived at the Lane from local amateurs Enfield, that the youth international inspired predictions of a long-term England career. Then, having made his League debut alongside the veteran Bill Nicholson in April 1953, he settled as understudy to no less a personage than Alf Ramsey, from whom he learned voraciously.

However, possibly the weight of expectation was detrimental and his rate of progress slowed so much that when the future England boss departed in 1955, Peter found himself losing out to Charlie Withers and Maurice Norman in the contest for the right-back berth. He persevered, though, winning a regular place in 1956/57, surviving a challenge from Johnny Hills during the following term, and emerging to play a full part in Tottenham's early-1960s triumphs.

One of the older members of that wonderful side – as the irreverent Jimmy Greaves, who as a boy had hunted the Baker autograph, never tired of reminding him – Peter nevertheless continued to offer stalwart service until mid-decade, seeing off one stern challenge from Mel Hopkins before the young Cyril Knowles arrived to take his place.

Still supremely fit, probably the best all-round sportsman at the club, Peter Baker emigrated to South Africa in 1965, becoming player-boss of Durban City before embarking on a successful business career in that country. He could depart happily and honourably, knowing that only a very fine player could have satisfied that ultimate perfectionist, Bill Nicholson, for so long.

**PETER RUSSELL BARKER BAKER**

BORN: Hampstead, London, 10 December 1931.
HONOURS: European Cup Winners' Cup 62/3. League Championship 60/1.
FA Cup 60/1, 61/2.

GAMES **344**
GOALS **3**

# BOBBY SMITH

· · · · · · · · · · · · · · · · · · · · · · · · · · · · · · · · · · · · · · · · ·

## 1955/56 → 1963/64

Bobby Smith was an immense individual in terms of physique, personality and, yes, footballing talent. Down the years there were always elitists who decried the bulky, bustling buccaneer of a centre-forward as crude and uncomely, the type who might have his uses as a battering ram but who lacked the necessary class for Spurs and England.

Yet while the broad-shouldered son of a Yorkshire miner could be awesomely aggressive – indeed, he put the fear of God into faint-hearted opponents and was not above heightening the effect with the kind of menacing mien beloved of boxers before a fight – it was scandalously unjust to write him off as a mere slugger.

The record books offer eloquent testimony, but more of that later; first, let the memory reveal the extent of Smith's skills. Most easily recalled, perhaps, are his rather similar goals against Leicester and Burnley in the FA Cup Finals of 1961 and 1962. In both cases he controlled the ball with one sure touch, wrong-footed his marker by sheer guile, then netted unstoppably.

Equally exhilarating was his strike as Spurs clinched the title at home to Sheffield Wednesday in April 1961: in a glorious blur of action he flicked the ball over one of his England colleagues, Peter Swan, then strode on to crash a first-time half-volley past another, Ron Springett. But for sheer artistry – and we are still talking about Bobby Smith – that was as nothing compared to his perfectly-judged chip over Spain's goalkeeper at Wembley in 1960, a moment that graced the international stage he was to occupy so fleetingly.

Now for those statistics. In his first five years at White Hart Lane, Smith became the highest scorer in Tottenham history; he exceeded 30 League and Cup goals in each of the four seasons between 1957/58, in which he notched 38 in 40 outings, and 1960/61, the year of the double; and for his country he hit the target 13 times in 15 games before being discarded.

All that must have seemed unthinkable to the fans who jeered him as a carthorse following his £18,000 purchase from Chelsea in December 1955, and it's true that his path to Stamford Bridge offered few clues to his ultimate destiny. Smith grew up never dreaming that he might make his living as a footballer and after leaving school he started work in the local pit as an apprentice blacksmith, shoeing the ponies which pulled the wagons of coal, a life of toil to which his bull-like build appeared to be ideally suited.

In his early teens he was a prodigiously strong but otherwise unremarkable full-back with Redcar Boys. Then one day the team's centre-forward didn't turn up, the rookie anvilman volunteered to replace him in the front line and he scored twice. Thereafter he never played in defence again, impressing so vividly as leader of the line that he was recruited as an amateur by Chelsea in 1948.

Still, though, there were obstacles to be overcome. At first homesick in London, soon he returned to Yorkshire. His father, anxious that the boy should avoid a lifetime of drudgery in the pit, was not unduly sympathetic, hurrying him back to the Bridge with the imprecation that he should show Chelsea what he was made of.

Gradually he did, but largely he languished in the shadow of England's Roy Bentley and duly he moved on, though the apparent absence of tactical acumen in his early Spurs appearances appeared to indicate why his progress as a Pensioner had been so ponderous.

But before long the goals flowed in profusion, manager Jimmy Anderson's judgement was vindicated and Tottenham's intensely demanding terrace critics took the burly, ebullient marksman to their hearts, making light of rare fits of smouldering ill temper characterised by unseemly interludes of flat-footed indolence.

At this time there were many Smith performances to savour, but especially satisfying was an Old Trafford hat-trick in November 1957 that lifted the north Londoners to victory over the pre-Munich Busby Babes and spawned talk of silverware. In fact, it would be several years before space was needed in the White Hart Lane trophy cabinet, but Smith's eminence grew rapidly and he was even tried as club captain. A happy-go-lucky soul who enjoyed himself freely and could hardly be described as a stickler for training, he was not an ideal choice as skipper and his reign was short.

But with Danny Blanchflower in charge, both Smith and Spurs prospered royally, and it was not until 1962/63, when he was dropped temporarily in favour of Les Allen, that his star began to fall. In the past he had seemed impervious to pain, sometimes taking the pitch with severely swollen ankles, but now, perhaps, the years of taking punishment as well as dispensing it were beginning to have an effect.

Thus in May 1964, with pace if not power diminished, Smith joined Brighton for a paltry £5,000 and scored heavily to help the Seagulls take the Fourth Division title. Thereafter he entered non-League football, his weight ballooned and he experienced hard times. But no amount of personal misfortune could deprive Bobby Smith of his place among Spurs' all-time greats. Whatever the snipers said, that was his by right.

| | |
|---|---|
| **ROBERT ALFRED SMITH** | |
| **BORN:** | Skelton, Yorkshire, 22 February 1933. |
| **HONOURS:** | European Cup Winners' Cup 62/3. League Championship 60/1. |
| | FA Cup 60/1, 61/2. 15 England caps (60-63). |
| **OTHER CLUBS:** | Chelsea 50/1-55/6 (74, 23); Brighton 64/5 (31, 18). |

| | |
|---|---|
| GAMES | **319** |
| GOALS | 210 |

# TERRY MEDWIN

## 1956/57 → 1962/63

Terry Medwin was a blond-thatched, fleet-footed attacker whose exhilarating right-flank dashes and goal-scoring menace took the eye throughout the late 1950s and early 1960s. Sadly for the Welsh international, the one season in which he was comprehensively eclipsed by constant rival Terry Dyson was 1960/61, when Spurs won the League and FA Cup double.

An £18,000 recruit from his home-town club of Swansea in May 1956, Medwin made a telling early impact in the number-seven shirt, helping Tottenham finish as League runners-up in his first term. He crossed the ball precisely, boasted a powerful shot in either foot and was sufficiently adept in the air to merit infrequent stints at centre-forward, the role in which he struck four times in the 6-0 home thrashing of Leicester in April 1959.

That day he capitalised implacably on the service of Danny Blanchflower, with whom he enjoyed a fruitful understanding on the right attacking flank – occasionally the two would stage-manage a bogus argument over a throw-in to catch opponents off guard.

However, it must be said that ruthlessness was not a prime characteristic of the Medwin game. Considerably more gifted than Dyson, he lacked some of the smaller man's spirit and aggression, leaving manager Bill Nicholson with a perpetually difficult choice. In favour of the former Swan was his strike rate – he netted 14 League goals in each of his first three Spurs campaigns – though ironically when he regained his place periodically in the post-double years he was less prolific.

To the satisfaction of the many who championed his cause, the genial Medwin played just enough games, deputising on either flank for Dyson and Cliff Jones, to earn a Championship medal in 1961, and made up for that year's Wembley absence by helping to beat Burnley in the 1962 final.

A broken leg on the 1963 summer tour of South Africa precipitated premature retirement, though later he returned to the professional game by coaching at Fulham, then serving Swansea as assistant manager to John Toshack.

**TERENCE CAMERON MEDWIN**
BORN: Swansea, Glamorgan, 25 September 1932.
HONOURS: League Championship 60/1. FA Cup 61/2. 30 Wales caps (53-62).
OTHER CLUBS: Swansea Town 51/2-55/6 (148, 59).

GAMES 216
GOALS 73

# TONY MARCHI

## 1949/50 → 1956/57 & 1959/60 → 1964/65

Rarely can a newspaper tag have been more unwelcome than the one foisted on Tony Marchi in 1960/61. The tall, elegant utility man was dubbed the best reserve in British football, a compliment of a kind but hardly ideal for a talented performer in his prime who could only kick his heels in frustration as his team-mates lifted the League and FA Cup double.

Marchi was, it should be stressed, a Spurs man heart and soul. London-born of an Italian father, he had been an ardent fan as a boy whose uncle, George Dorling, had once played for the club at junior level. So it was that he turned down Arsenal to sign for Arthur Rowe and made his debut as a teenage deputy for left-half Ron Burgess in the 1949/50 Division Two Championship side. Thereafter chances were few until the mid-1950s, when he inherited Burgess's shirt and became an influential team member.

The constructive Marchi game consisted of skill and vision combined with a reassuringly solid presence. He was a

composed, intelligent reader of play who exuded a certain arrogance, but as he strode confidently around the pitch there were times when he appeared to lack urgency. This impression, heightened by his meagre pace, fuelled the case of those who maintained he would never reach the highest class.

Nevertheless Marchi was an England 'B' international and Tottenham's much-respected club captain when he joined Lanerossi for £42,000 in 1957. Two years later, though Arsenal were coveting his services, a £20,000 fee brought him back to the Lane from his second Italian club, Torino, as the eventual replacement, or so the pundits thought, for Danny Blanchflower.

But the Irishman didn't see it like that and with Dave Mackay immovable in the other wing-half slot, Marchi was in the margins. However, as Spurs suffered injury problems after 1962, he was often in the side and his Italian experience was crucial in his role as an extra defender in European campaigns.

His reward was to replace the sidelined Mackay in the 1963 Cup Winners' Cup Final, and the biggest tribute to Tony is that Dave was barely missed in the 5-1 drubbing of Atletico Madrid. In 1965, Marchi left to manage non-League Cambridge City, then held the reins at Northampton Town.

| | |
|---|---|
| **ANTHONY VITTORIO MARCHI** | |
| **BORN:** | Edmonton, London, 21 January 1933. |
| **HONOURS:** | European Cup Winners' Cup 62/3. |
| **OTHER CLUBS:** | Lanerossi 57/8, Torino 58/9, both Italy. |
| **MANAGER:** | Northampton Town (67-68). |

| | |
|---|---|
| GAMES | 260 |
| GOALS | 7 |

# MAURICE NORMAN

· · · · · · · · · · · · · · · · · · · · · · · · · ·

## 1955/56 → 1965/66

Nature intended Maurice Norman to be a centre-half. To begin with, there was an awesomely powerful physique which would have served him splendidly had he made his living farming the fields of his native Norfolk; then, if 6ft 1in of muscular athleticism was not enough to make opposing marksmen quail, the effect of towering dominance was heightened by the shock of wavy black hair that stood out several inches from the crown of his head.

Not that Maurice – irreverently but affectionately dubbed 'Swede' by Jimmy Greaves, in reference to his bucolic background – conformed conveniently to the strong-but-limited stopper stereotype. Indeed, the Norman game was infused with highly distinctive character, never more evident than when he sallied out of defence, cantering down the centre of the pitch with neck outstretched and long limbs extended in unexpected directions, like some fantastic cross between runaway giraffe and quick-stepping spider.

Norman's enduring fame is assured by his presence as pivot in the League and FA Cup double-winning side of 1961, yet when he arrived at White Hart Lane from Norwich City in November 1955, in exchange for £18,000 and winger Johnny Gavin, he was a right-back.

Indeed, the quietly-spoken newcomer won England under-23 honours in both full-back berths and had to wait behind the less effective John Ryden before emerging as the long-term successor to Harry Clarke. It was not until the autumn of 1957 that he could call the central position his own, and even then there were occasions when he appeared nervy and lacking in confidence. But experience brought true authority and by the turn of the decade, Norman was exhibiting the attributes that made him a crucial cornerstone of Bill Nicholson's team.

Of paramount impact, of course, was his aerial ability at both ends of the pitch; he was one of the first centre-halves to make a habit of attacking excursions – none more productive than his important headed goal in an Eastertime encounter with Chelsea at Stamford Bridge in 1961, which Tottenham won 3-2 – and while his personal tally was hardly startling, the mere fact of his attendance was often enough to unsettle opponents into making costly mistakes.

As a tackler, he was usually firm though occasionally awkward, as if he couldn't decide with which foot to meet the ball, and he gave the impression of preferring interceptions, at which he was magnificently adept. So often the ball appeared sure to bypass Norman when a leg would shoot out to claim possession, sometimes with its owner seeming to perform contortions in mid-air.

His enviable sense of anticipation was underpinned by speed unusual in such a big man, enabling him to fill gaps left by more creative colleagues, to recover quickly if beaten and, not least, to compensate for a certain ponderousness on the turn. This latter weakness could make Norman vulnerable to quick, skilful centre-forwards who were given space to run at him, as Arsenal's David Herd demonstrated devastatingly with a two-goal display at Highbury in 1958. Overall, though, he was a formidable contributor to Tottenham's success, and his two years of regular England service in the early 1960s were well deserved.

Come 1965, by then in his thirties and operating once more at right-back, Norman suffered an horrific accident in a home friendly with a Hungarian Select XI, his leg being broken in five places. Despite a two-year fitness fight, during which his shinbone had to be reset, he was forced to retire, and Spurs had lost not only a marvellous player but also an impeccable ambassador for the game.

Testimony to both his attitude and his popularity came when local fans formed a team and christened it Norman FC. His reaction was to offer sincere encouragement and become club president. That said it all about Maurice Norman.

**MAURICE NORMAN**
BORN: Mulbarton, Norfolk, 8 May 1934.
HONOURS: European Cup Winners' Cup 62/3. League Championship 60/1. FA Cup 60/1, 61/2.
23 England caps (62-64).
OTHER CLUBS: Norwich City 54/5-55/6 (35, 0).

GAMES **413**
GOALS **19**

# RON HENRY

## 1954/55 → 1965/66

It was the biggest day in the history of Tottenham Hotspur; the gaze of the sporting world was riveted on Bill Nicholson's wondrous assembly of artists as they lined up against Leicester City at Wembley as white-hot favourites to complete the much-coveted League and FA Cup double.

But which of Spurs' extravagant firmament of stars would dazzle on the grand stage? Inevitably, the names of Blanchflower and Mackay, Jones and White, were on the pundits' lips; Smith, too, was mentioned as a possible key man. But when it came to this last, nerve-twanging obstacle between Spurs and eternal soccer glory, the popular heroes were, in general, less than scintillating – and the performer who took the eye most vividly was the unfussy, untrumpeted but utterly efficient left-back Ron Henry.

That afternoon the neat, compact Londoner, whose upright, correct carriage was strikingly reminiscent of Alf Ramsey, gave a well-nigh perfect display of positioning and tackling, interception and distribution, shackling the dangerous Howard Riley and barring all Leicester progress down the Tottenham left flank. Henry's all-round excellence was encapsulated in one dextrous manoeuvre that thwarted Albert Cheesebrough as he hared for the byline. It seemed that the winger had broken through, with Ron and his fellow defenders trailing, when the Henry leg snaked out to trap the ball and avert a potential crisis.

After the match many critics declared that the classy number-three was a natural for England, but with Ray Wilson and Mick McNeil then vying for a place in a successful national side, Henry had to wait two more years for his call-up. When it came, in Ramsey's first game as manager, England lost 5-1 to France and the Spurs man paid the penalty, never getting another chance at the top level.

To be consigned so summarily to the international scrapheap seemed rough justice on a splendidly consistent all-rounder who was renowned for his perfectly timed sliding tackles but whose subtle skill in ushering opponents into unprofitable avenues was perhaps even more valuable. Though Henry could appear ponderous on the turn, it was rare that a winger got past him, and critics of his heavy left-sided bias could not claim that it prevented him linking sweetly in the flowing passing movements for which Spurs became famous.

There had been a time, however, when it seemed he might never rise from the reserve ranks in which he spent the mid-1950s. After being spotted as a teenage outside-left when stationed at Woolwich during his National Service, Henry was converted into a left-half and made his senior debut as a centre-half before becoming a left-back – only to be confronted by an apparently immovable obstacle to his first-team ambitions in the form of Mel Hopkins.

But he refused to give up and in 1959 his patience was rewarded when the Welshman was sidelined by a serious injury. Even then, most observers judged that Henry would fill in only until Hopkins regained fitness, but they had reckoned without the deputy's determination. In the event, his form made it impossible for Bill Nicholson to drop him, he was ever-present throughout the 1960/61 double-winning campaign, and contributed nobly to subsequent triumphs.

Henry, who served briefly as skipper in the post-Blanchflower days, retained his place until knee trouble ended his senior tenure in the mid-1960s, but not before netting a belated first goal of his career in February 1965, his speculative 35-yarder against eventual champions Manchester United amazing and delighting a packed White Hart Lane.

There followed doughty service for the reserves and 'A' team, combined with a coaching stint in which his honesty and directness proved of immeasurable benefit to the club's young hopefuls. Few men have given more to the cause of Tottenham Hotspur than Ron Henry.

**RONALD PATRICK HENRY**
BORN: Shoreditch, London, 17 August 1934.
HONOURS: European Cup Winners' Cup 62/3. League Championship 60/1. FA Cup 60/1, 61/2. 1 England cap (63).

GAMES 289
GOALS 1

# BILL BROWN

1959/60 → 1965/66

Bill Brown didn't conform to the popular notion of what a goalkeeper should look like. He was tall, sure enough, but where the majority of top custodians boasted immense, muscular frames suggestive of barrier-like impregnability, Bill was lean and stringy and seemingly insubstantial; every line of the Brown figure was angular, an effect heightened by his aquiline features. But – and this was all that mattered – throughout Spurs' most fruitful era, he did his job magnificently.

The point was that the Scottish international was ideally tailored to Tottenham's needs. If the one occasional weakness in his game was collecting crosses, that was hardly calamitous with mountainous Maurice Norman in front of him, and in other respects Brown was impeccable.

Agile but unshowy, he was a superb shot-stopper possessed of keen reflexes, perceptive positional sense and unparalleled powers of concentration. This last-mentioned quality was crucial in the days when Spurs were accustomed to dominate matches and he might remain isolated for long periods.

It was reassuring for the fans – at least, those who could wrest their eyes momentarily from the attacking exploits of Blanchflower and company – to note their 'keeper half-crouching in an attitude of total involvement when all the action was taking place at the opposite end of the pitch. In his own mind, Brown kicked every ball and made every challenge, and often left the field looking drained after games in which he had been a virtual spectator.

Composure was another Brown attribute, particularly when the stakes were highest. He was never known to fail in a big match, performing immaculately in the FA Cup Finals of 1961 and 1962, in which he made a mockery of any supposed aerial fallibility. But it was during the triumphant Cup Winners' Cup campaign of 1963 that the spare, stringy Scot was seen at his admirable best, rarely more so than in the quarter-final first leg defeat by Slovan in Bratislava. Playing with a plaster across his nose after taking a heavy knock, he defied the Czechs with a series of stirring saves, limiting their lead to two and paving the way for eventual victory.

Then came two splendid semi-final displays against OFK Belgrade, but his *piece de resistance* was reserved for the final encounter with Atletico Madrid. By half-time Spurs were 2-0 up and apparently coasting, but then the Spaniards scored a penalty and for 15 minutes they peppered the Londoners' goal. As his fellow defenders reeled in the face of the onslaught, the 'keeper stood firm, coping heroically until the crisis had passed and three more Tottenham strikes secured the trophy.

It was the fourth major prize to come Brown's way since his £16,500 transfer from Dundee in June 1959, a transaction with cloak-and-dagger undertones as Bill Nicholson, wary of mounting competition from other clubs following his quarry's brilliant display against England at Wembley, rushed to jump on a night train north to be sure of closing the deal.

Although, at 27 and an established international, Brown had hardly represented a gamble in an age before Scottish net-minders became a prime source of material for English comedians, Spurs followers were relieved by his contribution after Ted Ditchburn's understudies had failed to make the grade.

The green jersey became Brown's personal property until spring 1964, when injuries began to erode his position, and a callow Irishman named Pat Jennings arrived that summer. For two seasons, veteran and youngster vied for the job, playing an almost equal number of games, but in the end there could be only one winner and in October 1966 the older man left for Northampton.

By then he had become his country's most capped custodian until his record of 28 appearances was surpassed by Alan Rough of Partick Thistle in 1979.

Brown, who later emigrated to Canada, left behind many friends in north London. They speak fondly of a modest fellow who smoked incessantly and never put on weight despite indulging a voracious appetite; and professionally, while Messrs Ditchburn and Jennings must take precedence, Bill Brown proved beyond doubt that he was worth his place in any team.

**WILLIAM DALLAS FYFE BROWN**

BORN: Arbroath, Scotland, 8 October 1931.

HONOURS: European Cup Winners' Cup 62/3. League Championship 60/1. FA Cup 60/1, 61/2. 28 Scotland caps (58-65).

OTHER CLUBS: Dundee 49/50-58/9 (214, 0); Northampton Town 66/7 (17, 0); Toronto Falcons, Canada, 67.

DIED: Simcoe, Ontario, 30 November 2004.

GAMES 264

GOALS 0

# DAVE MACKAY

## 1958/59 → 1967/68

The stature of Dave Mackay in Tottenham folklore is vast and indisputable; indeed, to imagine Spurs' great 1960s side without the vibrant Scot is to picture the Huns without Attila or the Alamo without Davy Crockett. Yet while it is right that so much is made of Dave's dynamic, warrior-like qualities – many have written that if Blanchflower was the brains of the team, Mackay was its heart – there is a danger of under-selling his sheer, unadulterated all-round talent.

In fact, his control was second to none, he was the cleanest striker of a ball at the club and he passed with the utmost precision. And how the mighty left-half revelled in his skill; in training he would astonish team-mates by volleying continuously against a wall from ten or even 15 yards, and anyone who doubts the difficulty of this trick should attempt it for themselves. A little later, as Spurs captain, he would run on to the pitch, kick the ball high in the air, then catch it infallibly on his instep, a subtle form of intimidation that demanded of his opponents: 'Can you compete with that?'

All this is not to say that the traditional image of Dave Mackay as indestructible powerhouse is a myth. Despite standing just 5ft 8in, he exerted an awesome physical presence, muscular thighs and a barn-door of a chest topped by features that were positively piratical. The man tackled like a granite avalanche, exuding a passionate will to win and apparently consumed by a devilish, ruthless relish for his work. Colleagues leapt to do his bidding as he drove them on, invariably by stirring personal example, often by melodramatic gesture and abrasive Caledonian invective.

Though lacking in outright pace, he bustled tirelessly between attack and defence, typically winning the ball, flicking a pass, then surging forward to receive the return. On reaching enemy territory, he could finish venomously, as he proved with a hat-trick against West Ham in 1962, and another potent weapon was a prodigiously long throw.

Addicted as he was to winning at everything – Mackay would pour his entire being into a casual game of snooker – it followed that he was devastated in defeat, a situation he strove so hard to avoid that in some 40 cup finals at all playing levels, he never finished on the losing side. Such unquenchable spirit was never more evident than in recovery from a twice-broken left leg; the first fracture came in a clash with Noel Cantwell of Manchester United in a European tie at Old Trafford in December 1963, the second nine months later on his comeback against Shrewsbury reserves. Such calamity would have ended the career of lesser men; in his case, it merely added to the aura of indestructibility that had enveloped him since his indomitable contribution to Tottenham's early-1960s triumphs.

Yet, unthinkably now, the Scottish international might never have arrived at the Lane. In March 1959, Bill Nicholson had been making overtures to Swansea Town's Mel Charles, and had the Welshman not opted for Arsenal he would almost certainly have joined Tottenham instead of Mackay. Later Bill maintained, perhaps diplomatically, that it was Dave he wanted all along, and certainly he was delighted to pay Heart of Midlothian £32,000 for the signature of the sought-after 24-year-old who had won every major honour open to him north of the border.

Soon he was integral, even indispensable, as the League and FA Cup double was completed, then the FA Cup retained, and it was a source of monumental frustration to Tottenham's flintily imperious titan when a stomach injury denied him European glory in 1963.

Come the middle 1960s, Mackay had taken over as skipper and, his mastery over ball and men undimmed, led Spurs to FA Cup Final victory against Chelsea in 1967. By then, he was operating in a mainly defensive role but the earlier years of midfield effort had exacted a toll and injuries became more frequent. Perhaps, too, he needed a new challenge and he found it with Derby County, whom he joined for £5,000 (a reduced fee in recognition of his services) in July 1968.

Under Brian Clough he played masterfully alongside centre-half Roy McFarland and in his first season helped the Rams lift the Second Division title, as well as sharing the Footballer of the Year award with Manchester City's Tony Book. Success in management followed, including a Championship at the Baseball Ground, but it is to his fabulous achievements as a Spur that Mackay owes his undying reputation.

Nicholson called him his best signing, which is some compliment from the man who enlisted Cliff Jones, John White and Jimmy Greaves. He has been compared to the hitherto peerless Duncan Edwards; and Matt Busby made no secret of the fact that he would have loved to rebuild Manchester United around his fellow Scot after the Munich air disaster of 1958. About the credentials of Dave Mackay, nothing more need be said.

| | |
|---|---|
| **DAVID CRAIG MACKAY** | |
| BORN: | Edinburgh, 14 November 1934. |
| HONOURS: | League Championship 60/1. FA Cup 60/1, 61/2, 66/7. |
| | 22 Scotland caps (57-65). FWA Footballer of the Year 69, shared. |
| OTHER CLUBS: | Hearts 53/4-58/9 (135, 25); Derby County 68/9-70/1 (122, 5); Swindon Town 71/2 (26, 1). |
| MANAGER: | Swindon Town (71-72); Nottingham Forest (72); Derby County (73-76); Walsall (77-78); Al-Arabi Sporting Club, Kuwait, (78-86); Alba Shabab, Dubai, (86-87); Doncaster Rovers (87-89); Birmingham City (89-91); Zamalek, Egypt, (91-93). |

| | |
|---|---|
| GAMES | 321 |
| GOALS | 51 |

# CLIFF JONES

## 1957/58 → 1968/69

Like a hungry cheetah at full stretch on the trail of its hapless prey, Cliff Jones running towards goal was a spectacle to take the breath away. The Welsh dasher was that rare and glorious being, a speed merchant with assured ball control, and he was undoubtedly the most thrilling, eye-catching entertainer in Spurs' greatest team.

Appearing to skim effortlessly over the ground, invariably he would dart beyond his markers before they had the chance to make a fair tackle. When he was fouled – often the only way to hinder his headlong flight – he would hurtle horizontally for yards after the impact, and it was tempting to look for scorchmarks on the turf.

Those charged with shackling the flying winger were faced with a nightmare dilemma. Should they jump in with a challenge which, should it fail, would leave them embarrassingly adrift of the action? Or should they beat a rapid retreat, hoping to usher their tormentor away from the immediate danger area? Either option was fraught with peril, especially as he differed from most of his rivals in that he could maintain his pace over long distances as well as deploying it in destructive short bursts.

Yet velocity and skill were not the only Jones qualities that became an integral part of the White Hart Lane success story in the early 1960s. Mention Cliff's name to many who saw him at his peak and they speak in awe of his matchless courage; indeed, no less a warrior than Dave Mackay described the wiry wingman as the most fearless player he ever knew.

This bravery was most evident in aerial combat, into which Jones threw himself body and soul. If there was the slightest sniff of a goal, the 5ft 7in dynamo would dive unhesitatingly among flailing feet – a fabulous full-length strike at home to Fulham in November 1960 comes to mind – or wrap himself around the woodwork in an effort to get a decisive touch. His timing was uncanny as he wormed into position to steal the ball from the foreheads of hulking opponents, though he took many sickening knocks and carries the scars to this day.

Naturally right-footed, Jones could play on either wing – left when Terry Medwin was in the team, right to accommodate Terry Dyson – but was particularly potent cutting inside from the left before streaking for goal or freeing a team-mate in the touchline space he had just vacated. However, he was perhaps most menacing when roaming free, and one of his characteristic thrusts through centre-field with a posse of petrified defenders retreating in front of him was a sight to savour.

Jones' success as a Spur came as no surprise to supporters in his homeland, who were used to following the family's fortunes – his father, Ivor, and uncle, Bryn, were Welsh internationals and his brother, also Bryn, played for five League clubs – but were gratified by the handsome manner in which he upheld the tradition.

Capped at 18, Jones starred for Swansea before a £35,000 deal, a record for a winger at the time, took him to White Hart Lane in February 1958. However, the road to glory can be rocky, as he discovered on his debut at Arsenal, whom he had looked certain to join only weeks earlier. The game finished 4-4 but Jones was disappointing, and as his form failed to improve over subsequent weeks, the Gunners fans gloated.

Still he helped Wales to reach the last eight of that summer's World Cup Finals in Sweden, but then the Jones fortunes dipped again when he broke his leg in a pre-season training collision with Peter Baker. Yet, perversely, the breathing space thus afforded by the enforced lay-off proved beneficial. On his return to action that December he seemed less overawed by the size of his fee, and soon he began to give awesome value for money.

Thereafter Cliff matured into arguably the world's finest flankman, sharing in Spurs' headiest triumphs and prompting Juventus to offer a then-monumental £100,000 for his services in 1962. Bill Nicholson was too wise to be tempted and Jones went on to complete ten years at the Lane, being the last member of the double-winning side to depart when he left for Fulham, aged 33, in October 1968.

Though hampered since 1965 by injuries to hamstring, knee and shoulder, he never ceased to give maximum effort and a flash of the old Jones magic could never be ruled out.

Throughout his career Cliff Jones remained a friendly, positive character who brought a spirit of enjoyment as well as moments of sheer inspiration to the game he loved. His youthful charges in north London, where he went on to teach PE, could count themselves as fortunate, indeed.

**CLIFFORD WILLIAM JONES**
**BORN:** Swansea, Glamorgan, 7 February 1935.
**HONOURS:** European Cup Winners' Cup 62/3. League Championship 60/1.
FA Cup 60/1, 61/2. 59 Wales caps (54-69).
**OTHER CLUBS:** Swansea Town 52/3-57/8 (168, 46); Fulham 68/9-69/70 (25, 2).

GAMES **372 (8)**
GOALS **159**

# JOHN WHITE

## 1959/60 → 1963/64

No major footballing talent since the war has plied his trade more subtly than John White, the slender Scottish schemer whose influence at the hub of the majestic Spurs side of the early 1960s can hardly be overstated. Rarely did he garner personal glory, often not catching the attention of supporters even in games dominated by his skills, but he was feted royally by fellow professionals, who recognised the scale of his contribution.

In fact, it was the likes of Danny Blanchflower and Dave Mackay, with whom he had shared an international stage, who had urged Bill Nicholson to sign him; they saw his golden gift of making others play – indeed, never has the tag of 'play-maker' been more apt – and coveted it for the Tottenham cause.

This priceless quality was based on a nigh-uncanny positional sense which earned White the nickname of 'The Ghost', a tag made all the more appropriate by his slim, almost ethereal figure and wan appearance. When Spurs went forward, he was an elusive, flickering wraith, flitting unobtrusively into space to ensure that attacks did not break down for the want of a passing option, then keeping the move flowing with an instant dispatch.

Though not as overtly entertaining as the ball-juggling Tommy Harmer, whom he ultimately replaced, White was endowed with superb control and vision. Invariably his deliveries were delivered with perfect weight, his tactical brain was sharp and he was the master of every technique, notably the chip – one that produced a goal at Nottingham Forest in October 1960 being an example to savour. The key was that White integrated his skills more successfully than Tommy, mainly because of his superior mobility and a deceptive strength that seemed unlikely to be housed in so willowy a frame.

Actually, as a teenager he had been turned away by both Rangers and Middlesbrough for being too slight, but Bill Nicholson, reluctant to reject an artist on the grounds of physique, was shrewd enough to investigate further and discovered that the teenage White had excelled as a cross-country runner, so stamina would be no problem. At a casual glance, he didn't offer the impression of being a workaholic, but closer examination revealed that he seldom stopped moving and thus was a nightmare to mark.

White, who had been offered to Charlton for £3,000 while at Alloa, his first club, arrived at White Hart Lane as a £20,000 capture from Falkirk in October 1959 while still doing his National Service. Stationed at Berwick, he was making regular 700-mile round trips to and from London, and the strain told as he faded towards the end of his early games.

But he toiled to improve his fitness, his lack of self-confidence eased gradually – in those days he was a shy lad whose penchant for practical jokes was yet to become evident – and when he settled in the south, eventually marrying the daughter of Tottenham assistant manager Harry Evans, his performances mushroomed in stature.

At first White, whose younger brother Tommy played at centre-forward for Hearts, Aberdeen and four English clubs, operated in tandem with Harmer, sometimes as twin inside-forwards, occasionally with the Scot on the wing. But as it became apparent that they were duplicating each other's jobs, and that two such artistic contributors could be construed as a luxury, the older man made way.

All Spurs' triumphs over the next three seasons owed plenty to the quiet, unfussy White input, none more so than victory in the 1963 Cup Winners' Cup. In the first round at home to Rangers he nodded two goals – White's strike rate is often underestimated, as he managed double figures in three of his four full terms at the Lane – and in the final he tormented Atletico Madrid with his passes, adding a smart goal for good measure.

By the summer of 1964, with Blanchflower newly retired, the commendably composed, misleadingly unobtrusive but increasingly productive schemer was set to assume extra midfield responsibility; a new phase in his career was about to begin. But on July 21, while practising alone at Crews Hill golf course, Enfield, he was caught in a thunderstorm and sheltered under an oak tree. Lightning struck, so savagely that his wedding ring was melted on his finger, and, at 26, John White was dead.

Just how good, or great, he might have become, no one will ever know for sure. But Blanchflower, at least, was in no doubt. As he put it, with typically profound eloquence: 'There were no boundaries for John . . . he was going to be a king.'

| | |
|---|---|
| | **JOHN ANDERSON WHITE** |
| **BORN:** | Musselburgh, Midlothian, 28 April 1937. |
| **HONOURS:** | European Cup Winners' Cup 62/3. League Championship 60/1. |
| | FA Cup 60/1, 61/2. 22 Scotland caps (59-64). |
| **OTHER CLUBS:** | Alloa Athletic 56/7-57/8; Falkirk 58/9-59/60 (27, 6). |
| **DIED:** | Crews Hill, Middlesex, 21.7.64. |

| | |
|---|---|
| GAMES | 221 |
| GOALS | 48 |

# LES ALLEN

## 1959/60 → 1964/65

The Spurs career of Les Allen fell victim to genius. After scoring 27 goals and playing in every match as Bill Nicholson's awe-inspiring side completed the League and FA Cup double in 1960/61, the chunky marksman looked set for a long and bountiful White Hart Lane tenure. Indeed at 24, with both youth and experience in his favour and while learning eagerly from team-mates of the highest quality, Allen seemed capable of sufficient improvement to add full international honours to the under-23 cap already garnered. But out of a clear sky, just seven months after Tottenham's twin triumph, there appeared a certain Jimmy Greaves.

Now while folklore has it that Jimmy ousted Les and that was the end of the story, it was not quite that simple. In fact, the two men played in harness for the newcomer's first dozen games, with Allen wearing the number-nine shirt until it was reclaimed by Bobby Smith. There followed a Smith-Allen battle for the role of spearhead throughout 1962/63 and it wasn't until after the arrival of Alan Gilzean in December 1964 that Allen slipped irrevocably out of contention.

The next summer signalled a £21,000 switch to Third Division Queen's Park Rangers, an anti-climactic departure in view of his early progress after arriving from Chelsea in exchange for Johnny Brooks in December 1959. Though Allen, ironically a teenage amateur with Spurs before turning professional at Stamford Bridge, had lately been confined to the Pensioners' reserves, his manager Ted Drake had dubbed him the best young footballing centre-forward in the top flight and Bill Nicholson was ready to back a hunch that he would flourish away from the boo-boys who had tormented him at Chelsea.

Pitched straight into the Tottenham first team, Allen was not slow in justifying that faith. Come January he endeared himself to his new fans by scoring twice against Arsenal at an ice-bound White Hart Lane, then trespassed towards the realms of fantasy in February, notching five in the 13-2 FA Cup replay drubbing of Crewe Alexandra.

Yet despite the strike rate – he finished that campaign with 15 goals in 19 outings – Allen was not a confident character, his basic shyness perhaps emphasised, at least temporarily, by transferring to a team containing so many stars. On the pitch his features were clenched invariably in the tensest of expressions, though certainly he had no occasion to feel inferior.

While his most commonly lauded attributes were strength on the ball, remarkable unselfishness and willingness to graft ceaselessly, Allen was blessed also with excellent control, a savage shot and, perhaps most significantly, the intelligence to apply his gifts to maximum effect. Many of his goals were of the so-called bread-and-butter variety, the product of gliding unobtrusively into dangerous positions, but there were spectacular moments, none more so than the waist-high volley against Sheffield Wednesday that decided both match and Championship in April 1961.

As a provider, too, Allen could be devastating, as his dribble past four Sunderland defenders to set up a Terry Dyson strike in the FA Cup quarter-final replay at White Hart Lane that same spring demonstrated exhilaratingly. All he lacked, and there had to be something, was outright pace; with that one addition to his game, he might have risen to the giddiest heights.

On retirement as a player, Allen sampled management, but even after he slipped out of the hot-seat at Swindon the family name was to return to prominence. His son, Clive, was destined to score freely for various clubs, but most notably for Spurs.

Yet despite the prolific achievements of Allen junior, and the lavish praise that he earned, there are those who maintain that the gifted son was never quite the equal of his less acclaimed father.

**LESLIE WILLIAM ALLEN**
**BORN:** Dagenham, Essex, 4 September 1937.
**HONOURS:** League Championship 60/1. FA Cup 60/1.
**OTHER CLUBS:** Chelsea 56/7-59/60 (44, 11); Queen's Park Rangers 65/6-68/9 (128, 54).
**MANAGER:** Queen's Park Rangers (69-70); Swindon Town (72-74); Aris Salonika, Greece.

| GAMES | 138 |
| GOALS | 63 |

# TERRY DYSON

· · · · · · · · · · · · · · · · · · · · · · · · · · · · · · ·

## 1954/55 → 1964/65

There is a school of churlish pundits who maintain, to this day, that Terry Dyson was an honest but essentially ordinary workman and was lucky to take his place in one of the greatest club sides of all time. They are, this writer would humbly submit, purveying hogwash.

What they ignore when advancing the claims of the more skilful Welshman, Terry Medwin, is that Tottenham's most significant triumphs – completing the League and FA Cup double in 1961 and taking Britain's first European trophy, the Cup Winners' Cup, two years later – were attained when the plucky Yorkshireman held sway in the constant struggle for supremacy between the two wingmen.

With artistry hardly in short supply in a team of all talents, what was needed to achieve a successful blend was a hyperactive beaver who could contribute in all areas of the pitch and who would donate his dying breath to the common cause. Bill Nicholson found him in Terry Dyson.

The son of leading northern jockey Ginger Dyson, sandy-haired Terry was, at 5ft 3in, the ideal size to take up the silk himself. Instead, after playing at non-League level for Scarborough, he signed for Spurs in 1954, the prelude to half a decade in the Football Combination relieved by only occasional senior outings.

Indeed, Dyson remained very much a reserve in status until the tail-end of 1959/60 when he won a place on merit, then cemented it by a series of sterling displays when Cliff Jones was injured at the start of the double campaign. Thereafter Medwin was dropped and his namesake prospered, linking effectively on the left flank with Dave Mackay but also roaming, now popping up alongside centre-forward Bobby Smith, then snapping at the heels of opponents in his own penalty area.

Admittedly the Dyson distribution was wild at times, and he was not always quick to spot the most profitable passing option, but he compensated amply by perpetual motion and bravery, and his finishing, too, could be lethal.

The crowd loved him for his enthusiasm – when he found the net his face radiated pure joy as his body launched into an ecstatic war dance – and respected him for aerial efforts hardly commensurate with his 1961 position as the League's smallest player. In fact, two of the most telling moments of that memorable year came from Terry's headers, the first when he outjumped the hulking Don Megson to lay on a goal for Smith in the title-clinching clash with Sheffield Wednesday, the second when he nodded precisely past Gordon Banks to complete the scoring in the FA Cup Final against Leicester City.

Understandably, Dyson started 1961/62 in confident vein, scoring five goals in three August days, including a hat-trick at home to Arsenal, but Medwin was a formidable rival and that winter, as Spurs strove for a second double, the Welsh international regained his place.

It was not in the Dyson nature to give up, however, and he fought back to take a crucial part in the 1963 Cup Winners' Cup campaign, scoring the winner in the semi-final first leg against OFK Belgrade before contributing the game of his life in the final 5-1 hammering of Atletico Madrid.

After helping to create the second goal for John White, Dyson made a vital saving tackle when Spurs were 2-1 up and floundering. Then he seized the initiative, increasing the lead with an admittedly flukey curler, laying on the fourth for Jimmy Greaves and adding the fifth himself with a venomous 25-yard shot after a slick exchange of passes with Tony Marchi.

No wonder Bobby Smith was moved to quip that the wee fellow ought to retire there and then, as he could never play as well again! In the event, Dyson went on to complete two more seasons in the first team, his irrepressible dressing-room presence a bonus to the morale of a side in the process of breaking up. Quite clearly, by the time he joined Fulham in June 1965, the case for Terry Dyson was open and shut.

| | | |
|---|---|---|
| **TERENCE KENT DYSON** | | |
| BORN: | Malton, Yorkshire, 29 November 1934. | |
| HONOURS: | European Cup Winners' Cup 62/3. League Championship 60/1. FA Cup 60/1. | |
| OTHER CLUBS: | Fulham 65/6 (22, 3); Colchester United 68/9-69/70 (56, 4). | |

| | |
|---|---|
| GAMES | 210 |
| GOALS | 55 |

# JOHN SMITH

## 1959/60 → 1963/64

It was through no shortfall of skill that wing-half cum inside-forward John Smith failed to make the grade as a Spur. Indeed, when he left West Ham for White Hart Lane, swapped for front-runner Dave Dunmore in March 1960, there was widespread belief that his imaginative passing and instinctive feel for the ball, so integral to the Hammers' 1957/58 Second Division title triumph, guaranteed the recently-capped England under-23 international a glowing future.

True, the sturdy Londoner was never the quickest mover, always having to watch his weight, but he was extremely fit and was seen by many as the long-term successor to Danny Blanchflower, already 34 at the time.

Unfortunately for Smith, the Irishman made a nonsense of his years, and Bill Nicholson achieved his magnificent midfield blend without the help of the talented newcomer. Thus he was relegated to the status of reserve, doing well enough as deputy for Blanchflower, John White or Dave Mackay but never making his services indispensable.

Come March 1964, the purchase of Alan Mullery made his position clear and he left for Coventry. A late career highlight came five years later when he helped Swindon Town deprive Arsenal of the League Cup in one of Wembley's most memorable upsets. Smith, who went on to sample management briefly, died prematurely in 1988.

**JOHN SMITH**
BORN: Shoreditch, London, 4 January 1939.
OTHER CLUBS: West Ham United 56/7-59/60 (127, 20); Coventry City 63/4-65/6 (35, 1); Leyton Orient 65/6-66/7 (39, 3); Torquay United 66/7-67/8 (68, 8); Swindon Town 68/9-70/1 (84, 9); Walsall 71/2 (13, 1).
MANAGER: Walsall (72-73); Dundalk, Northern Ireland.
DIED: Harlesden, London, 12 February 1988.

| | |
|---|---|
| GAMES | 24 |
| GOALS | 1 |

# JOHN HOLLOWBREAD

## 1958/59 → 1963/64

John Hollowbread was the sort of goalkeeper needed by any club striving for top honours. Not quite accomplished enough to claim the first-team spot for himself, nevertheless he was a solid performer who could be relied on to deputise for Bill Brown without letting the side down. In addition, he was impeccably loyal to the cause of Tottenham Hotspur, emphatically not the type to clamour for a transfer in a bid to establish himself elsewhere.

Spurs signed Hollowbread from non-League Enfield in 1952, and he demonstrated his patience by waiting six years for his senior debut. That came in August 1958, when he stepped in after Ted Ditchburn broke a finger. He impressed sufficiently with his all-round competence, particularly his bravery in diving at feet, to retain his place for the rest of that term.

But the arrival of Brown in June 1959 made Hollowbread's position clear and for the next five seasons he accepted the role of faithful understudy. Perhaps a spell in the limelight when the Scot was sidelined in the spring of 1964 heightened the Londoner's appetite for senior action, and come the summer, with the signing of Pat Jennings on the horizon, he joined Southampton for £2,000. John Hollowbread retired through injury in 1966.

**JOHN FREDERICK HOLLOWBREAD**
BORN: Enfield, London, 2 January 1934.
OTHER CLUBS: Southampton 64/5-65/6 (36, 0).
DIED: 12 December 2007.

| | |
|---|---|
| GAMES | 73 |
| GOALS | 0 |

# EDDIE CLAYTON

### 1957/58 → 1967/68

Loyal and steady, Eddie Clayton was limited to a century of senior outings over 11 campaigns with Spurs. For all but one of those seasons, the amiable, dark-haired Londoner never rose above the rank of reserve, leaving unanswered the question of whether he might have excelled at a slightly lower station in the top flight.

Certainly, an indication of the inside-forward cum wing-half's worth is that no less a judge than Alf Ramsey, then manager of Ipswich Town, expressed interest in signing him during the early 1960s, though when Clayton actually asked for a transfer in 1964, only lowly Lincoln City made a serious inquiry.

What is not in doubt is that the Clayton presence was a considerable asset to Bill Nicholson throughout his first ten years as a manager. Though Eddie was not always appreciated by demanding fans who expected him, unrealistically, to emulate the stars for whom he deputised – Messrs Harmer and White, Greaves and Allen, Mackay and Venables – he could be relied upon to fit competently into a team method with which he had been imbued since stepping out of local football in December 1957.

His service at half-back was sterling, but probably he was more accomplished in a forward role in which his capable passing and finishing skills – he possessed the important knack of keeping his shots low – were seen to best advantage.

Early in his career, naturally enough, Clayton had harboured aspirations of a regular first-team spot and four months after arriving he did his case no harm with a brace of goals on his top-flight debut, a 4-3 victory at Everton.

However, so intense was the competition for places that he was to remain on the sidelines almost perpetually until 1965/66, when he made 41 senior starts. Thereafter he slipped out of contention once more, finally relinquishing ambitions of betterment when, in March 1968 and aged 30, he accepted a move to Southend United.

After a little more than two seasons in the Fourth Division, Clayton left the League to serve Margate, then Aylesbury, before entering the teaching profession.

| EDWARD CLAYTON | | | |
|---|---|---|---|
| **BORN:** | Bethnal Green, London, 7 May 1937. | GAMES | **99 (4)** |
| **OTHER CLUBS:** | Southend United 67/8-69/70 (73, 16). | GOALS | **20** |

# JIMMY GREAVES

## 1961/62 → 1969/70

'A blinking little genius' was how Joe Mercer saw him; Dave Mackay recalled reverently how he took pressure off his team-mates by grabbing goals out of nothing; Pat Jennings reckoned he was such a complete player that he was worth his place whether he found the net or not! But however football folk chose to remember Jimmy Greaves, there was one point on which nearly all tended to agree: when it came to scoring goals, he was the best.

What placed Greaves apart from his peers, and from magnificent marksmen of other eras? Perhaps, if it is ever valid to make judgements that span the ages, it is that he was unique as a specialist finisher with outstanding all-round talent. What other full-time striker – a category that, of course, excludes the likes of the Old Trafford trinity George Best, Denis Law and Bobby Charlton – could pick the ball up in the centre circle and dribble past half a team before outwitting the 'keeper?

We're not talking about an isolated incident here; the man made a habit of it. There was the day at White Hart Lane in November 1962 when Leicester City's Gordon Banks had the dubious honour of retrieving the ball; Manchester United were the victims in October 1965; then it was poor Leicester's turn again in October 1968, this time Peter Shilton tasting humiliation as Jimmy paused impudently before applying the *coup de grace*.

There were plenty more similarly unforgettable efforts, goals of equal audacity, but they did not form his staple diet. The majority of Greaves' vast total – his career average of approximately three strikes every four matches is nothing short of phenomenal – came from inside the box and were the product of a rarefied combination of qualities. Wicked intelligence, instinctive anticipation, perfect balance, magnetic control, explosive pace, supreme confidence . . . it seems ridiculous, unfair even, but that entire cornucopia of riches was his to command.

Here was a gleeful opportunist who destroyed defences for fun, one moment drifting nonchalantly on the periphery of the action, the next darting unerringly to its heart. When the ball ran loose in half a yard of space, invariably he would be the first to move, and by the time some hapless marker had latched on to his shirt-tails it would be too late. Small but wirily muscular, Greaves could strike as firmly as the next man, but usually he opted for precision, passing the ball into the net, his customary accuracy giving 'keepers no chance.

The son of a London tube-train driver, Greaves was a soccer-mad infant prodigy who flopped his eleven-plus examination on purpose to avoid the chance of being sent to a rugby-playing grammar school. Soon he was scintillating in schoolboy football and was on the verge of joining Spurs, whom he supported, only to be overlooked during the managerial transition from Arthur Rowe to Jimmy Anderson. It was to prove a costly piece of confusion.

Instead of landing neatly in Tottenham's lap, Greaves was beguiled by an eloquent Chelsea scout who persuaded him to Stamford Bridge, where he exceeded even the most extravagant of expectations, enjoying four campaigns of unprecedented bounty culminating in a barely believable 41 League goals during 1960/61.

The following summer, fed up with the Football League's iniquitous maximum wage system – ironically, soon to be swept aside by the march of progress – and lured by visions of untold wealth, he switched to AC Milan. The upshot was half a season of pure hell, his free spirit proving unable to cope with the draconian disciplinary regime imposed by his new employers. Now he felt trapped, under-valued, victimised, and after four months of misery in Italy he was ecstatic when Spurs rode to the rescue.

Greaves returned to his beloved London for the peculiar fee of £99,999 – Bill Nicholson wouldn't run to six-figures! – and began by maintaining his tradition of scoring on debut at every level. Even by his standards, however, this time was special as he weighed in with a hat-trick at home to Blackpool, starting with a gravity-defying scissors-kick.

Soon the baggy-shorted Eastender with the jaunty air of an eternal schoolboy was contributing a deluge of goals that helped win the FA and Cup Winners' Cups, then did much to mask a gradual team decline as the decade wore on.

At times manager and colleagues alike despaired over his, shall we say, laid-back approach, and it's true that many blades of grass remained uncovered by the Greaves feet. But, as he might say himself, he did the business; and, as he would be too modest to add, there was no one who could match him. Nicholson, such a wise man, knew this and left well alone.

Greaves excelled for England, too, overshadowing all other strike rates with 44 goals in 57 matches; indeed, but for the strength-sapping jaundice that cost him four months of 1965/66, he would surely not have missed the final stages of the World Cup, a circumstance which left him devastated.

Eventually, in March 1970, he left for West Ham, valued at £54,000 in the Martin Peters deal. His Upton Park sojourn was not the happiest, and ahead lay the well-documented drink problems that threatened his very existence. Rehabilitation was followed by new stardom as a puckish TV pundit, a role in which he revelled. But to all those who saw him play, the name of Jimmy Greaves will always conjure up images of the greatest of all goal-poachers. Not for the first time, Joe Mercer had the measure of his man.

---

**JAMES PETER GREAVES**

**BORN:** East Ham, London, 20 February 1940.
**HONOURS:** European Cup Winners' Cup 62/3. FA Cup 61/2, 66/7. 57 England caps (59-67).
**OTHER CLUBS:** Chelsea 57/8-60/1 (157, 124); AC Milan, Italy, 61/2 (14, 9); West Ham United 69/70-70/1 (38, 13).

| | |
|---|---|
| GAMES | 381 |
| GOALS | 268 |

# DEREK POSSEE

## 1963/64 → 1965/66

Derek Possee, like Keith Weller, was an accomplished young forward who grew disaffected with perpetual reserve team football at White Hart Lane and decided on a fresh start elsewhere. Accordingly, in the summer of 1967 when the opportunity arose to follow his friend to Millwall in a £25,000 deal, the 21-year-old accepted and Spurs bade farewell to another talented prospect they could ill afford to lose.

Small and compact, Possee was a quick, darting raider who could operate on either flank. Indeed, such was his speed that he won sprint titles as a youth and gave up the chance of an athletics career in favour of soccer. Though not quite of Weller's all-round quality, he was brave, with sure ball control and blessed with good timing in his aerial work.

Possee's senior debut, at home to Aston Villa in January 1964, was a personal triumph marked by a goal and a magazine award for the best sporting performance of the week. But he was not offered anything approaching a settled senior sequence until 1965/66, when he did well enough before being consigned to the stiffs for another term.

Then followed his move to The Den, where he broke the Lions' League scoring record before returning briefly to the top flight with Crystal Palace.

**DEREK JAMES POSSEE**
BORN: Southwark, London, 14 February 1946.
OTHER CLUBS: Millwall 67/8-72/3 (223, 79); Crystal Palace 72/3-73/4 (53, 12); Orient 74/5-76/7 (80, 11).

GAMES **19**
GOALS 4

# KEITH WELLER

## 1964/65 → 1966/67

Keith Weller was the one that got away. In the mid-1960s, the young, ambitious north Londoner impressed mightily as an all-purpose forward whose talent was equalled only by his zest. But despite acquitting himself admirably whenever he deputised for one of the established stars, Weller was unable to claim a regular place.

Demoralised to find himself in a tunnel at the end of which he could discern no pinprick of light, he accepted a £20,000 move to Millwall in June 1967, leaving for The Den burning with desire to prove Spurs wrong. That he did so, going on to play for England as an attacking midfielder, became a harrowing slice of Tottenham history, but in fairness to the management, they were reluctant to let him go.

Just 21 at the time, Weller was a lovely, flowing, natural footballer endowed with exhilarating flair, the skill and pace to go past defenders, smooth passing ability, a savage shot, enviable versatility and an apparently bottomless reservoir of stamina.

He was never more outstanding than in Mexico on the club's 1966 summer tour, when his sheer dynamism in searing heat flabbergasted his toiling team-mates. Unluckily that was one trip Bill Nicholson did not make, and a potential White Hart Lane hero took his leave.

**KEITH WELLER**
BORN: Islington, London, 11 June 1946.
HONOURS: 4 England caps (74).
OTHER CLUBS: Millwall 67/8-69/70 (121, 38); Chelsea 70/1-71/2 (38, 14); Leicester City 71/2-78/9 (262, 37); New England Tea Men 78-80, Fort Lauderdale Strikers 80-84, Tacoma Stars 84, all USA.
DIED: Seattle, USA, 12 November 2004.

GAMES **19 (2)**
GOALS 1

# FRANK SAUL

. . . . . . . . . . . . . . . . . . . . . . . . . . . . . . . . . .

## 1960/61 → 1967/68

At 17, Frank Saul looked like hot property. Strong, eager and with no shortage of skill, the sandy-haired centre-forward played six games and scored three goals as deputy to Bobby Smith during Spurs' 1960/61 League and FA Cup double campaign.

At 18, he confirmed the impression of limitless potential, netting twice in the away leg of the European Cup clash with Feyenoord and showing maturity beyond his years; the future could hardly have beckoned more promisingly. But at 24, he departed for Southampton, a £40,000 makeweight in the deal that took Martin Chivers to White Hart Lane.

Where had all that youthful impetus gone? Disappeared, perhaps, with the buoyancy of a team that had declined from its 1961 peak. Certainly Saul would not be the first man to shine in a great side, then lose his lustre in less rarefied circumstances.

The turning point came in 1964/65 when, with Smith gone, he was given a substantial uninterrupted sequence as Jimmy Greaves' striking partner. Despite netting five times in the first four games, including a hat-trick at home to Burnley, Saul did not carry the consistent threat demanded of a Spurs spearhead. Accordingly, Alan Gilzean arrived in midwinter and thereafter the England youth international, who had shelved an ambition to join the Merchant Navy to turn professional, was edged towards the shadows.

Not that Saul, honest trier that he was, rolled over and died at the first hint of competition. He showed his mettle and versatility by adapting to a wide position, while remaining an able substitute in the centre, and was rewarded with at least 20 senior outings in each of his last four seasons as a Spur.

Two high spots came in the 1967 FA Cup, with decisive and beautifully dispatched goals against Nottingham Forest in the semi-final and Chelsea at Wembley. Clearly Saul deserved better than the supporters' jibes which came his way when his progress did not match early predictions, and when he left for The Dell in January 1968, he could do so with his head held high.

**FRANK LANDER SAUL**

BORN: Canvey Island, Essex, 23 August 1943.
HONOURS: FA Cup 66/7.
OTHER CLUBS: Southampton 67/8-69/70 (50, 2); Queen's Park Rangers 70/1-71/2 (43, 4); Millwall 71/2-75/6 (96, 4).

GAMES 126 (4)
GOALS 46

# LAURIE BROWN

## 1963/64 → 1965/66

Laurie Brown was the life and soul of any dressing room, a bluff north-easterner whose constant wisecracking masked an unswervingly serious approach to the game. Unfortunately, the unquenchable enthusiasm of a memorably endearing character was never matched by his footballing ability.

After winning England amateur international caps during early days with Bishop Auckland, Brown experienced life in the lower divisions before joining Arsenal, then moving to Tottenham for £40,000 in February 1964.

Though primarily a central defender, he was pressed into immediate service as an emergency spearhead, proving rather blunt in his first match, against his former club, in which he was bested by Ian Ure. Though brimming over with self-belief, Brown soon found himself out of the side, and he did not reclaim a regular place until reverting to centre-half in the spring of 1965.

Thereafter he performed loyally for a season and a half, his awkwardness on the ball offset by his aerial strength, before being replaced by Mike England and joining Norwich in September 1966. Nobody tried harder than Laurie Brown, and at White Hart Lane he is remembered with affection.

**LAURENCE BROWN**
BORN: Shildon, County Durham, 22 August 1937.
OTHER CLUBS: Darlington 58/9 (3, 0); Northampton Town 60/1 (33, 21); Arsenal 61/2-63/4 (101, 2); Norwich City 66/7-68/9 (81, 2); Bradford Park Avenue 68/9-69/70 (36, 1).
MANAGER: Bradford Park Avenue (69).
DIED: 1998.

| GAMES | 65 |
|---|---|
| GOALS | 3 |

---

# NEIL JOHNSON

## 1965/66 → 1970/71

On a crisp autumn afternoon in 1965, Spurs fans thought they had discovered a new star. League champions Manchester United were the visitors to White Hart Lane and their defence was shredded, comprehensively and repeatedly, by a 19-year-old outside-right who gave polished Irish international left-back Tony Dunne a rare chasing.

That day everything Neil Johnson attempted came off; he scored once and had a hand in two more goals as the Red Devils were eclipsed 5-1. Sadly for the young flankman, and for Tottenham, he would never again perform to such scintillating effect.

Johnson's principal assets were speed and directness. Indeed, he tore into the game with such all-consuming enthusiasm that he seemed in danger of screwing himself into the ground. Unfortunately, he lacked any degree of subtlety, his control and passing ability were poor for the top level, and although his tackling and tenacity made him handy as a one-on-one marker – he once did a creditably limpet-like job on Manchester City's Colin Bell – much of the time he looked out of his depth in the First Division.

After only two substantial senior sequences, in 1965/66 and 1968/69, Johnson remained in the reserves, sometimes at right-back, until joining Torquay in 1971.

**NEIL JOSEPH JOHNSON**
BORN: Grimsby, Lincolnshire, 3 December 1946.
OTHER CLUBS: Charlton Athletic on loan 70/1 (1, 0); Torquay United 71/2 (6, 1).

| GAMES | 31 (7) |
|---|---|
| GOALS | 6 |

# JIMMY ROBERTSON

## 1963/64 → 1968/69

The White Hart Lane faithful were dumbfounded when international winger Jimmy Robertson was exchanged for Arsenal's unproven David Jenkins in October 1968. Their sense of grievance increased as poor Jenkins fared dismally, making memories of the popular Scot all the more poignant and highlighting the uncharacteristic eccentricity of Bill Nicholson's most controversial deal.

Robertson was dripping with potential when he arrived from St Mirren for £25,000 in March 1964. Sure enough, within six months he had won a full cap – destined to be his only one – and soon his searing pace had installed him as a terrace favourite.

Rare was the full-back who could stay with the leggy 19-year-old flier if he was given the room to push the ball past and run, and though his control and crossing did not always match his velocity, the Robertson service offered a rich source of fodder for Jimmy Greaves and Alan Gilzean.

Capable of performing on either flank but more comfortable on the right, Robertson was at his most effective when operating at speed and following his instinct. At full stretch his delivery was likely to be accurate, while time for deliberation, it seemed, gave rise to mistakes.

Though never a prolific scorer, he could strike with brutal force as Manchester United discovered at the Lane in October 1965. On an afternoon of magical entertainment, Robertson advanced from the corner of the box to crash home an unstoppable rising shot and complete a 5-1 rout of the reigning champions.

Of more lasting significance was his opener against Chelsea in the 1967 FA Cup Final, in which he excelled, when an Alan Mullery effort rebounded into his path and he netted from 15 yards.

After switching to Highbury, Robertson was ousted summarily by Peter Marinello, and he left to shine first at Ipswich, then for Stoke. That he could have done a valuable job for Spurs during their mid-1970s travail is beyond doubt.

**JAMES GILLEN ROBERTSON**

| | |
|---|---|
| **BORN:** | Glasgow, 17 December 1944. |
| **HONOURS:** | FA Cup 66/7. 1 Scotland cap (64). |
| **OTHER CLUBS:** | Cowdenbeath 61/2 (25, 7); St Mirren 62/3-63/4 (52, 18); Arsenal 68/9-69/70 (46, 7); Ipswich Town 69/70-71/2 (87, 10); Stoke City 72/3-76/7 (114, 12); Walsall 77/8 (16, 0); Crewe Alexandra 78/9 (33, 0). |

| | |
|---|---|
| GAMES | **178 (4)** |
| GOALS | 32 |

## JEFF IRELAND

1957/58 → 1958/59

Right-winger Jeff Ireland had already made an impact as an amateur with the London FA when he turned professional in November 1957, and he made his senior debut three months later. However, soon he slipped out of the Spurs reckoning.

**JEFFREY JOHN CHARLES IRELAND**
BORN: Paddington, London, 1 December 1935.
OTHER CLUBS: Shrewsbury Town 59/60 (38, 4).

GAMES **3**
GOALS 0

## BILLY DODGE

1958/59 → 1959/60

A run of nine straight games as deputy to Danny Blanchflower early in 1958 demonstrated that wing-half Billy Dodge was no duffer, but he proved unable to emerge from the Irishman's substantial shadow and left White Hart Lane in the summer of 1962.

**WILLIAM CHARLES DODGE**
BORN: Hackney, London, 10 March 1937.
OTHER CLUBS: Crystal Palace 62/3 (3, 0).

GAMES **10**
GOALS 0

## FRED SHARPE

1958/59

Fred Sharpe was an accomplished wing-half, but competing for a place with Blanchflower and Mackay proved beyond him, even after netting the winner on his debut against Nottingham Forest. After nine years as a Spur he left in 1963 to begin an enterprising spell with Norwich.

**FREDERICK CHARLES SHARPE**
BORN: Greenwich, London, 11 November 1937.
OTHER CLUBS: Norwich City 63/4-68/9 (111, 0);
Reading 69/70-70/1 (64, 1).

GAMES **2**
GOALS 1

## LEN WORLEY

1959/60

England amateur international flankman Len Worley appeared to possess the talent to forge a career in professional football but opted for a future outside the game. His sole outing for Tottenham was as a replacement for Terry Medwin, who was playing for Wales.

**LEONARD FRANCIS WORLEY**
BORN: Amersham, Buckinghamshire, 27 June 1937.
OTHER CLUBS: Charlton Athletic 56/7 (1, 0).

GAMES **1**
GOALS 0

## KEN BARTON

1960/61 – 1963/64

After seven years on Tottenham's books, Ken Barton made his debut against Manchester United at Old Trafford in January 1961, but the steady right-back never seemed likely to dislodge the ultra-consistent Peter Baker as first choice.

**KENNETH REES BARTON**
BORN: Caernarfon, 20 September 1937.
OTHER CLUBS: Luton Town 64/5 (11, 0).
DIED: Chester, Cheshire, 6 September 1982.

GAMES **4**
GOALS 0

## JIMMY COLLINS

1961/62

The peak of inside-forward Jimmy Collins' career was enjoyed at the Goldstone Ground, after he had left Spurs for Brighton in October 1962. At White Hart Lane the skilful little Scot had been overshadowed by his illustrious countryman, John White.

**JAMES COLLINS**
BORN: Ayr, Scotland, 21 December 1937.
OTHER CLUBS: Brighton 62/3-66/7 (201, 44).

GAMES **2**
GOALS 0

## RON PIPER

1962/63

Inside-forward Ron Piper served both big north London clubs, playing as an amateur with Arsenal before turning professional with Tottenham in 1960, but his experience at senior level was limited to a sole outing, for Spurs at Blackburn in May 1963.

**RONALD DAVID PIPER**
BORN: Cresswell, Northumberland, 16 March 1943.

GAMES **1**
GOALS 0

## ROY LOW

1964/65 → 1966/67

Roy Low was a specialist half-back but capable of filling virtually any forward position, too, and he plugged several attacking gaps towards the end of 1964/65. He could never claim a regular place, but is often remembered as the club's first League substitute.

**ANTHONY ROY LOW**
BORN: Watford, Hertfordshire, 8 July 1944.
OTHER CLUBS: Watford 66/7-68/9 (26, 4).

GAMES **6 (2)**
GOALS 1

## STEVE PITT

### 1965/66

There were high hopes for little Steve Pitt, a lively winger with a penchant for scoring goals at youth and reserve level. However, he was only afforded one senior opportunity, at home to Blackpool in August 1965, before drifting out of contention.

**STEPHEN WILLIAM PITT**
BORN: Willesden, London, 1 August 1948.
OTHER CLUBS: Colchester United 69/70 (6, 0).

| GAMES | 1 |
|---|---|
| GOALS | 0 |

## ROGER HOY

### 1965/66 → 1967/68

The signings of Mike England in 1966 and Peter Collins a little more than two years later sounded the death-knell for the first-team aspirations of young stopper Roger Hoy. Duly the former full-back crossed London for a fresh start with Crystal Palace.

**ROGER ERNEST HOY**
BORN: Poplar, London, 6 December 1946.
OTHER CLUBS: Crystal Palace 68/9-69/70 (53, 6); Luton Town 70/1 (32, 0); Cardiff City 71/2-72/3 (16, 0).

| GAMES | 12 |
|---|---|
| GOALS | 0 |

## JOHN COLLINS

### 1965/66 → 1967/68

Wales under-23 international full-back John Collins, who collected five caps with Spurs and then two more with Portsmouth, could not force his way to the forefront at White Hart Lane, but went on to enjoy a worthwhile career in the lower divisions.

**JOHN LINDSAY COLLINS**
BORN: Bedwellty, Monmouthshire, 21 January 1949.
OTHER CLUBS: Portsmouth 71/2-73/4 (74, 0); Halifax Town 74/5-75/6 (82, 1); Sheffield Wednesday 76/7 (7, 0); Barnsley 76/7-79/80 (129, 1).

| GAMES | 2 |
|---|---|
| GOALS | 0 |

## ROY BROWN

### 1966/67

It was daunting enough having his namesake, Bill, ahead of him in the pecking order of Spurs goalkeepers, but when Pat Jennings arrived, too, it must have seemed like the final straw to Roy Brown, whose one League outing came at home to Blackpool in 1966.

**ROY ERIC BROWN**
BORN: Shoreham-by-Sea, Sussex, 5 October 1945.
OTHER CLUBS: Reading 68/9-69/70 (63, 0); Notts County 70/1-74/5 (113, 0); Mansfield Town 75/6 (1, 0).

| GAMES | 1 |
|---|---|
| GOALS | 0 |

## ROY WOOLCOTT

### 1969/70

Marksman Roy Woolcott had no difficulty in hitting the target for Spurs reserves, but was granted only one chance for the first team, against Ipswich at Portman Road in December 1969. The presence of Messrs Gilzean and Chivers had plenty to do with that.

**ROY ALFRED WOOLCOTT**
BORN: Leyton, London, 29 July 1946.
OTHER CLUBS: Gillingham on loan 71/2 (13, 5).

| GAMES | 1 |
|---|---|
| GOALS | 0 |

## KEN HANCOCK

### 1969/70 → 1970/71

Ken Hancock was a pair of safe hands who had won divisional titles with Port Vale and Ipswich when Bill Nicholson recruited him for £7,000 from Portman Road in March 1969 as cover for Pat Jennings. He lived up to his reputation for reliability before joining Bury.

**KENNETH PAUL HANCOCK**
BORN: Hanley, Staffordshire, 25 November 1937.
OTHER CLUBS: Port Vale 58/9-64/5 (240, 0); Ipswich Town 64/5-68/9 (163, 0); Bury 71/2-72/3 (35, 0).

| GAMES | 4 |
|---|---|
| GOALS | 0 |

## RAY CLARKE

### 1972/73

Subtle striker Ray Clarke proved there was life after the Lane, pocketing a Fourth Division title gong with Mansfield, then lifting the Dutch League and Cup double with Ajax. Later he seemed poised to star with Newcastle, only for injury to end his career at 28.

**RAYMOND CHARLES CLARKE**
BORN: Hackney, London, 25 September 1952.
OTHER CLUBS: Swindon Town 73/4 (14, 2); Mansfield Town 74/5-75/6 (91, 52); Sparta Rotterdam, Holland; Ajax, Holland; FC Bruges, Belgium; Brighton 79/80 (30, 8); Newcastle United 80/1 (14, 2).

| GAMES | 0 (1) |
|---|---|
| GOALS | 0 |

## TERRY LEE

### 1973/74

Terry Lee came late to keeping goal, having been a successful inside-forward as a schoolboy. The agile east Londoner turned professional with Spurs in 1970, was unbeaten at Newcastle in his only senior appearance four years later, then went on to do well for Torquay.

**TERENCE WILLIAM GEORGE LEE**
BORN: Stepney, London, 20 September 1952.
OTHER CLUBS: Torquay United 75/6-77/8 (106, 0); Newport County 78/9 (1, 0).
DIED: 22 June 1996.

| GAMES | 1 |
|---|---|
| GOALS | 0 |

# JOE KINNEAR

## 1965/66 → 1975/76

A pal's misfortune presented Joe Kinnear with the chance to prove his worth at White Hart Lane, though the talent, toughness and self-belief with which he capitalised on his windfall confirmed that, sooner or later, he would have reached the top regardless.

The irrepressible, dark-haired Dubliner had played a handful of senior games at the end of 1965/66 but, having been troubled by a blood clot on his thigh, appeared to face a lengthy wait in the reserves, when Phil Beal broke his arm in February 1967. Thus Kinnear inherited the right-back berth and retained it till the end of that season, which he climaxed as the popularly acclaimed man of the match in the FA Cup Final victory over Chelsea.

The former apprentice printer who had been discovered playing amateur football in St Albans – the Kinnear family had crossed the Irish Sea when he was seven – brought a comprehensive range of qualities to his game. Quick and bursting with untold energy, Joe was an exhilarating overlapper and polished passer, but didn't lose sight of his prime responsibility, that of defence. To that end he bit incisively in the tackle and covered his colleagues shrewdly, as he showed in the occasional accomplished display as sweeper.

Having made the first team, however, Kinnear was not to experience a smooth ride. In January 1969 his leg was broken in two places during a home clash with Leeds, and he was out for a year. On recovery, he was linked with Manchester United but that came to nothing, and he reclaimed his place for the League Cup triumphs of 1971 and 1973, and the UEFA Cup success of 1972.

Both between and after these highs, though, the Eire international was kept out on merit by Ray Evans and in August 1975, with Terry Naylor ready to don the number-two shirt, he joined Brighton.

After retirement he assisted his mentor, Dave Mackay, as coach at Doncaster, his lively personality fitting him well for the management career he began subsequently with Wimbledon.

| | |
|---|---|
| **JOSEPH PATRICK KINNEAR** | |
| BORN: | Dublin, 27 December 1946. |
| HONOURS: | UEFA Cup 71/2. FA Cup 66/7. League Cup 70/1, 72/3. |
| | 26 Republic of Ireland caps (67-76). |
| OTHER CLUBS: | Brighton 75/6 (16, 1). |
| MANAGER: | Wimbledon (92-99); Luton Town (01-03); Nottingham Forest (04). |

| | |
|---|---|
| GAMES | 252 (7) |
| GOALS | 2 |

# TERRY VENABLES

## 1965/66 → 1968/69

Terry Venables was a debonair schemer, extravagantly skilful and brimming with self-belief, whose prospects for glory seemed boundless when he crossed the capital from Chelsea to Tottenham in May 1966. At Stamford Bridge, as the League's youngest skipper, he had been a vital influence in the Tommy Docherty-led revival and, at 23, had won two England caps.

The £80,000 switch to White Hart Lane, a bastion of soccer sophistication, was surely tailor-made to suit his talents. Yet after three seasons of moderate accomplishment, Venables departed to Queen's Park Rangers, leaving behind an inescapable impression of anti-climax.

What went wrong? In retrospect, the answer appears simple enough – it was merely a matter of style. As the Blues' creative fulcrum, he was accustomed to deliberating on the ball before dispensing the immaculate passes that were his trademark; he was the conductor of an orchestra in which the musicians were well attuned to his thoughtful and creative promptings.

But Tottenham did things a different way, espousing a more fluid, one-touch game which thrived on constant movement; thus when the ball reached Venables, who had stamina in plenty but lacked pace, he interrupted the momentum. Naturally this frustrated the fans, who never really warmed to the solidly-built newcomer with the distinctive rolling gait, comparing him unfairly but not unexpectedly to his revered predecessor, the late John White.

Even so, the ever-ebullient Venables had his moments, notably at the climax of his first full season at the Lane when he helped lift the FA Cup at the expense of his former club, and not even his sternest critic could question his devotion to the job.

Scrupulous about his physical fitness, Venables also thought deeply about the game, ever analysing systems of play and devising free-kick routines, and his considered approach served him well after his £70,000 move to Loftus Road in June 1969. Way ahead was a high-profile career as a manager, and a loudly heralded return to White Hart Lane.

---

**TERENCE FREDERICK VENABLES**

**BORN:** Bethnal Green, London, 6 January 1943.

**HONOURS:** FA Cup 66/7. 2 England caps (64).

**OTHER CLUBS:** Chelsea 59/60-65/6 (202, 26); Queen's Park Rangers 69/70-74/5 (179, 19); Crystal Palace 74/5 (14, 0).

**MANAGER:** Crystal Palace (76-80); Queen's Park Rangers (80-84); Barcelona, Spain, (84-87); Tottenham Hotspur (87-91); England chief coach (94-96); Australia chief coach (96-97); Crystal Palace chief coach (98-99); Middlesbrough chief coach (00-01); Leeds United chief coach (02-03); England assistant manager (06-07).

| GAMES | 140 (2) |
| GOALS | 9 |

# ALAN MULLERY

## 1963/64 → 1971/72

Despite a career of high achievement, Alan Mullery has remained somehow underrated in comparison to many of his peers. In considering his merits, often there has been an element of 'Steady old Alan, he always did a reliable job.' Well so he did, but there was much more to it than that. In fact, throughout most of his eight-year White Hart Lane tenure, there was no more consistently excellent outfield player at the club, and after the departure of Dave Mackay in 1968, he became not only the side's captain, but also its heart.

From the moment in March 1964 when Spurs paid Fulham £72,500 for his services – Bill Nicholson made an unsuccessful attempt to sign England full-back George Cohen in the same deal – Mullery knew he faced a struggle for acceptance. Having inherited the number-four shirt vacated by the much-loved Danny Blanchflower, he was expected to replace the virtually irreplaceable. Soon some so-called fans were letting him know they felt he wasn't up to it; as well as the inevitable catcalls from the terraces, he encountered insults on the street and hate mail at home.

But if the morons thought they could frighten off the brash Londoner, they reckoned without the tempered steel at the core of both his character and his game. Rejecting the soft option of asking for a move, Mullery buckled down to reveal the all-round qualities that made him one of the most effective wing-halves in the land.

Sturdily built and with stamina to burn, he was never the most graceful of movers as he ferried his talents to every corner of the pitch, but such was his strength and skill that he was devilishly difficult to dispossess. In addition, he tackled abrasively, passed fluidly and packed a walloping shot, but equally important was his value as a motivator. Consumed by an insatiable desire to win, he drove on his colleagues and could be bitingly critical, which didn't exactly make him the most popular man at White Hart Lane but had a marked effect on team performance.

A landmark in the Mullery career was the 1967 FA Cup Final defeat of Chelsea, in which he was outstanding, and after which he appeared to gain in stature. Indeed, that year he secured a regular place in the England side that might have been his in 1964 had he not contrived to rule himself out of a tournament in Brazil by ricking his back while shaving, thereafter fading temporarily from the scene as Nobby Stiles of Manchester United staked his claim.

In 1968 Mullery became club skipper and entered his finest playing phase, which took in a stirring contribution to England's 1970 World Cup campaign. However, after holding aloft the League Cup in 1971, he began to suffer from a deep-seated pelvic strain, often finishing games in agony, and needed a four-month lay-off in the middle of the subsequent term.

On recovery he went on loan to Fulham and there were fears that he was finished, but they seemed laughable as he was recalled to lead Spurs into their UEFA Cup semi-final with AC Milan.

Not for the first time, Bill Nicholson had pulled a masterly stroke, his revitalised captain clinching the tie with a brilliant 20-yard volley at the San Siro, then going on to secure the trophy with a brave header – he knocked himself out in the process – in the second leg of the final against Wolves. Afterwards, cut off from his team-mates by milling fans, he embarked on a solo lap of honour with the trophy he had done so much to win.

That summer, still only 30, he returned to Craven Cottage for £65,000. Three terms on, as Footballer of the Year, he led Fulham to the FA Cup Final and still had a season's football left in him. It was difficult not to conclude that Alan Mullery, by then an MBE and on the brink of a combative managerial career, had been allowed to leave Tottenham far too soon.

**ALAN PATRICK MULLERY**
**BORN:** Notting Hill, London, 23 November 1941.
**HONOURS:** UEFA Cup 71/2. FA Cup 66/7. League Cup 70/1. 35 England caps (64-71).
FWA Footballer of the Year 75.
**OTHER CLUBS:** Fulham 58/9-63/4 (199, 13) and 71/2-75/6 (165, 24).
**MANAGER:** Brighton (76-81); Charlton Athletic (81-82); Crystal Palace (82-84);
Queen's Park Rangers (84); Brighton (86-87); Barnet (96-97).

| GAMES | 374 |
| GOALS | 30 |

# DENNIS BOND

## 1966/67 → 1970/71

Few, if any, players at White Hart Lane in the late 1960s were blessed with sweeter skills than Dennis Bond – and in a squad that included the likes of Greaves, Gilzean and Venables, that was saying something. The problem was that the young midfielder was not a natural athlete, his exceptional ability being concentrated more in his feet than his body, and he never achieved the consistency necessary for a top-level career.

Twenty-year-old Bond was seen as a gilt-edged investment when he was signed from Watford for £20,000 in March 1967. In training, he looked positively brilliant, his control, vision and passing accuracy enough to make the purists drool. He packed a tremendous shot, too, but it was seen all too rarely in games, in which he appeared to lack stamina in spite of a sturdy physique.

Occasionally, as in the European Cup Winners' Cup clash with Olympique Lyonnais at the Lane in December 1967, he looked the part, but competition for places proved too hot and in October 1970 he moved to Charlton Athletic.

A popular, breezy individual who enjoyed life to the full, he returned to Watford eventually and served them splendidly, but that could not disguise the fact that the tale of Dennis Bond was one of vast potential unrealised.

**DENNIS JOSEPH THOMAS BOND**
BORN:    Walthamstow, London, 17 March 1947.
OTHER CLUBS:    Watford 64/5-66/7 (93, 17); Charlton Athletic 70/1-72/3 (75, 3); Watford 72/3-77/8 (179, 20).

GAMES **23 (4)**
GOALS 1

# DAVID JENKINS

## 1968/69 → 1969/70

The demands on any young man joining a club of Spurs' stature are bound to be massive, but for David Jenkins the challenge was always going to be that little bit stiffer than the norm. The reasons were two-fold: first, the talented but inconsistent forward was arriving from Arsenal, the old enemy; second, he had been swapped for Jimmy Robertson, a proven and popular player.

In the eyes of many Tottenham fans, Bill Nicholson had dropped a rare transfer-market clanger, and in truth the Bristolian did little to dissuade them from that view following the surprise deal in October 1968. Though his goals at Stoke and at home to Queen's Park Rangers that winter were each worth a point, the former schoolboy star just did not convince.

Jenkins possessed a strong shot, good control and adequate pace, but sadly these ingredients in a potentially excellent mix never quite gelled. In addition there was a feeling that he lacked a bit of 'devil', and as the criticism mounted, so his confidence appeared to wither. New players were signed, he dropped in the pecking order, and in July 1972 he accepted a move to Brentford. However, neither with the Bees nor his subsequent clubs could David Jenkins fulfil his youthful promise.

**DAVID JOHN JENKINS**
BORN:    Bristol, 2 September 1946.
OTHER CLUBS:    Arsenal 67/8-68/9 (17, 3); Brentford 72/3 (18, 1); Hereford United 72/3-73/4 (22, 3); Newport County on loan 73/4 (6, 1); Shrewsbury Town 74/5 (2, 1); South African football; Workington Town 75/6 (6, 0).

GAMES **13 (4)**
GOALS 2

# ROGER MORGAN

## 1968/69 → 1971/72

Bill Nicholson's decision to pay £110,000 to Queen's Park Rangers for Roger Morgan in February 1969 had most White Hart Lane fans bubbling with enthusiasm. They didn't doubt that the identical twin of fellow winger Ian – also linked with Spurs but destined to remain a Ranger – could create for Tottenham's marksmen the same abundance of opportunities he had provided for former team-mate Rodney Marsh. After his first outing – at Loftus Road, coincidentally – in which he set up a goal for Jimmy Greaves, and his home debut against Wolves, on which he scored, they had little reason to revise their opinions.

However, after a brief settling-in period, the terrace mutterings began. Morgan exhibited commendable skill and could be an accurate crosser, usually finding space to dispatch the ball by jockeying for an angle rather than speeding past defenders, but he lacked consistency. Stepping up from Rangers – bound for a swift return to Division Two at the time of the deal – to a club with designs on the top prizes, the England under-23 international had something to prove; sadly, he never quite managed it.

To be fair, the second half of his Tottenham career was blighted by injury, which ruled him out of contention between October 1970 and January 1972. On his return there was some promise, including an enterprising display and a goal on his European debut against Arad in Romania, but fitness eluded him and he bowed out of the professional game.

For the happy-go-lucky Londoner, who admitted to modelling his image on George Best yet somehow never cut the most athletic of figures, this was a bitter pill after months of pain and hard work. A natural ball-player – both he and brother Ian had been talented young cricketers who had excited interest from three first-class counties – Morgan retained his sporting connection by becoming a Football In The Community officer at West Ham.

**ROGER ERNEST MORGAN**
BORN: Walthamstow, London, 14 November 1946.
OTHER CLUBS: Queen's Park Rangers 64/5-68/9 (180, 39).

GAMES **77 (3)**
GOALS **12**

# CYRIL KNOWLES

## 1964/65 → 1975/76

Cyril Knowles was a born entertainer. To the thousands of doting fans with whom he enjoyed a gleeful rapport, he exuded charisma, even in the traditionally unspectacular position of full-back. To his team-mates he was a zestful companion, beloved for his perpetual good cheer and addiction to practical jokes, but also respected for the toughness, dedication and sheer ability that lurked behind that contagious humour.

Indeed, it would be shameful to underplay the distinctive footballing merits that can be overlooked all too easily amid the strains of 'Nice One, Cyril', the pop record which he inspired and which earned him national cult status in 1973.

The Knowles game was a cocktail of swashbuckling adventure, lithe athleticism and jarring power, though it was principally the last-mentioned ingredient which transfixed the attention of his new colleagues after the one-time Yorkshire pitman arrived from Middlesbrough as a £45,000 virtual unknown in May 1964. In his first training session, the eager 19-year-old ran amok, tackling anything that moved with a wild abandon that had Dave Mackay calling for calm! Accordingly, Knowles applied restraint – sensible people didn't argue with Mackay – though throughout his career faint-hearted opponents were to quail at the vigour of his challenges, while acknowledging them to be fair.

But most vivid in the memory are images of his raiding overlaps, cultured distribution – after early rashness had been ironed out – and coolness in defensive crises. Knowles was in his element speeding down the flank, like some rampant premonition of Stuart Pearce, before releasing a made-to-measure cross, a service that proved particularly productive when the two Martins, Chivers and Peters, were in their prime.

As his experience grew, so did the renown of his left foot as an instrument of culture, picking out his targets with impeccable accuracy, though it must be admitted that there were moments when his confidence – some might say arrogance – in possession caused Tottenham hearts to flutter. Knowles had an occasional, disconcerting tendency to trap the ball on his own goal-line, then swagger forward selling outrageous dummies as he waltzed towards safety. Inevitably, such an eccentric talent was doomed to periodic aberrations, but it would be hard to find a fan who didn't reckon them a small price to pay for so much that was captivating.

Knowles' one obvious weakness was a lack of aerial prowess, surprising in a six-footer and on which canny opponents such as Don Revie's Leeds United were wont to prey. Overall though, he proved to be one of Bill Nicholson's most marked bargains, and only the brilliance of Ray Wilson and Terry Cooper prevented him from playing more than his four times for England.

At club level, Knowles spent his initial north London season at right-back, moving to the left to replace his retired erstwhile partner, Ron Henry, at the start of 1965/66. Thereafter he rarely relinquished the number-three shirt until a knee injury in December 1973 sidelined him for five months and warned of future problems.

Still ahead, however, was perhaps his most cherished display, at home to Leeds on the last day of 1974/75. Spurs had to win to be certain of staying up, and Cyril was the hero of the hour, cracking home a free-kick and a penalty as well as tormenting the visitors' defence incessantly in an unforgettable 4-2 victory.

The Knowles knee broke down repeatedly during the first half of 1975/76, and he was forced to retire, having shared in four cup triumphs during a stirring career. Keen to remain in football – unlike his gifted brother Peter, the Wolves forward who had left the game at 24 to concentrate on his faith as a Jehovah's Witness – Knowles went on to become a successful coach and manager.

But calamity was lying in wait. In August 1991 Cyril Knowles died of a brain tumour at the tragically early age of 47. The soccer world was distraught; it seemed impossible to believe that such a fervent lover of life was no more.

| | |
|---|---|
| **CYRIL BARRY KNOWLES** | |
| BORN: | Fitzwilliam, Yorkshire, 13 July 1944. |
| HONOURS: | UEFA Cup 71/2. FA Cup 66/7. League Cup 70/1, 72/3. 4 England caps (67-68). |
| OTHER CLUBS: | Middlesbrough 62/3-63/4 (37, 0). |
| MANAGER: | Darlington (83-87); Torquay United (87-89); Hartlepool United (89-91). |
| DIED: | Middlesbrough, Yorkshire, 31 August 1991. |

| | |
|---|---|
| GAMES | 505 (2) |
| GOALS | 17 |

# ALAN GILZEAN

## 1964/65 → 1973/74

The difference between Alan Gilzean and the majority of his peers was the gulf between a Van Gogh and a competent, even excellent painting by a lesser artist. A cursory glance at the canvases by anyone but a true connoisseur might offer the impression that there was little to choose between them; closer examination, of course, would reveal the subtlety of colour, composition and texture that lifted the Dutch master into a class of his own. So it was with 'The King of White Hart Lane', who provided Tottenham fans with everything they demand of their idols – sheer quality invested with character and style.

Pale, balding and frequently besuited, the intelligent Scot fitted the popular image of stockbroker or accountant rather than that of star centre-forward. Indeed, one irreverent team-mate reckoned that, even in his twenties, Gilzean looked the League's oldest player, while others spoke of an ungainly figure with one shoulder higher than the other.

But dress him in football kit, give him a ball and suddenly the butterfly emerged from the chrysalis. What made Gilzean special was a supreme delicacy of touch, especially with his head, that often defied belief. No one equalled his accuracy in nodding the ball in any direction, invariably employing the most minimal of glancing deflections rather than power. One moment there would seem little danger as a hopeful punt sailed towards the penalty area with 'Gilly' surrounded by a forest of huge opponents; the next he had timed his leap to perfection, letting the ball slide from his pate at whatever angle was required to wreak havoc.

On the ground, too, he was a professor of stealth and technique, creating an illusion of strolling as he slipped into space, controlled the ball deftly and laid it off with infinite cunning. So gently did Gilzean caress a football that he might have been wearing carpet slippers; in fact, he soaked his boots in hot water before every match to make them soft and ensure added feeling.

Sometimes in the heat of action, the players around him failed to read his intentions, but rarely would he appear ruffled, instead merely resuming his beat across the Spurs front line. Inevitably such a performer received copious punishment from desperate opponents, but he was not lacking in heart and accepted the blows as part of his job, preferring to retaliate with skill rather than violence. He was helped in this by enviable fitness which belied that superficially non-athletic appearance. In reality, he regularly outdid younger men in ten-lap races around the training ground.

Gilzean joined Tottenham in December 1964, a £72,500 capture from Dundee, with whom he had scored prolifically as a conventional spearhead, helping them win the Scottish title and reach the European Cup semi-finals. Dens Park boss Bob Shankly, brother of Liverpool's Bill, was not keen to part with his prize asset, but the persuasive Bill Nicholson, seeking to rebuild as his double side broke up, beat off opposition from Sunderland and Torino of Italy to strike a deal.

Soon it became evident that he could make goals as well as take them, and he featured in two celebrated partnerships without ever scoring heavily himself. First came 'The G Men' with Jimmy Greaves, his close friend; then, arguably to even more marked effect, he linked with Martin Chivers, whose colossal throw-ins he met so cleverly at the near post.

Alan served Tottenham until he was nearly 36, his deathless craft compensating royally for declining pace, and signed off with a goal at Newcastle on the final day of 1973/74. Thereafter Gilzean senior – his son Ian was a Spurs junior before switching to Dundee – played in South Africa and managed Southern League Stevenage before taking a job outside the game. Never, though, will Alan Gilzean be forgotten at White Hart Lane, where he gave so much pleasure. The fans loved him then, and they love him still.

**ALAN JOHN GILZEAN**
BORN: Coupar Angus, Perthshire, 22 October 1938.
HONOURS: UEFA Cup 71/2. FA Cup 66/7. League Cup 70/1, 72/3. 22 Scotland caps (63-71).
OTHER CLUBS: Dundee 59/60-64/5 (134, 113); Highland Park, South Africa, 74/5.

GAMES 430 (10)
GOALS 133

# PETER COLLINS

## 1968/69 → 1972/73

It was like some young and verdant giant oak crashing to the forest floor, while alongside him the gnarled survivors of many a storm continued, for the moment, to wave their branches in the breeze. When injury and consequent arthritis forced Peter Collins to retire from top-level football at the age of 26, it spelled calamity not only for a talented performer who looked capable of becoming the backbone of Spurs' defence for five more years at least, but also for a team in urgent need of long-term replacements for the experienced Mike England and Phil Beal.

It was little consolation that Collins had been something of a windfall in the first place, costing just £5,000 from non-League Chelmsford City in January 1968, with a further £4,000 to pay if he made ten senior appearances. In the event, the second instalment fell due during the following season when the strapping 6ft 1in stopper enjoyed 33 outings as injuries disrupted Bill Nicholson's plans.

Enormously strong, fearsomely hard and very quick for a big man, Collins couldn't equal England's ball skills, but he matched him in the air and his all-round game was improving steadily. The youngster's most rewarding term was 1970/71 when he shone in an early stint as deputy for Beal, then stood in for the sidelined Welshman from midwinter onwards and pocketed a richly deserved League Cup winners' medal for his pains.

Having returned to the reserve ranks in 1971/72, Collins continued to distinguish himself whenever called to the first-team colours, as against Rapid in Bucharest that December. But then ankle and knee problems developed and by the mid-1970s it was clear that the popular centre-half – dubbed 'Spud' and 'Farmer' by irreverent team-mates in reference to his rural roots – had no future at White Hart Lane. He went on to become player-boss of Southern League Folkestone, while Tottenham strove unavailingly for the rest of the decade to find a fitting successor to Mike England.

**PETER JOHN COLLINS**
BORN: Chelmsford, Essex, 29 November 1948.
HONOURS: League Cup 70/1.

GAMES 91 (10)
GOALS 5

# MIKE DILLON

## 1972/73 → 1973/74

The experience of central defender Mike Dillon highlights the uncertainty of football as a career, even for the most promising of youngsters who sample life in the senior ranks. An England schools and youth international, he helped Spurs win the FA Youth Cup in 1970, displaying all-round ability and abundant confidence, and praise was heaped upon him. At that stage, Dillon looked a banker to make the grade.

All was well on his senior debut, too, standing in for Phil Beal in a 4-1 victory at Old Trafford in the autumn of 1972, and over the next season and a half he proved a competent deputy both for Beal and for Mike England, including appearances in two European encounters. But despite the opportunity afforded by the impending departure of several senior rivals, Dillon failed to progress at the rate demanded by the Spurs management, illustrating the truisms that individuals develop at different speeds and that nothing can be taken for granted.

Perhaps a trifle short for his role at 5ft 10in, he was unable to dominate larger and more seasoned opponents, and after brief loan stints with Millwall and Swindon, Dillon left for New York to ply his trade alongside Pele.

**MICHAEL LESLIE DILLON**
**BORN:** Highgate, London, 29 September 1952.
**OTHER CLUBS:** Millwall on loan 74/5 (4, 0); Swindon Town on loan 74/5 (9, 0 ); New York Cosmos, USA, 85-78; Washington Diplomats, USA, 78.

| GAMES | 25 (4) |
| --- | --- |
| GOALS | 1 |

---

# TONY WANT

## 1967/68 → 1971/72

The shadows of Cyril Knowles and Joe Kinnear loomed large and dark for Tony Want. The gutsy little Londoner was a quick, aggressive left-back who played as if his life depended on it, but throughout his five-year sojourn on the fringe of Tottenham's senior squad he never quite made the breakthrough from reliable deputy to regular first-teamer.

England youth international Want, a stalwart of Spurs' successful Football Combination side of the late 1960s, made his debut when Kinnear was omitted for the home encounter with West Bromwich Albion in March 1968, playing in the number-three shirt with Knowles switching flanks.

But it was not until 1969/70, when the Irishman had broken his leg, that the loyal reserve was given a settled run. Tackling tigerishly and passing assuredly with his left foot, Want let no one down but failed to cement his place. It would have been understandable if he had become disheartened, but he battled on until he ousted Knowles on merit in 1971/72, only to perform disappointingly and be dropped again.

That summer he joined newly-promoted Birmingham City for £60,000, serving the Blues for six years before trying his luck in the United States.

**ANTHONY GEORGE WANT**
**BORN:** Shoreditch, London, 13 December 1948.
**OTHER CLUBS:** Birmingham City 72/3-77/8 (101, 1); Philadelphia Atoms 75-78; Minnesota Kicks 78, both USA.

| GAMES | 52 (4) |
| --- | --- |
| GOALS | 0 |

# MARTIN CHIVERS

## 1967/68 → 1975/76

The words seem extravagant in stark black-and-white, yet the case is so strong that it deserves to be made: for a couple of seasons in the early 1970s, Martin Chivers was the best all-round centre-forward in the world. There, it's said, and there is no shortage of vivid memories or expert opinion to support a contention certain to attract wider support with the addition of one simple qualification: when he was in the mood.

In terms of attributes for the job, Chivers lacked either none or only one, depending on your viewpoint. About his power and technique, flair and balance there could be no argument, and it was rare to find such a rich combination of qualities in a big man. Add intelligence and speed – he could seem ponderous, but it was a dangerous illusion as countless defenders left stranded by that ground-gobbling lope could testify – and the picture of an exceptional performer is almost complete.

And so to the one factor which some believe prevented Martin from attaining true greatness: the absence of 'devil', a killer streak, call it what you will. Certainly Bill Nicholson despaired at times, reckoning his gifted, muscular number-nine needed an injection of Bobby Smith-style aggression to fulfil his vast potential. The frustrated manager even urged defenders to clatter Chivers on the training field in a bid to provoke the flashes of fire he so longed to see and, as a result, his relationship with the sensitive striker became strained.

It all served to heap extra pressure on a man already carrying a massive burden of expectation due to the inescapable fact that if he didn't score, then Spurs' chances of victory were drastically reduced.

Chivers joined Spurs from Southampton in January 1968, valued at £125,000 in the deal that took Frank Saul to The Dell. After early goals, the newcomer hit a barren patch as the team struggled, but was picking up form when, that September at Nottingham Forest, he twisted his knee and was sidelined for a year.

Now his very career was in doubt, and on his return he had to rebuild confidence as well as fitness. Perhaps the turning point came in spring 1970 with the departure of Jimmy Greaves. Chivers appeared to relish fresh responsibility as chief goal-getter and over the next two terms his game ascended to new heights.

Meshing delightfully with Martin Peters and Alan Gilzean – how often that subtle duo capitalised on the long throw that became a Chivers hallmark – or going it alone, he was frequently virtually unstoppable. His two goals won the 1971 League Cup Final against Aston Villa, there were two more – a stunning 25-yarder after beating two men, and a soaring header – in the first leg of the 1972 UEFA Cup Final against Wolves at Molineux and, still more spectacular, a 35-yard free-kick of phenomenal velocity that provided a crucial away goal against Vitoria Setubal in March 1973.

But no single strike epitomised his blend of strength and delicacy more than one in a home clash with Stoke City in October 1970, when he surged infield from the left flank like some rampant tank before shrugging off the combative Denis Smith and outwitting the great Gordon Banks with the sweetest of 20-yard curlers.

It must be admitted that between such peaks were troughs of inconsistency, and it was then that the lack-of-bite brigade delivered their most poisonous barbs, notably when he failed to score as Poland dumped England out of the World Cup in 1973. Thereafter Chivers was never quite the same irresistible force, and in 1976 he joined Servette Geneva for £80,000.

Later in life he became a successful businessman involved in promoting Spurs' image; meanwhile, though arguments about his precise position in the club's order of merit might continue, few could deny that, on his day at least, Martin Chivers was unequalled among his contemporaries.

**MARTIN HARCOURT CHIVERS**

**BORN:** Southampton, 27 April 1945.
**HONOURS:** UEFA Cup 71/2. League Cup 70/1, 72/3. 24 England caps (71-73).
**OTHER CLUBS:** Southampton 62/3-67/8 (175, 97); Servette Geneva, Switzerland, 76/7-77/8; Norwich City 78/9 (11, 4); Brighton 78/9-79/80 (5, 1).

| | |
|---|---|
| GAMES | 355 (12) |
| GOALS | 174 |

# GRAEME SOUNESS

## 1971/72

Every club has suffered the mortification of letting a young player slip from their grasp only to see him re-emerge as a star on some rival stage. But that offered scant consolation to Spurs fans as they cast envious eyes towards Anfield, Italy and Ibrox, and noted the awesome progress of Graeme Souness. Even given the heroic deeds of Hoddle and Ardiles, the Tottenham cause could hardly afford to lose such a talent.

Having helped Spurs win the FA Youth Cup in 1970, the precocious Scot progressed quickly to the first-team fringe, making his one senior appearance as a substitute for Alan Mullery in Keflavik in September 1971. Already the Souness game was stamped with that familiar swagger: there was little pace but his passing was immaculate and his tackling brisk; undeniable, too, was a hint of petulance, though in fairness, at that age he was more sinned against than sinner.

With so much ability for all to see, the young man grew impatient on the sidelines, apparently believing he could do better than the established stars. Thus after returning homesick to Scotland, he signed for Middlesbrough before developing into one of the most influential British play-makers since the war. Of that magnificent career, all Tottenham followers had to savour was 26 minutes in Iceland . . .

|  | **GRAEME JAMES SOUNESS** |
| --- | --- |
| **BORN:** | Edinburgh, 6 May 1953. |
| **HONOURS:** | 54 Scotland caps (74-86). |
| **OTHER CLUBS:** | Middlesbrough 72/3-77/8 (176, 22); Liverpool 77/8-83/4 (247, 38); |
|  | Sampdoria, Italy, 84/5-85/6 (56, 8); Glasgow Rangers 86/7-89/90 (50, 3). |
| **MANAGER:** | Glasgow Rangers (86-91); Liverpool (91-94); Galatasaray, Turkey, (95-96); Southampton (96-97); |
|  | Torino, Italy, (97); Benfica, Portugal, (97-99); Blackburn Rovers (00-04); Newcastle United (04-06). |

| GAMES | 0 (1) |
| --- | --- |
| GOALS | 0 |

# PHIL HOLDER

## 1971/72 → 1973/74

Phil Holder was consumed by enthusiasm, slaving constantly throughout every match, and was brave to a degree that made hardened professionals wince. He lacked nothing in terms of skill or strength, either, and there was a time in the early 1970s when the squarely-built England youth international had a chance of overcoming the disadvantage of standing only 5ft 3in to fashion a top-flight career with Spurs.

That was during the regime of Bill Nicholson and his assistant, Eddie Baily, as demanding a duo as ever ran a football team and who honoured Holder for his phenomenal spirit. Indeed Bill, not noted for dispensing light-hearted nicknames, unbent sufficiently to accord the effervescent Londoner, who was one of 13 children, the title of 'Chief'.

But come autumn 1974, new boss Terry Neill found him surplus to requirements and, in the next February, Holder moved to Crystal Palace. In truth, he had never risen above the rank of reserve at White Hart Lane – impressing on occasions as a midfield deputy for his best friend, Steve Perryman – and was troubled both by injuries and a tendency to gain weight when unable to train. A natural motivator, Holder became a coach when his playing days ended, and worked under Perryman at Brentford until taking over as manager in 1990.

|  | **PHILIP HOLDER** |
| --- | --- |
| **BORN:** | Kilburn, London, 19 January 1952. |
| **OTHER CLUBS:** | Crystal Palace 74/5-77/8 (95, 5); Bournemouth 78/9-79/80 (58, 4). |
| **MANAGER:** | Brentford (90-93). |

| GAMES | 9 (10) |
| --- | --- |
| GOALS | 2 |

# RAY EVANS

## 1968/69 – 1974/75

If achievement were measured purely by speed, fitness and enthusiasm, then Ray Evans would have been England's right-back. As it was, he will be remembered as a strong and eager dasher, practically a winger in disguise, whose defensive qualities never quite equalled his invaluable attacking attributes.

Evans was at his most effective sprinting down the touchline before releasing any manner of centre – now long and raking to a distant Martin Chivers, next curving wickedly to Alan Gilzean on the near post – both ploys which created plenty of goals. He struck the ball with resounding crispness and his booming, accurate passes into the traditional inside-forward channels could transform defence into instant attack, while the fierce Evans shot was a potential threat to any goalkeeper within 30 yards of his right boot.

At the back, however, he was more adequate than outstanding, a tackler of variable precision and rather disappointing in the air for a tallish, solidly-built individual who deputised occasionally in central defence. At need, though, the former youth international could be a limpet-like marker, as he showed against Red Star Belgrade's influential Dragan Djajic at the Lane in November 1972.

After making his senior debut in March 1969, Evans was to spend three years as faithful understudy to Joe Kinnear before playing so well during a lengthy stint in 1971/72 that the more polished Irishman couldn't reclaim his place on regaining fitness. During the following season, the two men were given equal opportunities in the number-two shirt, before Evans established the ascendancy, missing only two games in 1973/74.

Frustratingly for the ebullient north Londoner, Kinnear was the incumbent for all three cup triumphs during the early 1970s, with his own 1974 UEFA Cup loser's medal offering little consolation. Come January 1975, with new boss Terry Neill bringing change, Ray Evans joined Millwall for £40,000, later performing solidly for Fulham and Stoke City.

| | |
|---|---|
| **RAYMOND LESLIE EVANS** | |
| **BORN:** Edmonton, London, 20 September 1949. | |
| **OTHER CLUBS:** Millwall 74/5-76/7 (74, 3); Fulham 76/7-78/9 (86, 6); Stoke City 79/80-81/2 (94, 1). | |

| GAMES | 174 (7) |
|---|---|
| GOALS | 4 |

# MIKE ENGLAND

## 1966/67 → 1974/75

**B**ill Nicholson acquired the services of Britain's best centre-half when he bought Mike England from newly relegated Blackburn Rovers in the summer of 1966. That, at least, was the judgement of most contemporary pundits – the merits of Jack Charlton of Leeds United and Sunderland's Charlie Hurley notwithstanding – and it was reflected in the £95,000 fee, then a Football League record for a defender.

A further indication of the big Welshman's worth was the identity of Spurs' chief rival in the race for his signature, a certain Matt Busby, who for months had been favourite to recruit England and had withdrawn surprisingly from negotiations at a late stage. Perhaps Spurs' immediate need was greater than Manchester United's – a recent injury had ended Maurice Norman's career, while veteran Old Trafford stopper Bill Foulkes was still in harness – but there was no doubt whose decision proved soundest in the long term.

For their money, Tottenham brought strength, stability and style to the heart of their defence, as well as adding a fearsome new option to their attacking armoury. Most instantly eye-catching of the England assets was his aerial might, which owed as much to intelligent timing as it did to a bonily angular 6ft 2in frame and a wide forehead which propelled the ball vast distances.

But unlike many traditional centre-halves, England could offer a respectable turn of pace and a degree of ball control and passing expertise of which plenty of midfielders would have been proud. If not under direct challenge, he could 'kill' a 70-yard drop-kick from the opposing goalkeeper with a single touch and his penetrating through-balls fashioned many an opening for the front-men.

In fact, apart from a slight vulnerability on the turn when faced by a nippy adversary, the only criticism to be levelled against the long-striding pivot's all-round expertise was a slight awkwardness in the tackle. He appeared to close clumsily on his target, often falling in a tangle which occasionally resulted in conceding free-kicks in perilous situations, as well as placing undue strain on his joints. This last-mentioned consequence might have been a factor in the knee problems that plagued him for years, to the extent that at times he played with heavy strapping and was known to take hot baths before games to aid mobility.

After his move from Ewood Park, England took several outings to settle before striking a vein of majestic form that was typified by his utter dominance of the dangerous Tony Hateley in that season's FA Cup Final victory over Chelsea.

Then in 1968/69, as Spurs struggled to find the net, he demonstrated his versatility with a six-game stint at centre-forward, partnering Jimmy Greaves and scoring twice. Indeed thereafter, having returned to the back, he seemed keener than ever to lend his power to the attack in timely exhilarating sorties.

The new decade started with frustration for England as injury deprived him of a League Cup medal in 1971, but despite frequently playing through considerable pain, which was etched on his features during matches, he made up for it in 1973 and excelled in the UEFA Cup triumph of the intervening term.

A forthright character who insisted on doing things right – back in 1966 he had threatened to quit football when Blackburn initially blocked his move – he rocked fans by departing White Hart Lane suddenly in spring 1975, reportedly disillusioned with the regime of new manager Terry Neill.

Two spells in Seattle and one with Cardiff rounded off his exploits on the pitch, before he spent most of the 1980s in charge of the national side he had served so nobly as a player, and in 1984 he was rewarded with an MBE for his services to the Welsh game.

Where does he stand in the pantheon of Spurs stars? Suffice it to say that when Bill Nicholson selected his dream XI, he pondered the hefty claims of Maurice Norman before opting for Mike England. In Tottenham terms, there could be no more meaningful tribute.

---

**HAROLD MICHAEL ENGLAND**
**BORN:** Holywell, Flintshire, 2 December 1941.
**HONOURS:** UEFA Cup 71/2. FA Cup 66/7. League Cup 72/3. 44 Wales caps (62-74).
**OTHER CLUBS:** Blackburn Rovers 59/60-65/6 (165, 21); Seattle Sounders, USA, 75-76; Cardiff City 75/6 (40, 1).
**MANAGER:** Wales (80-88).

GAMES  398
GOALS  19

# JIMMY PEARCE

## 1968/69 → 1972/73

The Tottenham team-mates of Jimmy Pearce had always believed he was a star in the making, and by 1972/73 he was beginning to prove them right. After four seasons of bright, promising contributions had fallen marginally short of establishing an automatic first-team slot, the skilful utility attacker was finally adding consistency to his comprehensive range of assets. Then, at 26 and on the threshold of his prime, Pearce suffered persistent knee pain that was linked to a rare bone condition, and he never played top-level soccer again.

Perhaps part of the reason for the fitful early progress was that the mild, self-deprecating local lad didn't realise just how good he was. Those who watched him as an England schoolboy had no such doubts, predicting a full international future, and he did enough in 1968/69, his first senior season, to confirm that here was a talent worth monitoring.

In full flight, Pearce was a thrilling performer, able to control the ball at high speed and blessed with a characteristic shimmy which took him gliding past defenders almost as if they weren't there. A crisp finisher with his right foot

and physically strong, he gave his most satisfying displays as a winger with a predilection for cutting inside, though he doubled effectively as a central striker.

However, he continued to flit in and out of the side, a frustrating situation underlined when he came on as substitute to score in the 1971 League Cup semi-final against Bristol City, yet was denied a place at Wembley. It was two years before Pearce made up for the disappointment, winning a medal for his part in the victory over Norwich City in the same competition.

At last, it seemed, his confidence was matching his ability and he was poised to become a major influence – and then came that shattering diagnosis. Pearce rested for a year before making a comeback with non-League Walthamstow Avenue; meanwhile, a declining Tottenham were left to rue the departure of a talent they could ill afford to lose.

| | | |
|---|---|---|
| **JAMES WILLIAM PEARCE** | | |
| BORN: | Tottenham, 27 November 1947. | |
| HONOURS: | League Cup 72/3. | |

| | |
|---|---|
| GAMES | **141 (52)** |
| GOALS | 35 |

# JIMMY NEIGHBOUR

## 1970/71 → 1976/77

Jimmy Neighbour was a winger of considerable natural gifts, a twister and turner who could mesmerise an opponent and bring a crowd to its feet, yet he remains something of a 'nearly man' in the Tottenham story.

Having risen through the club's junior ranks and turned professional in 1968, he found himself competing for a flank berth with Roger Morgan and Jimmy Pearce. This was no easy option and when Morgan suffered a long-term injury in 1970/71, then Pearce was tried and temporarily discarded, it was an opportunity on which the inexperienced Neighbour needed to capitalise convincingly.

That he did so to such effect, earning a place in the League Cup Final triumph over Aston Villa along the way, reflected great credit on the slightly-built 20-year-old, whose cause was strengthened by his ability to play on either flank.

Sadly for Neighbour, his momentum was halted abruptly by the purchase of Ralph Coates and a switch of formation from 4-3-3 to 4-4-2. Thereafter his opportunities were limited, and it was not until the appointment of Terry Neill as manager that he was given the extended senior sequence he craved.

Even then his elevation to first-team regular was delayed until 1975/76, but once in place he responded with the most captivating form of his career. Though he held on to the ball too long at times, his nimble footwork paved the way for a stream of accurate crosses, and he was ever willing to chase back when possession was lost.

Yet for such a clean striker of the ball, Neighbour did not score enough goals – three in 44 starts that term was a woeful return – which was a factor, presumably, in the decision of new boss Keith Burkinshaw to sell him to Norwich for £75,000 in September 1976.

The move was greeted with dismay by some fans who preferred Jimmy Neighbour to his replacement, Peter Taylor, their discontent being fuelled by that season's relegation and their former favourite's fine service at Carrow Road.

**JAMES EDWARD NEIGHBOUR**
BORN: Chingford, Essex, 15 November 1950.
HONOURS: League Cup 70/1.
OTHER CLUBS: Norwich City 76/7-79/80 (106, 5 ); West Ham United 79/80-82/3 (73, 5); Bournemouth on loan 82/3 (6, 0).

| | |
|---|---|
| GAMES | **134 (22)** |
| GOALS | 11 |

# MARTIN PETERS

## 1969/70 → 1974/75

**M**artin Peters was a sleek, ultra-professional performer who won the minds of Tottenham supporters without, perhaps, managing always to warm their hearts. That is no sleight on a man blessed liberally with every skill in the textbook, but whose mode of operation tended towards the subtle and unobtrusive. Cool and seemingly detached from the hurly-burly, Peters played the game with his brain, frequently seeing things that escaped his fellow players, let alone those watching from the stands and terraces. Accordingly, despite the cornucopia of honours that came his way during a fabulous career, it was not universally appreciated just how unremittingly excellent he was.

Indeed, his willingness to leave West Ham, aged 26 and approaching his prime, might have had plenty to do with a desire to escape from the all-encompassing shadows cast by Bobby Moore and Geoff Hurst, his co-heroes of England's 1966 World Cup triumph. Whatever the motivation, it was in March 1970, close to the transfer deadline, that Peters became Britain's first £200,000 footballer in the transaction which took Jimmy Greaves to Upton Park.

Though he scored with a header on his debut, a home defeat by Coventry City, Martin took time to gain widespread acceptance, but gradually the sheer quality of almost every Peters touch convinced the doubters of his pedigree. A clean striker of the ball, he underpinned his accurate distribution and lethal finishing by supreme positional awareness which enabled him to drift into space, creating danger from unexpected angles.

A lean, wiry six-footer, he was magnificent in the air, whether timing spring-heeled leaps to perfection or leaning forward imperceptibly to make wicked near-post deflections. Ever thoughtful, he could turn a game with a flash of intuition, a swift pass here, a little run there, without stirring a crowd with the more overt vigour of, say, a Mackay or a Mullery.

Thus doing his job quietly, elegantly, and sometimes courageously – his refusal to be intimidated by Rapid Bucharest's strong-arm tactics in Romania in December 1971 offered comprehensive proof of his steel – Peters became an increasingly influential part of the Tottenham set-up as trophy followed trophy in the early 1970s. He was the natural successor as captain when Alan Mullery left in 1972, earning the respect of his team-mates through personal example, tactical shrewdness and unquestionable integrity.

Though it is inevitable that victories linger longest in the memory, one of Peters' most inspirational displays came on a night of aggregate defeat, against Liverpool at White Hart Lane in the 1973 UEFA Cup semi-final second leg. The skipper was everywhere, prompting ceaselessly and scoring twice in a stirring fightback which was not quite enough to prevent the Merseysiders going through on the away-goals rule.

Peters maintained his standards admirably into mid-decade, but the side's fortunes slumped, leading to the resignation of Bill Nicholson and the surprise appointment of Terry Neill. The young Irishman found himself at odds with certain senior players and in March 1975, while a relegation battle was raging, a disagreement resulted in the ex-Hammer's £40,000 departure to Norwich City.

It might be argued that the price was fair for a 31-year-old, but Peters demonstrated that he had been released prematurely in the most effective way possible – by giving the Canaries five years of impeccable service, most of them in the top flight. At the end of the decade he switched to Sheffield United, with whom he tried management before opting for a future in insurance. One thing was certain, however; the player whom Alf Ramsey had once described as ten years ahead of his time had done enough to suggest that, no matter in what era he played, he would have excelled.

**MARTIN STANFORD PETERS**
**BORN:** Plaistow, London, 8 November 1943.
**HONOURS:** UEFA Cup 71/2. League Cup 70/1, 72/3. 67 England caps (66-74).
**OTHER CLUBS:** West Ham United 61/2-69/70 (302, 81); Norwich City 74/5-79/80 (207, 44); Sheffield United 80/1 (24, 4).
**MANAGER:** Sheffield United (81).

GAMES 260
GOALS 76

# PHIL BEAL

. . . . . . . . . . . . . . . . . . . .

## 1963/64 → 1974/75

If Bill Nicholson had ever felt moved to take out insurance against conceding goals through recklessness among his back four, it is easy to imagine the policy being delivered by Phil Beal; after all, the blond, moon-faced defender was guaranteed never to make a drama out of a crisis. A shrewd anticipator who was at his best sweeping up alongside centre-half Mike England, Beal tended to go unnoticed yet so often it was he who defused dangerous situations. Frequently it would be well after a game was over that Spurs' more reflective fans would begin to recall his timely interceptions, the cool efficiency in everything he did; indeed, that he had barely put a foot wrong.

The Beal footballing philosophy appeared to be based on a safety-first method in which over-elaboration had no place and the ball was returned carefully to 'keeper Pat Jennings if there was the slightest risk of squandering possession through a more ambitious option. Some observers felt him to be over-cautious and reckoned he did not make the most of commendable ball control, albeit with a heavy right-foot bias, and a sharp soccer brain. Presumably he believed he was using his ability in the best way possible, and could cite his longevity at the top level as compelling evidence.

Beal's path to recognition as a leading player was not an easy one. After being spotted by Spurs' assistant boss Harry Evans in county football, the England youth international, who had been considering a career in the Merchant Navy, signed as an amateur in 1960. He turned professional two years later but it was not until 1963 that he made his senior debut, deputising at right-half for Danny Blanchflower at Aston Villa.

The arrival of Alan Mullery in 1964 seemed to leave him in the cold, but fate took a hand when he came on at right-back for the seriously injured Maurice Norman in a home friendly against a Hungarian XI in November 1965. Beal impressed, was given a lengthy run in the number-two shirt, and by early 1967 appeared to be well established.

However, it was not to last. A broken arm put him out for the rest of the season, costing him an FA Cup Final appearance against Chelsea, and the following term found him changing roles regularly, filling every defensive position except goal and also excelling as an adhesively attentive one-on-one midfield marker. Yet despite missing few matches, Beal remained something of a 'bits-and-pieces' player and in January 1968 he was linked with Southampton as part of the deal that took Martin Chivers to north London.

Nothing came of that, though, and the departure of Dave Mackay in the summer brought about the turning point of his career. Now he settled into a sound and complementary central defensive partnership with Mike England. Beal was merely adequate in the air but with England around that didn't matter, while his own speed, durability and decisiveness offered crucial support to the big Welshman.

Of course, it took the fans who had idolised Mackay some time to accept his replacement and Beal endured unwarranted helpings of terrace stick, but eventually he wore down the critics to win both acceptance and affection. That landmark campaign of 1968/69 also saw his only senior goal, at home to QPR in January, and a memorable one it was; picking up the ball deep in his own half, he ran some 75 yards and completed a slick one-two interchange with Jimmy Greaves before clubbing an unstoppable drive from just outside the box.

Beal went on to play a major part in one UEFA Cup and two League Cup triumphs, while his extrovert, mickey-taking personality became ever more central to maintaining team morale. When he left for Brighton in July 1975, it became apparent that the merits of Phil Beal had long been taken for granted. He was sorely missed, both by a struggling side and by supporters who were becoming increasingly desperate.

**PHILIP BEAL**
BORN: Godstone, Surrey, 8 January 1945.
HONOURS: UEFA Cup 71/2. League Cup 70/1, 72/3.
OTHER CLUBS: Brighton 75/6-76/7 (10, 0); Los Angeles Aztecs, USA, 77; Memphis Rogues, USA, 78; Crewe Alexandra 79/80 (4, 0).

GAMES **417 (3)**
GOALS **1**

# PAT JENNINGS

## 1964/65 → 1976/77

It was like George Best being shunted off to Liverpool or Geoff Boycott dispatched across the Pennines to take guard for Lancashire; the world went crazy for Tottenham fans on that terrible day in August 1977 when Pat Jennings, the man they revered as the world's greatest goalkeeper, was sold to Arsenal – yes, Arsenal – for a piffling £45,000. Coming just three months after relegation to the Second Division, it seemed too much to take; and to rub salt into the most gaping of wounds, the man to whom Spurs boss Keith Burkinshaw had practically gift-wrapped Jennings was Terry Neill, his less than universally popular predecessor at White Hart Lane.

It was a bizarre incident, and a decision which Burkinshaw – while maintaining that the sale of the 32-year-old Ulsterman had appeared a reasonable option at the time – was later big enough to admit that, in retrospect, he would have reversed. Yet it served to highlight not only the glorious unpredictability of sport, but also the notoriously short memories of many supporters.

It seems unthinkable now, but the fact was that after Bill Nicholson paid Watford £27,000 for 19-year-old Jennings in June 1964, the one-time tree-feller and Gaelic footballer made such a nervous start that he became a target for mindless barrackers who demanded – and got, temporarily – the recall of the popular Bill Brown. So potentially damaging was the abuse that the manager was forced to appeal to the boo-boys to lay off, and it is a tribute to the Nicholson acumen that even in that dark hour, he retained faith in his man.

For Jennings there followed two seasons of sharing senior duty with Brown, gradually gaining confidence as his talent blossomed. Rangy, muscular and supremely fit, he was, it seemed, born to keep goal, albeit with an unorthodox style that was all his own.

One moment he was a benign but immovable giant who might have been plucking fruit in his orchard, that huge reach and safe pair of hands dominating the air around his net. The next he was a snake-charmer, hypnotising some unfortunate forward into shooting precisely when and where the master wished.

Jennings was a connoisseur of angles, an improviser supreme, adept at saving with feet, elbows or any other part of his anatomy. All this, combined with a composed, dignified bearing, made the job look easy, which was an absurd illusion, as all those privy to his thorough physical preparation and his tension as he built concentration before a match could testify.

The Jennings career was studded with spellbinding displays too numerous to mention, but there are examples which will lodge forever in this writer's memory: a series of fabulous saves over the two legs of the 1972 UEFA Cup Final against Wolves, including one astonishingly elastic stretch to tip over a chip after racing back 15 yards to reach the ball; the two penalty saves at Anfield in March 1973, diving right to frustrate Kevin Keegan, left to defeat Tommy Smith; and the drop-kicked goal against Manchester United in the 1967 Charity Shield at Old Trafford which left his opposite number, the splendid Alex Stepney, both dismayed and embarrassed.

Jennings helped Spurs lift four trophies and broke the club's appearance record, though his new mark was eclipsed later by Steve Perryman. On a wider front, he won player of the year accolades from writers (1973) and his fellow professionals (1976), and was awarded the MBE (1976) before heading for Highbury with nine years of top football – during which he stretched his international cap total to 119, then a world record – still ahead of him.

Sadly, he left the Lane with the feeling that he was no longer wanted. He never asked to go, but was not offered a new deal, a silence which upset and disappointed him. Soon it emerged that Keith Burkinshaw was in a telling minority in believing that Pat's day was done. Manchester United and Aston Villa both moved to sign him, but he opted to join the Irish enclave at Arsenal where, significantly, Neill handed him a four-year contract.

One of sport's most modest, yet enduring heroes had been allowed to depart prematurely from the scene of his greatest triumphs. In 1985/86 Jennings returned to serve Spurs briefly as first-team cover (he gave Everton similar assistance) and to hone his fitness for the 1986 World Cup.

**PATRICK ANTHONY JENNINGS**
BORN: Newry, Northern Ireland, 12 June 1945.
HONOURS: UEFA Cup 71/2. FA Cup 66/7. League Cup 70/1, 72/3. 119 Northern Ireland caps (64-86). FWA Footballer of the Year 73. PFA Footballer of the Year 76.
OTHER CLUBS: Watford 62/3-63/4 (48, 0); Arsenal 77/8-84/5 (237, 0).

GAMES 591
GOALS 1

# TERRY NAYLOR

1969/70 → 1979/80

Terry Naylor was hard and he was funny, a pugnacious, wise-cracking gladiator who gave sterling service in the Spurs back line during one of the leaner periods of White Hart Lane history.

The blond, brash north Londoner, a one-time porter at Smithfield Market, lacked plenty in finesse but nothing in confidence, as he showed at his first training session after turning professional with Tottenham. Walking calmly into the dressing room, he announced in matter-of-fact tones to the assembled stars: 'Anyone fancy dying today? 'Cause if they do, they should tackle me.' Naylor revelled in taking opponents on, both physically and verbally, and even on the practice field he was not a man with whom to trifle.

His senior breakthrough came in spring 1970, when he stood in for Phil Beal, and there followed several years spent primarily as a central defensive deputy – with occasional outings as a combative midfield trouble-shooter – before injury to left-back Cyril Knowles in December 1973 afforded him his longest sequence to date. Naylor took his chance avidly and thereafter filled every outfield defensive role, becoming a regular until the late 1970s.

As well as such splendid versatility, his chief assets were fitness, strength and an earthy refusal to accept defeat, all particularly priceless in the 1977/78 dogfight to rise from Division Two, but also he read the game with a shrewdness for which he received scant public credit.

Admittedly, the Naylor skills were not of the dainty variety, though he loved to get forward and his cross for Martin Peters to score the winner in the 1974 UEFA Cup quarter-final in Cologne was typical of many successful sorties.

That competition yielded his only medal – sadly of the loser's variety – but neither his spirit nor his humour flagged and when he left for Charlton Athletic in November 1980, the White Hart Lane scene was duller for his absence. Terry Naylor would never have won a place in a great Spurs side, but in times of struggle he was an absolute nugget.

**TERENCE MICHAEL PATRICK NAYLOR**
BORN: Islington, London, 5 December 1948.
OTHER CLUBS: Charlton Athletic 80/1-83/4 (73, 0).

GAMES **290 (14)**
GOALS 1

# KEITH OSGOOD

## 1973/74 → 1977/78

Keith Osgood was one of an alarmingly large White Hart Lane contingent during the mid-1970s: players who appeared on the verge of long and satisfying Tottenham careers, but who for a variety of reasons slipped anti-climactically from the scene.

The promising central defender, an England schoolboy and youth international, was three days past his 19th birthday when he received his senior call-up, leaving the bench to replace Phil Beal at Newcastle in May 1974. There followed a handful of stand-in appearances during the following autumn, but the key moment in Osgood's continued rise came that February when Mike England left the club.

Now the youngster stepped up, impressing immediately with his speed, agility and composure, and cementing his position with a courageous display at home to Leeds United in April. That day only a win would provide insurance against the drop to Division Two, and when Osgood played on with painful head and ankle injuries, deserving enormous personal credit for his part in a 4-2 victory, he signalled that a character of substance had arrived at the heart of Spurs' defence.

However, though he was competent in the air, at 5ft 11in Osgood did not dominate in the manner of his predecessor, and big Willie Young was drafted in alongside him. In other respects, his game developed satisfactorily, his smooth distribution and his knack of cracking home free-kicks from anything up to 35 yards drawing widespread approbation, leaving only the occasional lapse in concentration on which to work.

Thus, after two ever-present terms – with heavy speculation that he would follow Terry Neill to Arsenal having proved incorrect, and despite Spurs' relegation in 1976/77 – his White Hart Lane future seemed assured. But in midwinter 1978, a difference of opinion with boss Keith Burkinshaw preceded a £130,000 move to Coventry City, after which the Osgood career failed to fulfil all that early potential.

| KEITH OSGOOD | | |
|---|---|---|
| **BORN** | Isleworth, London, 8 May 1955. | |
| **OTHER CLUBS:** | Coventry City 77/8-78/9 (25, 1); Derby County 79/80-81/2 (69, 10); Orient 81/2-83/4 (36, 0); Cambridge United 84/5-85/6 (35, 1). | **GAMES** 126 (1) |
| | | **GOALS** 14 |

# JOHN PRATT

## 1968/69 → 1979/80

**O**nly the valiant, it's been said, should contemplate a life in football, a profession which demands steely resolution in all manner of ways. It needs obvious physical bravery to confront a ferocious tackle, or to play on with an injury; a different kind of courage is required to risk a piece of outrageous skill when the stakes are high, and yet another brand of fortitude to own up to a calamitous blunder; the list could go on.

But could there be anyone more stout-hearted than the player who faces concerted, frequently prolonged and mindless criticism from the terraces, yet who never hides or shirks, just keeps coming back for more? Such a man was John Pratt, who believed unshakeably in his own ability and whose appearance record for Spurs – more than 400 outings over 12 seasons – speaks volumes for both his strength of character and the esteem in which he was held by a succession of managers.

Pratt was an unselfish workhorse of the type every side needs, but who lacked the extravagant natural skills possessed by the majority of Tottenham midfielders down the years. Hence when the tide of battle was flowing the wrong way, he was a convenient scapegoat, for a time becoming a particular target of a vitriolic section on the Shelf.

In fact, as well as being prodigiously industrious – which did win him admirers, witness the 24,000 attendance for his testimonial game with Arsenal in 1978 – Pratt knew the game comprehensively and had a marvellous eye for an attacking opening. The problem was that he could not always make the most of it, his more ambitious passes tending to go astray, and that's when the condemnation would begin.

What the detractors chose to ignore was that although he gave the ball away a lot, he won it a lot, too, challenging combatively both in the air and on the ground. In addition, Pratt was a magnificent motivator, coaxing some team-mates while driving others, refusing to yield while the slightest shred of hope remained.

Then there were his goals, many of which were unleashed suddenly, spectacularly and at moments of vital importance, as Liverpool discovered when his unstoppable blast into the top corner of Ray Clemence's net set Spurs on the victory trail in a White Hart Lane League Cup quarter-final clash in December 1972. He went on to play a prominent part in lifting that trophy, though his sole Wembley appearance was marred by an injury which forced him out of the action after 20 minutes.

North Londoner Pratt, a former centre-half who deputised occasionally at the heart of Tottenham's rearguard, had spent a year in Brentford's youth team when he joined Spurs as an amateur on the recommendation of Terry Medwin. He made his League debut at Highbury in March 1969, but had to wait until 1971/72 for a settled senior stint, coming in for the sidelined Alan Mullery and finishing the campaign with a UEFA Cup winner's medal.

For the rest of the decade, Pratt's name was rarely absent from the teamsheet. In 1977/78 he was an ever-present as Spurs climbed out of the Second Division at the first attempt, and his standard of performance remained commendably consistent.

In the summer of 1980, aged 32 and having been displaced by new arrival Terry Yorath, Pratt opted for a fresh challenge across the Atlantic, starting a three-year association with Portland Timbers. Next came a return to the Lane, at first running the youth side, then the reserves, before a spell as assistant manager, which ended when Peter Shreeves was sacked in 1986. Thus Spurs bade farewell for a second time to one of their most dedicated loyalists.

| | |
|---|---|
| **JOHN ARTHUR PRATT** | |
| **BORN:** | Hackney, London, 26 June 1948. |
| **HONOURS:** | UEFA Cup 71/2. League Cup 72/3. |
| **OTHER CLUBS:** | Portland Timbers, USA, 80-82. |

| | |
|---|---|
| GAMES | **381 (34)** |
| GOALS | 49 |

# RALPH COATES

## 1971/72 → 1977/78

The devastation of Burnley fans when Ralph Coates was sold to Tottenham for £190,000 in May 1971 was overwhelming; at 25, the thickset midfielder-cum-flankman appeared to be on the verge of fully-fledged soccer stardom. Despite the Clarets' relegation, he had just completed a season of majestic personal performances, and Alf Ramsey had rewarded him with an England call-up. There were even some observers ready to extend a comparison with fellow north-easterner Bobby Charlton beyond the obvious similarity in hair-do, though such a parallel always reeked of wishful thinking.

Sadly, in the event, Coates was not to find a platform for greatness at White Hart Lane; rather his seven-year tenure was characterised by ceaseless, honest graft, illuminated by only the periodic shaft of brilliance. In the final analysis, without being a flop, he never quite matched his billing.

Certainly, expectations had been elevated to the skies, not only by the gnashing of teeth emanating from Turf Moor, but also because invariably Coates had looked a potential world-beater when Burnley had met Spurs. Anticipation was fuelled further by melodramatic rumours of how Bill Nicholson, alarmed at competition from other clubs, had dashed north to meet his quarry at a secret rendezvous. The fans felt that if their manager, whose judgement they trusted implicitly, was so keen then this fellow Coates must be quite a player.

Accordingly, Ralph's early contributions were seen as a marked anti-climax. Playing as an orthodox winger, he appeared over-anxious and even clumsy at times, his pace and strength not matched by his ball control and sense of direction. However, after a brief rest from the limelight he returned as a midfielder and, apparently revelling in the added responsibility for chasing back, proved far more effective.

On his day, there was no doubt that Coates could turn a match, most often through a sudden burst of acceleration or a flowing body-swerve that left defenders leaden-footed. He could cross well under pressure, too, but was prone to give a disappointing final ball when time and space were his for the taking. Equally frustrating was the Coates shot, a fearful weapon when delivered accurately but frequently lacking in precision, fizzing wide and wild like a bullet from the gun of a blindfolded cowboy.

The best of Ralph Coates was seen at Highbury in the final League match of his first campaign in north London, when he picked up the ball inside his own half, ran past several defenders and gave Arsenal 'keeper Geoff Barnett no chance with a high-quality finish. Less spectacular but even more welcome than a strike against the old enemy was his Wembley winner some ten months later in the League Cup Final against Norwich, a stinging cross-shot after joining the action as a substitute for John Pratt. The fact that Coates had been omitted from the starting line-up was an apt illustration of his fluctuating fortunes at that time, and it came as a timely boost for a modest, honest and personable character.

Now some of the tension seemed to lift from his game and 1973/74 saw a succession of freer, more confident displays – notably an inspired effort, both going forward and defending, against Dinamo in Tbilisi – along with four goals during Spurs' progress to the UEFA Cup Final, which was lost to Feyenoord.

For three seasons thereafter, Coates remained more often in the senior side than out of it, sometimes struggling on bravely while carrying injuries, without wielding the overall influence once expected. The relegation term of 1976/77 saw his last major involvement and he started only one Second Division match before a brief spell in Australia preceded a free transfer to Orient in October 1978.

Two admirable seasons at Brisbane Road completed a career that had flourished most productively away from the merciless microscope under which all those seeking success at White Hart Lane must perform.

**RALPH COATES**
BORN: Hetton-le-Hole, County Durham, 26 April 1946.
HONOURS: UEFA Cup 71/2. League Cup 72/3. 4 England caps (70-71).
OTHER CLUBS: Burnley 64/5-70/1 (216, 26); St George's, Sydney, Australia on loan 78; Orient 78/9-80/1 (76, 12).

| GAMES | 229 (19) |
| GOALS | 24 |

# IAN MOORES

## 1976/77 → 1978/79

Big, blond and bewhiskered, Ian Moores strode out at Old Trafford for his Tottenham League debut in September 1976 like some time-warp Viking bent on an afternoon of plunder. He snatched some booty, too, scoring as Spurs transformed a two-goal deficit into victory, but all too soon the pickings were to grow desperately thin, the rather cumbersome front-man struggling to hold his place, even as his new club dropped a division.

Moores had cost £75,000 from Stoke City following an enthusiastic recommendation from England trainer Les Cocker, who had been hugely taken with his showings as an under-23 international. As well as being an aerial threat in the penalty box, the ex-Potter could drop deep to play his part in building attacks, sometimes supplying a classy touch. Unfortunately he tended to ruin the effect by botching something basic, perhaps a straightforward one-two passing movement, and before long the fans lost patience with him.

The most bountiful day of Moores' disappointing White Hart Lane sojourn was in October 1977, when he contributed a hat-trick towards the 9-0 demolition of Bristol Rovers. However, a year later he was gone, a £55,000 fee taking him to Orient, whom he served competently for four seasons before his career petered out.

**IAN RICHARD MOORES**
BORN: Chesterton, Staffordshire, 5 October 1954.
OTHER CLUBS: Stoke City 73/4-75/6 (50, 14); Orient 78/9-81/2 (117, 26); Bolton Wanderers 82/3 (26, 3); Burnley on loan 82/3 (3, 0).
DIED: Stoke-on-Trent, Staffordshire, 12 January 1998.

GAMES 28 (4)
GOALS 8

---

# CHRIS McGRATH

## 1973/74 → 1975/76

The term 'enigma' is over-used when discussing gifted footballers who fail to do justice to their talent, but in the case of Chris McGrath it is singularly apt. The dark, softly-spoken Ulsterman had exquisite skill that might have graced either Tottenham flank for a decade, and he made a stirring start to his White Hart Lane career; but then, inexorably, he faded into obscurity.

McGrath was introduced to the senior ranks as an 18-year-old challenger for Jimmy Neighbour's wing role in autumn 1973 and soon was impressing with his ability to flow past defenders on either the outside or inside. Though he disappeared into his share of blind alleys and didn't always choose the right moment to pass, it was felt that such flaws were due merely to inexperience. McGrath proved particularly potent in that term's progress to the UEFA Cup Final, scoring five goals, including one that climaxed a thrilling dribble at home to Aberdeen.

But in the next two seasons, the Irish international's confidence appeared to evaporate and his form fizzled. In October 1976, still only 21, he joined Manchester United for £30,000, but fared no better at Old Trafford. A subsequent American sojourn offered scant consolation for what might have been.

**ROLAND CHRISTOPHER McGRATH**
BORN: Belfast, 29 November 1954.
HONOURS: 21 Northern Ireland caps (74-79).
OTHER CLUBS: Millwall on loan 75/6 (15, 3); Manchester United 76/7-80/1 (28, 1); Tulsa Roughnecks, USA, 81-82; South China, Hong Kong.

GAMES 38 (9)
GOALS 10

# JOHN DUNCAN

## 1974/75 → 1978/79

It might surprise many who recall John Duncan as an unorthodox, rather awkward centre-forward whose method of finishing sometimes owed as much to knee or shin as it did to instep or forehead; yet the fact remains that over the past three decades, only a select few Spurs strikers have boasted a better goals-to-games ratio than the angular Scot.

When new Tottenham manager Terry Neill signed Dundee's top marksman for £125,000 in October 1974, he was following a fruitful precedent; ten years earlier one Alan Gilzean had taken the same path from Dens Park to White Hart Lane, with fabulous results. However, the two players could hardly have offered a more vivid contrast. Where Gilzean had been the subtlest of artists, a master of the game's finer points, Duncan daubed his canvas with the broadest of brushes.

There was no doubt, though, that the newcomer delivered the goods. So what if, on occasion, he would shape to shoot one way and the ball would slew in an unexpected direction; the chances were that it would end in the net. Certainly, his control was not of the silky variety, but he could bring the ball down and shoot in one explosive movement, his predatory positional instinct was second to very few, and that distinctive stiff-backed run generated deceptive pace as he peeled away suddenly from defenders who never knew quite what to expect.

In his first term as a Spur, Duncan's goals played a crucial part in staving off relegation, then his quarter-century of League and Cup strikes in 1975/76 provoked unheeded calls for an international call-up. Significantly, he was sidelined by a back injury for most of 1976/77, when Tottenham went down, but was regularly on target as they bounced back at the first attempt.

With Keith Burkinshaw planning a radical team overhaul, John Duncan joined Derby for £150,000 in September 1978, later attracting plaudits as one of British soccer's more imaginative and articulate managers.

**JOHN PEARSON DUNCAN**
**BORN:** Lochee, Angus, 22 April 1949.
**OTHER CLUBS:** Dundee 68/9-74/5 (124, 62); Derby County 78/9-80/1 (36, 12); Scunthorpe United 81/2-82/3 (9, 0).
**MANAGER:** Scunthorpe United (81-83); Hartlepool United (83); Chesterfield (83-87); Ipswich Town (87-90); Chesterfield (93-00).

**GAMES** 118 (2)
**GOALS** 62

# CHRIS JONES

## 1974/75 → 1981/82

One stark statistic offers the most telling comment on the Spurs career of striker Chris Jones: over more than half a decade of being in first-team contention, he never stretched his end-of-season goal tally into double figures. Drawing attention to that sorry fact is not intended to belittle the popular Channel Islander, but is rather an attempt to explain why a player of undoubted talent was discarded when still in his mid-twenties.

In fact, there was no shortage of mitigating circumstances. For most of his senior tenure Jones was playing in a side that fell below the club's traditional quality, and only twice did he exceed 30 League outings in one term. Then there was the little matter of competition, at various times, from Messrs Chivers, Duncan, Armstrong, Moores, Lee, Falco, Archibald, Crooks and Gibson!

Yet Jones was by no means the poor relation when it came to qualifications for the job. Though slightly built, he made up for any shortfall in power with speed, effort and a splendid touch, which he employed intelligently to retain possession until a passing option materialised. Good in the air and a specialist in shrewd off-the-ball runs, he roamed productively to the flanks, from where he would whip in wickedly dipping shots and crosses.

One vivid instance of Jones at his best came against Aston Villa at the Lane in April 1977: back to goal and closely policed near the byline, he controlled a Glenn Hoddle pass on his thigh before swivelling to hit a fierce half-volley into the far top corner of the net. Of course, such a strike needs a dash of luck, and often that was one commodity Chris Jones lacked, his shots seeming to rebound from the woodwork with depressing frequency.

Come September 1982, with Garth Crooks and Steve Archibald rampant, his time ran out and he was freed to join Manchester City. But only later, with Orient, did his performances come close to matching his ability.

| | |
|---|---|
| **CHRISTOPHER HARRY JONES** | |
| BORN: Jersey, 18 April 1956. | GAMES **166 (19)** |
| OTHER CLUBS: Manchester City 82/3 (3, 0); Crystal Palace 82/3 (18, 3); Charlton Athletic 83/4 (23, 2); Orient 84/5-86/7 (107, 19). | GOALS **42** |

# WILLIE YOUNG

## 1975/76 → 1976/77

Raw talent, with the accent firmly on the 'raw' – that was Willie Young in September 1975 when Terry Neill crossed the Scottish border in his quest for a long-term successor to Mike England. Clearly, despite the reservations of some observers, the Spurs boss was deeply impressed by the potential of the towering red-headed stopper.

He parted readily with the £100,000 needed to prise him away from Aberdeen and was undeterred by a lurid reputation which owed something to a fiery playing style, but more to a recent lifetime ban imposed on the under-23 international by his country following an alleged incident in a Copenhagen nightclub.

Soon Young, though cumbersome and with ball skills which might charitably be described as basic, was winning the Spurs fans' approval with his aerial dominance, crunching strength and infectious enthusiasm. However, by mid-1976/77, after some shaky displays, the Scot was dropped by new boss Keith Burkinshaw and, still disinclined to bow his head to authority, he was ready to leave White Hart Lane.

Accordingly, that March he joined Arsenal in an £80,000 deal that saw him reunited with Terry Neill. At Highbury, 'Big Wullie' became something of a cult hero, prospering in a more settled side before assisting Nottingham Forest and sampling lower-division life, then leaving the game.

**WILLIAM DAVID YOUNG**
**BORN:** Edinburgh, 25 November 1951.
**OTHER CLUBS:** Aberdeen 70/1-75/6 (132, 10); Arsenal 76/7-81/2 (170, 11); Nottingham Forest 81/2-82/3 (59, 5); Norwich City 83/4 (6, 0); Brighton on loan 83/4 (4, 0); Darlington 84/5 (4, 0).

| GAMES | 64 |
|---|---|
| GOALS | 4 |

---

# ALFIE CONN

## 1974/75 → 1976/77

Alfie Conn had so much to offer, yet in the end delivered so little. When Bill Nicholson bought him from Rangers for £150,000 in 1974, he was hailed as a magical talent, a beguiling goal-maker and ruthless finisher who, at 22, had limitless potential. In truth, he made a better first impression with the fans, who were rapturous over his skills, than with the boss, who made no secret of his loathing for the Scot's hippy-length locks.

Fitness worries delayed Conn's full debut until January at Newcastle, where he responded with an impudent hat-trick, his blend of pace and control making the imagination reel. But his inconsistency and attitude could be infuriating: he demurred when new manager Terry Neill asked him to switch from roving entertainer to the left of midfield, and when he was applied to for more effort, it was not always forthcoming. Conn's two sides were illustrated against Leeds United in April 1975. With victory imperative to stave off relegation, he dribbled past three men to score brilliantly, then re-motivated the flagging visitors by sitting on the ball!

His form that term earned him two Scotland caps, but then injuries restricted his appearances during the next two seasons, before he joined Celtic for £60,000 in 1977. What a shame that, in recollecting the deeds of Alfie Conn, the negative so firmly outweighs the positive.

**ALFRED JAMES CONN**
**BORN:** Edinburgh 5 April 1952.
**HONOURS:** 2 Scotland caps (75).
**OTHER CLUBS:** Glasgow Rangers 69/70-73/4 (92, 23); Celtic 76/7-78/9 (39, 8); Pittsburgh Spirit, San Jose Earthquakes, both USA; Heart of Midlothian 80/1 (17, 3); Blackpool 80/1 (3, 0); Motherwell 81/2-82/3 (27, 3).

| GAMES | 38 (5) |
|---|---|
| GOALS | 7 |

# JOHN GORMAN

### 1976/77 → 1978/79

Even as the storm clouds of impending relegation gathered over White Hart Lane in the early winter of 1976, manager Keith Burkinshaw demonstrated by the purchase of John Gorman that Tottenham were seeking to play, rather than clog, their way out of trouble. That the battle was destined to be lost reflected no discredit on the swarthily dark left-back who, but for persistent knee problems, must surely have become a classy medium-term replacement for the recently retired Cyril Knowles.

Gorman had cost £60,000 from Carlisle, with whom he had enjoyed one term in the top flight before returning to Division Two. He was neither quick, nor graceful – his jerky, almost stuttering running action was unmistakable – but he was the possessor of an astute soccer brain. No hell-for-leather tackler, he preferred to jockey opponents away from the danger area, though it was his assured control and long, accurate passes down the left flank that spoke most eloquently of his quality.

Unfortunately, injury limited the Scot to 16 games in his first season at the Lane, wiped out the whole of his second and truncated his third, before he sought better luck in the Florida sunshine. By the 1990s, Gorman had recrossed the Atlantic to help his friend Glenn Hoddle to run first Swindon Town, and then England.

# JIMMY HOLMES

### 1976/77 → 1978/79

Jimmy Holmes had everything it took to become a long-term fixture on the left flank of Tottenham's defence; everything, that is, except luck. The amiable Dubliner was an emergency £120,000 acquisition from Coventry City on transfer deadline day in 1977, following a serious injury to John Gorman. Despite winning their two most recent matches, Keith Burkinshaw's men were in dire peril near the foot of the table and time was running out.

The Republic of Ireland international was quick to display his footballing pedigree. In attack he was an intelligent overlapper whose left-foot delivery to his forwards was outstanding, while his work at the back was brisk and decisive, based on sound positioning and a firm tackle.

However, despite Holmes' goal in a home victory over Leicester City in the season's last game, Spurs went down. An exemplary professional who applied himself unstintingly as they bounced straight back, he enjoyed an enterprising return to the top flight, his all-round skill proving effective during two spells in midfield. But then fate dealt a cruel blow: Holmes broke his leg on international duty in Bulgaria, and never played for Spurs again. Brief service with other clubs preceded a coaching post at Northampton Town.

# DON McALLISTER

## 1974/75 → 1980/81

Pace, strength and versatility were the hallmarks of Don McAllister, whose football would never have won commendations for culture, but who deserves an honourable mention in dispatches for doughty work during a period of Tottenham travail. Terry Neill signed the blond Lancastrian from Bolton Wanderers in February 1975, and for his £80,000 he got an honours graduate from the Burnden Park academy of tough tackling, made famous in the 1950s by Messrs Roy Hartle, Tommy Banks and assorted hard nuts.

Initially McAllister slotted in as a midfield ball-winner, then went on to give half a decade of solid service in the back four, performing at various times in every outfield defensive position. Some of his finest displays came in a central role alongside Steve Perryman during a 1977/78 campaign spent in the Second Division, though he could hold his own in the top flight, too, as he proved with two consistent seasons as the 1970s drew to a close.

He was used also as an occasional, extremely single-minded one-on-one marker, oozing implacable aggression and constituting an obstacle not to be taken lightly by any opposing play-maker.

If McAllister could have used the ball more creatively himself, he might have retained his place into the 1980s and taken his part in the exciting era then dawning at White Hart Lane. As it was, he was overtaken by more accomplished all-round footballers and his status slipped to that of reliable reserve, causing him to miss the two epic 1981 FA Cup Final encounters with Manchester City.

Thus it became clear that if McAllister wanted first-team football – and at 28 he was far from washed-up – his future lay elsewhere. Accordingly that August he crossed London to join Charlton Athletic for £40,000, half his purchase price, leaving Tottenham to feel they had got their money's worth from a man who had clocked up a double-century of senior outings.

| | | GAMES | 197 (5) |
|---|---|---|---|
| **DONALD McALLISTER** | | | |
| **BORN:** | Radcliffe, Lancashire, 26 May 1953. | GOALS | 10 |
| **OTHER CLUBS:** | Bolton Wanderers 69/70-74/5 (156, 2); Washington Diplomats, USA, 77; Charlton Athletic 81/2-82/3 (55, 6); Tampa Bay Rowdies, USA, 84; Rochdale 84/5 (3, 0). | | |

# PETER TAYLOR

## 1976/77 → 1980/81

One crucial flaw in Peter Taylor's footballing make-up prevented him from maturing into a Tottenham star whose lustre might have lit up White Hart Lane well into the 1980s. All the multi-talented, goal-scoring winger lacked during lengthy periods of his north London sojourn was confidence, a commodity of huge importance to all players but which to Taylor was the very lifeblood of his game.

When he arrived as a £200,000 recruit from Crystal Palace in September 1976, he was flying high. At Selhurst Park that flamboyant psychologist Malcolm Allison had kept Peter bubbling by informing him constantly what a marvellous player he was, thus extracting the last ounce of performance. Indeed, so scintillating had the Taylor form been that recently he had made light of his Third Division base to win four England caps.

But at Tottenham, he was under Keith Burkinshaw, a sound manager but one whose comparatively dour style could hardly have been in greater contrast to Allison's. Now Taylor faced the daunting task of replacing the popular Jimmy Neighbour without his regular fixes of confidence, and in a team doomed to relegation in his initial term, he struggled at times. Not that he could be dubbed a flop, totalling 30 League goals in his first three campaigns – a prolific return for a flankman and testimony to a venomous shot in either foot – and displaying, intermittently, a thrilling ability to beat a defender and deliver an accurate cross.

But so much was expected, and by the turn of the decade his consistency had dipped alarmingly. Thus in November 1980, out of the Spurs side and his international prospects in ruins at the tender age of 27, Taylor joined Orient for £150,000. After playing on in the lower divisions, then sampling the non-League scene, he left the game before returning as Steve Perryman's number-two at Watford, bursting with enthusiasm.

There followed an excursion into League management with his first club, Southend United, after which he became part of Glenn Hoddle's England regime. Later he was to hand David Beckham the captaincy during a brief caretaker spell in charge of his country before impressing in several other jobs.

| | |
|---|---|
| **PETER JOHN TAYLOR** | |
| **BORN:** | Rochford, Essex, 3 January 1953. |
| **HONOURS:** | 4 England caps (76). |
| **OTHER CLUBS:** | Southend United 70/1-73/4 (75, 12); Crystal Palace 73/4-76/7 (122, 33); Orient 80/1-82/3 (56, 11); Oldham Athletic on loan 82/3 (4, 0); Maidstone United (non-League); Exeter City 83/4 (8, 0). |
| **MANAGER:** | Southend United (93-95); Gillingham (99-00); Leicester City (00-01); England (caretaker 00); Brighton (01-02); Hull City (02-06); Crystal Palace (06-07). |

| GAMES | 128 (12) |
|---|---|
| GOALS | 33 |

# NEIL McNAB

## 1973/74 → 1978/79

Once upon a time – it seems worlds away now, but actually happened in the mid-1970s – Neil McNab was the recipient of what many considered to be the ultimate seal of soccer approval. He was pronounced, by a certain Bill Shankly, to be as fine a midfield prospect as there was in the land.

Yet despite joining Spurs when he was only 16 and too young to turn professional, the sandy-haired Scot was destined to spend the bulk of his career outside the top flight. Certainly such an outcome would have been unthinkable to Morton boss Hal Stewart, who waxed so lyrical about his prodigy that in February 1974 Bill Nicholson took a look for himself, then gambled £75,000 to take the boy south.

Though short and thin, Neil was deceptively powerful, a fiery character who dug hard in the tackle and possessed immense stamina; but the real appeal of the McNab game was his lovely skill. In training he could stroll the length of the pitch and back, casually bouncing the ball from foot to foot without letting it touch the ground; more practically, in matches he could worm his way past opponents and pass superbly.

He was not rushed, however, being nursed in the reserves with the occasional taste of the big time, until Terry Neill gave him a six-week senior run at the start of 1975/76. Judged to be not ready still, he continued to play most of his football in the Combination until 1977/78 when, with Spurs in Division Two, Keith Burkinshaw used him in every match.

Then came the turning point of McNab's career. Back in the top flight, Tottenham made their bold Argentinian investment and he was dropped. That November he joined Bolton for £250,000, going on to serve half a dozen more clubs, his performances improving as he matured.

Some say he was a brilliant youngster who failed to progress at the expected rate; others maintain that letting him go at 21 was a criminal waste. That he never scaled the game's giddiest peaks tends to bear out the Burkinshaw judgement, but had he remained at White Hart Lane, who knows?

**NEIL McNAB**
**BORN:** Greenock, Scotland, 4 June 1957.
**OTHER CLUBS:** Morton 72/3-73/4 (14, 0); Bolton Wanderers 78/9-79/80 (35, 4); Brighton 79/80-82/3 (103, 4); Leeds United on loan 82/3 (5, 0); Manchester City 83/4-89/90 (221, 16); Huddersfield Town on loan 91/2 (11, 0); Tranmere Rovers 89/90-92/3 (105, 6); Darlington 93/4 (4, 0).

**GAMES** 70 (10)
**GOALS** 3

## MARK KENDALL

### 1978/79 → 1980/81

Mark Kendall was the dark horse in the three-man race to replace Pat Jennings and become Tottenham's goalkeeper of the 1980s. But though he had youth on his side – the Welshman was junior by some seven years to both Barry Daines and Milija Aleksic – he couldn't make it count, and it can have been of precious little consolation that his rivals, too, were unable to step into the void filled eventually by Ray Clemence.

By far Kendall's most successful season was 1978/79, in which he missed only one League game between November and April and won an under-21 cap into the bargain. At that time there were hopes that the personable six-footer, who was not helped by a constant struggle to control his weight, might add much-needed consistency to all-round competence.

But errors, particularly of the positional variety, continued to mar otherwise excellent displays, and in September 1980 Kendall joined Newport for £45,000. After six years at Somerton Park, he played some of his finest football for Wolves before bowing out of the League at Swansea City.

**MARK KENDALL**
**BORN:** Blackwood, South Wales, 20 September 1958.
**OTHER CLUBS:** Chesterfield on loan 79/80 (9, 0); Newport County 80/1-86/7 (272, 0); Wolverhampton Wanderers 86/7-89/90 (147, 0); Swansea City 90/91-91/2 (12, 0); Burnley on loan 91/2 (2, 0).
**DIED:** 1 May 2008

| GAMES | 36 |
|---|---|
| GOALS | 0 |

## MICKY STEAD

### 1975/76 → 1977/78

Though all-round footballers inferior to Micky Stead have enjoyed lengthy First Division stints, it must be conceded that the sturdy full-back was not quite of top-flight calibre. Highly competitive in the tackle and a reliable passer, the blond Londoner was not the quickest of movers and in the three seasons in which he lurked on the fringe of the senior side, a regular berth seemed likely to remain beyond his compass.

When 19-year-old Stead made his first-team bow at Stoke in February 1976, he played well enough to retain his place for three matches, until injured first-choices Terry Naylor and Don McAllister regained fitness. Then he enjoyed a six-match run at the end of the following season as Jimmy Holmes' deputy.

But his future at White Hart Lane was clearly limited and, after a loan spell at Swansea, he joined Southend for £45,000 in September 1978. At Roots Hall, Stead found his true level, serving United doughtily before ending his playing days at Doncaster Rovers, where he became a coach.

**MICHAEL JOHN STEAD**
**BORN:** West Ham, London, 28 February 1957.
**OTHER CLUBS:** Swansea City on loan 76/7 (5, 1); Southend United 78/9-85/6 (297, 5); Doncaster Rovers 85/6-87/8 (85, 0).

| GAMES | 14 (1) |
|---|---|
| GOALS | 0 |

## COLIN LEE

### 1977/78 → 1979/80

As dream starts go, Colin Lee's at Tottenham was decidedly on the extravagant side. Two days after joining Spurs in a £60,000 move from Torquay in October 1977, the tall Devonian scored four times in the 9-0 annihilation of Bristol Rovers in front of the *Match Of The Day* cameras at White Hart Lane. It is almost superfluous to note that he never attained such heights again.

With an injury crisis at its height, the young marksman had arrived at a time of rare opportunity: instead of taking his place in a queue, as a raw newcomer from the bottom flight might expect, Lee won a regular place in the Second Division promotion fray. However, though wholehearted, he proved limited, an effective leaper for high balls beyond the far post but lacking the required sharpness on the ground.

Still, he helped to achieve the immediate objective, and made 26 starts, including a few as a makeshift defender, in Spurs' first term back among the elite. Then, in January 1980, a £200,000 fee took Lee to Chelsea, with whom he was converted eventually into a capable full-back.

**COLIN LEE**
**BORN:** Torquay, Devon, 12 June 1956.
**OTHER CLUBS:** Bristol City no games; Hereford United on loan 74/5 (9, 0); Torquay United 76/7-77/8 (35, 14); Chelsea 79/80-86/7 (185, 36); Brentford 87/8-88/9 (24, 1).
**MANAGER:** Watford (90); Wolverhampton Wanderers (98-00); Torquay United (caretaker 01); Walsall (02-04); Millwall (05); Torquay United (07).

| GAMES | 65 (6) |
|---|---|
| GOALS | 21 |

# BARRY DAINES

1971/72 → 1980/81

It is Barry Daines' misfortune to be remembered principally as the man in whom Keith Burkinshaw had so much confidence that he sold Pat Jennings to Arsenal in August 1977. It was a decision which enraged many Spurs fans, who were mystified on two counts: if Daines was that good, why had he not been hunted by other clubs since his debut in 1971, and why had he been content to remain an understudy for more than half a decade?

In fact, Daines was a competent all-rounder – better, perhaps, at stopping shots than claiming crosses – and the pick of the 'keepers tested by Tottenham during the interregnum between the Irishman and Ray Clemence. But despite the bold backing of his manager, based on some impressive displays when Jennings was injured during the relegation season of 1976/77, and an admirable, ever-present contribution to the subsequent promotion campaign, Daines appeared to lack self-belief.

This became evident on Spurs' return to the top flight, and culminated in Burkinshaw's preference of Milija Aleksic for the 1981 FA Cup Final.

Concluding understandably that the future could hold little for him at White Hart Lane, Daines opted to try his luck in Hong Kong, later serving Mansfield. However, despite the anti-climax, it would be wrong to under-value his loyal, ten-term contribution to the Tottenham cause. True, he was never in the Jennings class, but then, who was?

## GERRY ARMSTRONG

1976/77 → 1980/81

When Gerry Armstrong crossed the Irish Sea to join Tottenham in 1975, he was raw, hungry and ready for action – and without being disrespectful to one of the game's best-loved and most genuine characters, it might be said that the big striker had barely altered when he left for Watford five years later. Of course, there had been certain refinements to his method, but essentially Armstrong would always remain a prodigiously strong, unendingly selfless workaholic, not overburdened with ball skills but a colossus in the air and with heart enough for ten men.

Not that he was devoid of technique: his colleagues knew that they could knock the ball towards him and, having fought for it and won it, he could retain possession until reinforcements arrived. But as the Argentinian influence placed extra emphasis on touch play, Armstrong was not in his element at the Lane, and he didn't help his standing with the fans by battling on uncomplainingly when he was injured, thus unable to do himself full justice.

As stars were bought, his departure became inevitable, but a place in folklore was awaiting him. When the Ulsterman's spirited exploits in the 1982 World Cup, including the winning goal against Spain, earned him an award as British Player of the Tournament, a more popular accolade was difficult to imagine.

**GERARD JOSEPH ARMSTRONG**
BORN: Belfast, 23 May 1954.
HONOURS: 63 Northern Ireland caps (77-86).
OTHER CLUBS: Bangor, Northern Ireland; Watford 80/1-82/3 (76, 12); Real Mallorca, Spain, 83/4–84/5; West Bromwich Albion 85/6 (8, 0); Chesterfield on loan 85/6 (12, 1); Brighton 86/7-87/8 (42, 5); Millwall on loan 87/8 (7, 0).

| | |
|---|---|
| GAMES | 74 (24) |
| GOALS | 16 |

**BARRY RAYMOND DAINES**
BORN: Witham, Essex, 30 September 1951.
OTHER CLUBS: Bulova, Hong Kong, 81-83; Mansfield Town 83/4 (21, 0).

| | |
|---|---|
| GAMES | 173 |
| GOALS | 0 |

# MILIJA ALEKSIC

## 1978/79 → 1981/82

The ups and downs of football life were illustrated poignantly by the three-and-a-half-year White Hart Lane sojourn of goalkeeper Milija Aleksic. His ride on the Tottenham rollercoaster began with a £100,000 transfer from Luton Town in December 1978, joining Barry Daines and Mark Kendall as contenders for the job between Spurs' posts. His fortunes dipped as he was injured after two matches, declining even more drastically in January 1980 when he broke his jaw in a collision with Manchester United's Joe Jordan in an FA Cup replay at Old Trafford.

Poor Aleksic was due an upturn, but it did not come until the spring of 1981 when a knock to Barry Daines gave the Midlands-born son of a Yugoslavian father the opportunity to shine. He seized it avidly, playing so well that he retained his place for both FA Cup Final clashes with Manchester City. Now, his stock never higher, he had concrete hopes of becoming Tottenham's number-one, but suddenly Ray Clemence arrived and his prospects at the club took a final plunge.

In truth, Aleksic was no more than a competent all-round 'keeper, brave and with the sharp reflexes of a natural shot-stopper, but seemingly nervous when dealing with crosses. After returning to Luton on loan, he took up coaching in South Africa.

**MILIJA ANTONY ALEKSIC**
BORN: Newcastle-under-Lyme, Staffordshire, 14 April 1951.
HONOURS: FA Cup 80/1.
OTHER CLUBS: Plymouth Argyle 73/4-75/6 (32, 0); Luton Town 76/7-78/9 (77, 0); Luton Town on loan 81/2 (4, 0).

GAMES 32
GOALS 0

# TERRY YORATH

## 1979/80 → 1980/81

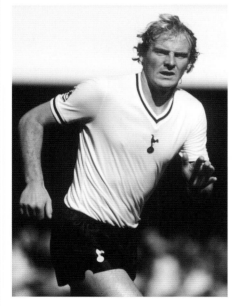

Mention Terry Yorath and most football fans will think of Leeds, where he spent nine seasons as an often under-appreciated member of one of post-war soccer's finest squads, or of Wales, whom he managed for five years. Yet somewhere between those peaks was an interlude at Tottenham which, though relatively uneventful, was completed with characteristic, full-blooded application.

Keith Burkinshaw signed Yorath from Coventry City for £275,000 in August 1979, seeing in him the battle-hardened warrior he desired to play alongside his centre-half. In this role, and in the more familiar midfield holding berth to which he was to revert, the rugged, blond Welsh international brought the abrasive tackle and nagging persistence which had served him so well at Elland Road.

Though his pace was sluggish, Yorath's distribution was more accomplished than many pundits would allow, and he possessed a shrewd grasp of tactics that he was not slow to share with colleagues on the pitch. However, after suffering injuries early in 1980/81, he was unable to reclaim a regular place in the face of stiff competition, and that summer he moved to Vancouver Whitecaps, later returning to these shores before launching a successful career in coaching and management.

**TERENCE CHARLES YORATH**
BORN: Cardiff, 27 March 1950.
HONOURS: 59 Wales caps (69-81).
OTHER CLUBS: Leeds United 67/8-76/7 (143, 10); Coventry City 76/7-78/9 (99, 3); Vancouver Whitecaps, Canada, 81-82; Bradford City 82/3-84/5 (27, 0); Swansea City 86/7 (1, 0).
MANAGER: Swansea City (86-89); Bradford City (89-90); Swansea City (90-91); Wales (88-93); Cardiff City (94-95); Sheffield Wednesday (01-02).

GAMES 58 (4)
GOALS 1

# RICKY VILLA

## 1978/79 → 1982/83

The two sides of Ricky Villa were laid bare in the 1981 FA Cup Final. In the first, drawn encounter with Manchester City he was sluggish, brooding, almost sulkily ineffective. In the replay he came alive, was suddenly bright and inventive, contributing two goals, including a winner that will stand forever as one of the finest Wembley has witnessed.

Though he had made two substitute appearances as Argentina had lifted the World Cup that summer, Villa was little known to British fans when, valued at £375,000, he accompanied his countryman Osvaldo Ardiles to White Hart Lane in July 1978. After outdoing his star stable-mate in pre-season training, the so-called 'Dark Horse of the Pampas' was quickly out of the starting stalls with a goal on his Spurs debut at Nottingham Forest, but soon found the going tougher than expected. Taking longer than Ardiles to settle in a strange land and hampered by injuries in his first English autumn, his form was patchy.

However, when Villa was on song, he was a stylish swashbuckler. Tall and bulky, his bullish strength made him hard to dispossess and his apparent ponderousness belied skills fit to grace any stage. His scorn for the orthodox took him swerving away from two

defenders to plant a booming 30-yarder into the Wolves net in the 1981 FA Cup semi-final, and it surfaced even more gloriously in the final replay.

On receiving the ball in the inside-left slot, he was confronted by a wall of opponents and most men would have passed. But Ricky surged on, went past Caton, Ranson and Caton again before gulling 'keeper Corrigan to give Spurs the trophy.

Yet this headiest of moments proved no cure for inconsistency and the Argentine's confidence, never noticeably resilient, took a further fearful buffeting when he was abused by opposing crowds over the Falklands conflict. Understandably, he left England in June 1983, taking his unpredictable talents to the USA. Later he played in Colombia before returning to his homeland, where eventually he went into politics. At the Lane, meanwhile, memories of Ricky Villa grow ever warmer in the rosy glow of retrospect.

| | |
|---|---|
| **JULIO RICARDO VILLA** | |
| BORN: | Buenos Aires, Argentina, 18 August 1952 |
| HONOURS: | FA Cup 80/1. 25 Argentina caps. |
| OTHER CLUBS: | Quilmes 70-74; Tucuman 74-76; Racing Club 76-78, all Argentina; Fort Lauderdale Strikers, USA, 83; Deportivo Cali, Colombia 84-85; Deportivo Defensa, Argentina. |

| | |
|---|---|
| GAMES | 169 (11) |
| GOALS | 25 |

# PAUL MILLER

· · · · · · · · · · · · · · · · · · · · · · · · · ·

1978/79 → 1986/87

For those purists who demand culture from their Spurs, Paul Miller was close to anathema. But as even the most savage critic of the rough-and-ready central defender would have to admit, he was a born survivor. For a large proportion of the time between his senior debut in spring 1979 and his ultimate unseating by Richard Gough in August 1986, Miller seemed on the verge of being replaced. John Lacy, Paul Price, Gary Stevens, they all might have been expected to sabotage the loquacious Londoner's first-team ambitions, but each time he rose to meet the challenge, pocketing three major cup medals in the process.

Though Miller's game boasted barely a shred of refinement, in certain circumstances he was mightily effective, his ruthless tackling and aerial power equipping him as an opponent with whom no one relished a confrontation, particularly when

he was operating in tandem with the formidable Graham Roberts.

But – and it was a sizeable but – he could be exposed mercilessly by clever, elusive forwards who dropped off him or who ran at him with the ball, and he could be drawn out of position too easily for comfort. As a result, Miller was subjected to periods as a crowd scapegoat that would have scuppered less buoyant characters, but he would emerge from them with his confidence and drive undiminished, cheerfully ready for whatever the football fates had in store for him.

To be fair, Miller's footwork improved with experience, and he became relatively adept at picking out his attackers with long, raking passes. He could play at full-back, too, and loved to get forward, contributing one of Tottenham's most valuable goals of the decade, a powerful header from a Mike Hazard corner in the drawn first leg of the 1984 UEFA Cup Final against Anderlecht in Belgium.

Miller – dubbed 'Max' by team-mates after the music-hall comedian with whom he shared both a surname and an aptitude for patter – left White Hart Lane for Charlton Athletic in February 1987, later seeing out his career in the lower divisions.

---

**PAUL RICHARD MILLER**

BORN: Stepney, London, 11 October 1959.
HONOURS: UEFA Cup 83/4. FA Cup 80/1, 81/2.
OTHER CLUBS: Charlton Athletic 86/7-88/9 (42, 2); Watford 88/9 (20, 0); Bournemouth 89/90-90/1 (47, 1); Brentford on loan 89/90 (3, 0); Swansea City 90/1 (12, 0).

GAMES 283 (4)
GOALS 10

# CHRIS HUGHTON

## 1979/80 → 1989/90

Chris Hughton was a thoroughly modern full-back, as far removed from the outmoded tradition of hulking clogger as it is possible to imagine, his game based on smoothness and movement without the hint of a jagged edge. Small and neat, light and searingly quick – at his peak, wingers tended to struggle in his wake, rather than vice versa – he was a potent overlapper and careful crosser, a legacy of his teenage days as a flankman.

When Spurs had possession, Hughton was ever ready to receive the ball, then keep the game flowing with thoughtful distribution, and when scoring opportunities presented themselves he could oblige skilfully. At the back he was equally calm and resourceful, more disposed to jockeying opponents out of position than robbing them with a thundering tackle.

Versatility was another Hughton asset, at least to the extent of being able to play on either defensive flank, though the right-footer's preference for playing on the left, an increasingly common vogue, did not win universal approval. Certainly he could be seen frequently switching the ball to his stronger side, but such was his dexterity that momentum was sacrificed only rarely.

Chris, who qualified to play for Eire as his mother hailed from Limerick, was working as a lift engineer when Spurs spotted him in junior football. After he turned professional in the summer of 1979, his impact was instant, and he missed only three League games during the season that followed.

Thereafter he shared in all Spurs' cup triumphs of the early 1980s, though as the decade grew old his form became fitful and he grew less assured of his place. Accordingly Hughton, whose brother Henry played for three League clubs, was given a free transfer in 1990, joining West Ham before lending his experience to Brentford in the new First Division.

Throughout an exemplary playing career, he remained a credit to the game and was welcomed back to Tottenham as a coach under Ossie Ardiles in 1993. Four years later he took charge of the first team in the one-match interregnum between Gerry Francis and Christian Gross, then stayed on to become the faithful number-two to a succession of managers through to Martin Jol, before joining Kevin Keegan's staff at Newcastle early in 2008.

**CHRISTOPHER WILLIAM GERARD HUGHTON**

| | |
|---|---|
| BORN: | West Ham, London, 11 December 1958. |
| HONOURS: | UEFA Cup 83/4. FA Cup 80/1, 81/2. 53 Republic of Ireland caps (79-91). |
| OTHER CLUBS: | West Ham United 90/1-91/2 (33, 0); Brentford 91/2-92/3 (32, 0). |
| MANAGER: | Tottenham Hotspur (caretaker, 97). |

| | |
|---|---|
| GAMES | 391 (9) |
| GOALS | 19 |

# MARK FALCO

## 1978/79 → 1986/87

It's an unpalatable fact but surely one for which his own teenage years as a denizen of the Shelf must have prepared Mark Falco: simply that being born in north London and graduating through Tottenham's junior ranks is anything but a passport to acceptance from the White Hart Lane faithful.

Local boys, it seems, are expected to do that little bit more to satisfy fans who are sometimes willing to make generous allowances for star imports. Thus despite a commendable goals-to-games ratio – the product of unceasing honest endeavour and vast strength coupled with considerably more natural ability than he was credited with – the former England youth international never received the terrace acclaim that was his due.

Part of the problem was that Falco's style was not easy on the eye. Tall and strappingly built, he could appear cumbersome, and in all fairness, compared to quicksilver contemporaries Archibald and Crooks, so he was. But when he ran on to a through-ball in his favoured inside-left slot, it took a good man to stop the Falco surge, which was apt to climax in a venomous low shot. Fearless and a constant menace in the air, he was effective at retaining possession, too, frequently taking the knocks and contributing the legwork that paved his colleagues' way to goal.

After scoring on his senior debut in May 1979, Falco lingered on the fringe of Spurs' squad until August 1981, when two Charity Shield goals against Aston Villa signalled the start of a five-week purple patch. But injury intervened and it was not until 1983/84 that he won a regular place.

Then came three prolific terms in which his tally never dipped below 20, yet always there was the feeling that just around the corner was an expensive buy and that he would have to make way. So it proved when Nico Claesen arrived and David Pleat dispatched the faithful Falco to Watford for a bargain £300,000 in October 1986. Maybe he fell short of the highest class, but Mark was an underrated asset to Tottenham and to each of the string of clubs he went on to serve.

**MARK PETER FALCO**
**BORN:** Hackney, London, 22 October 1960.
**HONOURS:** UEFA Cup 83/4.
**OTHER CLUBS:** Chelsea on loan 82/3 (3, 0); Watford 86/7 (33, 14); Glasgow Rangers 87/8 (14, 5); Queen's Park Rangers 87/8–90/1 (87, 27); Millwall 91/2 (21, 4).

GAMES 218 (20)
GOALS 92

# JOHN LACY

## 1978/79 → 1982/83

Lean, lanky Liverpudlian John Lacy might be described as Tottenham's silent signing. He joined in the summer of 1978, at the height of the commotion surrounding the arrival of Ardiles and Villa from Argentina, and thus tended to be overlooked. In fact, the 6ft 3in stopper was making his own piece of history as the first man whose fee, in the region of £200,000, was fixed by a Football League tribunal after Spurs and his former club, Fulham, failed to agree terms.

Lacy had profited much at Craven Cottage from the tutelage of Alan Mullery and Bobby Moore, alongside whom he had played in the 1975 FA Cup Final, yet there was no disguising the truth that his work with the ball at his feet was no match for his commendable aerial prowess. In those early days at White Hart Lane his control and passing were poor and an impatient crowd let him know it in time-honoured heartless fashion.

But where lesser men might have made their excuses and left, Lacy – an economics graduate who had not taken up football seriously until his university days – worked hard on his skills and, imperceptibly at first, attitudes began to change. Hard-boiled terrace critics who had protested that 'this mug can't play' ended up swallowing their words, even professing affection towards a player who had been willing to learn.

Of course, the improvement was relative, and after a niggling thigh injury had ruled him out of contention for the 1981 FA Cup Final, in which the vigorous young central defensive partnership of Graham Roberts and Paul Miller had performed effectively, the long-term prospects of a man approaching 30 were not bright.

However, Lacy remained at the Lane until August 1983, making 27 senior starts in his final season before moving to Crystal Palace for a year, then linking up with former Fulham team-mate John Mitchell at non-League St Albans and embarking on a career outside the game.

**JOHN LACY**
**BORN:** Liverpool, 14 August 1951.
**OTHER CLUBS:** Fulham 72/3-77/8 (168, 7); Crystal Palace 83/4 (27, 0).

GAMES **127 (6)**
GOALS **3**

# STEVE PERRYMAN

· · · · · · · · · · · · · · · · · · · · · · · · · · ·

## 1969/70 → 1985/86

Steve Perryman was that rarest of gems, a sure thing in an uncertain world. He remained the one constant factor as Spurs lifted a clutch of cups in the early 1970s, then slumped to relegation before rising to win further trophies and, at last, make a sustained title challenge. Throughout that dramatic decade-and-a-half, Steve shone as a footballer of superior all-round ability and, no less important, a character whose strength and honesty, affability and intelligence, were of incalculable value to the Tottenham cause.

That he won more medals and made more senior appearances – in excess of a thousand, including friendlies – than any other Spur, and counts an MBE (1986) and a Footballer of the Year award (1982) among his honours, is hardly surprising. That he won just one England cap, and that as a substitute, is a mystery to which only Don Revie and Ron Greenwood could ever have supplied a solution; Alf Ramsey, as the Perryman under-23 record shows, was grooming Steve for an international future when he lost his own job as national boss in 1974.

Perryman's marathon top-level tenure began in September 1969 when the baby-faced 17-year-old was pitchforked into League action after a handful of reserve games. Nothing too unusual about that, except that most such youngsters return to the 'stiffs' to continue the learning process. Not so the tough, enthusiastic midfielder, who kept his place among the stars, becoming indispensable through a biting tackle, persistence and a maturity beyond his years, a combination of which rendered irrelevant a certain deficiency in pace.

Perryman fitted perfectly into the Spurs style, winning the ball, moving it on and making himself available for an instant return pass. Some felt his elevation had come too early, and that by slaving so assiduously he was not doing justice to his impressive ball skills. Yet having broken through on the back of work rate, he was in no mind to slacken off and, certainly, Bill Nicholson wasn't complaining.

However, in 1971/72 Perryman endured a hiatus in form which, combined with a lack of goals that was to dog him throughout his career, gave grounds for concern. The challenge was met with typical fortitude as he battled on, underlining his recovery that spring with two beautifully volleyed edge-of-the-box strikes at home to AC Milan in the UEFA Cup semi-final. Nevertheless, with Spurs struggling early in 1974/75, the unthinkable almost occurred when he came close to joining Coventry City, but the move fell through after the shock resignation of Bill Nicholson.

Changes were afoot for Perryman, though. First, in March 1975, the departure of Martin Peters signalled his promotion to captain, a role in which he was to revel for ten years; then, towards the climax of the relegation dogfight in March 1977, he switched to a central defensive berth that might have been made for him.

Now the game opened up for Perryman, the more considered approach demanded at the back enabling his talents to blossom, and though he was not as aerially dominant as bigger men, his impeccable reading of situations could be trusted to neutralise the quickest and wiliest of opponents.

Though he revitalised the rearguard, it was too late to avoid the drop, and at season's end Liverpool tried to lure him north. Making a decision that encapsulated his personality, Perryman opted to stay, reasoning that as he had led his men down, it was his duty to lead them back, and so he did, going on to reap rich reward in the 1980s. By then he had become an overlapping right-back, tackling as implacably as ever but relishing also the long-delayed taste of adventure as he galloped forward to keep his strikers supplied with crosses.

Perryman closed a Spurs playing career of unparalleled achievement in March 1986, serving Oxford briefly before entering management. With both Brentford and Watford he proved eminently well-equipped as a boss, with his vast knowledge, sane values and commendable ethics. Then, in 1993, came a seemingly idyllic return to the Lane as number-two to Ossie Ardiles. Sadly, as discussed elsewhere in his book, it didn't work out, but that brief, unsuccessful homecoming could do nothing to tarnish the towering long-term attainments of Steve Perryman in the shirt of Tottenham Hotspur.

**STEPHEN JOHN PERRYMAN**

**BORN:** Ealing, London, 21 December 1951.
**HONOURS:** UEFA Cup 71/2, 83/4. FA Cup 80/1, 81/2. League Cup 70/1, 72/3. 1 England cap (82). FWA Footballer of the Year 82.
**OTHER CLUBS:** Oxford United 85/6-86/7 (17, 0); Brentford 86/7-89/90 (53, 0).
**MANAGER:** Brentford (87-90); Watford (90-93); Tottenham Hotspur (caretaker 94); IK Start, Norway, (94-95); Shimuzu S-Pulse, Japan, (96-00); Kashiwa Reysol, Japan, (01-02).

| GAMES | 852 (4) |
|-------|---------|
| GOALS | 39 |

# OSVALDO ARDILES

## 1978/79 → 1987/88

It might have been an old Argentinian proverb, more likely it was the product of his own shrewd soccer brain. Either way, Osvaldo Ardiles had a saying: 'Some people play with a round ball, others use a square one'. What he meant was that while certain players make life easy for themselves and their team-mates, creating time and space by delivering intelligent passes, unfortunately there are those who make a simple game deucedly difficult by not using their heads. Ossie, of course, was the living, breathing embodiment of the former category, a footballing philosopher whose intellect and instinct evoked memories of Danny Blanchflower, no less, bringing a new dimension to Spurs while making a vast impression on the English game as a whole.

When Keith Burkinshaw bought Ardiles from Huracan of Buenos Aires in July 1978, it was hailed as both a coup and a gamble. Tottenham fans were delighted at the acquisition of a performer who only weeks earlier had sprung to international celebrity as a leading light in his country's World Cup triumph. At £325,000, a comparatively modest fee facilitated by Argentina's financial recession, many felt that Tottenham had a rare bargain, though there was no shortage of cautionary voices questioning how Ardiles and his compatriot Ricky Villa would settle in north London.

Certainly as far as the diminutive schemer was concerned, doubt on that score was short-lived. Charming and articulate – he was trained as a lawyer – Ardiles swiftly secured a social niche, while showing all the dedication and mental strength his new life demanded. On the pitch, he worked hard to become accustomed to the extra pace of the First Division and was quick to learn certain unfamiliar defensive responsibilities. But more significantly, even as those minor adjustments were being made, Ardiles' creative game blossomed gloriously at White Hart Lane.

'The Little Master' brought to his work perfect ball control, distribution that was at once both artistic and workmanlike, and what seemed like his own radar system: 'I hear feet coming' was his deadpan explanation to colleagues mystified by his knack of detecting and avoiding unexpected challenges.

The Ardiles trademark was the instantly dispatched 15-yard pass, sometimes piercing a defence at a single stroke but more frequently the centrepiece of a quickfire midfield interchange. He was that rare phenomenon in England, a 'head-up' player, one who could make the ball do his bidding without glueing his eyes to it, thus having more chance to spot an opening; and all the time he wanted that ball, scooting everywhere in tireless search of it. Inevitably there were opponents who, gulled by his bird-like frame, believed that force could stem his flow, but they were wrong, reckoning without a wiry strength allied to beautiful balance and feisty determination.

By the time of his first English club honour, a 1981 FA Cup winner's medal, Ardiles was beloved of the Spurs supporters, and his integration into the local scene heightened his distress as nationalist fervour ran amok during the Falklands War. As a result of the conflict, he moved temporarily to Paris St Germain, missing the 1982 FA Cup triumph and not 'coming home' until January 1983.

Then began an epidemic of injuries that was to plague him for more than three years and the return to something near his best form in 1986, following two broken legs and a cartilage operation, was a comeback as remarkable as Dave Mackay's in the 1960s.

In 1987/88, aged 35, Ardiles was loaned to Blackburn before joining Queen's Park Rangers on a free transfer the following summer. There followed a managerial career that began brightly at Swindon, faltered at Newcastle, then picked up fresh momentum at West Bromwich. Depressingly, a brick wall was waiting at Tottenham, of all places, but that traumatic episode must never be allowed to erase the precious memories of the visionary Cordoban's playing pomp. Until the rise of Eric Cantona at Old Trafford, Ossie Ardiles was, by some distance, the British game's most successful foreign import.

**OSVALDO CESAR ARDILES**

| | |
|---|---|
| BORN: | Cordoba, Argentina, 3 August 1952. |
| HONOURS: | UEFA Cup 83/4; FA Cup 80/1. 63 Argentina caps (73-82). |
| OTHER CLUBS: | Instituto de Cordoba, Argentina, 69-73; Belgrano de Cordoba, Argentina, 74; Huracan, Argentina, 75-78; Paris St Germain on loan 82/3; Blackburn Rovers on loan 87/8 (5, 0); Queen's Park Rangers 88/9 (8, 0); Swindon Town 89/90 (2, 0). |
| MANAGER: | Swindon Town (89-91); Newcastle United (91-92); West Bromwich Albion (92-93); Tottenham Hotspur (93-94); Guadalajara, Mexico, (95); Shimuzu S-Pulse, Japan, (96-98); Dinamo Zagreb, Croatia, (99); Yokohama Marinos, Japan, (00-01); Al-Ittihad, Saudi Arabia, (01); Racing Club, Argentina, (02-03); Tokyo Verdy, Japan, (03-05); Beitar Jerusalem, Israel, (06); Huracan, Argentina, (07). |

| | |
|---|---|
| GAMES | 294 (18) |
| GOALS | 25 |

# STEVE ARCHIBALD

### 1980/81 → 1983/84

He was the darling of the White Hart Lane faithful; some of his team-mates warmed to him while others remained distinctly cool; manager Keith Burkinshaw, having paid handsomely for his services, rowed bitterly with him. But one thing was certain about Steve Archibald – everyone recognised his outstanding talent.

The slim, sandy-blond Glaswegian joined Spurs from Aberdeen in May 1980, fresh from playing a star role in taking the Scottish title to Pittodrie. The £800,000 fee was the biggest to pass between clubs on opposite sides of the border, but soon, as Archibald netted 25 times and tasted FA Cup glory at Wembley in his first English season, it became obvious that the north Londoners had sunk their capital into gilt-edged stock.

Here was a striker with wings on his heels. Eternally alert, he could flash past a defender as suddenly and unstoppably as an arrow from a bow, and could finish with apparently nerveless efficiency. Archibald boasted skill, subtlety and style in abundance, and was well served by a wiry resilience which enabled him to withstand heavy physical challenges. He brimmed with stamina, too, often roaming deep to join in the build-up to attacks, and could do a capable job in midfield at need.

Crucially, the Scot employed his many assets cleverly, constantly adapting to the ever-changing options around him, and making the most of the sumptuous service emanating from Messrs Hoddle and Ardiles. Particularly bountiful for the Tottenham cause was the scoring partnership he enjoyed with Garth Crooks, and those who would chide Archibald for a certain selfishness when confronted with the net – actually a required tendency for any successful marksman – should note that his deft touches supplied a more-than-acceptable number of 'assists'.

However, after that prolific introductory campaign, the Archibald bandwagon encountered a somewhat rockier road in 1981/82, when the winning of a second FA Cup medal was offset by injury absences and a leaner time in front of goal. There was one moment of archetypal Archibald to savour, though, when he held off two defenders before netting expertly in the League Cup Final defeat by Liverpool. The next term brought more consistent personal returns, but it was in 1983/84, his final season at White Hart Lane, that he reached his zenith, and that despite a well-publicised rift with Keith Burkinshaw.

The apparent cause was the player's insistence on leaving the field after being injured at home to Coventry City that August, while the manager, having used his substitute already, wanted him to stay on. Though quiet, Archibald was strong-willed and there were heated exchanges which failed to clear the air. Even after the striker returned to action with a thunderous 25-yard goal at Watford, the relationship remained intensely strained, a situation hardly conducive to team needs, and Archibald's attitude annoyed certain of his colleagues.

Such unwelcome distractions did not put him off his own game, though. Indeed, he struck his richest vein of form to date, scoring 29 goals and helping to secure the UEFA Cup, as well as showing his courage by playing through at least one game in severe pain.

Oddly, both men were due to leave White Hart Lane that summer, Keith resigning at season's end and Steve – dismaying the doting thousands who serenaded their hero with 'We'll Take More Care Of You, Archibald', to the strains of a topical TV advertising ditty – was sold to Barcelona in July for £1,150,000. Predictably for such an accomplished and self-confident performer, he flourished in Spain, before ending his career with further short spells in England and Scotland. Meanwhile, back at the Lane, his memory is cherished still.

**STEVEN ARCHIBALD**

| | |
|---|---|
| **BORN:** | Glasgow, 27 September 1956. |
| **HONOURS:** | UEFA Cup 83/4. FA Cup 80/1, 81/2. 27 Scotland caps (80-86). |
| **OTHER CLUBS:** | Clyde 74/5-77/8 (65, 7); Aberdeen 77/8-79/80 (76, 29); Barcelona, Spain, 84/5-87/8; |
| | Blackburn Rovers 87/8 (20, 6); Hibernian 88/9-89/90 (44, 15); Espanol, Spain, 89/90-90/1; |
| | St Mirren 90/1 (16, 2); Reading 91/2 (1, 0); Fulham 92/3 (2, 0); East Fife 94/5-96/7 (49, 7); |
| | Home Farm, Republic of Ireland, 96/7. |
| **MANAGER:** | East Fife (94-96); Airdrieonians (00-01). |

GAMES **187 (4)**
GOALS **78**

# GARTH CROOKS

· · · · · · · · · · · · · · · · · · · · · · · · · · · · · · · · · · · · · ·

## 1980/81 → 1984/85

'**B**lack Magic in the box' – a typically glib tabloid newspaper tag, but when Garth Crooks was at his effervescent best it was an apt one. Somehow it summed up more than his quicksilver, explosive contributions to the Tottenham attack, carrying with it a hint of glamour and tapping into the zestful personality of a performer who thrived on life at a big-city club. While some players from the provinces seem overcome by the razzmatazz which is an inescapable part of the White Hart Lane scene, Crooks appeared to be lifted by the limelight; indeed, when he was on a roll he exuded an infectious confidence that expressed a rare quality in the modern game, the sheer joy of playing football.

Born in the Potteries of Jamaican parents, Crooks had made an exciting impression with Stoke City, his home-town club, and as an established under-21 international was viewed as one of England's most promising young forwards when Keith Burkinshaw signed him for £600,000 in July 1980. He arrived in north London two months after the Scot, Steve Archibald, and before long the two had established a rapport which was to reap rich rewards. Friends off the field, they became a lethal strike combination on it, spearheading Tottenham's triumphant back-to-back FA Cup campaigns of the early 1980s and, importantly, catching the fans' imagination.

Though not the equal of Archibald in terms of ball control and all-round ability, the left-sided Crooks was to be no junior partner, as he indicated by netting on each of his first three League outings. Bouncy, fleet-footed and brave, he provided an ideal, constantly moving target for the passing masters in Spurs' ultra-creative midfield, and when given a chance at goal he could take it with waspish vigour.

One archetypal Crooks strike came in the 1981 FA Cup semi-final replay against Wolves, when he sprinted on to a supremely weighted through-ball from Glenn Hoddle before beating 'keeper Paul Bradshaw with ruthless accuracy. In fact, numerous memories of Crooks at his most effective relate to the FA Cup, in which he played 17 games for the club before tasting defeat: there was the smartly dispatched equaliser in the 1981 Final rematch against Manchester City, the slight miscue that knocked out Arsenal in January 1982 and the adroit volley that ended Leeds United's interest in the following round.

However, Garth's tenure at Tottenham was not spent solely on the crest of a wave. Injuries and the type of lean spell that plagues every marksman from time to time appeared to dent the Crooks confidence and 1983/84 saw him out of the side for long periods. That season, with the presence of Alan Brazil increasing the already keen competition for places, he was released on loan to Manchester United, but was given little chance to impress at Old Trafford and returned to the Lane understandably frustrated.

Yet he still had much to offer, as he demonstrated during the next term as another new acquisition, Clive Allen, faced fitness problems. That autumn Crooks grabbed two hat-tricks in eight days – one at Halifax in the League Cup, the other in a home UEFA Cup encounter with Sporting Braga – before going on to score in seven successive games at the turn of the year. Then he netted the goal against Liverpool that secured Spurs' first win at Anfield for 73 years, and had he not sustained a springtime injury, Tottenham's title challenge might not have faded away in quite the anti-climactic manner it did.

Despite this second wind, though, it became clear that Crooks' future lay elsewhere and that August he switched to West Bromwich Albion, later serving Charlton Athletic before retiring. An intelligent, articulate individual who had proved an able chairman of the Professional Footballers Association, he moved on eventually to a fulfilling media career. On the air, as on the pitch, Garth Crooks was a bundle of unbounded vitality, a definite case of Black Magic *on* the box.

**GARTH ANTHONY CROOKS**

BORN: Stoke, 10 March 1958.
HONOURS: FA Cup 80/1, 81/2.
OTHER CLUBS: Stoke City 75/6-79/80 (147, 48); Manchester United on loan 83/4 (7, 2); West Bromwich Albion 85/6-86/7 (40, 16); Charlton Athletic 86/7-90/1 (56, 15).

GAMES **177 (6)**
GOALS 75

# MIKE HAZARD

## 1979/80 → 1985/86 & 1993/94 → 1994/95

Mike Hazard was a richly gifted play-maker who decorated many games but dominated few. Thus, in his first and principal spell as a Spur, he was condemned to an in-and-out White Hart Lane existence languishing perplexedly in the shadow of Glenn Hoddle.

In retrospect, and after drooling over film clips of the bubbly-haired Wearsider's bewitching skills, it would be easy to berate successive Tottenham managers for not using him more frequently – only once did Hazard exceed 20 League starts in a season – but cooler consideration invites the unavoidable conclusion that neither Keith Burkinshaw nor Peter Shreeves can reasonably be blamed. Finding a regular place for one midfield artist whose contribution did not tally consistently with his talents may be expected of a club with Spurs' traditions, but accommodating two would have been unaffordably rash.

Certainly, though, it can be conceded that Hazard was monstrously unlucky to encounter such a formidable rival in his own camp, and it is telling that the majority of his most influential displays were made in Hoddle's absence, notably during early 1984/85. Then, he revelled in the role of chief creator, entertaining royally with an intoxicating combination of incisive passing and adventurous dribbles. In full flow, Hazard was an enthralling sight, all swerves and feints and shimmies. He was capable of carving his way through apparently inpenetrable rucks of opponents, and he struck the ball well, too, crossing perceptively and shooting powerfully, many of his goals coming from outside the box.

Tantalisingly, there were occasions when the Hazard-Hoddle chemistry was perfect – they gelled most irresistibly during one heartlifting period of mid-1981/82 – which served only to whet the appetite for what might have been. Eventually, Hazard lost patience with waiting for a regular slot and in September 1985 he joined Chelsea for £310,000.

Eight years later, following a successful interlude in harness with none other than Glenn Hoddle at Swindon, he returned to the Lane in a £50,000 deal. Though by then in his 34th year, Hazard produced some deliciously imaginative performances for Ossie Ardiles before retiring in 1995.

**MICHAEL HAZARD**
BORN: Sunderland, 5 February 1960.
HONOURS: UEFA Cup 83/4. FA Cup 81/2.
OTHER CLUBS: Chelsea 85/6-89/90 (81, 9); Portsmouth 89/90-90/1 (8, 1); Swindon Town 90/1-93/4 (119, 17).

GAMES **132 (39)**
GOALS 25

# TONY GALVIN

## 1978/79 → 1986/87

Tony Galvin was a rough diamond of a footballer whose presence among a collection of more sophisticated gems brought much-needed attacking balance to Spurs sides of the early and mid-1980s. In contrast to the subtlety and guile of Hoddle, Ardiles and company, the indefatigable Yorkshireman employed a full-frontal, hard-running approach that was apt to catch defenders cold by its sheer directness and simplicity. Indeed, especially on days when the artists were a little off-colour, there was something solidly reassuring in the sight of Galvin – head down, elbows out and socks around his ankles – bustling purposefully along his flank.

Though the Galvin style has been called naive, that is hardly surprising in view of his lack of a conventional soccer apprenticeship. While the majority of his contemporaries were learning their craft, Galvin was acquiring a university degree in Russian studies, only then joining Spurs as a £30,000 recruit from non-League Goole Town in January 1978.

His early progress was interrupted by a pelvic injury which sidelined him for almost a year, and it was not until January 1981 that he sprang to prominence. Then, though still in considerable pain, he scored in the FA Cup third round replay victory over Queen's Park Rangers and played a vigorous part during the rest of the campaign that ended triumphantly at Wembley.

Galvin built on this, becoming invaluable not only for forward sallies but also for tenacity in tackling back, and shared in all Spurs' successes of that era while forging an international career thanks to a grandparent from the Irish Republic.

Though naturally right-sided, he lined up most frequently on the left wing, from which he could cross ably with either foot or cut in and dash across the box before shooting. Some reckoned he was one-dimensional, but in the context of the team's need, the only valid criticism would be his relatively meagre goal tally. When Tony Galvin was sold to Sheffield Wednesday for £130,000 in August 1987, Spurs lost both an underrated player and a welcome down-to-earth influence.

**ANTHONY GALVIN**
**BORN:** Huddersfield, Yorkshire, 12 July 1956.
**HONOURS:** UEFA Cup 83/4. FA Cup 80/1, 81/2. 29 Republic of Ireland caps (82-89).
**OTHER CLUBS:** Sheffield Wednesday 87/8-88/9 (36, 1); Swindon Town 89/90 (11, 0).

| GAMES | 264 (11) |
| GOALS | 31 |

# GORDON SMITH

## 1978/79 → 1981/82

Injury marred the White Hart Lane career of Gordon Smith, an attacking full-back who never produced for Spurs the splendid form he had displayed for his former club, Aston Villa. Keith Burkinshaw paid the Midlanders £150,000 for the Scottish under-23 international in February 1979, content in the knowledge that he was acquiring a young defender with three seasons of experience in the top half of the First Division.

But after a handful of competent performances in 1979/80, both in the flank role and as a deputy for Paul Miller in the centre, Smith succumbed to knee problems and needed an operation in the spring. Despite working hard on the road to recovery, he impressed only rarely in a settled sequence at the outset of the following season, and he was dropped, thus missing out on the FA Cup Final clashes with Manchester City.

Thereafter his all-round accomplishment appeared no better than average and he never again held a regular place during a period in which competition for full-back places came from Miller, Chris Hughton and Don McAllister. Smith, who played in contact lenses, was allowed to join Wolves on a free transfer in August 1982, but suffered further injuries and bowed out of Molineux two years later.

**GORDON MELVILLE SMITH**
**BORN:** Glasgow 3 July 1954.
**OTHER CLUBS:** St Johnstone 72/3-75/6 (118, 11); Aston Villa 76/7-78/9 (79, 0); Wolverhampton Wanderers 82/3-83/4 (38, 3).

GAMES **40 (5)**
GOALS **1**

---

# PAUL PRICE

## 1981/82 → 1983/84

When Paul Price left Luton Town for Tottenham in June 1981, the 27-year-old central defender was at the crossroads of his career. For a recently-established Welsh international with nearly a decade of League experience behind him, the £250,000 move looked like the ideal turning; sadly, it was to prove a frustrating dead end.

Price suffered an early blow when an injury in his second match, at home to West Ham, sidelined him for several months, and when he returned the expectant crowd gave him little time to settle. However, he played well in the second half of the season, helping Spurs to reach Wembley twice, suffering League Cup defeat at the hands of Liverpool, then pocketing an FA Cup winner's medal at the expense of Queen's Park Rangers.

It might have been the platform for consolidation, but even allowing for fitness setbacks, Price's form thereafter was patchy. At his best he was a competent all-rounder, without ever suggesting he might become the dominant figure Tottenham needed. His final performance, in the morale-sapping League Cup reverse against Arsenal at White Hart Lane in November 1983, was particularly disappointing and it was hardly a surprise when he left for Minnesota the following summer. Later Price returned to the British scene at Swansea, then Peterborough.

**PAUL TERENCE PRICE**
**BORN:** St Albans, Hertfordshire, 23 March 1954.
**HONOURS:** FA Cup 81/2. 25 Wales caps (80-84).
**OTHER CLUBS:** Luton Town 72/3-80/1 (207, 8); Minnesota Kicks, USA, 77-78; Swansea City 84/5-85/6 (61, 1); Peterborough United 86/7-87/8 (86, 0).

GAMES **58 (4)**
GOALS **0**

# ALAN BRAZIL

## 1982/83 → 1983/84

There was no shortage of envious rivals when Keith Burkinshaw secured the signature of Alan Brazil in March 1983. Indeed, the Scottish international striker, a £450,000 buy from Ipswich Town, was one of the most wanted men on the First Division scene, a billing he justified with six goals in 12 outings for his new club that spring. Skilful and quick, Brazil boasted a wicked sidestep that could leave the tightest marker floundering as he bore down on goal, usually from his favoured left side, and was adept at confusing defenders by intelligent curving runs.

However, his confidence was fragile, and when it dried up after a barren spell early in 1983/84, he was unable to rise above a combination of injuries and stiff competition for places. When he was dropped, Brazil – essentially an easy-going fellow – clashed with his manager, and despite some valuable contributions, notably a goal in either leg of the UEFA Cup quarter-final against Austria Vienna, he departed to Old Trafford for £700,000 in June 1984.

Thus, while failing to get the best out of him, Spurs had profited financially from a player who was perhaps more suited to life at a relatively small-town club where the spotlight was less intense, a theory supported by his subsequent struggles with Manchester United.

**ALAN BERNARD BRAZIL**
**BORN:** Glasgow, 15 June 1959.
**HONOURS:** 13 Scotland caps (80-83).
**OTHER CLUBS:** Ipswich Town 77/8-82/3 (144, 70); Manchester United 84/5-85/6 (31, 8); Coventry City 85/6 (15, 2); Queen's Park Rangers 86/7 (4, 0); FC Baden, Switzerland.

| | |
|---|---|
| GAMES | 33 (5) |
| GOALS | 13 |

# TERRY GIBSON

## 1979/80 → 1982/83

Striker Terry Gibson goes down as one of the unluckiest players who failed to make the grade at White Hart Lane. On most of his senior outings, the 5ft 4in dasher showed all the qualities that once made him the hottest property in local youth football. Sharp and fiery, he made light of his lack of inches, buzzing everywhere across the front line, ferreting for defensive mistakes and often inducing them. But if he didn't happen to get a goal – and his ratio wasn't bad considering the fragmentary nature of his Spurs career – the fans, bred on expensive stars, called for the manager to brandish his chequebook.

Consequently Gibson, an archetypal chirpy Londoner who showed admirable spirit throughout his travails, was almost always near the end of the queue for a first-team berth. Many wondered why, especially those who saw him during his one settled run, some 19 games in early 1983 when he netted six times and demonstrated enormous potential.

That August, his Tottenham future clearly limited, Gibson accepted a £100,000 move to Coventry City, where he shone so brightly that Manchester United procured his signature. At Old Trafford, sadly, he was confronted once more by the star syndrome, being given few chances before leaving for Wimbledon, whom he helped to win the FA Cup in 1988.

**TERENCE BRADLEY GIBSON**
**BORN:** Walthamstow, London, 23 December 1962.
**OTHER CLUBS:** Coventry City 83/4-85/6 (98, 43); Manchester United 85/6-86/7 (23, 1); Wimbledon 87/8-92/3 (86, 22); Swindon Town on loan 91/2 (8, 1).

| | |
|---|---|
| GAMES | 22 (4) |
| GOALS | 7 |

## IAN SMITH

### 1975/76

Full-back Ian Smith could not progress beyond the fringe of the Spurs first team after wearing the number-two shirt twice as manager Terry Neill shuffled his defensive pack in the autumn of 1975. Later he fared little better with home-town club Rotherham.

**IAN RALPH SMITH**
BORN: Rotherham, Yorkshire, 15 February 1957.
OTHER CLUBS: Rotherham United 77/8 (4, 0).

| GAMES | 2 |
|---|---|
| GOALS | 0 |

## STEVE WALFORD

### 1975/76

Clearly Terry Neill liked the look of skilful utility defender Steve Walford, who followed the former Spurs boss to Arsenal for £25,000 in August 1977. The tall Londoner never quite became established at Highbury, but went on to peak with Norwich and West Ham.

**STEPHEN JAMES WALFORD**
BORN: Highgate, London, 5 January 1958.
OTHER CLUBS: Arsenal 77/8-80/1 (77, 3); Norwich City 80/1-82/3 (93, 2); West Ham United 83/4-86/7 (115, 2); Huddersfield Town on loan 87/8 (12, 0); Gillingham on loan 88/9 (4, 0); West Bromwich Albion on loan 88/9 (4, 0); Lai Sun, Hong Kong 89.

| GAMES | 1 (1) |
|---|---|
| GOALS | 0 |

## NOEL BROTHERSTON

### 1975/76

A solitary outing at home to Aston Villa in the League Cup was the only chance Irish winger Noel Brotherston was given to make his mark as a Spur. However, he went on to prove his worth during a decade at Blackburn, and became a regular choice for his country.

**NOEL BROTHERSTON**
BORN: Dundonald, Belfast, 18 November 1956.
HONOURS: 27 Northern Ireland caps (80-85).
OTHER CLUBS: Blackburn Rovers 77/8-86/7 (317, 40); Bury 87/8-88/9 (38, 4); Scarborough on loan 88/9 (5, 0).
DIED: 6 May 1995.

| GAMES | 1 |
|---|---|
| GOALS | 0 |

## MARTIN ROBINSON

### 1975/76 → 1977/78

Fans of Charlton will be best acquainted with the bright attacking qualities of Martin Robinson, who joined the Addicks for £15,000 in February 1978 after a mere handful of opportunities as a secondary striker with Spurs, then thrived at the Valley for six seasons.

**MARTIN JOHN ROBINSON**
BORN: Ilford, Essex, 17 July 1957.
OTHER CLUBS: Charlton Athletic 77/8-84/5 (228, 58); Reading on loan 82/3 (6, 2); Gillingham 84/5-86/7 (96, 24); Southend United 87/8-88/9 (56, 14); Cambridge United 89/90 (16, 1).

| GAMES | 5 (1) |
|---|---|
| GOALS | 2 |

## ANDY KEELEY

### 1976/77

Andy Keeley's tilt at the big time arrived at an awkward juncture for a young defender, as Tottenham were nosediving towards the Second Division. The England youth international showed initial promise but was released soon after Spurs' demotion.

**ANDREW JAMES KEELEY**
BORN: Basildon, Essex, 16 September 1956.
OTHER CLUBS: Sheffield United 77/8-80/1 (28, 0); Scunthorpe United 81/2-82/3 (77, 1).

| GAMES | 5 (1) |
|---|---|
| GOALS | 0 |

## STUART BEAVON

### 1978/79 → 1979/80

Stuart Beavon became a vastly influential midfield general for Reading throughout the 1980s, but with the world-class likes of Glenn Hoddle and Ossie Ardiles on the Tottenham scene, he was never likely to get much of a show at White Hart Lane during that decade.

**MICHAEL STUART BEAVON**
BORN: Wolverhampton, Staffordshire, 30 November 1958.
OTHER CLUBS: Notts County on loan 79/80 (6, 0); Reading 80/1-89/90 (396, 44); Northampton Town 90/1-92/3 (98, 14).

| GAMES | 3 (2) |
|---|---|
| GOALS | 0 |

## PETER SOUTHEY

### 1979/80

The tale of Peter Southey is one of stark tragedy. Considered an outstanding prospect, the diminutive full-back made his senior debut at home to Brighton in the League Cup in September 1979, but then fell prey to leukaemia, which claimed his life at the age of 21.

**PETER CHARLES SOUTHEY**
BORN: Putney, London, 4 January 1962.
DIED: Ham, Surrey, 28 December 1983.

| GAMES | 1 |
|---|---|
| GOALS | 0 |

## GIORGIO MAZZON

### 1980/81 → 1982/83

Defender Giorgio Mazzon was spotted by Tottenham excelling for his local club, non-League Waltham New Town, and he turned professional at White Hart Lane in April 1979. However, though he was versatile enough to double as a midfielder, a long-term breakthrough proved beyond him.

**GIORGIO MAZZON**
BORN: Waltham Cross, Hertfordshire, 4 September 1960.
OTHER CLUBS: Aldershot 83/4-88/9 (195, 6).

| GAMES | 4 (3) |
|---|---|
| GOALS | 0 |

## PAT CORBETT

1981/82 → 1982/83

Tall, strong defender Pat Corbett made a sensational impact as an attacker on his senior debut, leaving the bench to net a late winner at Southampton in October 1981. However, he could not make a lasting impression at his premier discipline, and soon he moved on.

**PATRICK AVALON CORBETT**
BORN: Hackney, London, 12 February 1963.
OTHER CLUBS: Orient 83/4-85/6 (77, 2).

| GAMES | 3 (2) |
|---|---|
| GOALS | 1 |

## SIMON WEBSTER

1982/83 → 1983/84

Tottenham, the first of Simon Webster's eight League clubs, never saw the best of the slim six-footer, who later developed into a muscular, dominant stopper, notably with Charlton. As a Spur he never got beyond the stage of a rookie filling in for injured regulars.

**SIMON PAUL WEBSTER**
BORN: Earl Shilton, Leicestershire, 20 January 1964.
OTHER CLUBS: Exeter City on loan 83/4 (26, 0); Huddersfield Town 84/5-87/8 (118, 4); Sheffield United 87/8-89/90 (37, 3); Charlton Athletic 90/1-92/3 (127, 7); West Ham United 94/5 (5, 0); Oldham Athletic on loan 94/5 (7, 0); Derby County on loan 95/6 (3, 0).

| GAMES | 2 (1) |
|---|---|
| GOALS | 0 |

## ROBERT BRACE

1983/84

Teenage attacker Rob Brace barely figured in the Tottenham story, his sole senior appearance being as a substitute at Southampton in May 1984 when manager Keith Burkinshaw put out a severely weakened team shortly before the UEFA Cup Final.

**ROBERT LEON BRACE**
BORN: Edmonton, London, 19 December 1964.

| GAMES | 0 (1) |
|---|---|
| GOALS | 0 |

## IAN CULVERHOUSE

1983/84

During his illustrious tenure at Carrow Road, Ian Culverhouse proved himself to be a high-quality all-purpose defender, particularly at full-back. Whether he might have scaled even loftier peaks had Spurs not sold him to Norwich for £50,000 in 1985, we shall never know.

**IAN BRETT CULVERHOUSE**
BORN: Bishop's Stortford, Hertfordshire, 22 September 1964.
OTHER CLUBS: Norwich City 85/6-94/5 (296, 1); Swindon Town 94/5- (97, 0).

| GAMES | 1 (1) |
|---|---|
| GOALS | 0 |

## ALLAN COCKRAM

1983/84

The zenith of midfielder Allan Cockram's career came under Steve Perryman at Brentford, whom he helped to reach the FA Cup quarter-finals of 1989. Earlier, at White Hart Lane, he had been unable to shine in competition with so many international rivals.

**ALLAN CHARLES COCKRAM**
BORN: Kensington, London, 8 October 1963.
OTHER CLUBS: Bristol Rovers 85/6 (1, 0); Brentford 87/8-90/1 (90, 14); Reading 91/2 (6, 1).

| GAMES | 2 |
|---|---|
| GOALS | 0 |

## DAVID LEWORTHY

1984/85 → 1985/86

Spurs paid non-League Fareham Town £5,000 for former Pompey attacker David Leworthy in August 1984. Duly he shaped promisingly, made his senior Tottenham entrance against Arsenal in April 1985, but before the year was out he joined Oxford for £250,000.

**DAVID JOHN LEWORTHY**
BORN: Portsmouth, 22 October 1962.
OTHER CLUBS: Portsmouth 81/2 (1, 0); Oxford United 85/6-88/9 (37, 8); Shrewsbury Town on loan 87/8 (6, 3); Reading 89/90-91/2 (44, 7).

| GAMES | 8 (4) |
|---|---|
| GOALS | 4 |

## TIM O'SHEA

1986/87 → 1987/88

Tim O'Shea was a utility player, best suited as a defender or holding midfielder. Once on Arsenal's books and a Republic of Ireland youth international, he couldn't carve a niche at Tottenham but went on to enjoy a productive stint at Gillingham.

**TIMOTHY JAMES O'SHEA**
BORN: Pimlico, London, 12 November 1966.
OTHER CLUBS: Newport County on loan 86/7 (10, 0); Leyton Orient 88/9 (9, 1); Gillingham 88/9-91/2 (112, 2); Eastern, Hong Kong.

| GAMES | 1 (2) |
|---|---|
| GOALS | 0 |

## SHAUN CLOSE

1986/87 → 1987/88

It would have taken a truly outstanding marksman to impose himself at a club where Clive Allen was in prime form, and the task proved beyond Shaun Close. Having decided that his fellow Londoner was surplus to requirements, Terry Venables sold him to Bournemouth for £70,000.

**SHAUN CHARLES CLOSE**
BORN: Islington, London, 8 September 1966.
OTHER CLUBS: Bournemouth 87/8-89/90 (39, 8); Swindon Town 89/90-92/3 (44, 1); Barnet 93/4 (27, 2).

| GAMES | 6 (6) |
|---|---|
| GOALS | 2 |

# RICHARD COOKE

## 1982/83 → 1985/86

Small, slim and with legs that might have been borrowed from a sparrow, Richard Cooke looked in danger of being snapped in half by the first crunching tackle that came his way. However, the speedy north Londoner was deceptively resilient, managing to ride most challenges and, on his day, his non-stop running posed a threat to most defenders.

One of two young wingers pushing for senior recognition in the mid-1980s – his direct style on the right offering an effective contrast to the trickier approach of left-flank partner Ally Dick – he enjoyed a promising debut at Luton in November 1983, netting crisply from the edge of the box after being set up by Steve Perryman.

But after a four-match run, the 18-year-old found it impossible to hold his place in the face of fierce competition, and during subsequent sporadic appearances Cooke's rather frenetic efforts made little impact.

By 1986/87 his senior prospects had receded and, after a loan spell with Birmingham, he moved to Bournemouth. At Dean Court Cooke forged a worthy career outside the top flight, but it was something of an anti-climax for a one-time England youth and under-21 international whose signature Tottenham had beaten Arsenal and Chelsea, among others, to secure. Worse was to come, however, when injury ended his playing days in 1993.

**RICHARD EDWARD COOKE**
BORN: Islington, London, 4 September 1965.
OTHER CLUBS: Birmingham City on loan 86/7 (5, 0); Bournemouth 86/7-88/9 (72, 16); Luton Town 88/9-90/1 (17, 1); Bournemouth 90/1-92/3 (53, 2).

| GAMES | 12 (5) |
|-------|--------|
| GOALS | 2 |

# ALLY DICK

## 1981/82 → 1985/86

When Ally Dick was dancing past defenders for Scotland schoolboys like some latter-day Jimmy Johnstone, there was never the slightest doubt of his ability to reach the top. Duly he continued to dazzle at youth level and when he made his League debut at home to Manchester City in February 1982, the youngest player ever to appear for Spurs in the Football League at 16 years 301 days and still an amateur, the slim left-flanker's accession to fully-fledged stardom seemed only a matter of time.

But somehow it never happened. Despite the skill and pace, the talent for crossing and the powerful shot, there was something missing. Perhaps Dick lacked the necessary hunger for success, maybe he received too much attention too soon, possibly he was not strong enough to withstand the injuries that came his way.

Whatever the reason, after some promising performances in 1983/84 – when he picked up a UEFA Cup winner's medal as a substitute for Gary Mabbutt in the second leg of the final against Anderlecht – he faded from contention and in the summer of 1986 joined Ajax on a free transfer.

The identity of his purchasers bore eloquent testimony to the young Scot's potential, but he never made the grade in Amsterdam, either, and after unsuccessful attempts to break through at Wimbledon, Brighton and elsewhere, Ally Dick was lost to the game.

**ALISTAIR JOHN DICK**
BORN: Stirling, Scotland, 25 April 1965.
HONOURS: UEFA Cup 83/4.
OTHER CLUBS: Ajax, Holland, 86/7.

| GAMES | 21 (4) |
|-------|--------|
| GOALS | 2 |

# GARRY BROOKE

## 1980/81 → 1984/85

If making the grade for Spurs could be likened to a 20-hurdle race, then only at the 19th obstacle did Garry Brooke take a tumble. As a teenager, the bright, chunky midfielder was a fabulous prospect, and the two FA Cup winner's medals he collected as a substitute in 1981 and 1982 seemed unlikely to remain his only honours. But, hampered by both soccer injuries and those sustained in a car crash, he never stepped up from invigorating number 12 to first-team regular.

Brooke's first senior impact came on Boxing Day 1980 when, fresh from a beneficial loan spell in Sweden, he netted twice on his full debut at home to Southampton. Indeed, his powerful long-range shooting, for which he employed negligible backlift and thus was apt to catch defences unawares, was a lethal asset, but he was no one-trick merchant. His control was impeccable, he crossed well from his habitual berth on the right flank and his quick-stepping, almost comical running style generated deceptive pace.

But too often he would choose the wrong passing option or fail to find space at the right time, accordingly interrupting the flow of attacks, and in July 1985 he was allowed to join Norwich. After a brief stint at Carrow Road, the shrewd little Londoner drifted, somewhat surprisingly, towards footballing obscurity.

**GARRY JAMES BROOKE**
**BORN:** Bethnal Green, London, 24 November 1960.
**HONOURS:** FA Cup 80/1, 81/2.
**OTHER CLUBS:** Gais, Sweden, on loan 80/1; Norwich City 85/6-86/7 (14, 2); Groningen, Holland, 86/7; Wimbledon 88/9-89/90 (12, 0); Stoke City on loan 89/90 (8, 0); Brentford 90/1 (11, 1); Reading 90/1 (4, 1).

| GAMES | 63 (38) |
|---|---|
| GOALS | 18 |

# GARY O'REILLY

## 1980/81 → 1983/84

Gary O'Reilly played international football for two countries, captaining England schoolboys and then, thanks to a parental qualification, representing the Republic of Ireland at youth level. But he found that forging a First Division future was an altogether more formidable proposition.

Intelligent and confident, O'Reilly was a tall, long-striding full-back with the powerful physique to double as a centre-half. Though aerially effective, strong in the tackle and adept at thrusting forward to join in attacks, he hindered his cause by an occasional tendency to dwell on the ball in dangerous situations, a habit that can be self-destructive even for those with more skill than he had at his disposal.

O'Reilly's senior career had begun promisingly with isolated stand-in duties and seemed poised for take-off when he excelled in the 1982 Charity Shield clash with Liverpool. That term was his best, with 30 first-team starts, but as his fallibility became apparent he lost ground in the ever-brisk struggle for a regular place, and in August 1984 he joined Brighton.

Gary O'Reilly's finest hour was to come at Wembley in 1990 when he gave Crystal Palace the lead against Manchester United in the FA Cup Final, though a loser's medal was his only reward.

**GARY MILES O'REILLY**
**BORN:** Isleworth, London, 21 March 1961.
**OTHER CLUBS:** Brighton 84/5-86/7 (79, 3); Crystal Palace 86/7-90/1 (70, 2); Birmingham City on loan 90/1 (1, 0); Brighton 91/2 (28, 3).

| GAMES | 48 (8) |
|---|---|
| GOALS | 0 |

# GRAHAM ROBERTS

## 1980/81 → 1986/87

The question that echoed around Highbury on New Year's Day 1986, roared from the throats of several thousand exulting Spurs fans, could have only one answer. 'Who put Charlie in the stand?' they inquired of their Arsenal counterparts, in reference to a *blitzkrieg* of a tackle which had deposited a certain Mr Nicholas among the spectators. On receiving no satisfactory reply from the nonplussed North Bank, they filled the blank themselves with a thunderous homage to Graham Roberts.

That incident illustrated luridly both the root and the nature of the ruthless central defender-cum-midfielder's popular appeal. And yet there was a paradox. Keith Burkinshaw once described Roberts as being of 'the Duncan Edwards type', and while that might rank as one of the more hysterical managerial remarks of our time, the message that the Spurs boss was attempting to convey was valid: simply that his often-controversial ball-winner was a far better all-round player than most people allowed.

Roberts cut an unlikely figure as a fairy-tale hero, yet the sequence of events culminating in his elevation to the ranks of Tottenham Hotspur and England positively reeked of *Boys' Own* fantasy. In the spring of 1980, having been rejected by Southampton, Bournemouth and Portsmouth, he was plying his trade as a fitter's mate in a shipyard and playing part-time for Weymouth. He was recommended to Bill Nicholson, by then a scout, during a casual conversation with a stranger on a railway platform, and was signed subsequently for £35,000, then a record fee for a non-League player. Some 12 months later, having established himself at centre-half, he was helping his new club to victory over Manchester City in the 100th FA Cup Final.

On his graduation to the senior side, it became clear that Roberts was the north Londoners' most formidable 'hard man' since Dave Mackay. Neither the tallest nor the quickest of defenders, nevertheless he would win challenges through sheer ferocious desire, and it must be said that there were occasions when his zeal got the better of him. He was prone to lose his temper, and while some opponents may have wilted, it's a fact that uncontrolled aggression can be counter-productive against wily operators with the nous to turn tantrums to their own advantage. Hence, when the red mist descended, Roberts was more likely to commit himself to tackles in dangerous situations or be drawn out of position.

In general, of course, his physical might was of enormous value, yet it should not eclipse entirely his largely unsung creative ability, which was most evident during his mid-1980s spells as Glenn Hoddle's midfield minder. In that role, Roberts displayed habitually unplumbed depths of subtlety, controlling the ball with ease and passing both accurately and constructively. A further bonus from pushing the dreadnought on to the offensive accrued from his power of shot, as shown by long-range goals at home to Bruges in November 1984 and Everton five months later.

Often the option of using Roberts as occasional midfielder proved profitable, notably when he plundered a hat-trick against his home-town club, Southampton, in March 1982. But certainly the most valuable Roberts strike was reserved for a loftier occasion, the 1984 UEFA Cup Final against Anderlecht. Near the end of the home second leg, Graham – deputising as captain in place of the suspended Steve Perryman – prodded the ball in from close range to set up the penalty shoot-out in which the spoils were claimed. His contribution that night, his stirring example in the vanguard of a glorious fightback, typified all that was best about him.

When a £450,000 fee took him to Glasgow Rangers in December 1986, it would have been a rare Spurs fan who did not experience a pang of regret for a departing hero. Whatever his critics may say, that is how Graham Roberts will be remembered at White Hart Lane.

**GRAHAM PAUL ROBERTS**

BORN: Southampton, 3 July 1959.
HONOURS: UEFA Cup 83/4. FA Cup 80/1, 81/2. 6 England caps (83-84).
OTHER CLUBS: Glasgow Rangers 86/7-87/8 (55, 3); Chelsea 88/9-89/90 (70, 18); West Bromwich Albion 90/1-91/2 (39, 6).
MANAGER: Clyde (05-06).

GAMES 277 (11)
GOALS 36

# JOHN CHIEDOZIE

## 1984/85 → 1986/87

The merciless roasting John Chiedozie inflicted on Chelsea left-back Doug Rougvie at White Hart Lane in November 1984 stands as a telling microcosm of the fleet-footed Nigerian's career. That day Chiedozie danced past the big Scot repeatedly and with an ease that embarrassed neutral observers. Yet just as Spurs didn't capitalise on the little winger's sparkling display – the match ended in a 1-1 draw – so he never made the most of a promising platform for long-term success.

Chiedozie, whose family had left Africa for London when he was 12, had earned a glowing reputation with Orient before joining Spurs for £350,000 from Notts County in August 1984. That season he flourished on the right flank as Peter Shreeves' enterprising 4-2-4 system sustained Tottenham's title challenge into April.

But next term his progress was hindered both by injury and the arrival of Paul Allen and Chris Waddle. All too soon, despite a moderately productive spell as a central striker, Chiedozie lost momentum. Some felt his immense speed cost him quality of distribution, or maybe the physical knocks had taken their toll; arguably this open, easy-going character – his grin of pleasure when he scored positively lit up the pitch – needed a little more drive. Whatever the root of his decline, John Chiedozie was freed in May 1988 and soon had left the professional game.

**JOHN OKAY CHIEDOZIE**
**BORN:** Owerri, Nigeria, 18 April 1960.
**HONOURS:** 9 Nigeria caps.
**OTHER CLUBS:** Orient 76/7-80/1 (145, 20); Notts County 81/2-83/4 (111, 15); Derby County 88/9 (2, 0); Notts County 89/90 (1, 0); Chesterfield 89/90 (7, 0).

GAMES **64 (11)**
GOALS **14**

---

# TONY PARKS

## 1981/82 → 1987/88

One glorious night does not a career make, as few footballers know better than Tony Parks. The young goalkeeper's supreme moment came in May 1984, when he sealed UEFA Cup triumph for Spurs with his second save of the penalty shoot-out which climaxed the final at White Hart Lane. Springing to his feet, he celebrated ecstatically with his team-mates, but sadly for the north Londoner, there was to be no further joy from his Tottenham career.

His appearance against Anderlecht was the culmination of a splendid spell that spring as deputy for the injured Ray Clemence. But, perhaps unready to handle the limelight which followed his great achievement, Parks returned to Clemence's shadow for the next three seasons, and when another chance came his way in 1987/88, there was little sign of his erstwhile confidence.

An athletic, impressive shot-stopper who was not quite as reliable at claiming crosses, he soon found the supporters on his back and after a mid-season spell of 19 consecutive games he was dropped in favour of new signing Bobby Mimms. With his prospects at the Lane clearly bleak, Parks accepted a £60,000 move to Brentford that summer, but didn't settle and headed north to resurrect his fortunes with Falkirk.

**ANTHONY PARKS**
**BORN:** Hackney, London, 28 January 1963.
**HONOURS:** UEFA Cup 83/4.
**OTHER CLUBS:** Oxford United on loan 86/7 (5, 0); Gillingham on loan 87/8 (2, 0); Brentford 88/9-90/1 (71, 0); Fulham 90/1 (2, 0); West Ham United 91/2 (6, 0); Stoke City on loan 92/3 (2, 0); Falkirk 92/3-95/6 (112, 0); Doncaster Rovers on loan 97/8 (6, 0); Scarborough 98/9 (15, 0); Halifax Town 99/00-00/01 (6, 0).

GAMES **48 (1)**
GOALS **0**

# DANNY THOMAS

## 1983/84 → 1986/87

Those footballers who bemoan their luck at the slightest setback – and every profession is burdened with its share of whingers – would do well to remember the distressing case of Danny Thomas. In March 1987, while playing arguably the best football of his career, the 25-year-old full-back was cut down by a controversial tackle from Queen's Park Rangers' Gavin Maguire that provoked fury on the White Hart Lane terraces, and he never played again. It was a savage blow for the sunny, universally-liked Midlander who had been tipped only recently to resume the England career he had begun while with his first club, Coventry City.

Keith Burkinshaw paid £250,000 to take Thomas from Highfield Road in June 1983, and though he didn't settle immediately, by the middle of his first season he was showing the qualities that had elevated him to the international ranks.

Capable of operating on either defensive flank, he was elastically athletic, an attacking overlapper of flashing pace and unending enthusiasm. He was no soft touch in the tackle, either, and was an effective one-on-one marker, a role in which he had been employed periodically during midfield days with the Sky Blues. However, though not unskilful, his control did not match his speed and he was not at his best when given time to deliberate on the ball, factors which contributed to the loss of his place for lengthy spells during the mid 1980s.

Undaunted, Thomas worked hard and after new boss David Pleat restored him to the side in December 1986, he hit new peaks, linking smoothly with Chris Waddle and looking every inch a top-notch performer. Then came that fateful impact from Maguire's boot and ten months later, in January 1988, he was forced to retire.

Ever positive, though, he refused to slink away in despair and qualified as a physiotherapist, going on to serve West Bromwich Albion in that capacity. The story of Danny Thomas offers an object lesson to everyone connected with the game.

**DANIEL JOSEPH THOMAS**

**BORN:** Worksop, Nottinghamshire, 12 November 1961.
**HONOURS:** UEFA Cup 83/4. 2 England caps (83).
**OTHER CLUBS:** Coventry City 79/80-82/3 (108, 5).

| | |
|---|---|
| GAMES | 103 (13) |
| GOALS | 1 |

# RAY CLEMENCE

## 1981/82 → 1987/88

A few months earlier it would have seemed inconceivable, but suddenly in the autumn of 1981, one of the world's finest goalkeepers had something to prove. That August Ray Clemence, who with Liverpool had swept the honours board so clean and for so long, had joined Tottenham in a £300,000 deal – and he had made a distinctly shaky start.

After a dose of uncertain handling in the Charity Shield clash with Aston Villa, seven goals flashed past him in his first two League games at White Hart Lane, and the whispers began. Was it possible that *anyone* might have looked good behind that superb Liverpool defence, and that all these years the England 'keeper had been overrated? Had he grown complacent in Anfield's pastures of plenty? Or, more bluntly, was he just plain past it?

So much balderdash, of course, and before long he was back to his inspirational best, if anything stronger for the experience and having showed that his magnificent ability was matched by immense strength of character.

In fact, more fascinating than the temporary blip in Clemence's form had been both his decision to head south in the first place and Keith Burkinshaw's choice of a 33-year-old custodian when, earlier in his managerial reign, he had dispensed with 32-year-old Pat Jennings, presumably on the basis of age. Clemence explained his motivation for walking away from the near-certain prospect of continuing glory on Merseyside as the need for a fresh challenge, while clearly Burkinshaw had revised his views on the shelf-life of goalkeepers; taken together, these unexpected circumstances spelt marvellous news for Tottenham.

However, even apart from that aforementioned indifferent start, Clemence's first term in north London must go down as a bitter-sweet interlude. His quarter-final exploits against Eintracht Frankfurt had kept Spurs in the European Cup Winners' Cup, but one horrific bungle against Barcelona, allowing an innocuous 40-yarder to sneak through his hands, set his side on the way towards semi-final elimination. Then there was a splendid League Cup Final performance against his old friends from Liverpool, which was to count for nothing as the Reds won in extra time. But at least the season was to end happily, with an FA Cup winner's medal, destined to remain Clemence's only club honour in his playing days at the Lane, thanks to Wembley victory over Queen's Park Rangers.

As the 1980s wore on, the Clemence standard showed no signs of slipping. As a 'sweeper-keeper' in the Anfield tradition pioneered by Tommy Lawrence, he needed a close understanding with his team-mates and achieved it, organising them vociferously and efficiently. With this system in place, Clemence's agility, bravery and high-class handling, allied to a finely honed positional sense and fierce concentration, offered as formidable a last line of defence as could be found in the First Division. If there was a weakness to his game – and this is nit-picking, indeed – it was his poor kicking of a dead ball, but that was a tiny price to pay for so much that was outstanding.

In 1984/85, after the disappointment of being sidelined for the previous term's UEFA Cup triumph, Clemence was a prime factor in Tottenham's most credible Championship challenge for more than 20 years. Satisfyingly, he reserved one of his most memorable displays for the Kop, pulling off a string of acrobatic saves to preserve a 1-0 lead as the visitors recorded their first win at Anfield in almost three-quarters of a century.

Even in his 40th year, Clemence remained as consistent as ever and when he suffered a groin injury at Norwich in October 1987, the fans were not unduly alarmed, expecting to see him back between the posts within a couple of weeks. In the event, he was never to return, instead accepting a coaching post with the club, which led to his appointment as assistant to chief coach Doug Livermore in 1992.

A breezy character who laughs a lot but who is deadly serious about the game, Ray Clemence MBE – he received the award in 1987 for his services to football – went on to manage Barnet before being recruited by Glenn Hoddle as England's specialist goalkeeping coach.

---

**RAYMOND NEAL CLEMENCE**

BORN: Skegness, Lincolnshire, 5 August 1948.
HONOURS: FA Cup 81/2. 61 England caps (72-83).
OTHER CLUBS: Scunthorpe United 65/6-66/7 (48, 0); Liverpool 69/70-80/1 (470, 0).
MANAGER: Barnet (94-96).

| GAMES | 332 |
| GOALS | 0 |

# IAN CROOK

1981/82 → 1985/86

Ian Crook was Glenn Hoddle's heir apparent as Spurs' schemer-in-chief, but he was denied the chance to prove that his slim shoulders could carry such an onerous mantle. The young wingman-turned-midfielder was a superb technician with a football: he could drive it, clip it, bend it, chip it, or spin it any which way, and all with an astonishing accuracy that is profoundly rare in the modern game. The natural sweetness of the Crook passing repertoire was enhanced by contact with the likes of Hoddle and Ardiles, and when he was given his senior debut as a substitute in May 1982, his prospects glowed.

However, the three consecutive starts Crook made thereafter proved to be his longest first-team run and, amidst mutterings that he didn't chase and couldn't tackle, the gifted 23-year-old joined Norwich for £80,000 in June 1986. Of course, Hoddle was to leave in 1987, and had he made his decision a year earlier it is possible that the younger man would have been retained.

Thereafter Crook matured gradually, habitually haunting his former employers with classy displays – his 30-yard winner at Carrow Road in spring 1991 was especially rewarding – and come 1992/93 he was making the play, subtly and delightfully, as the Canaries soared along blithely at the top of the Premier Division for much of that campaign.

# MARK BOWEN

1983/84 → 1986/87

Mark Bowen was an ordinary midfielder who became an excellent full-back – but not in time to carve out a career at White Hart Lane. Despite beavering enthusiastically and scoring a creditable number of goals for the reserves, it was not until the young Welshman dropped back that a senior breakthrough seemed feasible. After making his debut at home to Coventry in August 1983, Bowen remained on the fringe of a crowded squad, enjoying short first-team stints in mid-1983/84 and spring 1985.

By then playing on the left despite being right-footed, he rose above the trauma of gifting Trevor Steven a goal in the crucial title clash with Everton that April to impress with generally crisp defensive work and a voracious appetite for getting forward. But his hopes were dashed by the purchase of Mitchell Thomas in the summer of 1986 and a year later, despite having underlined his promise by winning full caps, Bowen was allowed to join Norwich.

Subsequently, as he and other ex-Spurs flourished at Carrow Road, some Tottenham fans criticised their management over the exodus of talent. In fact, in most cases – and certainly in Bowen's – the moans were not audible at the time of the move, being voiced only with the convenience of hindsight.

---

**IAN STUART CROOK**
BORN: Romford, Essex, 18 January 1963.
OTHER CLUBS: Norwich City 86/7-96/7 (341, 18);
Sanfrecce Hiroshima, Japan.

| | |
|---|---|
| GAMES | 11 (13) |
| GOALS | 1 |

**MARK ROSSLYN BOWEN**
BORN: Neath, Glamorgan, 7 December 1963.
HONOURS: 41 Wales caps (86-97).
OTHER CLUBS: Norwich City 87/8-95/6 (320, 24);
West Ham United 96/7 (17, 1); Shimizu S-Pulse,
Japan, 97; Charlton Athletic 97/8-98/9 (42, 0);
Wigan Athletic 99/00 (7, 0).

| | |
|---|---|
| GAMES | 17 (3) |
| GOALS | 2 |

# RICHARD GOUGH

## 1986/87 → 1987/88

To most Tottenham fans, Richard Gough was a gift from the gods. They had been longing for a truly outstanding centre-half since the departure of Mike England some 11 years earlier, and in August 1986 the tall, red-haired Scot strolled down from Mount Olympus and got on with the job.

In the interests of strict accuracy, Gough arrived from Dundee United – after David Pleat had missed out on signing England's Terry Butcher – and from his coolly authoritative debut at Villa Park it was apparent immediately that the £750,000 international represented impeccable value for money.

The basic requisites of any standard stopper, aerial power and a stern tackle, were present and correct but, glory of glories, there was more. Here was a number-five with the skill to retain possession of the ball and pass it accurately, a player who seemed always to have time, a sure mark of class in any sport.

As matches went by, the evidence of Gough's prowess grew ever more conclusive. His astute positional sense, the certainty with which he marshalled the defence and the development of an intuitive partnership with Gary Mabbutt – both men got forward effectively, but such was their understanding that rarely did gaps appear at the back – all augured magnificently for the future. Indeed, Gough's appointment as skipper at Charlton on New Year's Day 1987 appeared to fall into the 'job-for-life' category, and his leadership was a telling factor in Tottenham's progress to the FA Cup Final in his first season.

Then disquieting rumours began to circulate in the Scottish press that Richard Gough was set to re-cross the border and sure enough, that October, news broke that Spurs were to lose their new bulwark to Rangers for £1.5 million.

Some pointed to the handsome profit, but there was black despair on the terraces. It seemed the Gough family could not settle in England, which was of little consolation to fans who would have moved heaven and earth to keep their hero; and more than half a decade without a fitting replacement rendered their reaction entirely understandable.

| | |
|---|---|
| **CHARLES RICHARD GOUGH** | |
| **BORN:** | Stockholm, Sweden, 5 April 1962. |
| **HONOURS:** | 61 Scotland caps (83-93). Scottish PFA Footballer of the Year 86. Scottish FWA Footballer of the Year 89. |
| **OTHER CLUBS:** | Dundee United 80/1-85/6 (165, 23); Glasgow Rangers 87/8-96/7 (294, 25); Kansas City Wizards, USA, 97 (17, 0); Glasgow Rangers 97/8 (24, 1); San Jose Clash, USA, (19, 2); Nottingham Forest 98/9 (7, 0); Everton 99/00-00/01 (38, 1). |
| **MANAGER:** | Livingston (04-05). |

| GAMES | 65 |
|---|---|
| GOALS | 2 |

# GLENN HODDLE

## 1975/76 → 1986/87

His touch was exquisite, his vision sublime; he was by a massive margin the most bounteously gifted English footballer of his age. Yet Glenn Hoddle will be remembered not only as a ball-playing master, but also as an unwitting vehicle for the Great Debate on the direction of modern soccer. Were his supreme, if sometimes sedate skills out of place in a game dominated increasingly by work rate, pace and strength? Should he really have missed almost as many England games as he played? Because of those barren spells when the magic lay frustratingly dormant, was he a dispensable luxury? From White Hart Lane, where even to ask such questions might be seen as sacrilege, comes a thunderous negative on all three counts, a verdict echoed in the hearts and minds of all those who believe there is a place for beauty in sport.

The imagination and accuracy of the long-distance pass, the delicacy and precision of the unexpected chip, the sudden ferocity of the scoring volley, and the casual, yet inevitable curve of the free-kick around a defensive wall on its way into the net; truly such wonders were a joy to behold. Countless instances of artistry clamour for recollection, so where do we begin?

Let's try his fourth full season, by which time he had already overcome a serious knee injury, tasted the despair of relegation, been tested in the hurly-burly of the Second Division, and made enough concessions to honest toil as might be deemed reasonable by any manager seeking a blend of complementary talents rather than a team of identical robots.

That term – it was 1979/80 – saw Hoddle score 22 times for Tottenham, and one sensational edge-of-the-box volley at home to Manchester United might have been expected to win a 'Goal Of Any Season' competition; that is if the judges ignored an effort against Nottingham Forest which he clubbed home from 18 yards after the ball had travelled the length of White Hart Lane, from keeper Aleksic, to Armstrong, to Jones, to Hoddle and into the net without touching the ground.

Of course, he created more than he scored, and this craft was illustrated breathtakingly in the 1981 FA Cup semi-final replay against Wolves, when he freed Garth Crooks with a raking through-ball with the outside of his left foot. But if future historians scour old video-tapes seeking one piece of footage to define the magic of Hoddle, then they will settle, surely, on his goal at Watford in 1983. Receiving the ball on the right side of the box, some 15 yards out and at an acute angle to goal, he feinted one way, made space with a deft back-flick, then half-swivelled to chip gently into the far corner of the net. It all seemed to happen in slow motion, and was so perfect in execution that it might have been choreographed.

But what of the other side of the coin? Undeniably, there were dog days when the action would pass Hoddle by, and some felt that by the mid-1980s he was inclined to eschew the simple in favour of the needlessly spectacular. Admittedly, too, he had little pace, though after all, his passes allowed others to do his running for him. Indeed, how lethal he was behind the jet-propelled Archibald and Crooks, and how tantalising to reflect on what he might have achieved in harness with the greyhound Lineker.

Certainly there was no doubting Hoddle's athleticism, as he proved as Spurs' emergency 'keeper, and those who questioned his desire for combat might ponder on a rare brand of courage which team-mates declare he possessed in abundance, that of taking responsibility for the ball, no matter how tight the situation.

When David Pleat sold him to Monaco for around £1 million in July 1987, the loss to the Football League was colossal. Perhaps he felt stale, more likely unappreciated; whatever, Hoddle flourished in France before injury threatened his future. His subsequent attainments at Swindon and Chelsea, both as father-figure on the pitch and as one of the country's most enlightened coaches, gladdened the souls of purists everywhere.

That success opened the door for Glenn Hoddle to fulfil his international destiny at last, as England manager, and therein lies a tale of heartache and disillusion which was to be echoed frustratingly by his subsequent stint in charge at White Hart Lane. But whatever his perceived shortcomings as the club's manager, he will be feted as long as Spurs exist for his pure, untrammelled brilliance on the field of play.

| | |
|---|---|
| **GLENN HODDLE** | |
| BORN: | Hayes, Middlesex, 27 October 1957. |
| HONOURS: | FA Cup 80/1, 81/2. 53 England caps (79-88). |
| OTHER CLUBS: | Monaco, France, 87/8-90/1 (87, 30); Swindon Town 91/2-92/3 (65, 1); Chelsea 93/4- 94/5 (31, 1). |
| MANAGER: | Swindon Town (91-93); Chelsea (93-96); England (96-99); Southampton (00-01); Tottenham Hotspur (01-03); Wolverhampton Wanderers (04-06). |

| | |
|---|---|
| GAMES | **480 (12)** |
| GOALS | **110** |

# CLIVE ALLEN

## 1984/85 → 1987/88

It was like a record with only one groove: 'And the first goal for Spurs was scored by number seven, Clive Allen!' In 1986/87, the striker's season of supreme grace, those words became a gloriously monotonous refrain from White Hart Lane announcer Willie Morgan, its inevitability reflecting the fans' confidence in their prolific hero. Quite simply, whenever Allen had a chance they expected him to hit the target and if he missed they were genuinely shocked. That term he netted 49 times in 54 appearances, including two as substitute, shattering Jimmy Greaves' club record for a single campaign that had stood for nigh-on quarter of a century and which, in the modern era of blanket defence, had appeared certain to remain inviolate.

In fact, without emulating the great Jimmy's all-round brilliance – no out-and-out goal merchant since the Second World War has done that – Allen did possess certain Greaves-like characteristics. There was the instinct for taking up dangerous positions, the knack of twisting his body to shoot for goal no matter how awkwardly the ball fell, the ability to wrong-foot defenders with a single touch before turning in the tightest of spaces, and the accuracy of his finish, frequently with a firm sidefoot. There was also utter single-mindedness and a voracious edge that kept him sharp to the end of every match, no matter how many chances he might have squandered earlier – witness two hat-tricks, both plundered in the last ten minutes, against West Ham and Norwich in early 1987.

Clive, it seemed, had been put on this earth to score goals. The son of Les Allen, a leading marksman for Tottenham's revered League and FA Cup double-winning side, and nephew of Reading forward Dennis, he had absorbed soccer lore throughout his upbringing and made it tell from the moment he turned professional. He arrived at the Lane in August 1984, a £700,000 purchase from Queen's Park Rangers, a few weeks after winning his first full cap.

In contrast to his decidedly lacklustre international form, Allen's two-goal Spurs debut at Goodison installed him as an instant fans' favourite and he linked pleasingly with Mark Falco as Peter Shreeves' team topped the table that autumn. It was a heady period but it was not to last: that December Allen picked up a debilitating groin injury which was to keep him on the sidelines for a year. On his return, not surprisingly, he was slow to regain his momentum, and it was not until the spring of 1986 that the goals began to flow once more.

That, of course, was the prelude to Allen's Golden Season, which started fruitfully enough, then grew ever more bountiful after new manager David Pleat's November decision to play Clive as a lone raider in front of a five-man midfield. Revelling in the consequent space and helped by confusion among opponents uncertain about whom to mark, he capitalised ruthlessly on exceptional service from Messrs Hoddle, Waddle and Co, and the one regret come May – despite the personal consolation of the two major player of the year awards – was that Tottenham had no trophy to show for so much exciting football. Third in the League and losing semi-finalists in the League Cup, they had appeared on course to lift the FA Cup after Allen's near-post header had given them a second-minute Wembley lead, only for Coventry to fight back and deny them.

Nevertheless, 1987/88 dawned full of promise, only to prove traumatically anti-climactic. Allen, no doubt hindered by over-inflated expectations, struggled to find the net and at season's end, with the club sliding ever deeper into off-the-field travail, he accepted a £1 million transfer to Bordeaux.

A year later he was back in England, serving three clubs in as many seasons, playing well but with the game's peaks drifting ever more surely beyond his reach. It can be argued that, somehow, Clive Allen never achieved all that might have been expected of a man with his fabulous gift. But this much is sure: it will take one very fine striker to erase his name from the Spurs record books.

| | |
|---|---|
| **CLIVE DARREN ALLEN** | |
| BORN: | Stepney, London, 20 May 1961. |
| HONOURS: | 5 England caps (84-88). FWA Footballer of the Year 87. PFA Footballer of the Year 87. |
| OTHER CLUBS: | Queen's Park Rangers 78/9-79/80 (49, 32); Arsenal, 1980, no games; Crystal Palace 80/1 (25, 9); Queen's Park Rangers 81/2-83/4 (87, 40); Bordeaux, France, 87/8-88/9 (19, 13); Manchester City 89/90-91/2 (53, 16); Chelsea 91/2 (16, 7); West Ham United 91/2-93/4 (38, 17); Millwall 93/4 (12, 0); Carlisle United 95/6 (3, 0). |

| | |
|---|---|
| GAMES | **124 (11)** |
| GOALS | **84** |

# JOHNNY METGOD

## 1987/88

When Glenn Hoddle left White Hart Lane in the summer of 1987, Spurs needed a thoroughbred to fill the creative void in central midfield, and who could have seemed better qualified than a man who had operated in that role for those high priests of flair football, Real Madrid? Thus David Pleat paid Nottingham Forest £250,000 for Johnny Metgod and Spurs fans were anticipating eagerly the cultured passing for which the elegant Dutchman was renowned, while positively slavering over the prospect of his spectacular speciality, the dead-ball blast that created the optical illusion of gathering pace in flight.

The first surprise came when Metgod spent much of the season's opening game on the bench, and puzzlement increased when he made only three senior starts that autumn. But worse was to follow for the tall, balding play-maker, as Pleat departed and new boss Terry Venables' team selection made it clear that he was surplus to requirements.

With his chances further hampered by injury, a move seemed inevitable and after returning to senior duty for the last four games of the season, Metgod joined Feyenoord for £175,000. Back in Holland, he specialised as a sweeper and it was in that position that he helped his countrymen remove Spurs from the European Cup Winners' Cup in 1991/92.

**JOHANNES ANTONIUS BERNARDUS METGOD**
**BORN:** Amsterdam, Holland, 27 February 1958.
**HONOURS:** 21 Holland caps (78-83).
**OTHER CLUBS:** DWS Amsterdam; Haarlem 75/6 (32, 1); AZ 67 Alkmaar 76/7-81/2 (195, 26), all Holland; Real Madrid, Spain, 82/3-83/4 (49, 1); Nottingham Forest 84/5-86/7 (118, 15); Feyenoord, Holland, 88/9-93/4 (164, 13).
**HONOURS:** Excelsior Rotterdam (96-97 and 04-05); Feyenoord (caretaker 97).

| | |
|---|---|
| GAMES | **7 (7)** |
| GOALS | **0** |

---

# NICO CLAESEN

## 1986/87 → 1987/88

Terrace opinion was sharply divided on the merits of Nico Claesen. There were those who reckoned the Belgian striker never fitted comfortably into English football, while others maintained that his industry, speed and a strike rate that was highly respectable for a man still settling in a foreign country might have qualified him for an extended stay.

He arrived in October 1986, a £600,000 acquisition from Standard Liege, having enhanced his reputation hugely in that summer's World Cup finals. Elusive to mark and with a strength that belied his lack of inches, he was used, at first, as a conventional front-runner alongside Clive Allen, impressing on his debut in a 1-0 win at Anfield. But soon David Pleat experimented with tactics and Claesen suffered as a somewhat fitful member of the five-man midfield which served the Londoner so well.

When he was dropped periodically, he was unhappy and it showed – omission from the 1987 FA Cup Final starting line-up caused the deepest hurt – yet he shouldered his burden manfully and in 1987/88, back in his favoured forward role, he all but matched Allen's tally for that season despite playing far fewer games. However, new boss Terry Venables, struggling to stabilise a Spurs boat that was rocking alarmingly, preferred other options, and in August 1988 Claesen returned to his homeland, joining Antwerp for £550,000.

**NICOLAS PIETER JOSEF CLAESEN**
**BORN:** Leut, Belgium, 1 October 1962.
**HONOURS:** 36 Belgium caps (83-90).
**OTHER CLUBS:** Patro Eisden and Seresien, Belgium; Stuttgart, Germany, 83/4-84/5; Standard Liege, Belgium, 85/6-86/7; Antwerp, Belgium.

| | |
|---|---|
| GAMES | **45 (18)** |
| GOALS | **23** |

# STEVE HODGE

### 1986/87 → 1987/88

The Spurs career of Steve Hodge caught fire in his first game but flickered only fleetingly thereafter, the flame soon to subside in dismal anti-climax. After the left-sided midfielder's admirable efforts for England in the 1986 World Cup finals, it seemed that David Pleat could congratulate himself for persuading Aston Villa to part with the skilful 24-year-old for £650,000 the following December. That impression was strengthened by his Boxing Day debut at home to West Ham in which he scored one fine goal and set up another. But after a two-goal flourish against his former club in January, and despite another brace against Watford in that term's FA Cup semi-final, he lost his way.

Blessed with boundless vitality and an insatiable desire to get forward, while not ignoring defensive chores, Hodge seemed always to be about some urgent mission, and his incisive incursions into opposing penalty areas should have added a new dimension to Spurs' attack.

But too often he scurried to little effect, rarely making optimum use of his lovely left-foot touch or supplying the lethal whipped crosses for which he was known. His disappointing form was linked, almost certainly, to his disenchantment with London life, and it was no surprise in August 1988 when he rejoined his first club, Nottingham Forest, for £550,000.

**STEPHEN BRIAN HODGE**
**BORN:** Nottingham, 25 October 1962.
**HONOURS:** 24 England caps (86-91).
**OTHER CLUBS:** Nottingham Forest 81/2-85/6 (123, 30); Aston Villa 85/6-86/7 (53, 12); Nottingham Forest 88/9-90/1 (82, 20); Leeds United 91/2-93/4 (54, 10); Derby County on loan 94/5 (10, 2); Queen's Park Rangers 94/5 (15, 0); Watford 95/6 (2, 0); Leyton Orient 97/8 (1, 0).

| GAMES | 53 (1) |
|-------|--------|
| GOALS | 9 |

# BOBBY MIMMS

### 1987/88 → 1989/90

Poor Bobby Mimms! No professional footballer, indeed no human being, should be forced to endure public ridicule of the nature and degree heaped upon his head after Terry Venables drafted in the England under-21 goalkeeper to help stabilise Spurs' jittery defence in February 1988. For three games after his £375,000 move from Everton, all went well. But then he conceded a soft goal to Arsenal's Alan Smith at Highbury, several more errors followed and for the rest of the season he was pilloried mercilessly by press and fans alike.

The early months of 1988/89 brought no respite for Mimms, whose confidence had reached a low ebb. Though technically a sound all-rounder, he was now failing to dominate his six-yard box, let alone his penalty area, and suffered some horrible afternoons, notably during the home defeat by Derby in November.

Despite the mounting pressure, raised a notch or two by the arrival of Erik Thorstvedt, Mimms kept a succession of clean sheets in December and might have been turning the corner, but then came a shock FA Cup exit at Bradford and the axe descended. Thereafter the Yorkshireman remained a reserve until December 1990 when a £250,000 transfer took him to Blackburn, where there awaited a deserved and commendable renaissance.

**ROBERT ANDREW MIMMS**
**BORN:** York, 12 October 1963.
**OTHER CLUBS:** Rotherham United 81/2-84/5 (83, 0); Everton 85/6-87/8 (29, 0); Notts County on loan 85/6 (2, 0); Sunderland on loan 86/7 (4, 0); Blackburn Rovers on loan 86/7 (6, 0); Manchester City on loan 87/8 (3, 0); Aberdeen on loan 89/90 (6, 0); Blackburn Rovers 90/1-95/6 (128, 0); Crystal Palace 96/7 (1, 0); Preston North End 96/7 (27, 0); Rotherham United 97/8 (43, 0); York City 98/9-99/00 (63, 0); Mansfield Town 99/00-00/01 (45, 0).

| GAMES | 44 |
|-------|-----|
| GOALS | 0 |

# CHRIS WADDLE

## 1985/86 → 1988/89

To Tottenham Hotspur fans in the late 1980s fell the joy and the privilege of watching Chris Waddle mature from an exciting but wayward talent into one of the world's most accomplished forwards. Yet back in the autumn of 1985, that progress seemed anything but inevitable. Slouching diffidently, almost forlornly, on the fringe of the action, like some gauche farmhand longing for the end of an exhausting day in the fields, Waddle cut an unlikely figure for a soccer hero. Even when he received a pass, the image of ungainliness persisted for a moment as he crouched wanly over the ball. But then a sloping shoulder would drop still further, the long, lean body would sway beguilingly before gathering pace, and he would be gone.

On a good day defenders would fall away from him like chaff before the wind as he cut a swathe through their ranks; on a bad one he would disappear into some blind alley, there to be mugged, robbed and left wearing an expression of confusion. Contrast that with the confident, pulsating performer of 1988/89; now the ball came to him as a friend, a plaything, the instrument of his art, and in his use of it Chris Waddle became a genuine star.

The shy north-easterner, who had worked in a sausage-seasoning factory before winning England caps with Newcastle United, had made a telling impact during the Magpies' first season back in the top flight when he joined Spurs in July 1985. Immediately he set about repaying his fee – £590,000, set by a transfer tribunal – with two headed goals on his debut at home to Watford, but then came that exasperating patch as he struggled to build self-belief.

Come 1986/87 there were encouraging signs of consistency, and new manager David Pleat deserved credit for switching Waddle from his original beat, on his natural left side and in the centre, to the right flank. From that new location he would cut inside to devastating effect, or roam free, creating havoc with his adhesive skills and intelligent distribution.

It was, perhaps, in November 1986 at Oxford – where he scored twice, including a delicate curler after a delicious dribble – that the supporters accepted their gifted gangler as something special, and his verve was demonstrated to a wider audience in that term's FA Cup Final. Just two minutes into the game, his extravagant body-swerve wrong-footed a line of Coventry defenders before he crossed for Clive Allen to open the scoring in a match that was to end in such bitter disappointment.

Alas, there was further frustration lying in wait, for the player himself and for a side sorely in need of inspiration following the departure of Glenn Hoddle. Waddle spent much of 1987/88 sidelined with heel and hernia problems but, happily, it was a prelude to pure gold. In 1988/89, he contributed what was arguably the most scintillating season of football by a Spurs player that decade, finally realising his full potential, becoming the team's fulcrum and accordingly being crowned by fans as the new 'King' of White Hart Lane.

Some of his goals are etched indelibly on thousands of memories: the tight-angled drive after a surging run at home to Norwich in February, the 35-yard chip in the cloying mud at Southampton four days later, and the brilliant brace against Aston Villa that brought the Lane to its feet in March. Often it seemed that no one could take the ball from him, and as well as topping the goal chart with 14 strikes he created countless chances for others.

Picture then the utter consternation among the fans when, that July, he moved to Marseille for £4.25 million. It is said that, desperately though they needed the cash, Spurs left the decision to Waddle; he accepted the opportunity, overcame similar (but less protracted) problems of adjustment to those encountered at first in London, and went on to heady achievement in France before returning to England with Sheffield Wednesday. What if he had stayed at the Lane with Messrs Gascoigne and Lineker? Well, it's conceivable that Spurs might have been the most beautiful-to-watch bankrupts British football has ever seen . . .

**CHRISTOPHER ROLAND WADDLE**

| | | |
|---|---|---|
| **BORN:** | Felling, County Durham, 14 December 1960. | |
| **HONOURS:** | 62 England caps (85-91). FWA Footballer of the Year 93. | |
| **OTHER CLUBS:** | Newcastle United 80/1-84/5 (170, 46); Marseille, France, 88/9-91/2 (107, 22); Sheffield Wednesday 92/3-95/6 (109, 10); Falkirk 96/7 (4, 1); Bradford City 96/7 (25, 6); Sunderland 96/7 (7, 1); Burnley 97/8 (31, 1); Torquay United 98/9 (7, 0). | **GAMES** 172 (1) |
| **MANAGER:** | Burnley (97-98). | **GOALS** 42 |

# VINNY SAMWAYS

## 1986/87 → 1993/94

The pinched, sallow features still wore that characteristic expression of startled anxiety, the shoulders remained slightly hunched as if bearing some enormous burden, but the furrowed brows of bewildered opponents revealed an infinitely more telling story. Yes, in the spring of 1993, after years of flattering to deceive, the lovely play-making talents of Vinny Samways appeared to be approaching full bloom. Alas, it was not to be.

As a teenager, the skilful Londoner had excited rare anticipation among the White Hart Lane cognoscenti. Then skipper of Spurs reserves, he had shone in the Football Combination and exhibited such total command over the ball that he was slated for a starry future.

Duly Samways enjoyed his first settled sequence the following term, which confirmed the exquisite class of his passing, the sureness of his touch and the subtlety of his thinking, and he was accorded the status of an uncut jewel. In 1988/89, however, progress was expected at a more rapid rate than he managed, and it may be that he did not benefit from the all-enveloping midfield presence of new arrival Paul Gascoigne.

Thereafter Samways, already honoured by England at under-21 level, tended to float on the periphery, showing flashes of delightful insight but irritating fans by dallying. Often, too, he would take the safe option, acquiring for his pains the terrace tag of Vinny Sideways.

Come 1990/91 there was talk of a transfer, but then he dazzled in the FA Cup semi-final and final triumphs, against Arsenal and Nottingham Forest respectively, and he was expected to flourish in Gascoigne's absence. Instead Samways floundered, and after his delicate gifts were omitted from the side when pitches became heavy the following term, the spectre of eventual failure grew agonisingly real.

Then 1992/93 brought renewed hope. Roaming at will behind the front men, he ceased merely making pretty patterns and began consistently to lacerate defences with penetrating distribution. But though inspirational in bursts during 1993/94, Vinny Samways plateaued and joined Everton for £2.2 million in the summer. Sadly, Goodison Park was to prove the premature graveyard of an English top-flight career which had once promised so much.

| | |
|---|---|
| **VINCENT SAMWAYS** | |
| **BORN:** | Bethnal Green, London, 27 October 1968. |
| **HONOURS:** | FA Cup 90/1. |
| **OTHER CLUBS:** | Everton 94/5-95/6 (23, 2); Wolverhampton Wanderers on loan 95/6 (3, 0); Birmingham City on loan 95/6 (12, 0); Las Palmas 96/7-01/02 (160, 6); Sevilla 02/03 (10, 0), both Spain; Walsall 02/03-03/04 (42, 2); Algeciras, Spain, 04/05 (18, 1). |

GAMES **213 (33)**

GOALS **18**

# BRIAN STATHAM

### 1987/88 → 1988/89

When Tottenham's turbulent, sometimes desperate 1987/88 campaign was reviewed, there were precious few causes for satisfaction, but one, it seemed, was the emergence of young Brian Statham. After making his debut as a substitute at Southampton on Boxing Day, the African-born right-back won a regular place in February and retained it in some style until season's end, when he was rewarded with an England under-21 call-up.

Neat, quick and skilful, Statham looked a fair bet to settle in as long-term successor to Danny Thomas, and he began 1988/89 in firm possession of Spurs' number-two shirt. But though he was not conspicuously poor, his form had declined and after six games, with the rearguard as a whole looking increasingly insecure, he was replaced by Gary Stevens.

Surprisingly in view of his earlier success, Statham never played another game for Spurs in major competition, a combination of injury and the club's plethora of defenders keeping him in the background for more than three years. His luck changed finally when Phil Holder took him on loan to Brentford in February 1992 and he helped the Bees win the Third Division title. A £70,000 transfer followed and Statham consolidated in the new First Division, forging an impressively consistent full-back partnership with former Tottenham team-mate Chris Hughton.

**BRIAN STATHAM**
BORN: Harare, Zimbabwe, 21 May 1969.
OTHER CLUBS: Reading on loan 90/1 (8, 0); Bournemouth on loan 91/2 (2, 0); Brentford 91/2-96/7 (166, 10); Gillingham 97/8 (20, 0).

GAMES 22 (5)
GOALS 0

---

# CHRIS FAIRCLOUGH

### 1987/88 → 1988/89

Nottingham Forest fans saw it in the mid-1980s, supporters of Leeds United came to swear by it, but in between at White Hart Lane, it was a vexingly elusive commodity. We're talking here about the best form of Chris Fairclough, an England under-21 centre-half who had long been coveted by Tottenham when he was signed by David Pleat in the summer of 1987. The transfer – a tribunal set the fee at £387,500 – mystified observers who saw no need to improve on the Gough-Mabbutt partnership, though the confusion was quick to lift as the Scot departed that October.

Fairclough was never an abject failure, rather something of a disappointment in view of his apparently vast potential. Brave and a superb athlete, he was extremely quick, competent on the ball and good in the air when well placed for headers. But there was the rub: his positioning within the Spurs defensive framework was at fault too often for comfort.

Nevertheless, Fairclough was ever-present throughout Tottenham's troubled 1987/88 campaign, but after unconvincing performances the following term, he joined Leeds on loan in March, a £500,000 cheque later making the move permanent. At Elland Road he rediscovered his touch, and was outstanding as his new team lifted the title in 1992. Later he excelled for Bolton, too, all of which was great for Chris Fairclough, galling for Spurs.

**COURTNEY HUW FAIRCLOUGH**
BORN: Nottingham, 12 April 1964.
OTHER CLUBS: Nottingham Forest 82/3-86/7 (107, 1); Leeds United 88/9-94/5 (193, 21); Bolton Wanderers 95/6-97/8 (90, 8); Notts County 98/9 (16, 1); York City 98/9-99/00 (37, 0).

GAMES 70
GOALS 5

# GARY STEVENS

## 1983/84 → 1989/90

Tottenham fans who reckoned they knew a high-class footballer when they saw one were questioning their own judgement in the autumn of 1983. Just a few months earlier they had eulogised the FA Cup Final performance of Brighton's Gary Stevens, whose late equaliser had forced Manchester United to a Wembley replay, and had been overjoyed when Keith Burkinshaw had paid £300,000 for the 21-year-old central defender during the summer. But when understandable initial nervousness in the famous white shirt showed scant sign of abating, terrace indulgence was quick to evaporate and was replaced by something distressingly close to verbal bullying.

At this crucial juncture, with his expensive acquisition's confidence in tatters, the manager acted decisively by switching him to midfield, producing a marked improvement in form. That term Stevens impressed in the latter stages of the successful UEFA Cup campaign, and by 1984/85 he was a revelation. Adopting the role of general factotum to the play-makers, he exerted such an influence, albeit unobtrusive, that by October he had won his first England cap.

Stevens did the simple things well, tackling firmly and passing safely, and though he looked rather stiff and unimaginative on the ball, that hardly mattered alongside the likes of Glenn Hoddle or Mike Hazard. Indeed, there are shrewd observers who trace the first real cracks in Tottenham's title campaign to the moment that March when damaged knee ligaments ended Gary's season.

Thereafter the Stevens career was plagued by injury, notably a broken shoulder sustained in an aerial challenge with Wimbledon's John Fashanu in November 1986 and further severe knee trouble, which dated from a notorious challenge by Vinny Jones some two years later. On his return Stevens served at right-back but never became fully re-established and in March 1990 he was sold to Portsmouth for £250,000. Sadly, despite dedicated effort, fitness remained elusive and in 1991 he was forced to retire, staying close to the game as a media pundit.

**GARY ANDREW STEVENS**

| | |
|---|---|
| BORN: | Hillingdon, Middlesex, 30 March 1962. |
| HONOURS: | UEFA Cup 83/4. 7 England caps (84-86). |
| OTHER CLUBS: | Brighton 79/80-82/3 (133, 2); Portsmouth 89/90-90/1 (52, 3). |

GAMES **187 (13)**
GOALS **9**

# MITCHELL THOMAS

## 1986/87 → 1990/91

When David Pleat secured the services of Mitchell Thomas from Luton Town, his own former club, in the summer of 1986, it seemed that he had signed an outstanding prospect for a bargain fee. The Hatters had wanted £500,000 for their flamboyant England under-21 international left-back, but the new Spurs boss couldn't agree and a tribunal cut the asking price by half. The long term was to suggest this was a wise decision.

Yet Thomas' form during his first season at White Hart Lane tended to support Luton's case. At that time reassuringly sound at the back, he was an ebullient attacker who belied his 6ft stature by fluid dribbles and high-speed dashes that could leave opponents in a heap. This enterprising start was marred slightly by his unsuccessful attempt to cope with Coventry's Dave Bennett in the FA Cup Final, but majority opinion saw this as an isolated off-day.

Thereafter Thomas continued competently enough until, with Terry Venables now in charge, he was given opportunities in midfield. Strong and skilful, at times he appeared well equipped for the work but performed inconsistently, and occasionally with a certain eccentricity that earned him the terrace status of a minor cult figure.

In the end his contribution was not enough and, as he switched back and forth between roles, his standing as a first-team regular became eroded. The best and worst of Mitchell Thomas were illustrated in two home games during autumn 1988: against Manchester United he won a tackle outside his own area before splitting the Reds' rearguard with an incisive crossfield pass to Chris Waddle, who scored; then, faced by Derby's Ted McMinn, he was given a chasing and faulted for two goals.

Inexplicably, as time went by the Thomas defensive technique appeared less reliable, his positional play provoking particular unease, and when West Ham proffered a £500,000 cheque in August 1991, it was in the best interests of all concerned that he sought a fresh start. However, it was not until a subsequent return to his Kenilworth Road roots that Mitchell regained his best form.

**MITCHELL ANTHONY THOMAS**
BORN: Luton, Bedfordshire, 2 October 1964.
OTHER CLUBS: Luton Town 82/3-85/6 (107, 1); West Ham United 91/2-92/3 (38, 3); Luton Town 93/4-98/9 (185, 5); Burnley 99/00-01/02 (99, 0).

| GAMES | 176 (22) |
| --- | --- |
| GOALS | 8 |

# PAUL ALLEN

· · · · · · · · · · · · · · · · · · · · · · · · · · · · · · · ·

## 1985/86 → 1993/94

Those who revel in graphs with zigzag lines depicting peaks and troughs would be less than fascinated by a diagram illustrating the level of Paul Allen's performances in the late 1980s and early 1990s. It would consist of little more than one straight line, a horizontal testimony to the diminutive midfielder's quite staggering consistency.

Though public accolades were sparse for an unspectacular contributor to the Tottenham cause, there was no doubt about his worth among football insiders; to them Allen was the perfect professional, an archetypal players' player. Traditionalists who would decry the fact that his habitual role, ferrying up and down the right flank, might have been filled in days of yore by a tricksy (but unpredictable) winger should not address their criticism to Allen, but to the modern game itself, of which he was a typical product.

Not that the third member of the footballing Allen family to play for Spurs – he was preceded at White Hart Lane by his uncle, Les, and cousin, Clive – was denied his share of the media spotlight. His profile was high, indeed, as a rookie at West Ham in 1980 when, aged 17 years and 256 days, he became the youngest player in a Wembley FA Cup Final.

Paul acquitted himself creditably as the Hammers beat Arsenal, receiving special attention as the victim of a cynical foul by Willie Young, and was hailed as a star of the future. Come the summer of 1985, by which time he had added England under-21 honours to his record 23 youth caps, both Liverpool and Arsenal were in the hunt for his signature, but a £400,000 fee, decided by a transfer tribunal, took him to Tottenham.

Initially all went well, Allen performing effervescently and scoring on his debut at home to Watford, but soon his form dipped as he strove to fit into the Spurs set-up. Then, just as he showed signs of attaining the regular degree of excellence that was to become his hallmark, he was shaken by anxiety about his daughter's health. Eventually she recovered, Allen's relief was evident in his ever-growing confidence on the pitch and thereafter he proved, almost invariably, a welcome beacon of reliability in a mercurial, frequently-changing side.

Even so, when big transfer targets were in the wind, such an unshowy individual could appear dispensable and in 1989 manager Terry Venables accepted a £700,000 bid from Millwall. But Allen, though temporarily out of favour, opted to stay and lost no time in regaining his place, going on to play arguably the most effective football of his career over the next three seasons.

The Allen game was based on tireless running, gutsy determination in his challenges and shrewd positional play, but while he was not the man to lay waste to defences with Hoddlesque distribution, no one could belittle his all-round technique, which improved steadily with experience. A modest character, ever willing to learn, Paul was versatile, too, capable of forsaking his usual right-sided role to become a driving force in central midfield, switching to the left to accommodate less adaptable colleagues or even filling in competently at full-back.

His touch and intelligence were never demonstrated more effectively than in the 1991 FA Cup semi-final victory over Arsenal, when he combined sweetly with Paul Gascoigne to set up the second goal for Gary Lineker, and in the final, when his incisive run paved the way for Paul Stewart's equaliser. Equally, when the tide was flowing against Spurs, Allen could be a heart-lifting figure, sprinting defiantly into enemy territory, searching for an opening when all seemed lost.

Then there was his pride, in himself and his club, so evident when the absence of Gary Mabbutt and Neil Ruddock elevated him to captain at home to Everton in September 1992. Typically, he responded with a spirited display and a goal to underline yet again that, although he was approaching the veteran stage, replacing him would be no mere formality. As Tottenham struggled to avoid relegation in the campaign following Paul Allen's £550,000 move to Southampton in September 1993, that much was vividly evident.

**PAUL KEVIN ALLEN**

**BORN:** Aveley, Essex, 28 August 1962.
**HONOURS:** FA Cup 90/1.
**OTHER CLUBS:** West Ham United 79/80-84/5 (152, 6); Southampton 93/4-94/5 (43, 1); Luton Town on loan 94/5 (4, 0); Stoke City on loan 94/5 (17, 1); Swindon Town 95/6-96/7 (37, 1); Bristol City 96/7 (14, 0); Millwall 97/8 (28, 0).

GAMES 351 (20)
GOALS 28

# TERRY FENWICK

## 1987/88 → 1992/93

Some footballers are cherished by fans in the manner of chosen sons, basking in favour even when playing like drains; others are eternal scapegoats, cast out as pariahs without hope of redemption. Not even the most casual visitor to the Lane could harbour doubts into which category Terry Fenwick fell. The game was given away not so much by the barrage of derision that greeted any mistake by the north-easterner, more the knowing groans from sizeable sections of the Tottenham 'faithful' even when he was performing well.

Of course, it was unfair; 'Fen' was competent enough most of the time. Certainly, Terry Venables thought so, having managed him at Crystal Palace and Queen's Park Rangers, then paid £550,000 in December 1987 to make the versatile 28-year-old England defender his first major Spurs signing.

At the time, morale was low in a struggling side, and the Fenwick brief was to bring steel and method to a slack rearguard. But work rate, professionalism and presentable technique could not disguise lack of pace, a tendency to stray out of position and tackling that could be crude.

Starting at centre-half, he never looked the part and soon he was subjected to barracking, with some critics using him, maybe, as a surrogate aunt sally for Venables. True, he embodied the backs-to-the-wall spirit needed in Spurs' current plight, but the point was that, even in the medium term, the fans didn't want a team with its back to the wall.

Later Fenwick, whose vocal imprecations to colleagues when he was playing badly himself sat ill with many observers, though not with his manager, performed more ably as sweeper and then right-back, but anonymously in occasional midfield outings.

His strength of character was evident in the way he ignored the abuse, as it was in coming back after injuries, including a broken leg and a broken ankle, and a spell in prison for drink-driving. Come September 1993, his Tottenham day was done and he was freed to join Swindon Town. But as his former team-mates discovered to their cost, with 'Fen' gone, there was a lot of terrace vitriol going spare . . .

**TERENCE WILLIAM FENWICK**
BORN: Seaham, County Durham, 17 November 1959.
HONOURS: 20 England caps (84-88).
OTHER CLUBS: Crystal Palace 77/8-80/1 (70, 0); Queen's Park Rangers 80/1-87/8 (256, 33); Leicester City on loan 90/1 (8, 1); Swindon Town 93/4-94/5 (28, 0).
MANAGER: Portsmouth (95-98); Northampton Town (03); San Juan Jabloteh, Trinidad and Tobago.

GAMES **116 (3)**
GOALS **10**

# JOHN POLSTON

## 1986/87 → 1989/90

There was widespread disenchantment among Tottenham fans when 22-year-old central defender John Polston was sold to Norwich City in July 1990. The general feeling was that the blond Londoner was exactly the type of poised, stylish operator around whom the club's future should be built. The grievance was fuelled by the identity of Polston's new employers – the success at Carrow Road of Ian Crook, Ian Culverhouse and Mark Bowen had already caused considerable discontent, albeit mostly retrospective – and also by the apparent folly of dispensing with a promising, home-grown youngster when transfer cash was in such short supply.

In fact, Spurs' financial plight was probably a major factor in the deal, any injection of funds being welcome at the time, though the board were considerably miffed when a tribunal fixed the fee at only £300,000. In further mitigation of the sale, it's true that Polston, like the unchangingly excellent Gary Mabbutt, was at his best alongside a stopper. However, the skill and composure he revealed during a sequence of outings in early 1990 had convinced supporters of the Polston pedigree, and certainly his conception and execution of a goal at home to Charlton, which featured a flowing, end-to-end passing movement, supported their view. During 1992/93, when John was a bulwark in the Canaries' bold bid for the Championship, recriminations at the Lane became bitter, indeed.

**JOHN DAVID POLSTON**
BORN: Walthamstow, London, 10 June 1968.
OTHER CLUBS: Norwich City 90/1-97/8 (214, 8).

| | |
|---|---|
| GAMES | 20 (8) |
| GOALS | 1 |

# GUY BUTTERS

## 1988/98 → 1989/90

Guy Butters brought a gust of bracing fresh air to Spurs' back line when he was drafted in as a third centre-half in November 1988. No matter that he conceded an unlucky own-goal on his senior debut in a League Cup replay at Blackburn, the 19-year-old stopper's uncomplicated, uncompromising approach gave the rearguard a solidity which previously had been sadly lacking. Standing 6ft 3in, fearsomely strong and with limitless heart, Butters dominated in the air and tore into tackles with the minimum of ceremony.

As a bonus, in his first League game he balanced his goal account with a powerful header at home to Wimbledon, but more importantly, he defended with a consistency that eluded some of his senior colleagues and retained his place deservedly until the end of the season.

Alas, the following term Butters looked a different player. After a succession of poor displays, culminating in a veritable stinker at Villa Park, he was left out to regain confidence, only to perform equally shakily on his return. In happier economic times, Tottenham might have been content to allow such a promising youngster to develop further in the reserves, but with cash at a premium and with Portsmouth offering £325,000, Butters headed south in September 1990.

**GUY BUTTERS**
BORN: Hillingdon, Middlesex, 30 October 1969.
OTHER CLUBS: Southend United on loan 89/90 (16, 3); Portsmouth 90/1-96/7 (154, 6); Oxford United on loan 94/5 (3, 1); Gillingham 96/7-01/02 (159, 16); Brighton 02/03- (187, 8).

| | |
|---|---|
| GAMES | 37 (2) |
| GOALS | 1 |

# PAUL GASCOIGNE

## 1988/89 → 1990/91

Volatile and hyperactive, maniacally intense, even quite ludicrous at times – no, not Gazza, just a humble writer pondering how to do some sort of justice to the rarest, most enthralling British talent of a footballing generation. Of course, all the above conditions have been ascribed to our hero at various junctures, and with every justification, but what mattered most, all that really counted for the fans, was the spellbinding brilliance that flowed from Paul Gascoigne when the ball was at his feet.

But what was it that made this garrulous, excessive north-easterner of simple tastes and boundless insecurities, for whom Tottenham cheerfully wrote a £2 million cheque to Newcastle in July 1988, so different from the rest? When on parade in all his splendour, his passing and vision could make the heart sing, his free-kicks could be savage or subtle but invariably sensational, he was strong, enthusiastic and was not afraid of hard work.

But it was none of these things. No, Gascoigne's uniqueness, the entire ethos of his game in its pomp, was based on his mastery of the dying art of dribbling. During those three tempestuous but enchanting seasons with the Spurs cockerel carried proudly on his barrel chest, his surges from midfield that left a trail of bewildered defenders in his wake became as much a trademark as the Gazza nickname. When the Muse was with him, he could outwit opponents at will: now swerving past regally, keeping them at a distance as though refusing to admit mere commoners to his presence; next moving in tantalisingly close, before the toes twinkled, the ball was switched this way and that, and he was gone.

A telling microcosm of the Paul Gascoigne phenomenon was afforded by the 1991 FA Cup campaign, by which time his World Cup tears – whether they were shed in patriotism or in self-pity (or both) became irrelevant – had enshrined him as a media plaything more marketable than any personality British sport had yet known. Considering the inordinate pressure thus created, his contribution was astounding, and though it ignored the admirable tenet that football is a team game, for once it felt right to assert that one man took his side to the final.

After playing a merely mortal role in the third-round victory over Blackpool, the once-portly play-maker – the roll of fat had receded since his Spurs debut, when Newcastle fans had pelted him with *Mars* bars – ascended to a more celestial plane. Against Oxford in the fourth and Portsmouth in the fifth, his extravagant skills and clinical finishing claimed the spoils; by failing to clear his lines at home to Notts County in the quarter-final he offered the opening from which the visitors went ahead, before destroying them with a perfectly judged late strike – and all this while carrying a groin injury that was to need an operation before the semi-final. Come that glorious day, Gascoigne excelled even himself, giving Tottenham a fifth-minute lead over Arsenal with a 30-yard free-kick of awesome velocity that was to take its place in Wembley folklore, playing an inspired part in the second goal and generally holding centre stage.

And so to Gazza's blackest sporting hour, the final against Nottingham Forest. Carrying an impossible burden of expectation, he made a fool of himself in front of the world, being lucky to escape dismissal for one early challenge, then crippling himself with a second wild tackle.

He was stretchered away in discredit, a victim of self-destruction, and even as Spurs won the Cup their very future was in doubt, so desperately did they need the £8.5 million that Lazio had agreed to pay for Gascoigne. It's history now that after taking a year to recover, he moved for £5 million, showed the Italians what he could do, then lit up the Scottish scene with Rangers and re-emerged as one of England's premier hopes for international glory before embarking gradually on a debilitating downward spiral in his personal affairs.

Off the pitch he has been, by turns, funny, gross, endearing, petulant, almost always over the top, a tantalising cocktail of coruscating talent and banal boorishness. As tales of his creeping depression, his alcoholism and various other crippling problems have been broadcast, he has become enveloped in a cloak of impending tragedy – and we're talking here about the genuine human variety, not the contemptibly glib sporting version bandied so mindlessly in sections of the media.

But it is for his football that we want to preserve and cherish his image in our minds, and although at the time of writing his attempts to manage or coach have petered out in pathos, how uplifting it would be if a redemptive niche could be found for him, so that even yet he could be a major force for good in the game which he adores. May what is left of his life, and he only turned 40 in the spring of 2007, be sullied as little as is realistically possible by further controversy and the commercial machine. To hell with the hype and the money men; to the fan in the stand, Paul Gascoigne was a player beyond price.

| | |
|---|---|
| **PAUL JOHN GASCOIGNE** | |
| **BORN:** | Gateshead, County Durham, 27 May 1967. |
| **HONOURS:** | FA Cup 90/1. 57 England caps (88-98). |
| **OTHER CLUBS:** | Newcastle United 84/5-87/8 (92, 21); Lazio, Italy, 92/3-94/5 (41, 6); Glasgow Rangers 95/6-97/8 (74, 30); Middlesbrough 97/8-99/00 (41, 4); Everton 00/01-01/02 (32, 1); Burnley 01/02 (6, 0); Gansu Tianma, China, 03; Boston United 04/05 (4, 0). |

| | |
|---|---|
| GAMES | **110 (2)** |
| GOALS | **33** |

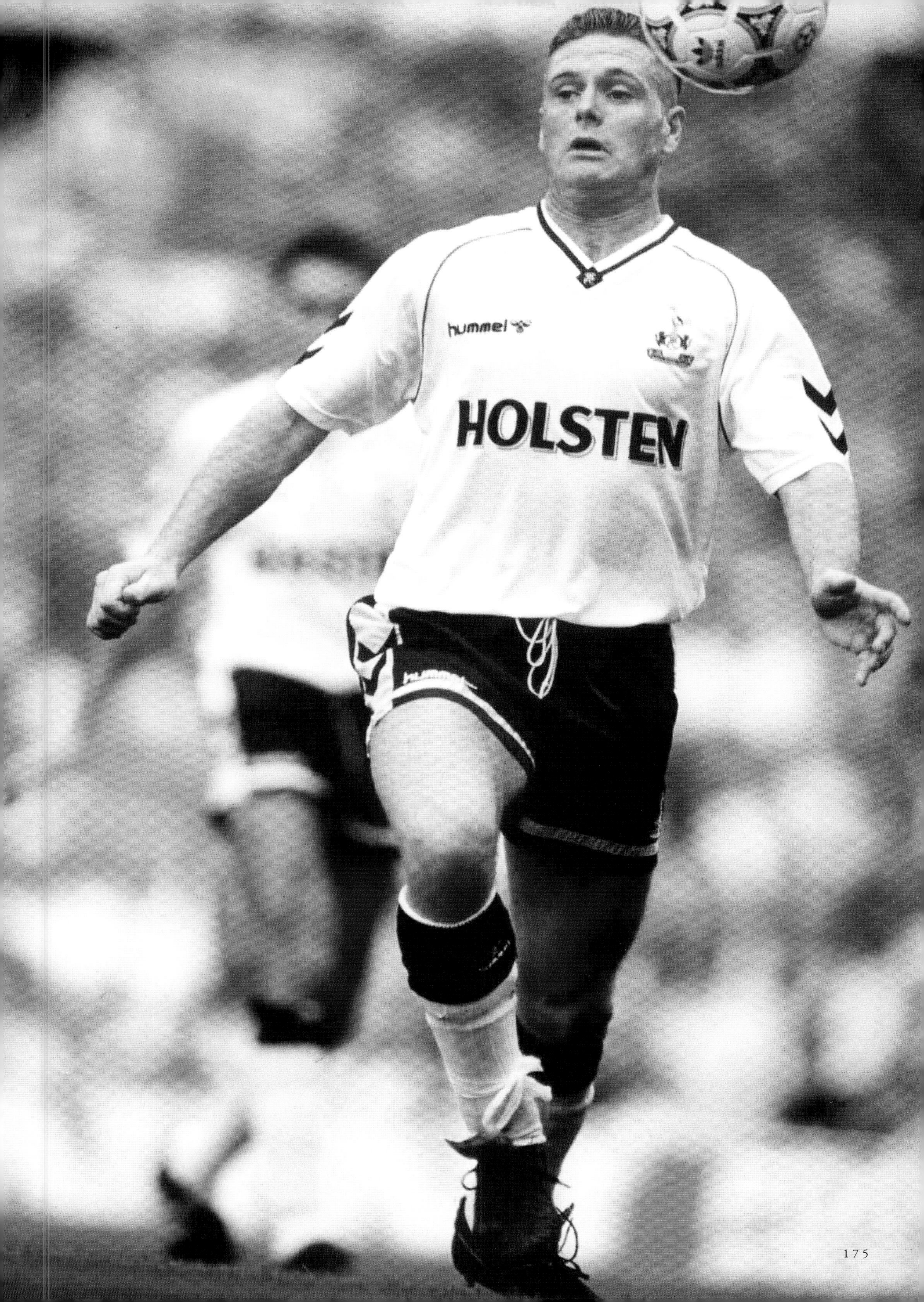
hummel
HOLSTEN

# NAYIM

. . . . . . . . . . .

## 1988/89 → 1992/93

Nayim was a connoisseur's delight, a true soccer thoroughbred whose presence brought spice and guile to the Tottenham midfield. Indeed, some seasoned observers maintain that, but for a certain lack of pace, the multi-talented, Moroccan-born Spaniard might have blossomed into an international star.

Having been groomed at Barcelona by Terry Venables, Nayim later became surplus to the Catalonians' requirements and in November 1988 Terry, by now *in situ* at White Hart Lane, signed his protege on loan. So promisingly did he perform during a handful of outings that spring that, come June, the north Londoners opted to make the transfer permanent, securing the swarthy ball-artist for a bargain £400,000 as a makeweight in the Gary Lineker deal.

Thereafter he tended to drift in and out of the side – sometimes through injury and sometimes, perhaps, because his Continental style was deemed too subtle for English demands – but it was a fact that Spurs looked far more inventive when Nayim was patrolling their left flank. His deft, penetrative passing, magnetic control and intelligent running carried a constant whiff of the unexpected, and no one at the club struck the ball more crisply. Against all that was an occasional tendency to loiter on the fringe of the action, and a penchant for extravagant penalty-area tumbles that did not endear him to opponents.

Arguably Nayim's most consistent senior sequences came in the first half of 1990/91 and after New Year in 1993, but surely his most dazzlingly memorable moment came in the League Cup at Southend in October 1989. Surrounded by defenders and facing away from goal, he flicked the ball over his head, eluded his markers and slotted the ball between the 'keeper's legs. More widely appreciated was a splendid FA Cup quarter-final hat-trick at Manchester City in 1993, at a time when rumours of his departure were rife. Sure enough, a few weeks later he joined Real Zaragoza for £500,000, leaving many fans to feel sad that the chant of 'Nayeeeeem' would no longer echo around White Hart Lane.

| | |
|---|---|
| **MOHAMED ALI AMAR** | |
| BORN: | Ceuta, Morocco, 5 November 1966. |
| HONOURS: | FA Cup 90/1. |
| OTHER CLUBS: | Barcelona 86/7-87/8 (7, 0); Real Zaragoza 93/4-96/7 (123, 5); Logrones 97/8-99/00 (67, 5), all Spain. |

GAMES **119 (26)**
GOALS 18

# PAUL MORAN

### 1986/87 → 1993/94

Paul Moran was a high-class schoolboy athlete who ran for Enfield Harriers; but what he always wanted was to run for Spurs. And so he did, making his debut at Everton in May 1987, then subsequently demonstrating speed, skill and fire in spasmodic outings as a utility forward over the next six seasons.

Sadly though, 'Sparrow', so dubbed for his slight build and skinny legs, found it impossible to rise in the pecking order above a succession of costly signings – he endured the arrival of Walsh and Stewart, Lineker and Durie, Anderton and Sheringham – and was hindered further by injuries.

Through it all Moran, who served four other clubs on loan, maintained commendable confidence, as he showed at home to Sheffield Wednesday in October 1989 when, put through on goal but with the unmarked Lineker lurking nearby, he opted coolly to find the net himself.

Come July 1994, still only 26 but with regular promotion clearly beyond him, Moran was freed to join Peterborough United. Later he entered the non-League ranks with his home-town club, Enfield.

**PAUL MORAN**
**BORN:** Enfield, London, 22 May 1968.
**OTHER CLUBS:** Portsmouth on loan 88/9 (3, 0); Leicester City on loan 89/90 (10, 1); Newcastle United on loan 90/1 (1, 0); Southend United on loan 90/1 (1, 0); Peterborough United 94/5 (7, 0).

| | |
|---|---|
| GAMES | **18 (30)** |
| GOALS | 2 |

# SCOTT HOUGHTON

### 1991/92

The Tottenham crowd, not always the most tolerant of taskmasters where home-grown talent is concerned, could not be faulted for their treatment of Scott Houghton. Indeed, in 1991/92 they clasped the chunky little midfield flankman to their collective bosom with a fervour that extended, in some sections, to mild outrage when his promising cameo displays as substitute were not rewarded with a first-choice sequence.

Standing only 5ft 5in, Houghton radiated vigour and enthusiasm, and his readiness to run boldly at hulking defenders struck a chord with fans who felt, at times, that their side's engine-room was too passive. His contribution against Luton at the Lane in November was particularly dramatic as he enlivened proceedings with two goals, one of them a speculative long-shot from near the touchline.

But as more and more youngsters rose through the ranks, Scott was given no senior opportunity in 1992/93 and he was released on loan. A return to first-team reckoning would have required exceptional form, which was not forthcoming, and in August 1993 he moved to Luton Town on a free transfer.

**SCOTT AARON HOUGHTON**
**BORN:** Hitchin, Hertfordshire, 22 October 1971.
**OTHER CLUBS:** Ipswich Town on loan 90/1 (8, 1); Gillingham on loan 92/3 (3, 0); Charlton Athletic on loan 92/3 (6, 0); Luton Town 93/4-94/5 (16, 1); Walsall 94/5-95/6 (78, 14); Peterborough United 96/7-98/9 (70, 13); Southend United 98/9-00/01 (79, 9); Leyton Orient 00/01-01/02 (42, 6); Halifax Town 01/02 (7, 0).

| | |
|---|---|
| GAMES | **0 (14)** |
| GOALS | 2 |

# JOHN MONCUR

### 1986/87 → 1991/92

They called him 'The Loan Ranger' at White Hart Lane, so frequently did he temp with other clubs, but John Moncur deserved a reputation which better fitted his undoubted skills. The blond schemer was a precise passer, a delightful manipulator of the ball and a persuasive dummy salesman. However, his presence could seem as lightweight as his build, and the athleticism and stamina he displayed in training were not always evident in matches.

It hardly helped the young Londoner that, after sampling senior action for the first time in May 1987, he was never given a settled run. Of course, the major problem was the presence of Paul Gascoigne as chief play-maker, and by the time Gazza had gone, it was almost as if John had been hovering on the brink for too long.

Those who championed the Moncur cause recall wistfully his imaginative performance at Derby in February 1990 and when he joined Swindon for £80,000 in March 1992, they wished him well. Nurtured by Glenn Hoddle, Moncur's subtle talent flourished in Wiltshire before he made the most of his full creative potential at last, with West Ham.

**JOHN FREDERICK MONCUR**
**BORN:** Stepney, London, 22 September 1966.
**OTHER CLUBS:** Doncaster Rovers on loan 86/7 (4, 0); Cambridge United on loan 86/7 (4, 0); Portsmouth on loan 88/9 (7, 0); Brentford on loan 89/90 (5, 1); Ipswich Town on loan 91/2 (6, 0); Swindon Town 91/2-93/4 (58, 5); West Ham United 94/5-02/03 (175, 6).

| | |
|---|---|
| GAMES | **11 (13)** |
| GOALS | 1 |

# GARY LINEKER

· · · · · · · · · · · · · · · · · · · · · · · · · · · · · · · · · · · · · · ·

## 1989/90 → 1991/92

There is a theory that any team containing Gary Lineker was never quite as good as its results suggested, the inference being that he compensated for collective shortcomings by the well-nigh unparalleled efficiency with which he did his job. Naturally, the man himself would be far too modest to accept such a contention, but with all due respect to his Tottenham colleagues during three goal-laden seasons, it carries an unmistakable ring of truth. Like any marksman born of woman, Lineker missed his share of opportunities, but his priceless art – for such it was, as sure as any schemer's most delicate touch – lay in spurning fewer than any of his peers.

So what elevated the personable Midlander to the uttermost peak of his profession? Searing pace is the answer most frequently trotted out but, as the plethora of fleet-footed under-achievers scattered around the divisions tends to suggest, that is a gross over-simplification. Certainly Lineker's speed was central to his success, but it was the intelligent application of that prize asset which set him apart. He was a brilliant reader of the game whose timing of runs into the area behind defenders was metronomically precise. In tighter situations he would lead his marker astray with a sudden dart away from goal, only to spin off the hapless 'shadow' just as the ball was played into the space thus vacated.

Then, of course, there was that ultimate skill which gives meaning to all the others: the knack of putting the ball in the net. Lineker could perform this notoriously difficult act clinically and repeatedly, evoking the deadliness and composure, if not the all-round ability, of one Jimmy Greaves. He took time when none seemed available, his instinct for stealing a yard in the most densely crowded goalmouth and his almost uncanny anticipation of a football's flight-path paying handsome dividends. He had a geometrician's feel for angles, an intuition for selecting the correct mode of shot – sidefoots and power-drives, chips and nudges, all were kept in their rightful place – and carried an aerial threat that was underrated at opponents' peril.

His critics would have it that he was useless without waiter-service, that only rarely would he fashion an opening himself, but as a specialist at the top level that was scarcely a weakness, witness his record. A further carp related to his lack of contribution outside the box, but that he was not always a passenger away from the front line was shown twice at Old Trafford in autumn 1989. First he dragged Gary Pallister out of position before setting up a League Cup goal for Vinny Samways, then three weeks later he cut in from the left flank to score with a 20-yard bender in a League encounter.

However, beyond all the analysis, the bare facts of Lineker's Tottenham career speak for themselves. Arriving from Barcelona in June 1989 – at £1.2 million, the 28-year-old star was one of the bargains of the decade – he went six matches without scoring before hitting a hot streak that saw him finish the season as the First Division's leading marksman. His middle term at the Lane was disrupted by injury, but despite a lean spell he managed 19 in major competitions, including two crucial efforts in the FA Cup semi-final victory over Arsenal.

Then in a 1991/92 campaign clouded by the serious illness of his baby son, he displayed remarkable resilience to strike no less than 35 times in 50 outings, probably saving Spurs from relegation and being rewarded with the writers' Footballer of the Year award. That summer the England captain failed narrowly to beat Bobby Charlton's scoring record for his country before retiring from the international scene and heading for Japan, his £900,000 move to Grampus Eight having been announced some months earlier. Thus Gary Lineker departed the English game held in a universal affection rivalled only by the aforementioned Mr Charlton himself, since when he has heightened his profile still further as the amiably emollient host of *Match of the Day*.

**GARY WINSTON LINEKER**
BORN: Leicester, 30 November 1960.
HONOURS: FA Cup 90/1. 80 England caps (84-92). FWA Footballer of the Year 86, 92. PFA Footballer of the Year 86.
OTHER CLUBS: Leicester City 78/9-84/5 (194, 95); Everton 85/6 (41, 30); Barcelona, Spain, 86/7-88/9 (99, 44); Grampus Eight, Japan, 92/3-93/4.

GAMES 138
GOALS 80

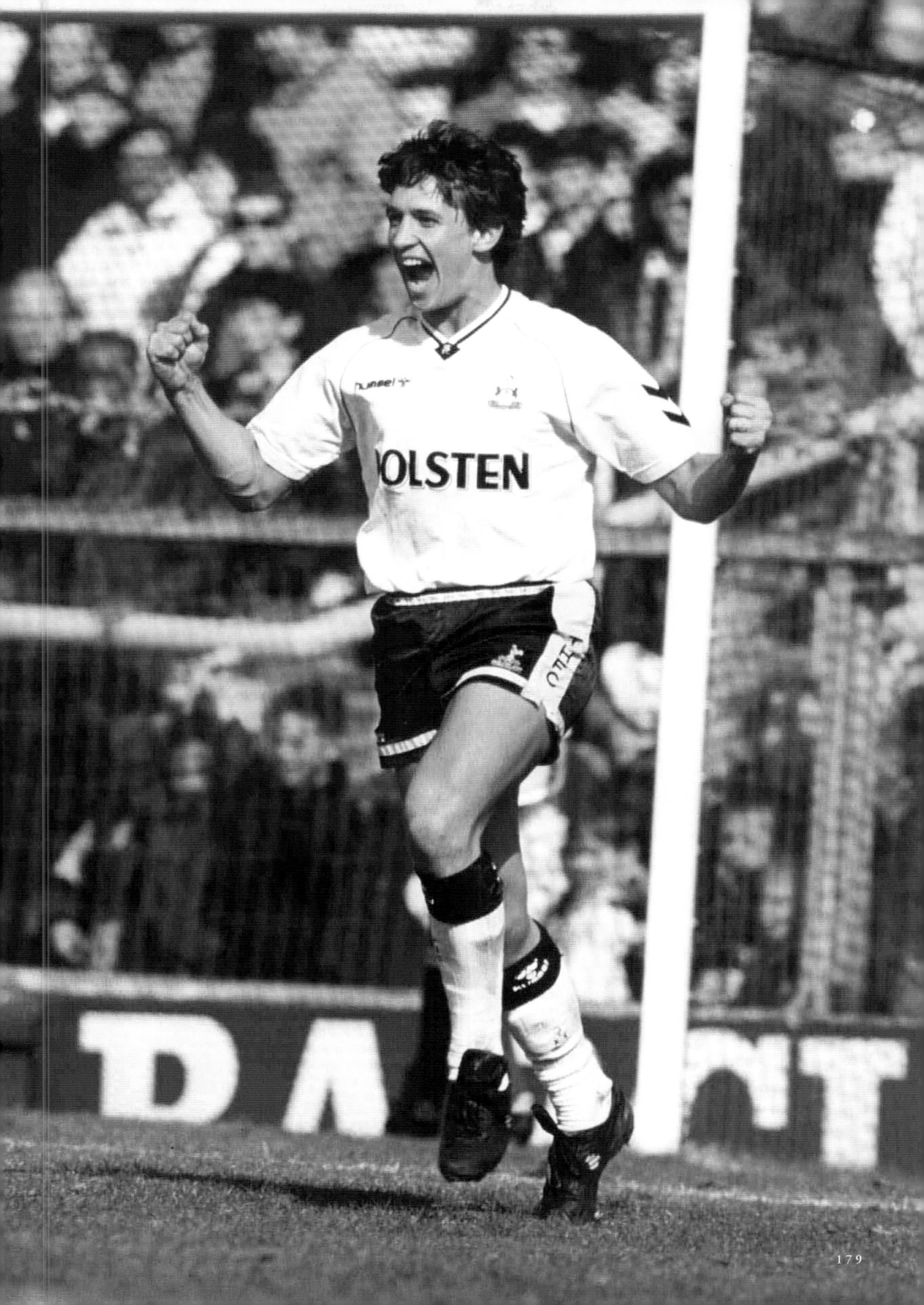
OLSTEN

# GARY MABBUTT

## 1982/83 → 1997/98

If money talks, and big money talks the loudest, then often during the 1980s the noise from White Hart Lane was deafening as millions poured from the club coffers to recruit some of the game's finest and most flamboyant talent. By comparison, the £105,000 it took to persuade Bristol Rovers to part with Gary Mabbutt in August 1982 was little more than a muffled whisper; the reverberations, however, went on and on, and what a satisfying, reassuring, often uplifting sound it turned out to be.

Certainly, it would be difficult to overstate the importance of Mabbutt to the Tottenham cause. His versatility alone – midfielder, central defender, full-back, even emergency striker, he did the lot – made him well-nigh indispensable to a succession of managers; and that's without considering his loyalty, industry and a brand of single-minded dedication that, if it could be bottled for consumption by less disciplined individuals, would find an avid market among overwrought bosses everywhere.

In fact, but for that last-mentioned quality, Mabbutt would never have become a leading player. Neither extravagantly gifted, nor particularly quick, he strove unstintingly from early boyhood – inspired by his father Ray, the former Bristol Rovers stalwart, and working in tandem with his brother Kevin, who played for Bristol City and Crystal Palace – to make the utmost of his natural athleticism, zest and will-power.

Mabbutt's desire to succeed in the game he loved was never shaken, not even by the shattering discovery as a 17-year-old that he was diabetic, a handicap he conquered to the extent that Bobby Robson dubbed him 'The Bionic Man'. Indeed, so impressed was the England manager by Gary's instant adaptation to the top flight that he awarded the young Bristolian his first full cap some two months after his move to north London, and it was to surprise many observers when future international appearances proved so intermittent.

Early seasons at the Lane were spent mostly in midfield – his first yielded ten League goals, just one short of top-scoring Steve Archibald – and despite finding himself out of the side for part of Peter Shreeves' first term at the helm, Mabbutt remained a valuable asset who was improving with experience. Even so, it took a switch to the centre of defence in 1985/86 to bring out the best in a performer who, in more forward positions, was not always at home with Spurs' traditional flowing movement. Now, though, he was majestic, employing his fastidiously honed abilities to full effect and radiating the unfussy composure that became a trademark.

Though standing only 5ft 9in, Mabbutt was brilliant in the air, the timing of his spring-heeled leaps winning duel after duel with giant opponents, while his strong, clean tackling was a joy and his shrewd anticipation defused countless threats on goal.

In 1986/87, Richard Gough and Mabbutt were the fans' dream ticket at the rearguard's core, and it was supremely galling to end an exhilarating season with no honours, especially so for Gary, who against Coventry at Wembley became only the second man to score for both teams in an FA Cup Final. Soon after that, having spurned reported advances from Liverpool, he replaced the departed Scot as skipper and in the years that followed no one did more to keep his club ticking over on the pitch while turmoil reigned in the boardroom.

Thus it was gratifying in 1991 when Mabbutt's smile, such a constant part of the Spurs scene, appeared – wider than ever – between two arms that were holding aloft the FA Cup. Thereafter his playing standard remained high and when he came back from injury in autumn 1992, he transformed a hitherto porous defence, helping new partner Neil Ruddock look twice the player he had been.

As the years rolled on, Mabbutt continued to astonish with his resilience. In early 1994, for example, he recovered from a shattered eye socket, the result of a clash with Wimbledon's John Fashanu, to help lift Spurs clear of relegation.

Two more seasons of imperturbable excellence ensued, then he missed the whole of 1996/97 after breaking his leg on the opening day. The end? No way! He bounced back the following term, aged 36 but still not out of his depth, before being given his freedom by Spurs in spring 1998 with the promise of a job for life if he wanted it.

Perhaps outsiders did not appreciate his full worth, but at White Hart Lane, Gary Mabbutt MBE will be remembered always as the most consistent and best-loved player of a supremely difficult era, and an impeccable ambassador for both his club and his sport.

**GARY VINCENT MABBUTT**
BORN: Bristol, 23 August 1961.
HONOURS: UEFA Cup 83/4; FA Cup 90/1. 16 England caps (82-92).
OTHER CLUBS: Bristol Rovers 78/9-81/2 (131, 10).

GAMES **587 (26)**
GOALS 38

# GUDNI BERGSSON

## 1988/89 → 1992/93

Gudni Bergsson made himself useful at White Hart Lane without ever managing to suggest that he would become indispensable. The slim, blond utility man, who could play at full-back or in midfield but was at his best sweeping alongside the centre-half, was quick, tackled briskly and relished the chance to get forward, but his control and distribution tended to detract from the overall effect.

Bergsson, rejected by Aston Villa after a 1985 trial, stepped out of his native Icelandic league for a midwinter loan with Spurs in 1988 and found himself at right-back in a home encounter with Luton on Boxing Day. He gave the first of a commendable series of displays and in February was awarded a full contract.

Thereafter he enjoyed sporadic senior sequences – his most settled spell being in 1991/92 under Peter Shreeves – but the signings of Neil Ruddock, Dean Austin and Jason Cundy that summer dented his aspirations considerably. In March 1995, a £65,000 deal took Bergsson to Bolton, with whom he struck the finest form of his English sojourn, going on to captain his country.

**GUDNI BERGSSON**
**BORN:** Iceland, 21 July 1965.
**HONOURS:** Iceland caps.
**OTHER CLUBS:** Valur, Iceland; Bolton Wanderers 94/5-02/03 (270, 23).

| GAMES | 62 (25) |
|---|---|
| GOALS | 2 |

# JOHN HENDRY

## 1990/91 → 1993/94

Promising striker John Hendry was accorded few senior opportunities at Tottenham, despite making a favourable impression on his rare outings. The slim, wiry Glaswegian had failed to make his breakthrough at Dundee but had attracted attention with a prolific spell on loan with Forfar Athletic when Terry Venables hazarded £50,000 on raw potential in July 1990.

Hendry's initial progress at White Hart Lane was hampered by injuries, but when his chance came in the spring of 1991, he took it. After scoring a debut goal at Norwich, he netted with a looping header at Old Trafford on his second full appearance, and at that stage looked a fine prospect. Adept at loping inconspicuously into dangerous positions, capable of turning sharply and possessing a neat first touch, Hendry carried the perpetual threat that he might steal a goal from nothing. But he was condemned to languish during the next three terms and, with competition for places hotting up, he left for Motherwell in 1995.

**JOHN MICHAEL HENDRY**
**BORN:** Glasgow, 6 January 1970.
**OTHER CLUBS:** Dundee 88/9 (2, 0); Forfar Athletic on loan 89/90 (10, 6); Charlton Athletic on loan 91/2 (5, 1); Swansea City on loan 94/5 (8, 2); Motherwell 95/6-97/8 (35, 3).

| GAMES | 5 (15) |
|---|---|
| GOALS | 5 |

# DAVID TUTTLE

## 1990/91 → 1992/93

Whatever doubts Spurs fans harboured about central defender David Tuttle, they need have had none about his character. Making his League debut at Stamford Bridge in December 1990, the 18-year-old six-footer was handed the task of shackling Kerry Dixon. Within five minutes, the experienced marksman had put Chelsea ahead and proceeded to give Tuttle such a chasing that manager Terry Venables withdrew his rookie stopper from the action at half-time.

In the face of such trauma, the confidence of many players might have withered, but Tuttle was made of stern stuff. Come the spring he was back in the side, tackling solidly and eager to learn, and in September 1991 sampled the smoother side of the soccer coin, scoring with a fierce drive at home to Hajduk Split.

However, the England youth international then suffered an injury that ruled him out for the season, enduring similar bad luck while on loan to Peterborough the following term. The path to Spurs' first team proved a rocky one but a £350,000 move to Sheffield United in August 1993 put plucky Tuttle's career back on track.

**DAVID PHILIP TUTTLE**
**BORN:** Reading, 6 February 1972.
**OTHER CLUBS:** Peterborough United on loan 92/3 (7, 0); Sheffield United 93/4-95/6 (63, 1); Crystal Palace 95/6-99/00 (81, 5); Barnsley 99/00 (12, 0); Millwall 99/00-02/03 (23, 0); Wycombe Wanderers on loan 01/02 (4, 0).
**MANAGER:** Millwall (caretaker 05-06); Swindon Town (caretaker 06).

| GAMES | 14 (4) |
|---|---|
| GOALS | 1 |

# STEVE SEDGLEY

## 1989/90 → 1993/94

When Steve Sedgley headed for White Hart Lane as a £750,000 recruit from Coventry City in July 1989, there was one telling factor in favour of the spindly north Londoner's chances of success – his heart was already there. Having cheered Spurs from the terraces as a boy and actually played for them at junior level, before being rejected and taking his talents to Highfield Road, he must have felt he was going home.

However, the path that lay ahead was by no means smooth. Sedgley was bought as a midfield anchorman, his doughty defensive qualities seen as the ideal counterbalance to the ebullient skills of Paul Gascoigne. It was a role he had filled regularly for England under-21s but in which he now failed to impress. Though staunchly determined and capable of passing well with his left foot if given the time, he appeared sluggish and awkward, a considerable disappointment.

But during his first campaign as a Spur, Sedgley was switched to central defence in an emergency and displayed instant poise,

linking effectively with Gary Mabbutt in a composed, generally solid partnership. Though prone to occasional bloomers – a rash pass here, a missed tackle there – suddenly at 21 he was a bright prospect again, remaining first choice until the end of 1990/91 and pocketing an FA Cup winner's medal in the process.

Then a ponderous display at Southampton on the opening day of the new term signalled a period of uncertainty that saw him flitting in and out of the side, and come 1992/93, with Neil Ruddock and Jason Cundy fresh on the scene, there was an inescapable feeling that he would become one of the club's many 'nearly men'.

Sedgley, however, had not read that particular script and, benefiting from injuries to others, he enjoyed two competent spells in his old midfield niche, the second marked by a smartly executed strike in the FA Cup quarter-final win over Manchester City at Maine Road. During 1993/94 he excelled both as a midfielder, contributing crucial goals in the fight against relegation, and as a defensive deputy for the sidelined Mabbutt, before making a £1 million summer move to Ipswich.

**STEPHEN PHILIP SEDGLEY**
**BORN:** Enfield, London, 26 May 1968.
**HONOURS:** FA Cup 90/1.
**OTHER CLUBS:** Coventry City 86/7-88/9 (84, 3); Ipswich Town 94/5-96/7 (105, 15); Wolverhampton Wanderers 97/8-00/01 (106, 9).

GAMES **187 (24)**
GOALS **10**

# PAUL STEWART

## 1988/89 → 1991/92

The old saying that you can't make a silk purse from a sow's ear held little credence for Spurs fans of the early 1990s; after all, in the case of Paul Stewart, they had seen the evidence with their own eyes. The burly centre-forward cost £1.5 million from Manchester City in the summer of 1988, and early indications were not encouraging. After missing the first four games through suspension for earlier misdemeanours, he endured a traumatic debut at home to Manchester United.

Coming on as a substitute palpably consumed with urgency to impress, he charged around like a man possessed until, near the end and with the scores level, he won a penalty. Terry Fenwick shaped to take the kick but Stewart, on a high, pressed his own claim, was given precedence – and slammed the ball against the crossbar. Further ignominy awaited as six games passed without a goal; even worse, he didn't look the part, appearing crude, ponderous and out of his depth.

Stewart's situation barely improved in the first six months of 1989/90 when, with new partner Gary Lineker garnering the glory, his blunt bludgeoning was exposed mercilessly by the gleaming rapier alongside. However, to his eternal credit, the bustling Mancunian tried ceaselessly, never hiding from the ball and refusing to make excuses as he endured a run of appalling luck in front of goal. Inevitably though, for a player to whom confidence was everything, the strain began to tell and his bearing on the pitch began to reflect the frustration and depression he must have been feeling.

A turning point of sorts arrived in March when, after being demoted to the reserves in favour of Paul Walsh, he was called off the bench and sealed a home victory over Liverpool with a marvellous soaring header in front of the TV cameras. Suddenly self-belief was rediscovered and the goals began to flow, one in particular, against Coventry at the Lane in April, prompting his most caustic critics to goggle with amazement. Taking possession inside the penalty box with his back to goal, Stewart flipped the ball up and over a marker's head before swivelling to lash an acute-angled volley into the net from ten yards.

However, the following season had begun in ominous fashion, with just one strike in 17 League outings, when three days before Christmas, at home to Luton, the Stewart fortunes were transformed in the unlikeliest of circumstances. With Spurs reduced to nine men by the dismissals of Nayim and Van den Hauwe, Paul dropped back to midfield, where he was a revelation. The fact that he scored twice to win the match was the least of it; what transfixed the eye was his new assurance, the unimagined delicacy of his touch, the accuracy and perception of his passing, all underpinned by stamina, strength and the aggression of a natural ball-winner.

For a handful of matches he returned to the front line before settling in midfield, proving that with the extra time his new role allowed, and without the pressure of having to find the net, he could make a handsome contribution. Stewart remained on song for the rest of the season, reserving the culmination of his rebirth for the grandest of settings, at Wembley in the FA Cup Final against Nottingham Forest. He played superbly throughout, capping his display with a ruthlessly executed equaliser, a low cross-shot from some 12 yards.

Stewart's form during the next term confirmed his progress – indeed, frequently he was the most impressive Spur on view – and he earned an England call-up, the very idea of which would have been risible only a year earlier. The fans, though, were not allowed to bask for long in their new hero's glory. Family reasons dictated a move north and in July 1992 Paul Stewart joined Liverpool for £2.3 million. It was a dream transfer for a wholehearted, and yes, gifted player who had experienced more than his share of nightmares. Unfortunately he failed to make the most of his Anfield opportunity, slipping out of the top grade with startling rapidity.

---

**PAUL ANDREW STEWART**

BORN: Manchester, 7 October 1964.

HONOURS: FA Cup 90/1. 3 England caps (91–92).

OTHER CLUBS: Blackpool 81/2-86/7 (201, 56); Manchester City 86/7-87/8 (51, 26); Liverpool 92/3-93/4 (32, 1); Crystal Palace on loan 93/4 (18, 3); Wolverhampton Wanderers on loan 94/5 (8, 2); Burnley on loan 94/5 (6, 0); Sunderland 95/6-96/7 (36, 5); Stoke City 97/8 (22, 3).

GAMES **167 (5)**

GOALS 37

# JASON CUNDY

### 1991/92 → 1995/96

The sight of Jason Cundy tackling mid-air on several occasions against Sheffield Wednesday in September 1992 highlighted vividly the major defect in the game of an otherwise promising central defender. Unarguably he was fast, fearless and ferocious, but also the enthusiastic stopper was prone to making rash challenges when prudence dictated a little restraint. That afternoon at Hillsborough, he looked out of his class against skipping, skilful opponents, and not long afterwards he lost his place to Gary Mabbutt.

England under-21 international Cundy arrived at White Hart Lane in spring 1992 on loan from Chelsea, where he had been accorded rabid terrace popularity. Bristling with aggression, aerially powerful and a fierce tackler, he did enough during the rest of the season to persuade Spurs to strike an £800,000 deal that summer, and as the new term began he formed a daunting partnership with Neil Ruddock.

Cundy played well at times and enjoyed one moment of undiluted bliss, when his lusty 50-yard punt caught the wind and sailed into the Ipswich net for a freak goal at Portman Road. But faulty positioning and impetuosity marred his defensive work and the axe fell. Later he was tried briefly as a holding midfielder before injury halted his progress. In October 1996, Cundy joined Ipswich in a £200,000 deal, subsequently triumphing over cancer to continue his career.

**JASON VICTOR CUNDY**
BORN: Wandsworth, London, 12 November 1969.
OTHER CLUBS: Chelsea 90/1-91/2 (41, 1); Crystal Palace on loan 95/6 (4, 0); Bristol City on loan 96/7 (6, 1); Ipswich Town 96/7-98/9 (58, 5); Portsmouth 99/00 (9, 0).

GAMES **25 (3)**
GOALS 1

# ANDY GRAY

### 1991/92 → 1993/94

As a driving force in the Crystal Palace midfield, Andy Gray could be guaranteed to impose himself on his Spurs counterparts. Hence when the combative, accomplished Londoner moved to White Hart Lane on loan in February 1992, his ineffective form was a sore letdown to expectant fans. In retrospect, however, that was not vastly surprising. Gray, not always the easiest character to handle, had been at odds with Palace boss Steve Coppell and had put on weight after ceasing to train.

Nevertheless, that summer Tottenham parted with £900,000 to acquire his services on a permanent basis and in subsequent outings – mostly in his familiar central slot rather than the right-flank role of the previous campaign – he looked more like the player who had won an England cap in 1991.

At his best Gray could inspire a team, both with an appetite for the fray that ensured he was near the heart of any rumpus and good all-round technique that encompassed a savage shot, aerial power, underrated creativity and a havoc-inducing long throw. But he remained unpredictable and, troubled both by injuries and by brisk competition for places, he was never more than a useful squad member. Andy Gray's talent was unquestioned; his ability to harness it consistently was another matter.

**ANDREW ARTHUR GRAY**
BORN: Lambeth, London, 22 February 1964
HONOURS: 1 England cap (91).
OTHER CLUBS: Crystal Palace 84/5-87/8 (98, 27); Aston Villa 87/8-88/9 (37, 4); Queen's Park Rangers 88/9 (11, 2); Crystal Palace 88/9-91/2 (90, 12). Swindon Town on loan 92/3 (3, 0); Marbella, Spain; Falkirk 95/6 (16, 0); Bury 97/8 (22, 1); Millwall 97/8- (12, 1).

GAMES **23 (10)**
GOALS 3

# PAT VAN DEN HAUWE

## 1989/90 → 1992/93

Pat Van den Hauwe was a Jekyll-and-Hyde footballer. One minute the Welsh international left-back might control the ball beautifully before clipping a precise pass to a colleague, his technique earning approbation from the most demanding of judges. But the next he would plough into an opponent with all the subtlety of a runaway bulldozer, demonstrating luridly why a baleful element among supporters of his previous club, Everton, gloried in christening him 'Psycho-Pat'.

Undeniably the versatile defender, so combative in the air and an able central stopper at need, did little throughout his stormy career to defuse his image as an archetypal 'heavy'. The dead-eyed stare, the designer stubble, his very demeanour during a game, they all served to emphasise and perpetuate the menacing persona that become his trademark.

Having helped to take two League titles and the European Cup Winners' Cup to Goodison Park, 28-year-old Van den Hauwe moved to White Hart Lane for £575,000 in August 1989. He marked his arrival with two bookings in his first three games, then settled capably into the side, going on to become popular with the fans in a jokey, anti-hero type of way.

True, unnecessary fouls put the side under pressure at times, and moments of excess like the waist-high tackle on Luton's Iain Dowie which earned him a sending-off at the Lane in December 1990 were clearly reprehensible, but in general the good – which included crossing accurately and delivering a devastating long throw – outweighed the bad.

Van den Hauwe, whose hopes of playing for his native Belgium disappeared when he opted out of National Service, surely would have won more caps for Wales, his adopted country, but for a tiff with the management. Nevertheless, his ambition remained undiminished and he assisted in Spurs' FA Cup triumph of 1991.

After one more season as a first-team regular, younger men reduced him to the role of occasional substitute and he was freed to complete his playing days with Millwall. By then Pat Van den Hauwe had given all his employers ample value for money.

**PATRICK WILLIAM ROGER VAN DEN HAUWE**

**BORN:** Dendermonde, Belgium, 16 December 1960.
**HONOURS:** FA Cup 90/1. 13 Wales caps (85-89).
**OTHER CLUBS:** Birmingham City 78/9-84/5 (123, 1); Everton 84/5-89/90 (135, 2); Millwall 93/4-94/5 (27, 0).

GAMES **140 (6)**
GOALS **0**

# DEAN AUSTIN

## 1992/93 → 1996/97

There was a time when Dean Austin was slated not only as Spurs' right-back for the foreseeable future, but also as a long-term England candidate. Somewhere along the way, that most sanguine of scripts went alarmingly awry.

The slim six-footer arrived at White Hart Lane in June 1992, following in Justin Edinburgh's footsteps from Southend, who were not happy at being used as purveyors of full-backs to the top-flight aristocracy. Indeed, when a tribunal set the fee at £375,000, rising to £525,000 after an agreed number of games, the Shrimpers' outraged chairman announced a ban on future transfers to Tottenham.

At first it seemed as though the north Londoners had secured a rare bargain. Austin won a senior berth that August and soon was being hailed as a major discovery. There were particular plaudits for his attacking style, which encompassed the pace and skill to go past opponents and the ability to deliver a teasing cross. Clearly the defensive side of his game needed some attention, but it appeared that the rudiments were all in place and experience was expected to produce the finished article.

Austin progressed satisfactorily throughout his first campaign with Spurs, but a broken leg suffered at home to Oldham in September 1993 destroyed his impetus and, with new arrival David Kerslake now competing for his place, he seemed less confident when he regained fitness later that term. Nevertheless he was preferred to Kerslake by new boss Gerry Francis, who reinstated him on a regular basis in November 1994, and for the ensuing season and a half he was an integral part of a radically tightened rearguard.

But after missing the last weeks of 1995/96 with an ankle injury, he was sidelined by knee trouble for much of 1996/97, during which Stephen Carr established his own claim. On subsequent senior outings Austin seemed less than assured, especially in his distribution, and while a settled run in the team might have helped, his hopes of that were scuppered by knee damage which ruled him out for most of 1997/98. Though Dean Austin was still only 28, with all that early potential as yet unfulfilled, he was given a free transfer at season's end.

**DEAN BARRY AUSTIN**
BORN: Hemel Hempstead, Hertfordshire, 26 April 1970.
OTHER CLUBS: Southend United 89/90-91/2 (96, 2); Crystal Palace 98/9-02/03 (142, 6).

GAMES **140 (10)**
GOALS **0**

# JUSTIN EDINBURGH

## 1990/91 → 1999/2000

Justin Edinburgh suffered his share of brickbats from the paying customers after being lauded as a hugely promising young left-back in the early 1990s. But despite the periodic jibes, directed mainly at a tendency to be caught out of position, he retained a certain affection among the majority of White Hart Lane regulars. The reason? It was as plain as the navy blue cockerel emblazoned on his chest. More than anything else, it seemed, Edinburgh wanted to play for Tottenham Hotspur.

He was spotted by the north Londoners as a precocious teenager with Southend United, and he spent the opening months of 1990 on loan at the Lane. While there were no senior opportunities, and he rejoined the Shrimpers to help clinch promotion to the Third Division, Edinburgh had shown enough potential for Tottenham to secure his services on a permanent basis for £150,000 that summer.

Though undeniably green, he won an unexpectedly early breakthrough as the squad was depleted by injuries, impressing with his incisiveness in the tackle and all-round eagerness. Against that was a tendency towards impetuous challenges in dangerous situations and the patent need to curb a quick temper. The initial verdict, however, was overwhelmingly favourable.

Edinburgh completed his first year as a Spur with splendidly efficient displays in the FA Cup semi-final clash with Arsenal and the final victory over Nottingham Forest, and he appeared to be in the team to stay. However, the next term his rate of progress slowed, perhaps an inevitable hiatus for one so young. Reassuringly he soldiered through the lean patch, and by spring 1993 was noticeably more poised and mature.

All sorted then? Not exactly. Throughout the mid-1990s, fluctuations of form fuelled the argument propounded by his growing number of doubters and, from the Edinburgh viewpoint, the arrival of Clive Wilson in 1995/96 was ominous. But Justin's stock was raised by his ability to fill in at right-back and he appeared in more than half of Spurs' games throughout the decade.

One of his last memorable performances, in the 1999 League Cup Final against Leicester City, would illustrate Edinburgh at his best and worst. During a dour contest he had stayed stone solid until 30 minutes from time, when his petulance emerged and a silly slap around the face of Robbie Savage earned Tottenham's longest-serving player a red card. Fortunately Spurs edged the game 1-0 and Edinburgh became the only man to collect two medals for the club during the 1990s. When he was offloaded to Portsmouth for £175,000 in March 2000, if the feeling remained that his pomp had not quite lived up to expectations, well . . . at least his heart was in the right place.

**JUSTIN CHARLES EDINBURGH**
**BORN:** Basildon, Essex, 18 December 1969.
**HONOURS:** FA Cup 90/1. League Cup 98/9.
**OTHER CLUBS:** Southend United 88/9-89/90 (37, 0); Portsmouth 99/00-01/02 (35,1).

GAMES **246 (30)**
GOALS 1

# NEIL RUDDOCK

## 1986/87 → 1987/88 & 1992/93

For a maddeningly brief interlude, the thunderous 1992/93 renaissance of Neil Ruddock was shaping to become one of the most significant events in Spurs' post-Nicholson era. Though there was no shortage of 'Bad Boy Makes Good' headlines to salute his formidable form, they did scant justice to the massive influence wielded by the glowering man-mountain who brought steel, confidence and something less definable – sheer presence, perhaps, begins to describe it – to the core of Tottenham's rearguard.

Alas, at season's end 'Razor', so dubbed in reference to the cutting edge of his game as much as to the heavyweight boxer who shared his surname, became embroiled in a contractual dispute at the Lane. The outcome, greeted with desperation by fans who had bid premature farewells to so many of their favourites in recent seasons, was a £2.5 million transfer to Liverpool, a move which was to prove less than fulfilling for all concerned.

Thus ended Neil Ruddock's second Tottenham tenure. The first had begun in March 1986 when he had arrived as an exceedingly raw, 17-year-old recruit from Millwall, costing £50,000 and without a senior outing to his name. He represented a distinct gamble and it was a year before he made his full debut, as a substitute in an FA Cup quarter-final victory at Wimbledon.

There followed sporadic chances over the next 12 months – he scored Spurs' goal in the FA Cup disaster at Port Vale in January 1987 – and though Ruddock didn't claim a regular place, he did enough to suggest that former manager Peter Shreeves had made a shrewd investment.

However, with cash at a premium, new boss Terry Venables accepted a £300,000 offer in June 1988 and the 20-year-old stopper returned to The Den, only to be consigned once more to the 'stiffs'. Before long he switched to Southampton, where finally he was given the extended opportunity his potential deserved and he made giant strides, soon earning an England under-21 call-up.

Unfortunately, the Ruddock file revealed an appalling disciplinary record that, at one time, threatened his very future in the game. Nevertheless, in May 1992 when Spurs were casting around for the dominant centre-half they needed so urgently, they could find no more suitable target than the rugged Londoner, whose £750,000 fee was settled by a tribunal.

Events proved that Venables could hardly have been wiser in shrugging off any embarrassment involved in re-signing a player with whom he had once dispensed, and in running the risk of Ruddock's well-publicised attempts to curb his temper ending in failure.

The 'second coming' began auspiciously with a superb defensive performance – at The Dell, ironically enough – but in his third League outing, 'Razor' was sent off for two bookable offences. He professed himself mortified, took his punishment on that stubbly square chin and vowed not to let the side down again, proving as good as his word.

More gratifying still was Ruddock's form and his effect on team morale. Paired with Jason Cundy in the term's opening months, he played extremely well but, in a defence that continued to ship goals wholesale, he did not always receive due personal credit. However, when Cundy was replaced by the immaculate Gary Mabbutt, results improved and Ruddock was thrown into stark relief as the high-quality bulwark he had become.

Aggression personified, he was a towering authority in the air at either end of the pitch and tackled like a torpedo, though almost invariably within the laws of the game. In addition, he revealed a hitherto-untrumpeted delicate left-foot touch, which was highlighted in the FA Cup fifth-round clash with Wimbledon. Several times he broke free on the flank and delivered some telling crosses, one of which resulted in a goal for Darren Anderton. Of course, there was still time to confront and vanquish that ultimate warrior centre-forward, John Fashanu.

Having impressed when deputising as skipper, Ruddock emerged as the prime long-term captaincy candidate and as spring arrived he became an increasingly talismanic figure to supporters, the slightest prospect of losing him through injury causing a communal shudder. Then came the Anfield bombshell and Tottenham's sorely-needed defensive bedrock was gone. Neil Ruddock, who was destined to experience more turbulence and untold frustration on Merseyside, will be remembered in north London as a wild youngster who grew up late but in a hurry, becoming an instant folk hero in the process. But what will always rankle is the thought of what the big fellow might have achieved had he opted to spend his prime at White Hart Lane.

**NEIL RUDDOCK**

| | |
|---|---|
| **BORN:** | Wandsworth, London, 9 May 1968. |
| **HONOURS:** | 1 England cap (94). |
| **OTHER CLUBS:** | Millwall 88/9 (2, 1); Southampton 88/9-91/2 (107, 9); Liverpool 93/4-97/8 (115, 11); Queen's Park Rangers on loan 97/8 (7, 0); West Ham United 98/9-99/00 (42, 2); Crystal Palace 00/01 (20, 2); Swindon Town 01/02 (15, 1). |

| GAMES | 55 (3) |
|---|---|
| GOALS | 4 |

# PAUL WALSH

## 1987/88 → 1991/92

That Paul Walsh never emerged as one of England's premier stars of the late 1980s is a cause for considerable bafflement, tinged with sadness. Here was a footballer with scintillating talent who worked hard and played for two great clubs; yet as he entered his thirties, all he had to look back on was a tantalising collage of cameo achievements.

Walsh joined Spurs from Liverpool in February 1988, ending an Anfield stint which could not be classed a flop but, mainly through injuries and bad luck, had failed to ignite. For his £500,000, Terry Venables had enlisted a quicksilver entertainer capable of thrilling crowds with his speed and control, his knack of riding tackles and selling dummies matched by slick distribution and, on his day, a waspish finish.

However, as the hirsute Londoner partnered first Clive Allen, then Paul Stewart and Chris Waddle, he never attained sufficient consistency, and Gary Lineker's arrival in 1989 was a chronic blow to his aspirations. Thus for his last three years at the Lane, Walsh found himself cast repeatedly as a substitute or as Lineker's deputy.

In the latter role he could be sure that no matter how well he played – his splendid three-goal display at home to Sheffield United in October 1990 is a perfect example – he would be back on the bench for the next game, a woeful situation for a man who had won England caps as a 20-year-old.

Walsh received a certain sympathy from the terraces, especially in 1989 and 1990 when many fans preferred him to Stewart, but though he had his chances, he never made it impossible for Venables to drop him.

Of course from a manager's viewpoint, Walsh was ideal number-12 material, a performer whose late introduction could invest urgency into the most sterile of encounters, yet it must be admitted that he threatened to turn more matches than he actually did.

Paul Walsh and Spurs parted company in May 1992 when he switched to Portsmouth in a £400,000 deal, going on to an enterprising stint with Manchester City before ending his career back at Pompey.

**PAUL ANTHONY WALSH**

**BORN:** Plumstead, London, 1 October 1962.
**HONOURS:** FA Cup 90/1. 3 England caps (83-84).
**OTHER CLUBS:** Charlton Athletic 79/80-81/2 (87, 24); Luton Town 82/3-83/4 (80, 24); Liverpool 84/5-87/8 (77, 25); Queen's Park Rangers on loan 91/2 (2, 0); Portsmouth 92/3-93/4 (74, 14); Manchester City 93/4-95/6 (53, 16); Portsmouth 95/6 (21, 5).

| GAMES | 98 (58) |
| --- | --- |
| GOALS | 21 |

# GORDON DURIE

## 1991/92 → 1993/94

Throughout his 27-month tenure at White Hart Lane, Gordon Durie remained Tottenham's most expensive acquisition – and one of their most frustrating. The Scottish international forward, a £2.2 million signing from Chelsea in August 1991, was potentially a fabulous player. Fast and strong, skilful and intelligent, he was willing to run himself into the ground and numbered a ferocious shot, delightful distribution and aerial power among his talents. Yet over the course of two and a bit injury-marred campaigns, that ostensibly captivating cocktail produced less heady intoxication than flat disillusionment.

In retrospect, it was ominous that a cynical section of Stamford Bridge fans had seen fit to rechristen their striker 'Groin Strain' instead of the more affectionate 'Juke-Box.'. However, this was far from the minds of his new followers as he made a sprightly start as a Spur, scoring on his debut at Southampton and contributing several more early-season strikes.

But there followed a chronic, six-month goal drought, during which Durie's industry could not be faulted but his confidence and fitness level suffered, and by summer there were disturbing rumours that he was on the point of joining Glasgow Rangers. However, he stayed to begin his second term in fine fettle, and when Teddy Sheringham arrived to share his front-running burden, Durie started to justify his fee with some brilliant all-round displays.

Then came disaster: he was charged by the FA with feigning injury, effectively branded a cheat, and until his name was cleared late in the year the slur combined with fitness worries to produce an understandably debilitating effect. At one point Durie was dropped because the management felt he was mentally unfit to play, which upset many fans, and reportedly he came close to the much-trumpeted Ibrox move. Then, in the spring, injury ruled him out for the rest of the campaign.

Though the side had been increasingly buoyant in his absence, the red-haired marksman regained his place at the outset of 1993/94. But with many supporters questioning whether his heart was in the club and, more pertinently, new boss Ossie Ardiles dissatisfied with his commitment, it came as no surprise that November when a £1.2 million fee took Gordon Durie to, yes, Glasgow Rangers.

**GORDON SCOTT DURIE**

| | |
|---|---|
| BORN: | Paisley, Renfrewshire, 6 December 1965. |
| HONOURS: | 43 Scotland caps (87-98). |
| OTHER CLUBS: | East Fife 81/2-84/5 (81, 26); Hibernian 84/5-85/6 (47, 14); Chelsea 85/6-90/1 (123, 51); Glasgow Rangers 93/4-97/8 (126, 44); Heart of Midlothian 00/01 (16, 3). |

GAMES **78**
GOALS **17**

# JASON DOZZELL

## 1993/94 → 1996/97

From an imaginative young play-maker with hopes of an international future to the whipping boy of merciless verbal bullies – such was the miserable ordeal of Jason Dozzell in the shirt of Tottenham Hotspur.

Ossie Ardiles, the man who had tipped the slender six-footer for England honours, had a heavily vested interest in his progress, having paid Ipswich Town £1.9 million for his creative services in August 1993. On the face of it, the Spurs manager had pulled off a considerable coup, even at that hefty tribunal-fixed price. After all, Dozzell had nearly 400 senior games behind him, thus offering rare experience in a 25-year-old to complement his evident natural ability. At first he radiated

quality, controlling the ball with calm assurance and passing it perceptively and accurately over distances both long and short. In addition, his height made him handier in the air than most midfielders and, having known spells as a striker at Ipswich, he was an able finisher.

Overall, he seemed perfectly equipped for his pivotal role at the front of Ossie's midfield diamond, operating just behind Gordon Durie and Teddy Sheringham, but as relegation trouble loomed early in 1994, Dozzell's confidence ebbed away. Now the crowd, with impeccable timing, began to chide him and his game became so distressingly indecisive that in 1994/95 he was no more than a fringe player, a forlorn figure engulfed by the shadows of newly-signed stars.

Season 1995/96 brought some improvement, the arrival of Gerry Francis providing fresh opportunity, and the beleaguered East Anglian totalled 34 senior outings, finishing the campaign with a flash of class which summed up his vast potential. At Newcastle in a match the home side had to win to stand a chance of the title, Dozzell controlled the ball immaculately, duped his challengers with a delightful shimmy and slid a perfect low shot into the corner of the net.

Thus he had shattered the Magpies' hopes, but his own long-term ambitions were to fare no better. Dozzell had his chances in 1996/97 and made the occasional telling contribution, such as a glorious late header to earn victory over Wimbledon in April. But he remained a target for fans' abuse and it came as no surprise when he was freed to return to Ipswich, sadly unfulfilled, in October 1997.

---

**JASON ALVIN WINANS DOZZELL**
BORN: Ipswich, Suffolk, 9 December 1967.
OTHER CLUBS: Ipswich Town 83/4-92/3 (332, 52) and 97/8 (8, 1); Northampton Town 97/8 (21, 4); Colchester United 98/9-00/01 (90, 9).

GAMES 81 (19)
GOALS 14

# NICK BARMBY

### 1992/93 → 1994/95

Of all the exits from White Hart Lane during a particularly turbulent period in the club's history, the most perplexing was that of Nick Barmby. After all, he was once the most sought-after schoolboy star in the land; he had plumped for Spurs ahead of a host of top clubs, then displayed his thoroughbred wares to such thrilling effect in the top flight that, come the summer of 1993, it seemed reasonable to conclude that the unspoilt Humbersider was the outstanding English talent of his generation. Yet, just two years later, he was sold to Middlesbrough for £5.25 million and dismayed Tottenham fans were left to wonder, not for the first time, exactly what was going on.

At the time of his breakthrough, the chunky 5ft 6in attacker's game was a bounteous, bubbling bundle of delights, but by far its most astonishing feature was maturity. Though only 19, he wielded the influence of a man in his prime, bringing others into play with his vision and awareness, invariably making the appropriate pass at the optimum moment and lubricating team movement by his perceptive running off the ball.

Whether operating up front, in midfield or somewhere in between, Barmby scampered eagerly, all bustling pace and perky audacity. Adhesive of touch, combative of tackle and strong enough to shield the ball under severe challenge, he carried a constant and varied threat to even the most mobile opponents.

After making his senior debut in September 1992, Barmby gave notice of his special ability with a series of precocious displays that autumn and early winter, his all-round prowess being thrown into vivid relief. In playing terms he resembled his hero, Peter Beardsley, and seemed set fair to become the Geordie's long-term international successor. But 1993/94 brought injury woe, a succession of shin operations leaving him apparently debilitated, and though he enjoyed a substantial return to form in 1994/95, earning an England call-up in the process, he was never quite the 'old' Nick Barmby.

Even so, it came as a severe jolt when he departed, amid hotly denied rumours of homesickness for the north. His subsequent experiences on Teesside, on Merseyside and at Leeds were to prove distressingly anti-climactic for a performer of such glorious ability.

| | |
|---|---|
| **NICHOLAS JONATHAN BARMBY** | |
| **BORN:** | Hull, Humberside, 11 February 1974. |
| **HONOURS:** | 23 England caps (95-01). |
| **OTHER CLUBS:** | Middlesbrough 95/6-96/7 (42, 8); Everton 96/7-99/00 (116, 18); Liverpool 00/01-01/02 (32, 2); Leeds United 02/03-03/04 (25, 4); Nottingham Forest on loan 03/04 (6, 1); Hull City 04/05- (100, 19). |

| | |
|---|---|
| GAMES | **100 (8)** |
| GOALS | 27 |

# GED McMAHON

### 1994/95 → 1995/96

While ludicrous reports of 'a new George Best' were greeted with deserved disdain by the wise heads on Tottenham's coaching staff, there is no denying that Ged McMahon created a genuine frisson of excitement after crossing the Irish Sea to ply his artistic trade in north London.

The 18-year-old winger or wide midfielder was recruited at a cost of £100,000 from Ulster club Glenavon by Terry Venables in July 1992 and, with his lavish mixture of skill, vision and pace, lost little time in stoking high expectations for his future. McMahon was a

confident lad whose game carried a thrilling touch of audacity but, like countless flankmen before him, a lack of consistency was to block his progress.

After an impressive loan spell at Barnet, he made his senior Spurs debut towards the end of 1994/95 and won his first full caps that summer. However, he failed to cement a place when given a handful of chances the following autumn, and he joined Stoke City for £450,000 in September 1996.

**GERARD JOSEPH McMAHON**
BORN: Belfast, 29 December 1973.
HONOURS: 17 Northern Ireland caps (95-97).
OTHER CLUBS: Glenavon, Northern Ireland;
Barnet on loan 94/5 (10, 2); Stoke City
96/7-97/8 (52, 3); St Johnstone
97/8-99/00 (50, 1).

| GAMES | 12 (8) |
|-------|--------|
| GOALS | 0 |

---

# STUART NETHERCOTT

### 1992/93 → 1996/97

Stuart Nethercott was a pugnacious young central defender whose usefulness was enhanced by his ability to fill three further roles, as midfield anchor, roving man-marker and full-back. However, despite winning England under-21 caps, the former Arsenal schoolboy never demonstrated the overall quality expected of a Spurs regular.

Immensely robust, Nethercott was a formidable tackler and a thumping header of the ball, but he could appear cumbersome and his reading of the game was not always impressive. He was most vulnerable when confronted by quick, clever opponents such as Everton's Anders Limpar, who embarrassed him mightily during the 1995 FA Cup semi-final defeat at Elland Road.

After breaking through under Doug Livermore in spring 1993, Nethercott was given further chances by both Ossie Ardiles and Gerry Francis, but the steady influx of expensive newcomers gradually eroded his position until he was rarely required even for stand-in duties. Accordingly, in 1997/98 Nethercott was released to join Second Division Millwall, perhaps finding his natural level.

**STUART DAVID NETHERRCOTT**
BORN: Chadwell Heath, Essex, 21 March 1973
OTHER CLUBS: Maidstone United on loan 91/2 (13, 1); Barnet on loan 91/2 (3, 0);
Millwall 97/8-03/04 (215, 10); Wycombe Wanderers 03/04-04/05 (51, 1).

| GAMES | 36 (26) |
|-------|---------|
| GOALS | 1 |

---

# DARREN CASKEY

### 1993/94 → 1995/96

The essential uncertainty of a career in football is illustrated aptly by the case of Darren Caskey. In the early 1990s the Basildon-born midfielder captained England's youth team and was deemed a hot property before playing a senior club game. A long-term Spurs future was widely predicted, and duly he enjoyed a settled sequence under Ossie Ardiles in 1993/94.

An energetic and tidy all-rounder, Caskey went some way towards confirming his potential, and it was felt that a tendency to fade in the later stages of games would disappear as he matured. However, star arrivals limited his opportunities in early 1994/95, after which new boss Gerry Francis opted for experience and Caskey was sidelined.

There were occasional outings as a deputy – he excelled in Tottenham's trouncing of Manchester United on New Year's Day 1996 – but further buys dimmed his prospects even more and a month later he joined Reading for £700,000. Though Caskey was young enough still to forge a top-flight future, his fortunes varied with the Royals, and he never quite made the impact expected of him for such a long time.

**DARREN MARK CASKEY**
BORN: Basildon, Essex, 21 August 1974.
OTHER CLUBS: Watford on loan 95/6 (6, 1); Reading 95/6-00/01 (202, 35); Notts County 01/02-03/04 (114, 10); Peterborough United 04/05 (4, 0); Virginia Beach Mariners, USA, 05-06; Rushden & Diamonds 05/06 (18, 1).

| GAMES | 29 (14) |
|-------|---------|
| GOALS | 5 |

# ERIK THORSTVEDT

## 1988/89 → 1994/95

Entertainer, cult hero, larger-than-life character, Erik Thorstvedt became much more than a mere goalkeeper to Tottenham loyalists during the Venables era, a colourful and flamboyant but occasionally uncertain period that, curiously enough, reflected his own personal contribution.

The blond, 6ft 4in Norwegian international – how naturally he wore his nickname of 'Erik the Viking' – had long harboured ambitions to play in England, having impressed in trials with Queen's Park Rangers, Spurs and Arsenal, but it was not until December 1988 that he was able to obtain a work permit, allowing Venables to complete his £400,000 purchase from IFK Gothenburg.

Drafted in to replace the troubled Bobby Mimms, Thorstvedt suffered a traumatic debut at home to Nottingham Forest in January when, in front of a huge TV audience, he gifted the winner to Nigel Clough and looked generally uneasy.

As he sought to adjust to English football, in which 'keepers are expected to exert more physical presence than elsewhere, there were further scares and another clanger against Charlton before the turning point came at Southampton.

Having brought down Alan Shearer at the edge of the box, he faced the possibility of a red card; but the referee showed mercy, Thorstvedt grew in confidence and made a series of fine saves. At the final whistle, to mark his first clean sheet, he threw his gloves to the travelling Spurs fans; both a custom and a rapport were born.

Subsequently, though his style appeared disconcertingly casual at times, Thorstvedt proved himself a high-class performer. Though he could be a little slow to reach low shots and was occasionally fallible on crosses, not many balls eluded his spidery reach, which also made him an effective smotherer of close-range threats.

However, Ian Walker was a dark cloud on the Thorstvedt horizon and after being unseated by the younger man for two lengthy spells, injury-plagued Erik succumbed finally to the youthful challenge in 1994/95. He was freed to join Wolves in the summer of 1996 but never played a senior game for the Molineux club.

| ERIK THORSTVEDT | | |
|---|---|---|
| **BORN:** | Stavanger, Norway, 28 November 1962. | |
| **HONOURS:** | FA Cup 90/1. 97 Norway caps (82-96). | |
| **OTHER CLUBS:** | EIK Tomsberg 82-83 (44, 0); Viking Stavanger 84-85 (38, 0), both Norway; | |
| | Borussia Moenchengladbach, West Germany, 86/7 (12, 0); IFK Gothenburg, Sweden, 87-88 (22, 0). | |

| | |
|---|---|
| GAMES | 217 (2) |
| GOALS | 0 |

# RONNY ROSENTHAL

### 1993/94 → 1996/97

Some footballers endear themselves to spectators as much by their bearing as by their specific deeds on the pitch. Such a man was Ronny 'The Rocket' Rosenthal, an effervescent character who played the game with a smile and communicated his evident enjoyment to the fans.

Having forged a reputation at Liverpool as a swashbuckling, hectically fast 'supersub', the Israeli international moved to Tottenham for £250,000 in January 1994. With Teddy Sheringham injured, Rosenthal served as a striker until season's end, and didn't fare badly, but unexpectedly it was as a left-sided midfielder that he compiled most of his century of Spurs appearances.

Kopites goggled to see their erstwhile loose cannon in such a relatively disciplined role, and while it is unlikely that he would have played as frequently but for Tottenham's perennial injury crisis, he did a splendid job before the arrival of Andy Sinton facilitated his free transfer to Watford in the summer of 1997.

Rosenthal left behind some happy memories, none more so than the spectacular hat-trick at Southampton in March 1995 which transformed a two-goal deficit into a crushing FA Cup replay victory. And all after former Anfield colleague Bruce Grobbelaar had greeted his arrival on the pitch with a gesture which seemed a tad less than complimentary!

**RONNY ROSENTHAL**
BORN: Haifa, Israel, 11 October 1963.
HONOURS: 55 Israel caps (84-97).
OTHER CLUBS: Maccabi Haifa, Israel; FC Bruges, Standard Liege, both Belgium; Liverpool 89/90-93/4 (74, 21); Watford 97/8-98/9 (30, 8).

| | |
|---|---|
| GAMES | 65 (35) |
| GOALS | 11 |

# ANDY TURNER

### 1992/93 → 1994/95

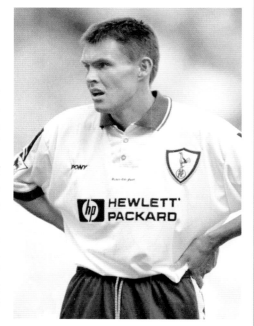

Andy Turner's failure to make the grade as a Spur is all the more saddening for the vast potential he displayed as an effervescent rookie during 1992/93. The presence of his name in the senior line-up on the opening Saturday produced quizzical frowns among all but that coterie of dedicated enthusiasts who follow their club at junior levels.

They were not surprised at the 17-year-old's inclusion on the left side of midfield because they knew what he could do; and in snatches, that day at The Dell and in subsequent senior outings, it became apparent to a wider audience that Andy was one to watch.

The Turner combination of skill and grit quickly made him a crowd favourite. A former England schoolboy whose dual nationality enabled him to switch allegiance to the Republic of Ireland (he was rewarded with an early under-21 call-up), Turner impressed with his neat passing, tenacity in chasing back and the sort of savage left-foot finish that brought a late winner at home to Everton in September.

He showed admirable coolness, too, but above all it was his speed that took the eye, troubling the most fleet-footed of opponents, especially on his occasional outings up front. Thereafter, though, Andy Turner could never force himself to the head of the crowded queue for first-team places and in September 1996 he joined Portsmouth for £250,000.

**ANDREW PETER TURNER**
BORN: Woolwich, London, 23 March 1975.
OTHER CLUBS: Wycombe Wanderers on loan 94/5 (4, 0); Doncaster Rovers on loan 94/5 (4, 1); Huddersfield Town on loan 95/6 (5, 1); Southend United on loan 95/6 (6, 0); Portsmouth 96/7-97/8 (40, 3); Crystal Palace 98/9 (2, 0); Rotherham United 99/00-00/01 (36, 1); Rochdale on loan 00/01 (4, 0); Northampton Town 02/03 (3, 0).

| | |
|---|---|
| GAMES | 8 (15) |
| GOALS | 4 |

# KEVIN SCOTT

1 9 9 3 / 9 4 → 1 9 9 5 / 9 6

# DAVID KERSLAKE

1 9 9 3 / 9 4 → 1 9 9 5 / 9 6

The memory of Kevin Scott is not cherished by the majority of Spurs supporters. The tall centre-half was bought by Ossie Ardiles to reinforce a creaking defence in February 1994 and, to be fair, he demonstrated plenty of pluck as relegation was avoided.

However, the unfortunate north-easterner was barracked cruelly for rash challenges which conceded penalties and free-kicks at crucial junctures, and was perceived as less than dominant in the air. His positional play was slammed, too, and the panning he received was enough to leave anyone's confidence in shreds.

Ardiles had rated Scott highly since managing him at Newcastle, where the left-sided stopper had spent five seasons as a first-team regular. But after helping to achieve promotion to the top flight in 1992/93 he was dropped and it was hoped that his £850,000 move south would revitalise his career.

Unable to command a Tottenham place in 1994/95, Scott was loaned to Port Vale, then suffered knee injuries with which he battled bravely but which severely hampered his attempts to return to senior contention. In January 1997 a £250,000 deal took him to Norwich where, happy to report, he regained something like the form of his Tyneside prime, albeit briefly.

David Kerslake made an enterprising start for Tottenham after his £450,000 transfer from Leeds United in September 1993, only to become the forgotten man of White Hart Lane after Gerry Francis replaced Ossie Ardiles as manager.

The pacy right-back, bought after Dean Austin suffered a broken leg, was very much an Ardiles favourite, the pair having prospered together at Swindon. A former midfielder, he was known best for his expertise as an overlapper and crosser, though in fairness he appeared adequate, if not outstanding, in defensive situations.

Illness and injuries limited his outings in 1993/94, though the presence of Austin always meant that competition for a place would be brisk. However, Kerslake held sway at the outset of 1994/95, and he was part of Ossie's gung-ho early autumn adventure which enthralled briefly, only to end in despair.

November brought the managerial change and Kerslake was ousted by Austin, never to command a regular berth again, though he remained a Spur until joining Ipswich in the summer of 1997.

**KEVIN WATSON SCOTT**
**BORN:** Easington, County Durham, 17 December 1966.
**OTHER CLUBS:** Newcastle United (227, 8); Port Vale on loan 94/5 (17, 1); Charlton Athletic on loan 96/7 (4, 0); Norwich City 96/7-97/8 (33, 0); Darlington on loan 98/9 (4, 0).

| GAMES | 16 (3) |
|-------|--------|
| GOALS | 1 |

**DAVID KERSLAKE**
**BORN:** Stepney, London, 19 June 1966.
**OTHER CLUBS:** Queen's Park Rangers 84/5-89/90 (58, 6); Swindon Town 89/90-92/3 (135, 1); Leeds United 92/3 (8, 0); Swindon Town on loan 96/7 (8, 0); Ipswich Town 97/8 (7, 0); Wycombe Wanderers on loan 97/8 (10, 0); Swindon Town 97/8-98/9 (24, 0).

| GAMES | 40 (4) |
|-------|--------|
| GOALS | 0 |

# ILIE DUMITRESCU

## 1994/95 → 1995/96

A mention of Ilie Dumitrescu to most Tottenham fans will produce a wistful smile, perhaps a shrug, and a few fond memories of a diverting fantasy which flickered vividly but all too fleetingly. The enigmatic Romanian midfielder arrived in north London in August 1994, fresh from a series of eye-catching displays in the World Cup Finals and from captaining his former club, Steaua Bucharest, to their domestic title.

At first glance Dumitrescu looked a bargain, even at £2.6 million. Operating on the extreme left of Ossie Ardiles' 'Famous Five', he was a bewitching entertainer, a serial nutmegger endowed with coruscating skills who thrived on the freedom to roam. Quick and strong, he demanded the ball constantly and carried it thrillingly, his progress studded by slick one-two passing movements which were a delight to behold.

Dumitrescu's favourite ploy was to receive the ball deep and near the left touchline, then run at defenders before dropping his shoulder, swerving inside and cutting a diagonal swathe across the opposing rearguard. He did it so often that it became predictable but, at least for a while, knowing it was going to happen and stopping it were two vastly different propositions.

However, before long opponents began countering the Dumitrescu menace by ushering him into blind alleys and simply crowding him out. As a result his fabulous footwork amounted to nothing and his penetrative incursions declined into fanciful and unproductive meanderings. If the situation rung alarm bells with Ardiles, then clearly it was utter anathema to his successor as manager, Gerry Francis, and it was no shock when Dumitrescu was loaned to Sevilla in December, a casualty of much-needed measures to tighten the side.

There was a brief recall in early 1995/96 but a Spurs exit was plainly beckoning and in March 1996 it materialised, after protracted work-permit difficulties, in the form of a £1.5 million transfer to West Ham. Sadly, Dumitrescu didn't flourish at Upton Park either, duly departing for a fresh start in Mexico. Happily, back at Tottenham there was no bitterness. After all, better to have loved and lost . . .

| | ILIE DUMITRESCU | |
|---|---|---|
| **BORN:** | Bucharest, Romania, 6 January 1969. | |
| **HONOURS:** | 62 Romania caps (89-98). | |
| **OTHER CLUBS:** | Steaua Bucharest, Romania, 86/7 (2, 0); FC Olt, Romania, 87/8 (31, 1); Steaua Bucharest 88/9-93/4 (163, 71); Sevilla, Spain, on loan 94/5 (13, 1); West Ham United 95/6-96/7 (10, 0); Futbol America, Mexico, 96-97; CF Atlante, Mexico, 97-98; Steaua Bucharest 98/9 (7, 3). | |
| **MANAGER:** | Otelul Galati (00-01); FCM Bacau (01-02); Brasov (02-03), all Romania; Egaleo, Akratitos, AEK Athens, Kallithea, PAOK, all Greece. | GAMES **18 (2)** |
| | | GOALS **5** |

# GICA POPESCU

## 1994/95

Gheorghe 'Gica' Popescu was an immensely accomplished and versatile footballer of world stature, but his part in the Spurs story proved frustratingly minimal. He was recruited at a cost of £2.9 million from PSV Eindhoven in September 1994 as Ossie Ardiles attempted to underpin his side's undoubted attacking flair with a much-needed infusion of midfield and defensive stability.

The Tottenham boss dubbed Gica 'the final piece in my jigsaw', a term employed frequently by managers making one last desperate throw of the dice. At this point, however, Ardiles had every right to be genuinely optimistic that the man who had been such a towering influence as Romania's sweeper during USA '94 was exactly what his unbalanced team needed.

In fact Popescu, who spent most of his short Tottenham sojourn as a deep-lying midfield anchorman and was employed only rarely in his international role, did play a telling part in Spurs' recovery from their autumn slump and their subsequent climb up the table, but only after Ardiles was dismissed. Frequently an oasis of calm in the midst of general mayhem, Popescu was a strolling prompter whose skill, vision and anticipation were outstanding and whose attacking instincts were reflected by three splendid goals, notably the neatly-steered winner at home to Arsenal in January 1995.

Yet there was a certain languid air about the elegant six-footer which could be disturbing in defensive situations – occasionally a casual back-pass would put colleagues under unnecessary pressure – and little attempt was made to disguise his distaste for chasing balls that had eluded him.

Nevertheless, when Popescu was injured against Wimbledon in February his influence was sorely missed during the lengthy absence that followed, and had he and Tottenham concluded that they were good for each other, their long-term union surely would have borne bountiful fruits.

Instead Gica Popescu and Gerry Francis agreed on a parting of the ways and in May 1995 the 27-year-old Romanian, whom Alan Sugar was later to declare could be kept out of action by a cracked eyelash, was sold to Barcelona for approximately the price of his original purchase.

**GHEORGHE POPESCU**

**BORN:** Calafat, Romania, 9 October 1967.

**HONOURS:** 115 Romania caps (88-03).

**OTHER CLUBS:** Universitatea Craiova 84/5-89/90 (103, 22); Steaua Bucharest on loan 87/8 (13, 1), both Romania; PSV Eindhoven, Holland, 90/1-94/5 (109, 24); Barcelona, Spain, 95/6-96/7 (59, 9); Galatasaray, Turkey, 97/8-00/01 (110, 5); Lecce, Italy, 01/02 (28, 3); Dinamo Bucharest, Romania, 02/03 (8, 0); Hannover, Germany, 02/03 (14, 1).

| GAMES | 28 |
| GOALS | 3 |

# TEDDY SHERINGHAM

## 1992/93 → 1996/97 & 2001/02 → 2002/03

The cascades of vitriol which descended on Teddy Sheringham's head when he returned to White Hart Lane to play his first game for Manchester United following his bombshell move to Old Trafford in July 1997 were inversely proportionate to the affection in which he was previously held by long-suffering Tottenham supporters. After all, he had been a Spurs follower himself and, on arrival, in a £2.1million deal from Nottingham Forest in August 1992, he had been at pains to stress that sporting the beloved cockerel on his chest was all his heart desired.

Thereafter, having endured an uneasy settling-in period when he was jeered by a small but vociferous faction of 'fans' who failed to perceive the delicious subtleties of the Sheringham game, he became the most popular player at the club. In fairness to the self-assured Londoner, by the time he exchanged cockerel for Red Devil in a quest for honours which seemed increasingly likely to elude him at the Lane, he had provided impeccable value for money.

Sheringham's distinctive combination of intelligence and technique made him arguably the most effective deep-lying English centre-forward of the 1990s, an exquisitely perceptive linker of play as well as, at his best, a lethal marksman. As a teenage upstart at Millwall, he had been harangued for his lack of pace and told he was too lazy to make it in the top flight. But those critics had ignored his lightning-quick footballing brain, which was of infinitely more worth than the excess of huffing and puffing which characterised countless front-runners of lesser wit.

Teddy excelled at dropping into space between forwards and midfield, an area where many markers were loth to follow. His first touch was invariably sure, his finishing range covered the whole gamut from delicate placement to full-blooded blast and his aerial prowess as both a scorer and a provider was tremendous. Strike partners were known to get earache from his vocal imprecations, but he was a perfectionist who demanded the finest standards from himself and those around him. Indeed, it is no coincidence that most of his regular co-workers tended to prosper, and no less a judge than Jurgen Klinsmann described Sheringham as the best he had played alongside.

Remarkably, in view of his initial difficulties, he topped the Premier League's scoring charts in 1992/93, then started the following campaign in similarly prolific vein. A severe knee injury cost him five months of 1993/94, yet still he contributed 16 goals in 19 starts, the most impressive goals-to-games ratio of his Tottenham tenure. During 1994/95 the mantle of chief sharpshooter shifted to the German star, under whose tutelage Sheringham thrived, and subsequently Teddy moved on to a new plane of accomplishment which saw him emerge as the preferred international partner for Alan Shearer.

In his earlier days he had mastered two brands of attacking football – the long-ball method under George Graham at The Den and the precision-passing style of Brian Clough's Forest – and by the end of his first Spurs stay, he had become an adaptable all-rounder of the highest order. Sheringham's value to the team was incalculable and it became evident during prolonged absences through injury in 1996/97 that perhaps they relied on him too much.

Thus the consternation at the Lane was overwhelming when Teddy joined United, being unveiled as a natural replacement for the recently retired Eric Cantona. Dismayed fans, angered that Alan Sugar had accepted half his asking price from Old Trafford, felt the switch was confirmation of the unspoken truth that Tottenham had become a second-class power. But, considering his magnificent service in north London, there was no genuine cause to begrudge a supreme professional four silverware-laden years in Manchester.

Even then Sheringham, still lean and chiselled, was proud of his reputation as the Peter Pan of the Premiership. When will he retire, the pundits asked, after the 33-year-old struck the equaliser for United during their astonishing European Cup Final comeback in Barcelona? He must be finished now, they said as, two years later, he became one of the oldest players to win awards from both the football writers and his fellow professionals.

But in the subsequent summer of 2001, Glenn Hoddle offered Sheringham the chance to return to Tottenham as club captain, and he relished the opportunity, arriving for training at Chigwell with the gusto of an ambitious teenager. Every day the new skipper would stay on when his team-mates had gone home, working assiduously on his technique before completing 100 press-ups and sit ups.

Initially the hard work paid off as his rich scoring patch helped fire Spurs to the League Cup Final, and he earned an England recall. But in July 2003 managerial upheaval provoked a switch to Portsmouth, where the veteran surprised most observers by continuing to flourish. Come 2006, by then in West Ham's colours, he became the first 40-year-old to score in the Premiership. After 23 years in the job, Teddy Sheringham was still bathing in the sunshine of the modern game's longest Indian Summer.

| | | GAMES | 270 (7) |
|---|---|---|---|
| **EDWARD PAUL SHERINGHAM** | | | |
| **BORN:** | Highams Park, London, 2 April 1966. | | |
| **HONOURS:** | 51 England caps (93-02). FWA Footballer of the Year 01. PFA Footballer of the Year 01. | | |
| **OTHER CLUBS:** | Millwall 83/4-90/1 (220, 93); Aldershot on loan 84/5 (5, 0); Nottingham Forest 91/2-92/3 (42, 14); Manchester United 97/8-00/01 (104, 31); Portsmouth 03/04 (32, 9); West Ham United 04/05-06/07 (76, 28); Colchester United 07/08 (19, 3). | GOALS | 125 |

# JURGEN KLINSMANN

## 1994/95 & 1997/98

If ever a club needed a hero it was Tottenham Hotspur in the summer of 1994. Banned from the FA Cup and with 12 Premiership points deducted before they had kicked a ball, the beleaguered north Londoners were in calamitous straits, the new season looming like a bottomless pit of despair. Enter Jurgen Klinsmann, whose impact could hardly have been greater had he strode into White Hart Lane in a suit of shining armour and set up a round table in the centre circle.

Certainly there was something knightly about the charismatic German, whose footballing achievements were hailed universally yet who had been demonised by British fans for what they perceived as undue theatricality in the vicinity of opponents' penalty areas. Immediately on arrival, Jurgen disarmed his critics with an exquisitely judged line in irony, asking for the whereabouts of local diving schools. Then, after scoring on his debut against Sheffield Wednesday, he celebrated by hurling himself to the Hillsborough turf in an affable parody of his own reputation.

Thereafter Klinsmania spread like wildfire, fanned in equal proportions by on-the-field derring-do and off-the-field charm, modesty and astuteness. On his home debut he scored with an explosive scissors-kick, one of a brace in a 2-1 victory over Everton, and he became the riveting focal point of the brief but intoxicating interlude in which Ossie Ardiles experimented with his 'Famous Five' forward line. When that particular bubble burst, as it was bound to do, the 30-year-old marksman demonstrated his substance by continuing to flourish under the more pragmatic regime of Gerry Francis.

Klinsmann, who finished the campaign with 29 goals in 50 senior outings, was a truly magnificent centre-forward. Acute intelligence and polished all-round technique were buttressed by pace and strength, courage and determination in ample quantities, but his most vivid characteristic was ruthlessness. Prowling among defenders, he could seem restrained, almost casual at times, like an overfed wolf casting an idle eye over a field of grazing sheep. But give him the faintest whiff of an extra morsel and he was at their throats, yards of seemingly secure space consumed in a couple of lightning strides, ready for yet another kill.

For all that lethal grandeur, however, he was an unfussy performer, ever willing to do the necessary as well as the flamboyant, and he proved an ideal foil for Teddy Sheringham, whose game profited hugely from their all-too-short association.

Having contributed seminally to Spurs' climb up the table and their progress to an FA Cup semi-final (the penalties for financial irregularities having been commuted to a fine), Klinsmann was an overwhelmingly popular choice as the writers' Footballer of the Year and supporters indulged in joyous fantasies concerning his second term at the Lane.

Then came devastation. That summer the messiah-like figure who had transformed the Tottenham mood so comprehensively, engendering genuine hope where there had been creeping desolation, announced that he had new fields to conquer and departed to Bayern Munich for £1.3 million.

He left half-way through a two-year contract and some of those who had come to cherish Klinsmann felt betrayed. Certainly Tottenham chairman Alan Sugar did, brandishing the hitherto hallowed number-18 shirt and declaring famously that it wasn't even fit for washing his car. But the majority, while mourning the loss of their talisman, swallowed their disappointment, reminded themselves that he had given impeccable value for money and bid him an affectionate adieu.

Just as well, in the circumstances. After adding voraciously to his already enviable collection of medals, Jurgen, now 33, returned to Spurs in December 1997, a fee of £175,000 securing his services from Sampdoria for the remainder of the season. Once again the club was in crisis but this time the globetrotting German was past his playing peak, a shadow of the dashing crusader of yore.

Nevertheless his galvanising presence and undiluted professionalism added much-needed toughness to the team's psyche and his farewell flourish, a four-goal salvo against Wimbledon in the campaign's penultimate match when points were still at a premium, was pure Klinsmann. Thus, despite his well-publicised differences with coach Christian Gross, Jurgen Klinsmann's second coming must go down as a success. As for the first, the scale of his impact was impossible to exaggerate.

| | JURGEN KLINSMANN | | |
|---|---|---|---|
| BORN: | Goppingen, Germany, 30 July 1964. | | |
| HONOURS: | 108 Germany caps (87-98). FWA Footballer of the Year 95. | | |
| OTHER CLUBS: | Stuttgart Kickers 81/2-83/4 (61, 22); Stuttgart 84/5-88/9 (156, 79), both Germany; Internazionale, Italy, 89/90-91/2 | | |
| | (95, 34); Monaco, France, 92/3-93/4 (65, 29); Bayern Munich, Germany, 95/6-96/7 (65, 31); Sampdoria, Italy, 97/8 (8, 2); | | |
| | Orange County Blue Star, USA, 03 (8, 5). | | GAMES 68 |
| MANAGER: | Germany (04-06); Bayern Munich (08-). | | GOALS 38 |

# DARREN ANDERTON

## 1992/93 → 2003/04

Gerry Francis once ventured the opinion that Darren Anderton had the potential to achieve for Spurs what Eric Cantona did for Manchester United and, in terms of pure ability, the former White Hart Lane boss's assessment did not seem wholly fanciful. But there was a problem. While the tempestuous Frenchman rarely missed a match – at least, not through injury – the would-be Tottenham talisman was absent from action for vast stretches of his expected prime.

A cruel catalogue of maladies – mostly of the groin variety though there were knee and hamstring problems, too – demoralised Darren at a time when he should have been underlining his stature as one of England's most extravagantly gifted performers. Indeed, to list the Anderton attributes is to assemble an *Identikit* picture which comes tolerably close to most people's vision of the ideal footballer. Assured control, fluent distribution, devastating acceleration and a fulminating shot were underpinned by a keen football brain and an irreproachable work rate. He was in the David Beckham class as a crosser and, despite his rather slender build, he was no pushover in the tackle. True, he was not outstanding in the air for a six-footer, but to dwell on that in the face of so much that is excellent would be more than a tad uncharitable. To top it all, he was an engagingly modest chap, oozing decency and every parent's image of a perfect role model, which made it all the more frustrating that, particularly between 1995 and 1998, new Spurs fans could be excused for asking 'Darren Who?'

In retrospect, there was an ominous foretaste of future difficulties during the autumn of 1992, following Anderton's £2 million summer move to Tottenham from Portsmouth. He began disappointingly and supporters started making unfavourable comparisons between the coltish 20-year-old and former hero Chris Waddle. Eventually the newcomer's missing spark was traced to a hernia condition and by the New Year, after an operation, the real Darren Anderton stood up. Suddenly there was confidence where there had been doubt. Now he was flowing past defenders before whipping in the sort of wickedly curving centres that Teddy Sheringham had met previously only in his dreams, or shooting for goal on his own account. More dangerous on the right than on the left, but at his best floating free, Anderton was a major reason for a marked upturn in team fortunes.

Sadly Spurs' improvement did not continue during the following campaign, but Darren's did, resulting in an England debut that attracted lavish international praise. Season 1994/95 brought further advances, first as a member of Ossie Ardiles' briefly exhilarating Famous Five and then as part of new boss Gerry Francis' tighter midfield unit. Anderton's burgeoning reputation was underlined that summer by a £5 million bid from Manchester United, who wanted him to replace Andrei Kanchelskis, but he affirmed his loyalty to the Tottenham cause and 1995/96 beckoned alluringly. His absence from the opening games with a seemingly minor strain was seen as a temporary inconvenience, a view borne out by his return in September when his form in his preferred position of central midfield, particularly during a 3-1 victory at Sheffield Wednesday, hinted at world class. But then began a period of utter and seemingly endless frustration. A hernia sidelined him for almost all the remainder of that term, and after recovering to take part in Euro '96, he managed only a handful of intermittent Premiership starts in 1996/97.

The sorry situation continued into 1997/98, provoking widespread pessimism among fans, who expected him to break down every time he made it on to the pitch. Disillusioned with false dawns, many felt that in terms of team-building, Tottenham should simply presume Anderton was not going to be there and buy accordingly. Then, if he were able to make a sustained return, what a marvellous bonus it would be. Few would doubt that had Francis been able to fulfil his intention of building the team around Darren Anderton then the player would have developed into a practically priceless asset. Indeed, the manager might even have kept his job! But harsh reality dictated otherwise.

A glorious strike for England in the 1998 World Cup against Columbia reminded Spurs fans of his sumptuous capabilities, but soon after returning home he succumbed once more to serial fragility, then a switch to a central midfield anchor role did little to massage his influence. When Anderton was released in the summer of 2004 it remained maddening to reflect that one of Tottenham's most gifted creators of the modern era had missed so many games during his dozen years in north London. But it was a touching testament to brittle old 'Sicknote', and his capacity to thrill when his limbs were in full working order, that the club medics whom he had stretched so sorely were as overwhelmingly sad to see him leave as all the other lovers of high-quality football in the White Hart Lane community.

**DARREN ROBERT ANDERTON**

| | |
|---|---|
| BORN: | Southampton, Hampshire, 3 March 1972. |
| HONOURS: | League Cup 98/9. 30 England caps (94-01). |
| OTHER CLUBS: | Portsmouth 90/1-91/2 (62, 7); Birmingham City 04/05 (20, 3).; Wolverhampton Wanderers 05/06 (24, 1); Bournemouth 06/07- (48, 9). |

| | |
|---|---|
| GAMES | 329 (29) |
| GOALS | 48 |

# RUEL FOX

· · · · · · · · · · · · · · · · · · · ·

## 1995/96 → 1999/2000

If only Ruel Fox had always played for Spurs as he did at home to Arsenal in November 1995. That day, a month after his £4.2 million arrival from Newcastle, the little flankman captivated the eye, outwitting defenders like some effervescent imp dancing past a collection of garden gnomes. Running from deep, mostly down the right touchline but roving menacingly to all forward areas, he dispatched a stream of accurate crosses and inspired a rousing 2-1 victory.

Unfortunately, that delicious display was to prove more of an exception than the real Ruel. Oh, the England 'B' international contributed plenty of pleasing interludes during matches in each of his first four campaigns at the Lane, tormenting opponents wickedly with his mesmeric dribbling skills, but he made a habit of failing to seize a game and moulding it in the unarguable fashion his ability appeared to warrant. It has to be mentioned, too, that there were far too many occasions when he was a peripheral figure, working back faithfully and clearly trying to get involved, but dithering in possession, crossing erratically and finishing abominably.

Gerry Francis signed Fox to supply some attacking penetration in the protracted absence through injury of Darren Anderton and, following those early fireworks against the Gunners, he did enough to suggest during the remainder of 1995/96 that he might fit the bill. The fans liked the Fox style and, for a while, were prepared to live with his inconsistency, but 1996/97 brought problems. Ruel suffered some niggling injuries and the manager's espousal of wing-backs cost him his place at times, hardly conducive to underpinning confidence which may have been dented as critical voices began to make themselves heard at home games.

However, there was cause for renewed optimism in August 1997 when he shone against Aston Villa at White Hart Lane, scoring once and setting up two for Les Ferdinand. Then came a sumptuous strike against Carlisle in the League Cup, when he received the ball with his back to goal, swivelled to dupe two markers and netted emphatically. But despite becoming more consistent eventually under new boss Christian Gross, Fox seemed no more given to decisive contributions and for every flash of genuine quality there would be multiple instances of flattering to deceive.

His role would be dramatically reduced following the arrival of George Graham as manager, and after failing to win a starting berth even for Spurs' reserves, in August 2000 he leapt at the opportunity of a £200,000 move to West Bromwich Albion, whom he helped to reach the Premiership. Later Fox opened a restaurant in Ipswich, then coached and played for the Caribbean island of Montserrat. As to his enduring impact at White Hart Lane, that was debatable. Was he an entertainer? Yes, sometimes. But was he a match-winner? All too rarely.

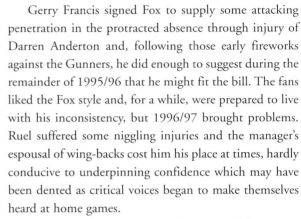

| **RUEL ADRIAN FOX** | | GAMES | **114 (15)** |
| --- | --- | --- | --- |
| BORN: | Ipswich, Suffolk, 14 January 1968. | GOALS | 15 |
| OTHER CLUBS: | Norwich City 86/7-93/4 (172, 22); Newcastle United 93/4-95/6 (58, 12); West Bromwich Albion 00/01-01/02 (58, 2). | | |

# ANDY SINTON

## 1995/96 → 1998/99

He was never going to drown in an ocean of public praise, yet Andy Sinton ranks as one of the canniest signings of Gerry Francis' managerial reign. Indeed, the boundlessly enthusiastic Geordie was the club's most consistent attacking player during 1996/97, and Tottenham's toil in the subsequent campaign might have been significantly less severe had his personal contribution not been interrupted so drastically by injury.

Sinton was a left winger cum midfielder blessed with an accomplished all-round technique and extensive nous accumulated while paying his dues around all four divisions and on the international stage. His work rate was prodigious, he had considerably more flair than most critics allowed and, to top it all off, he was almost foolhardily brave in a Bryan Robson sort of way. In fact, the last-mentioned attribute could be a drawback, as his refusal to duck out of even the most unequal challenge frequently deposited him unceremoniously on to the casualty list.

The Sinton purchase for £1.5 million from Sheffield Wednesday in January 1996 surprised many observers, who reckoned that Spurs should be aiming higher than a so-called journeyman who was nudging 30 and whose fitness record at Hillsborough had been chequered. But Francis had employed Andy to tremendous effect at Queen's Park Rangers and had terrific respect for a performer whose diverse abilities had been rewarded with a dozen England caps under Graham Taylor.

Replacing Ronny Rosenthal on the left flank, Sinton enjoyed a characteristically tidy debut in a goalless draw at Liverpool in February, then cemented his place before falling victim to injury before season's end. There were those who snorted at the setback, saying it was predictable, but they were made to eat their words the following term when Sinton played some of the finest football of his career, particularly in an all-too-brief stint in a Cantona-like support role behind the strikers.

Revelling in the unaccustomed freedom, he expressed himself with a creativity which might have blossomed still more luxuriantly had he been given the opportunity some years earlier. However, team circumstances dictated a return to the wider position and, when fitness allowed, Andy Sinton continued to fill it, passionately but unobtrusively, until he was freed in the summer of 1999 to finish his career with a spirited spell at Wolves.

| | |
|---|---|
| **ANDREW SINTON** | |
| BORN: | Cramlington, Northumberland, 19 March 1966. |
| HONOURS: | League Cup 98/9. 12 England caps (91-93). |
| OTHER CLUBS: | Cambridge United 82/3-85/6 (93, 13); Brentford 85/6-88/9 (149, 28); Queen's Park Rangers 88/9-92/3 (160, 22); Sheffield Wednesday 93/4-95/6 (60, 3); Wolverhampton Wanderers 99/00-01/02 (72, 3). |

| | |
|---|---|
| GAMES | 76 (24) |
| GOALS | 7 |

# DAVID HOWELLS

## 1985/86 → 1997/98

A little more luck, a lot more credit; David Howells deserved them both during a largely untrumpeted but enormously productive and influential White Hart Lane career. It is instructive that his all-too-frequent absences, usually through injury but occasionally through managerial whim, tended to coincide with periods of Tottenham travail, and that on his return, invariably, the team displayed infinitely more backbone, purpose and composure. Howells let no one down, either leading the attack in his early senior days or in subsequent stints shoring up the centre of defence, but it is as a midfield anchorman, prowling watchfully in front of the back line, that the affable all-rounder was at his most effective.

Ample evidence of his excellence was available in 1989/90 and 1990/91 when the Howells blend of reliability and intelligence – spiced, it should be said, with periodic shafts of imagination – allowed Paul Gascoigne the freedom his genius demanded. But perhaps the most vivid illustration of David's immense worth came in the second half of 1994/95. Having been discarded, or at least chronically under-used, by Ossie Ardiles, he became a veritable bulwark of the side under Gerry Francis, performing with metronomic consistency in his unglamorous but crucial role as Spurs' security blanket and helping to tighten all aspects of team play. In the seasons that followed, fitness permitting, his dependability was of Gary Mabbutt proportions and, in Tottenham terms, praise doesn't come higher than that.

The teenage Howells had arrived at the Lane as a striker good enough to win England youth and under-19 caps. He made an early impact on the senior scene with the winning goal against Sheffield Wednesday at Hillsborough in February 1986 and his combination of skill, industry and aerial prowess – he displayed an enterprising knack of arriving late in front of goal – hinted at riches in store. But competition for a marksman's place was intense, and soon the six-footer's comprehensive abilities were deployed in midfield, with the occasional spell as an emergency defender underlining his versatility.

One deficiency in Howells' game was lack of pace, and it's true that on occasion he could be bypassed by nippy, slick-passing opponents. But usually his canny positional play and vast experience in the holding position allowed him to cope admirably and, at need, he could tackle with a force which belied his relatively slender build. As a passer he was underrated, because in most situations he was content to feed the ball quickly and unfussily to better-placed colleagues. Yet Howells possessed the vision and technique to split a defence with a perfect long-distance dispatch, as he showed when freeing Ruel Fox to set up the first goal for Nicola Berti in the rousing, sorely needed victory at Blackburn in February 1998.

He retained his old eye for goal, too, being equally capable of striking with spectacular precision or battling for the messy tap-in. And for those who decried him as anonymous, what about his display at Nottingham Forest in October 1990? That afternoon Howells equalised with a delightful 20-yard curler, made a dramatic clearance from his own line, then immediately strode forward to nod a late winner. That's the sort of anonymity most managers would kill for.

Unfortunately, David suffered frequent injuries, disrupting his own career impetus as well as weakening the side immeasurably. Indeed, the immediate task facing Christian Gross would have been considerably less daunting with a fully-fit Howells to call upon. At senior representative level, he never progressed beyond his selection for the Football League in 1990 which, in truth, given the quality of his rivals for recognition, was an accurate reflection of his niche in the top-flight scene.

Though David Howells celebrated his thirtieth birthday during 1997/98, and had experienced apparently serious differences of opinion with Gross, he remained a dedicated professional who, given less time on the treatment table, appeared to have plenty still to offer at Premiership level. However, at the end of a trying season he was given a free transfer and Spurs bade farewell to one of their doughtiest servants.

**DAVID HOWELLS**
BORN: Guildford, Surrey, 15 December 1967.
HONOURS: FA Cup 90/1.
OTHER CLUBS: Southampton 98/9 (9, 1); Bristol City on loan 98/9 (8, 1).

GAMES 289 (48)
GOALS 27

# STEPHEN CARR

## 1993/94 → 2003/04

White Hart Lane could rest easy when Stephen Carr was scampering up and down Tottenham's right touchline. He was a comfort blanket with which to tuck home supporters into their seats. The Irish full-back, for all his squat appearance and scuttling gait, became a veritable linchpin of the side, diligent and vastly accomplished in every element of his game.

By the autumn of 1999 Spurs fans already knew that in Carr their team possessed a flank defender of truly exceptional talent, but just how comprehensively gifted he was they discovered during a heated showdown with Manchester United. Striding through curtains of torrential rain, he latched on to a loose ball some 30 yards from goal before unleashing a bullet of a shot that flew unerringly into the far top corner of 'keeper Mark Bosnich's net. It was one of the Lane's most memorable strikes of the decade.

After winning a regular place for the first time in 1996, Carr seemed to get better and better. It was just reward for a young Dubliner with steely determination who had left his home-town in his early teens for trials at Arsenal. But it didn't work out for him at Highbury and Tottenham gave him a chance. The ink had barely dried on his YTS forms when he was handed a surprise call-up to the first-team squad, But after playing two senior games in a week as a 17-year-old in September 1993 – following injury to Dean Austin and shortly before the arrival of David Kerslake – the floppy-haired full-back went back to basics at junior level for the next three years.

He was recalled to the top flight by Gerry Francis in September 1996 and performed with admirable composure, retaining his place for all but a handful of games until season's end. His progress continued under both Francis and Christian Gross in 1997/98, when he was Spurs' only Premiership ever-present and rose to the verge of full international status.

At a time when everyone at the club was under severe pressure, Carr's advances were to be applauded. His defensive contribution was generally solid, though there were positional aberrations and occasionally his decision-making – principally whether to pass his way out of trouble or to dispatch the ball in the direction of row Z – caused palpitations in the stands and, no doubt, on the bench. But his industry, stamina and enthusiasm were beyond reproach and his penchant for accelerating down the right wing provided an important attacking outlet. True, his crossing needed to be more consistent – such a common complaint, even at the highest level – but Stephen showed himself capable of impeccable delivery, notably at Middlesbrough in October 1996, when his exhilarating 50-yard dash past Emerson and Curtis Fleming set up a successful strike for Teddy Sheringham.

Carr boasted self-belief beyond his years. Though not a ranter or bellower, he was nothing loth to cast a scowl at a more experienced team-mate should a pass go carelessly astray. His finest years as a Spur were undoubtedly between 1997 and 2001, when he emerged as one of the Premiership's elite in his position. He starred as the club savoured some long-awaited silverware in the shape of the League Cup in 1999, and praise was rightfully heaped on him during the subsequent term.

Following that fulminating strike against United, a television commentator declared that Carr would never score a goal of that pedigree again. But he did, only eight months later. Against Sunderland he won a header in his own half, before beating two defenders and galloping virtually the full length of the pitch. Then, as he raced towards the 18-yard area, Stephen stopped in his tracks and sent a deft flick over the advancing 'keeper. Deservedly he was named the club's player of the year that same week. Surely this was Tottenham's captain in waiting?

But even as the gushing superlatives rang in his ears, Carr saw his fortunes take a tumble at the end of the next campaign, as knee problems left him sidelined and increasingly frustrated for a year. When he returned there seemed to be a new edge to his game; his dark locks had been shaved and he appeared to have adopted a cut-throat attitude to match. It seemed that those Irish eyes were smiling no more, especially as he struggled with his form and quibbled lengthily over a new contract. In August 2004, when it became crystal clear that one of White Hart Lane's favourite sons was determined to fly the nest, the Spurs directors reluctantly accepted Newcastle United's £2 million offer to take him to Tyneside.

**STEPHEN CARR**
BORN: Dublin, 29 August 1976.
HONOURS: League Cup 98/9. 44 Republic of Ireland caps (99-07).
OTHER CLUBS: Newcastle United 04/05- (78, 1).

| GAMES | 265 (5) |
| GOALS | 8 |

# ESPEN BAARDSEN

## 1996/97 → 1998/99

Espen Baardsen was barely out of his teens when whispers of 'another Schmeichel' began to reverberate optimistically around White Hart Lane. Sadly, the California-raised Norway international never came remotely close to becoming the influential figure that Tottenham supporters craved so passionately to stand between their posts. Yet, in fairness to the immense raw potential of the 6ft 5in custodian, it had required no quantum leap of the imagination to visualise a scenario in which he might develop along similar lines to Manchester United's Danish colossus.

After arriving in north London in the summer of 1996 on a free transfer from San Francisco All Blacks, Baardsen was quick to impress, earning a place on the substitutes' bench for most of that Premiership campaign before replacing the injured Ian Walker for 45 minutes against Liverpool in May. That afternoon at Anfield, he made a series of splendid diving saves, but perhaps it was his calm, almost nonchalant air as Steve McManaman and company buzzed around his goal which spoke most eloquently of his big-time possibilities.

That impression was reinforced during the opening months of 1998 when, with Walker sidelined again, Baardsen stepped into the demotion dogfight. Soon Spurs fans were acclaiming his athleticism and acute reflexes, and although there was an obvious need for improvement in his positional play, and he wasn't always making the most of his height and weight in close aerial combat, his potential seemed limitless.

Continued plaudits, though qualified, were heartening. For instance, at Old Trafford in January the Norwegian was a model of all-round proficiency until he dropped a cross, allowing Ryan Giggs to score, after which he appeared utterly unfazed by the mishap. At home to Leicester the following month, a stunning deflection from Emile Heskey was followed by a spill which cost a goal, but that characteristic self-possession came to his aid and there was no suggestion of further errors. Best of all, in the Lane encounter with fellow strugglers Bolton in March, he protected a 1-0 lead with a stupendous dive to his left to tip away a long-distance scorcher from Jimmy Phillips.

Work to do? There was oceans of it, but while Baardsen had the physical resources to make the grade, it seemed he lacked the mental toughness to force his way into first-team reckoning. The arrival of Neil Sullivan saw him slump to third place in the pecking order, and following short spells at Watford and Everton he quit football at the age of 25, having lost his appetite for the game. Later he became a business analyst based not far from White Hart Lane, those premature Schmeichel comparisons seeming more than a little fanciful.

| PER ESPEN BAARDSEN | | |
|---|---|---|
| **BORN:** San Rafael, USA, 7 December 1977. | | |
| **HONOURS:** 4 Norway caps (98-00). | **GAMES** | **27 (2)** |
| **OTHER CLUBS:** San Francisco All Blacks, USA; Watford 00/01-01/02 (41, 0); Everton 02/03 (1, 0). | **GOALS** | 0 |

# CLIVE WILSON

## 1995/96 → 1997/98

Having started his Spurs career in his 34th year, Clive Wilson exceeded the expectations of most pundits in giving three campaigns of consummately professional service to the White Hart Lane cause. True, as the amiable Mancunian's tenure lengthened steadily, supporters wondered why a club of Tottenham's stature should be relying on such a gnarled veteran, and Christian Gross did attempt to draft in Andy Hinchcliffe midway through 1997/98. But none could take issue with the wisdom of Gerry Francis in acquiring out-of-contract Wilson from Queen's Park Rangers, where the two had prospered together for so long, on a free transfer in June 1995.

Best employed at left-back but adaptable enough to play on the right or in midfield, Wilson was a splendid all-round footballer, comfortable in possession, a smooth and reliable passer and a penetrative overlapper. Utterly unflappable in moments of crisis, he was not prone to hasty neck-or-nothing challenges; instead he would jockey opponents intelligently, not committing himself until the odds were in his favour, an unshowy but effective style of defending.

A telling example of the Wilson expertise came at home to Newcastle United in the October of his first and finest season as a Spur. In the first half Clive was given an almighty chasing by a rampant Keith Gillespie, who must have been relishing the prospect of the second period. But after the break the balance of power was reversed as Wilson used all his experience, refraining from tackles and concentrating on positional play, frustrating the Ulsterman and neutralising his menace by ushering him repeatedly away from the danger area.

In the summer of 1997 Wilson underwent ankle surgery and there was understandable speculation about his future. But he returned to fitness in time for a recall at the outset of the Gross reign and, though there were inevitable signs of slowing down, his canny reading of the game and classy technique carried him through. After that it seemed unreasonable to expect more, but what a commendable Indian summer Clive Wilson had known.

| | |
|---|---|
| **CLIVE EUCLID AKLANA WILSON** | |
| **BORN:** | Manchester, 13 November 1961. |
| **OTHER CLUBS:** | Manchester City 81/2-86/7 (98, 9); Chester City on loan 82/3 (21, 2); Chelsea 87/8-89/90 (81, 5); Manchester City on loan 86/7 (11, 0); Queen's Park Rangers 90/1-94/5 (172, 12); Cambridge United 99/00 (27, 0). |

| GAMES | 78 (4) |
|---|---|
| GOALS | 2 |

# COLIN CALDERWOOD

## 1993/94 → 1998/99

Colin Calderwood was handed the formidable task of replacing warrior and cult hero Neil Ruddock at the core of Tottenham's rearguard and, while it would be a gross exaggeration to assert he received universal acclaim for his efforts, the calm, experienced Scot made a brave fist of it. After all, Calderwood's doughty central-defensive displays won him a full international debut at the age of 30 and he never disgraced himself on the world stage. In addition, he rendered assistance to Tottenham as a reliable anchorman in front of the back line, even operating as a conventional if extremely limited midfielder on occasions.

But if Spurs had their money's worth after Ossie Ardiles paid Swindon Town £1.25 million for his former County Ground skipper in the summer of 1993 – the tribunal-set fee was three times Ardiles' original offer – the ride was not always a smooth one for the dedicated Calderwood. He

settled well enough initially, impressing with his strength, industry and composure, but as Spurs' devastatingly disappointing 1993/94 campaign dragged on, he lost his place to newcomer Kevin Scott through a combination of injuries and ragged form. That summer there was talk of a move to Celtic, or even back to Swindon, but he remained at the Lane to join in the swashbuckling start to the subsequent term, at times toiling in impractical semi-isolation between the back four and the forwards.

Happily, the arrival of Gerry Francis saw Calderwood return to central defence, where he performed with such admirable consistency that he attracted the attention of Scotland boss Craig Brown. The 1995/96 campaign, during which he forged a solid partnership with Sol Campbell, was his most effective to date and he capped it by excelling for his country in Euro '96.

A niggling knee problem dogged him throughout much of 1996/97, but he soldiered on selflessly, missing only a handful of games. However, having turned 32 in the January and with Messrs Scales and Vega fresh on the scene, Calderwood's Tottenham future appeared tenuous. Typically, though, he persisted, striving manfully if mundanely in midfield when necessary in 1997/98 and the early months of 1998/99, while continuing to deputise at the back. In March 1999 the versatile veteran was sold to Aston Villa for £225,000, playing on until his middle thirties, then embarking on a promising managerial career. For a footballer who didn't make his top-flight debut until his 29th year, Colin Calderwood could consider himself commendably fulfilled.

| COLIN CALDERWOOD | | |
|---|---|---|
| **BORN:** | Stranraer, Wigtownshire, 20 January 1965. | |
| **HONOURS:** | 36 Scotland caps (95-99). | |
| **OTHER CLUBS:** | Mansfield Town 81/2-84/5 (100, 1); Swindon Town 85/6-92/3 (330, 20); Aston Villa 98/9-99/00 (26, 0); Nottingham Forest 99/00-00/01 (8, 0); Notts County on loan 00/01 (5, 0). | |
| **MANAGER:** | Northampton Town (03-06); Nottingham Forest (06-). | |

GAMES **186 (13)**

GOALS **8**

# IAN WALKER

· · · · · · · · · · · · · · · · · · · · · · · · · · · · · · · ·

## 1990/91 → 2000/01

Opinions diverged sharply over the merits of Ian Walker. There were those who sang the praises of the flamboyant goalkeeper, citing his rapid rise to England international stature as proof of his excellence. Others denounced him as flashy but unreliable, admitting that he was a fine shot-stopper while maintaining that he lacked physical presence and that the primary cause of his acrobatics was that he didn't claim enough crosses.

There appeared to be no such doubts when the chant of 'Ian the Saxon' took its place in the Shelf repertoire during the autumn of 1991. The label, of course, referred to the nickname of regular custodian Erik 'The Viking' Thorstvedt, beloved of Lane regulars but out of whose shadow his rookie rival looked increasingly likely to step. Walker, the son of former Norwich and Everton boss Mike Walker, seemed to be a natural, displaying an exhilarating all-round aptitude for his work, exuding confidence in abundance and communicating readily to the fans his evident enjoyment of the game.

After making his debut at Norwich in April 1991, he earned protracted first-team sequences on merit in each of the next three seasons, attracting plaudits for his acute reflexes, courage at feet and quickness of recovery, though always there was the rider that he needed to improve his aerial work. By 1994/95 Walker was a Tottenham regular, emerging with credit from the severe defensive pressure endured throughout much of Ossie Ardiles' reign, then consolidating impressively under Gerry Francis. Indeed, during November and December 1995 he kept a clean sheet for more than 600 minutes of football, an achievement followed soon by his first England cap.

It seemed, then, that Walker had laid a solid base for future eminence and steady progress was anticipated, but the subsequent campaign proved difficult. There were some shaky club performances and he received an over-the-top media mauling for his perceived error in conceding Gianfranco Zola's goal for Italy against England. Following that Wembley trauma the Walker game never quite regained its former assurance and there was a worrying edginess about many of his displays during late 1997. After he was sidelined by a shoulder injury in January, thus affording a lengthy senior opportunity to Espen Baardsen, Walker came back well. In terms of faith, though, the damage had been done. Despite keeping a clean sheet in the 1999 League Cup Final, he never seemed wholly convincing again and he had become second choice to new arrival Neil Sullivan by the outset of 2000/01. His pride was hurt – and for Ian his £2.5 million switch to Leicester City during the following summer could not come soon enough.

---

**IAN MICHAEL WALKER**

BORN: Watford, Hertfordshire, 31 October 1971.

HONOURS: League Cup 98/9. 4 England caps (96-04).

OTHER CLUBS: Oxford United on loan 90/1 (2, 0); Leicester City 01/02-04/05 (140, 0); Bolton Wanderers 05/06- (0, 0).

| GAMES | 308 (3) |
| --- | --- |
| GOALS | 0 |

# SOL CAMPBELL

## 1992/93 → 2000/01

What would become of Tottenham without the inscrutably commanding presence of Sol Campbell at the centre of their frequently flummoxed defence? As the new millennium commenced, apprehensive regulars at White Hart Lane did not want to know. It was a question to send a collective shudder down their spines, yet it was ominously insistent.

Anxious supporters understood all too well that if there was one Spur who was coveted perennially by Europe's top clubs, then certainly it was the formidably athletic, coolly charismatic Eastender. Indeed, there was more than a hint of resignation in the stands that a transfer was inevitable. Unfortunately, to countless Tottenham loyalists, the pity was that when Campbell did opt finally to move, his destination was Arsenal, the most resented of all their rivals.

Life at the Lane was bound to be disorientating for the muscular stopper, performing admirably and being feted at the top level with England, then returning to scrap manfully but often desperately to extract Spurs from the mire. There was an ever-growing danger that one of the most vaunted young defenders of his generation might be worn down by constant adversity. Clearly, the need to reconcile that immense talent with natural ambition was a pressing one, a fact which became increasingly evident as the strain began to show in some of Sol's displays during his final months at the club.

Campbell's path to eminence had not been straightforward. In his early days he was in danger of becoming a victim of his own versatility, being a sweeper as a 12-year-old before moving back and forth between midfield and forward roles, then enjoying his first settled senior stint as a left-back during 1993/94. Thereafter, though, he performed predominantly in a central defensive position, emerging majestically to succeed Gary Mabbutt as the rearguard's undisputed kingpin and team captain by the time he was 23.

The Campbell attributes were legion. Tall, agile and awesomely strong, he was quick for his size and tackled assuredly, invariably timing his challenges skilfully and endeavouring to remain on his feet. Less tangibly but of crucial importance, he appeared mature beyond his years, wearing his composure around him like a cloak, and he was capable of sustaining fierce concentration throughout lengthy periods of pressure. But most striking of all was his judicious reading of the action, his anticipation of where the next moment of crisis would occur, thus enabling instant and decisive intervention.

Undoubtedly Campbell's involvement with England improved his all-round technique, most notably the precision of his distribution, which could tend towards the wayward. Also, as the caps piled up, his positioning appeared ever more sound and he looked increasingly confident in deciding when to carry the ball forward and when to release it early. Eventually he grew into his leadership role at Tottenham, too. While he was not a natural organiser, he appeared to relish the opportunity of geeing up his team-mates with fearsome shrieks and bellows.

Campbell always seemed able to shrug off criticism as part of the learning process. Following a minor blip, his form hit a serenely immaculate standard for both club and country during 1998, then a year later he skippered Spurs to League Cup glory. In truth, Sol gave a somewhat shaky display against Leicester in the final, but he battled courageously to help ensure his side's clean sheet.

Still, though, he had more to learn before beginning to justify the tag bestowed upon him by a mass-circulation magazine, whose cover blurted daftly: 'Sol, quite possibly the best defender in the world.' With Campbell's reputation thus hyped to colossal proportions, Tottenham's board were left with the unenviable task of trying to persuade him to stay and lead a White Hart Lane revolution. But in the summer of 2001, he admitted at last that the club could not match his aspirations. Despite more lucrative offers from abroad, his choice was Arsenal, who had been, coincidentally, the last team he had faced for Spurs.

The fall-out, the vitriol, the undiluted hatred from so-called supporters were unprecedented. And while fans still speak of their anger, it was plain to see why Sol had defected. Of course, the matter could have been handled with more dignity, but from Campbell's career point of view, if he could make such enormous personal advances at Tottenham, to what giddy heights might he climb with – and let's be painfully frank – a more successful club? The answer came in the shape of League titles, FA Cups and a goal in a Champions League Final.

Whatever his erstwhile followers thought of Campbell's switch – and the description of his transfer by the Supporters' Trust as 'the ultimate act of betrayal' suggested he never received many good luck cards from N17 – it was not fair to label him a Judas. Some might say, though, that his middle name – Jeremiah – was tolerably apt.

---

**SULZEER JEREMIAH CAMPBELL**

| | |
|---|---|
| BORN: | Newham, London, 18 September 1974. |
| HONOURS: | League Cup 98/9. 73 England caps (96-). |
| OTHER CLUBS: | Arsenal 01/02-05/06 (135, 8); Portsmouth 06/07- (63, 2). |

GAMES **304 (11)**

GOALS **15**

# CHRIS ARMSTRONG

## 1995/96 → 2000/01

If this was a fair world, and perseverance in the face of adversity received its due reward, then Chris Armstrong could have counted on a chestful of medals. However, given the luck he endured at the Lane, he had no need to reach for the polish.

From the moment his £4.5 million move from newly-relegated Crystal Palace was mooted, Armstrong hardly received the star treatment. In all honesty, most Spurs fans were less than ecstatic about the prospect of the raw north-easterner replacing their talismanic German, especially with the brilliant Dennis Bergkamp checking in at Highbury, and there was press-fuelled confusion over Teddy Sheringham's enthusiasm for his new striking partner.

What Armstrong needed was a flying start; what he got was a two-month Premiership goal drought, which provoked a barrage of scathing criticism. He reacted by standing tall, straining every sinew in every game, never hiding from the ball no matter how scarred his confidence might have been – and he prevailed. The crossroads came at Goodison in October, where he beat Neville Southall with an audacious (desperate?) volleyed lob from 25 yards, and it was as though the weight of the world had been lifted from his shoulders. Now the goals began to flow, 22 of them by season's end, and suddenly supporters were praising the manager's acumen in signing him.

What had attracted Gerry Francis? Extreme pace, mostly, underpinned by bull-like strength, formidable aerial prowess, a powerful shot and endless willingness to chase for everything. Undeniably there was plenty of scope for improvement: frequently his off-the-ball runs lacked subtlety, his awareness of passing options was sketchy, his first touch was not always adhesive and he was inordinately right-sided. But Armstrong was eminently coachable; his advance, even in the short term, was immense and a bountiful future beckoned.

In fact, the roof was about to fall in. After the England 'B' international netted twice at Blackburn on the opening day of 1996/97, an ankle injury turned the season into one of despair and thwarted comebacks. The following term brought further protracted foot and ankle problems which sidelined him for much of the long fight against relegation. He would go on to shuttle in and out of the side, though a shock call-up to the England squad in 1999 and a tremendous strike against Everton in 2000 suggested he might mount a revival. But his groin problems persisted and when his contract expired in the summer of 2002, a new deal was not forthcoming, so he joined Bolton on a free transfer. Like every footballer, what Chris Armstrong had needed most of all was a modicum of good luck. Sadly, his was nearly all bad.

| | |
|---|---|
| **CHRISTOPHER PETER ARMSTRONG** | |
| **BORN:** Newcastle, 19 June 1971. | **GAMES** 144 (29) |
| **OTHER CLUBS:** Wrexham 89/90-90/1 (60, 13); Millwall 91/2-92/3 (28, 5); Crystal Palace 92/3-94/5 (118, 45); Bolton Wanderers 02/03; Wrexham 03/04-04/05 (59, 13). | **GOALS** 62 |

# STEFFEN IVERSEN

## 1996/97 → 2002/03

As Ole Gunnar Solskjaer was rocketing to stardom during 1996/97, informed sources were suggesting that, with all due respects to Manchester United's latest dazzler, he wasn't the finest young Norwegian marksman of his generation. That accolade they reserved for Steffen Iversen, and while their assessment proved a mite far-fetched, there is little doubt that, fitness permitting, Spurs' £2.6 million signing from Rosenborg had the makings of an exceptional performer.

Iversen arrived at White Hart Lane in December 1996 and, a mere three days after helping to beat AC Milan at San Siro, he made his Tottenham debut at Coventry. On his back was the number 18 which will be associated forever with Jurgen Klinsmann and, at once, there were similarities beyond the blond hair, tall frame and upright stance. Like his illustrious predecessor, Steffen appeared neat and earnest and played the game with a certain dash. Strong and agile, quick and skilful, he displayed an endless appetite for the fray and an intelligent appreciation of team requirements, while hinting constantly at an explosive personal contribution.

He settled quickly, linking effectively with Teddy Sheringham, but apart from a Boxing Day brace at home to Southampton he did not enjoy much early luck in front of goal and was guilty of some alarming misses. Then, shortly after an exhilarating hat-trick at Sunderland in March 1997 had boosted his confidence, Iversen suffered a knee injury which sidelined him for the remainder of the campaign. Nevertheless he had furnished ample evidence in his 16 successive outings to explain why Gerry Francis had trailed him so single-mindedly for eight months and been so hugely delighted to pip a posse of European giants for his signature.

Clearly Iversen was a key component to the Tottenham game plan for 1997/98, which heightened the blow when he hurt an ankle in August. Disappointment deepened to gloom when he aggravated the condition on Norway under-21

duty, and on subsequent club outings he looked uncharacteristically lacklustre, neither self-assured nor, it must be presumed, fully fit. Duly in January 1998 it was announced that a knee operation was needed and his season was over. Frustrated fans could only console themselves that Iversen, still only 21 at the outset of 1998/99, had time aplenty on his side.

Indeed, he returned to the fold with renewed vigour, picking up a League Cup medal and leading Tottenham's European charge the following season with several talismanic displays. There was genuine hope for his Tottenham future, but the arrival of Sergei Rebrov and later the return of Sheringham provided problems. With increased competition, Iversen looked shorn of confidence and, in a dramatic fall from favour, he was freed to join Wolves with a year remaining on his contract. After a season of struggle at Molineux, the Norwegian enjoyed a renaissance in his homeland, helping first Valerenga, then his former club Rosenborg to lift the domestic League title. Steffen Iversen was a Viking hero once more.

**STEFFEN IVERSEN**
BORN: Oslo, Norway, 10 November 1976.
HONOURS: League Cup 98/9. 71 Norway caps (98-).
OTHER CLUBS: Rosenborg, Norway, 94-96 (50, 18); Wolverhampton Wanderers 03/04 (16, 4); Valerenga, Norway, 04-05 (29, 11); Rosenborg 06- (44, 30).

GAMES 137 (40)
GOALS 47

# RAMON VEGA

## 1996/97 → 2000/01

After a distinctly wild and woolly start to his White Hart Lane sojourn, Ramon Vega began to show signs, albeit intermittent ones, of becoming the solid citizen needed so desperately alongside Sol Campbell at the heart of the Tottenham rearguard. However, after a tolerably consistent sequence of performances laced by some enterprising attacking contributions in the early spring of 1998, uncertainty resurfaced. Once again he was reacting to danger rather than anticipating it and there were games when a goal seemed imminent whenever he was involved, at either end of the pitch.

Gerry Francis had tracked the 6ft 3in stopper since his impressive displays for Switzerland during Euro '96. After that tournament Spurs were beaten to the punch by Cagliari, but Vega did not settle in Italy and when he became available for £3.75 million in January 1997, the north Londoners were quick to close the deal.

Early indications, however, were worrying. Of course, it was to be expected that the imposing Swiss would need a period of acclimatisation to the English game, but his initial hesitancy was so marked that cynics were beginning to wonder why Cagliari had been so keen to do business. Clearly Vega was powerful in the air, but he appeared off the pace of the action, there was a tendency to linger dangerously on the ball and his positional play was questionable. Injuries and a suspension did not help and by season's end there was a serious question-mark against his name, certainly in the minds of most fans.

His form continued to be erratic, but there was a gradual improvement which accelerated following the arrival of Christian Gross, under whom Ramon had won Swiss title medals with Grasshoppers of Zurich. Now, while still not immune to defensive lapses, he seemed more decisive, tackles were crisper and his venomous aerial menace in opposition penalty boxes produced several goals.

The overall upturn was demonstrated tellingly in the 3-0 victory at Blackburn in February 1998 when he snuffed out comprehensively the potent Chris Sutton. That day, instead of giving his opponent space to turn, Vega sat tight on Sutton, concentrating unrelentingly and earning deserved man-of-the-match accolades. His gradual progress continued in the following term, when his last-ditch tackle on Leicester's Emile Heskey in the League Cup Final secured Tottenham some long-awaited silverware.

But Vega needed to be more reliable if he was to become a viable long-term cornerstone of New Tottenham, and with the rapid emergence of a batch of young defenders, he faded from the first-team reckoning. In December 2000 he was loaned to Celtic, whom he helped to claim Scotland's domestic treble, before accepting a free transfer to Watford during the following summer.

---

**RAMON VEGA**

**BORN:** Olten, Switzerland, 14 June 1971.

**HONOURS:** League Cup 98/9. 28 Switzerland caps (93-96).

**OTHER CLUBS:** Grasshoppers, Switzerland, 90/1-95/6 (166, 13); Cagliari, Italy, 96/7 (14, 0); Celtic on loan 00/01 (18, 2); Watford 01/02 (27, 1); Creteil, France, 02/03.

| GAMES | 70 (14) |
|---|---|
| GOALS | 8 |

# ALLAN NIELSEN

## 1996/97 → 1999/2000

If it's not too blatant a contradiction in terms, midfielder Allan Nielsen was an exceedingly good ordinary type of player. Bought by Gerry Francis for £1.65 million from Brondby in September 1996, the blond Danish international offered all the practical virtues, such as industry and composure, stamina and strength, as well as limitless dedication to his profession. In addition, he controlled the ball competently, could play a neat pass, even the occasional cute one.

Most memorable for Spurs followers, however, was his eye for goal, never exhibited more crucially than in the dying seconds of the 1999 League Cup Final. Scampering nimbly between a posse of wrong-footed Leicester defenders, he dived horizontally to head home Steffen Iversen's deflected cross, illuminating the hitherto drab Wembley encounter and securing Tottenham's first trophy for eight years. Clearly Francis's judgement had been vindicated, especially as Nielsen's undeniably worthy contribution was made in the face of serial injury problems and during a less-than-auspicious interlude in Spurs' history.

On arrival, understandably, he took time to adapt to the English game, looking starkly prosaic in several early appearances, and there was a feeling among some fans that, although he contributed six goals in his first Premiership campaign, more might be expected of a man once voted footballer of the year in his native land.

During the anxious autumn of 1997, it seemed that Francis might share those misgivings and when Nielsen was omitted from the side he indicated that he might seek employment elsewhere in a bid to maintain his claim for a place in Denmark's 1998 World Cup plans. However, he was recalled by Christian Gross and laboured nobly, sometimes in his favoured central position, at others on the left flank of midfield, even helping out as an emergency left-back towards the end of the season.

To underline his usefulness, he popped up with several immensely important goals, including the sharply-taken half-volley which ensured a point at home to Arsenal in December (especially sweet), and the slightly scuffed cross-shot which defeated Bolton in a tense relegation clash at the Lane in March. As the scrap at the bottom of the table intensified, Allan's psychological steel grew more apparent and there were times when his energy fuelled the team.

Neither a conventional play-maker nor a common workhorse, then, but something in between. A something which, considering Tottenham's plight at the time, was acceptable, indeed. However, during 1999/2000 he became a casualty of progress as extra transfer funds sparked a minor revolution at the Lane, and during the summer he joined Watford for £2.25 million.

| | ALLAN NIELSEN |
|---|---|
| **BORN:** | Esbjerg, Denmark, 13 March 1971. |
| **HONOURS:** | League Cup 98/9. 44 Denmark caps (95-02). |
| **OTHER CLUBS:** | Bayern Munich, Germany, 90/1 (1, 0); Odense 91/2-93/4 (55, 9); FC Copenhagen 93/4-94/5 (26, 3); Brondby 94/5-96/7 (42, 11), all Denmark; Wolverhampton Wanderers on loan 99/00 (7, 2); Watford 00/01-02/03 (101, 19); Herfolge Boldklub, Denmark, 03/04. |
| **MANAGER:** | Herfolge Boldklub 03-05. |

| | |
|---|---|
| GAMES | **94 (21)** |
| GOALS | 18 |

# LES FERDINAND

## 1997/98 → 2002/03

When a player joins the club he supported as a boy, especially if he is a dashing centre-forward and the deal involves a record fee, the customary scenario involves excitement and fulfilment for footballer and fans alike. But through no fault of his own, Les Ferdinand's £6 million move from Newcastle United to Spurs in the summer of 1997 was never like that. To begin with, it made little sense to supporters that 31-year-old Teddy Sheringham was being sold for £3.5 million while Les, a mere eight months the departing hero's junior, was costing nearly twice that amount.

Then, after the newcomer had made a commendably bright start with three goals in four games, he was sidelined by a torn stomach muscle before suffering a knee injury which plagued him for much of the campaign. To make matters worse, when Les did make the starting line-up he failed to hit the target in 14 outings at a time when goals were needed urgently. What made this so frustrating for everyone concerned was that the amiable ex-van driver had proved conclusively with both Queen's Park Rangers and Newcastle that, when given appropriate service, he was a prolific marksman.

Former Magpies boss Kevin Keegan put it rather aptly: 'We've bought a monster so we've got to feed him.' Duly Kevin ensured that the muscular six-footer's appetite was catered for and the result was half a century of goals over two seasons, a PFA Footballer of the Year award for 1995/96 and an England place.

What Ferdinand wanted most, however, was to impress in a Tottenham jersey, a hope born in the 1970s when, as a schoolboy, his parents stopped him watching a game, fearing a black person might not be welcome at the Lane. It seems a depressing indictment of terrace racism of that time, yet Ferdinand's enthusiasm was never crushed by it. Instead he would develop into one of the most underestimated footballers of his era; a formidable talisman with all the natural credentials to banish such bleak beginnings.

In many ways, he was of the same ilk as fellow non-League graduate Cyrille Regis. In full flight, Les Ferdinand was a truly fearsome sight, a memorable amalgam of pace and power who was at his most effective when pounding after a long ball into space or a pass threaded between defenders. His vast upper-body strength enabled him to shrug off opponents, he carried a savage right-foot shot and his prodigious leaps from a standing start offered an added dimension to his menace Though he lacked nimbleness in delicate situations, he was not without skill, and his unselfishness and willingness to defend from the front made him an ideal team man.

As a Spur, encouraging bursts of form suggested that given an injury-free run and a game plan which accommodated his strengths, Les might live out some of those childhood dreams. Certainly there was plenty of high-flying endeavour to savour for the spearhead who piloted a helicopter in his spare time. A League Cup hat-trick in nine minutes at home to Bolton in December 2001 preceded a strike against Fulham which was something of a milestone. It was the Premiership's ten thousandth goal, and, typical of the generous Ferdinand, he gave his £10,000 winnings to charity.

But these were glistening highlights in a largely frustrating time for a man who, aside from a solitary Wembley success in 1999, never received the medals, or indeed plaudits, his talent warranted. He had arrived at the Lane as the third most prolific striker in Premiership history, yet, during his five-and-a-half season tenure, he never managed more than ten goals in a League campaign. That ranked as one of his greatest regrets, but the fact was that he had been overwhelmed by his injuries. Having grown accustomed to floating like a butterfly at previous clubs, this boxing addict would be forced to roll with the punches in N17.

After his final two terms were dogged by a ragged Achilles tendon, the challenge of younger men proved insuperable. He had been squeezed out of the starting line-up since the signing of Robbie Keane from Leeds and in January 2003 he joined West Ham for £200,000, later serving Leicester, Bolton and Reading before laying aside his boots in his 39th year and embarking on a career as a TV pundit. Meanwhile his personal following at White Hart Lane remained fervent, reckoning whimsically there was only one fitting valedictory accolade for this true footballing gent. Arise Sir Les . . .

**LESLIE FERDINAND**

BORN: Acton, London, 8 December 1966.

HONOURS: League Cup 98/9. 17 England caps (93-98). PFA Footballer of the Year 96.

OTHER CLUBS: Queen's Park Rangers 86/7-94/5 (163, 80); Brentford on loan 87/8 (3, 0); Newcastle United 95/6-96/7 (68, 41); West Ham United 02/03 (14, 2); Leicester City 03/04 (29, 12); Bolton Wanderers 04/05 (12, 1); Reading 04/05 (12, 1).

| GAMES | 123 (26) |
|---|---|
| GOALS | 39 |

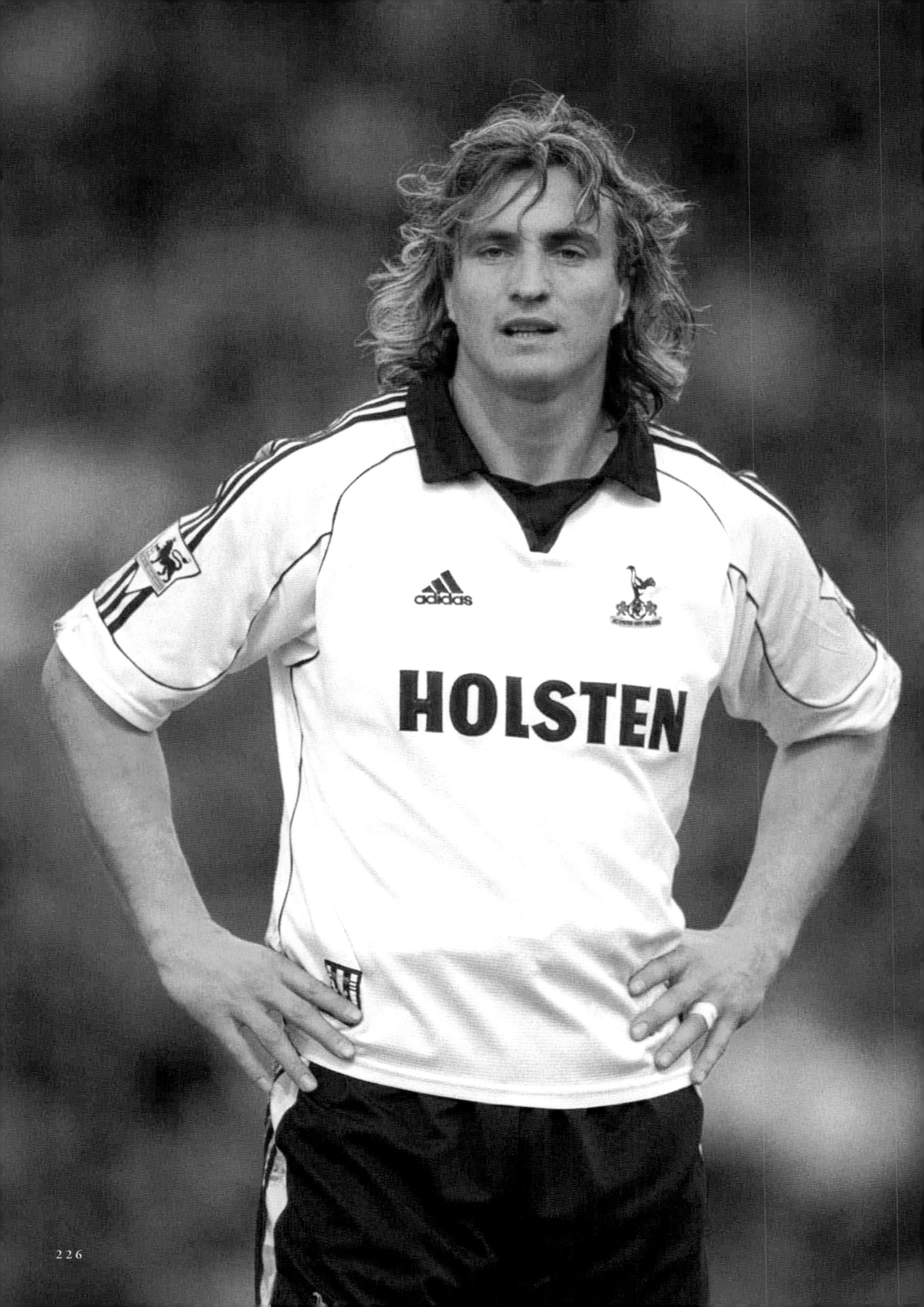
adidas
HOLSTEN

# DAVID GINOLA

## 1997/98 → 1999/2000

A great writer, and that term is used advisedly, once set down in print his ideas on selecting a favourite footballer. 'He is the player who may disappoint sometimes with a ragged, off-form performance, and yet over the years stays clear and bright in the memory. He is the player we bring to mind first when we ask ourselves what football looks like when we enjoy it most.' And then later: 'He does not make a crowd think murder; what he gives them is delight.' In his glorious book, *The Football Man (Collins, 1968)*, Arthur Hopcraft was talking about Bobby Charlton. In the context of the Premiership some 30 years later, this humble scribe would have looked no farther than David Ginola.

Tottenham's mettlesome thoroughbred was a D'Artagnan in football kit, all seductive skills and dash as he stretched out, as free as the wind, to embrace sporting beauty in an increasingly regimented world. Yes, he could be infuriatingly impractical, and there were accusations of indolence, but for Spurs in the dying years of the old millennium he cut an inspirational figure, a shaft of shining light in a time of often dim mediocrity.

Ironically enough, Ginola was purchased by one arch-pragmatist from another. Gerry Francis paid Newcastle United's Kenny Dalglish £2.5 million for the controversial French-Italian in the summer of 1997, seemingly a transaction inspired on Tottenham's side by growing discontent among Lane regulars about their side's perceived lack of flair and on Newcastle's by their manager's preference for consistent efficiency over wayward creativity.

In all honesty, David's start as a Spur was indifferent, and the cynics brayed about the inevitability of it all. Even so, there was no doubt, both before Francis was supplanted by Christian Gross but more particularly afterwards, that the so-called dilettante was working his socks off, whether operating as a roving striker, a midfield play-maker or, less frequently and not as influentially, in his old Newcastle role as a winger. In general, gone were the days when dispossession was greeted by little more than a sigh and a gesture; indeed, a certain amount of chasing back occurred, and even tackling was not unknown. Of course, it would be idle to deny that sometimes Ginola didn't pass when he should have, or that he retained a tendency to switch off, momentarily and probably involuntarily, when he lost the ball. That was the price – usually insignificant, occasionally not – for so much that was sublime.

What set him apart? Well, the grace and the style were captivating enough but they were not going to win matches on their own. That was down to the loping runs past defenders who couldn't predict his progress because of his effortless technique with either foot; to the exquisite drag-backs which made a mockery of crude challenges; to the precision of perfectly weighted through-balls and sumptuous cross-field dispatches; to both the delicacy and the power of his shooting.

Examples cry out to be chronicled, too many to mention here; but one contribution, his scintillating individual display in a 3-3 home draw with Liverpool in March 1998, summed up the appeal of Ginola with satisfying completeness. On a dramatic afternoon which highlighted the strengths and deficiencies of both teams, he made goals for Klinsmann and Vega and conjured up a special one of his own. After swaying past several opponents as he cut in from the right flank, David threaded a 25-yard left-footer into the only corner of Brad Friedel's net that was not guarded, combining audacity, vision and astonishing accuracy in one blindingly brilliant manoeuvre.

About two minutes from the end, with his side 3-2 up, the undisputed architect of what seemed to be imminent victory was substituted and spectators all around the ground rose as one to applaud him. How sad, but typical of Spurs' season, that such a joyous outpouring of emotion should be tarnished by a late Liverpool equaliser.

Even better was to come. The Frenchman's performances in 1998/99 were sensational, and praise poured from all quarters as he was voted player of the year both by the football writers and his fellow footballers. Unlike Clive Allen, who also received that double accolade as a Spur, Ginola was rewarded not for the quantity of his goals but for the way in which he took them. There was so much that dazzled; for instance, the mesmerising waltz past five defenders capped by a roaring shot into the roof of the Barnsley net, which still ranks as one of the greatest goals to grace the FA Cup.

So often that term, fans would walk away from a Spurs match reflecting that the only moments worth remembering had been furnished by David Ginola, as he fulfilled the Hopcraft criteria to the letter. But in 1999/2000 his golden standard slipped and, following a feud with coaching staff, he was sold to Aston Villa for £3 million. By now his best years were gone, but the question was still worth asking of those who had spurned him: if there isn't room for one such as Ginola, then what is the point of the game?

| | |
|---|---|
| | **DAVID DESIRE MARC GINOLA** |
| **BORN:** | Gossin, France, 25 January 1967. |
| **HONOURS:** | League Cup 98/9. 17 France caps (90-95). FWA Footballer of the Year 99. PFA Footballer of the Year 99. |
| **OTHER CLUBS:** | Toulon 85/6-87/8 (81, 4); Racing Paris 88/9-89/90 (61, 8); Brest 90/1-91/2 (50, 10); Paris St Germain 91/2-94/5 (115, 32), all France; Newcastle United 95/6-96/7 (58, 6); Aston Villa 00/01-01/02 (32, 3); Everton 02/03 (5, 0). |

GAMES **126 (1)**
GOALS 21

# STEPHEN CLEMENCE

## 1997/98 → 2002/03

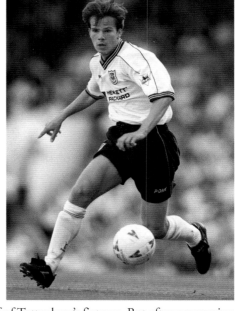

Stephen Clemence was a cultured young midfielder who seemed to have every chance of developing into an outstanding Premiership performer. All he needed was time and patient nurturing – and more support than certain 'fans' at White Hart Lane were prepared to offer him during a difficult period in 1997/98.

Having made his senior debut as a 19-year-old in the first game of the season, left-sided Clemence enjoyed an uninterrupted run of 12 appearances during which he revealed intelligence, vision and a willingness to work. On the debit side, some of his passing was over-ambitious, resulting in possession being lost, and he was not always able to assert himself in a struggling side against more experienced opponents. Cue for encouragement from the stands? Far from it. After a couple of anonymous performances, the son of former Tottenham hero Ray Clemence was targeted for abuse. Not surprisingly his confidence was jolted, his form fell away and he was omitted.

To his credit, he came again and his tough initiation stood him in good stead. Over the following two years he featured from the start in more than half of Tottenham's fixtures. But after progressing encouragingly, the England under-21 international was dogged by injury in 2001/02, then formidable midfield rivals were signed and in January 2003 he was sold to Birmingham City for £250,000 plus top-ups. At least Stephen could leave with his head held high. He had never given in to the terrace harassment – his father must have been extremely proud.

**STEPHEN NEAL CLEMENCE**
BORN: Liverpool, 31 March 1978.
OTHER CLUBS: Birmingham City 02/03-06/07 (121, 8); Leicester City 07/08- (31, 2).

GAMES **84 (25)**
GOALS 3

---

# JOSE DOMINGUEZ

## 1997/98 → 2000/01

A diverting but frustratingly unreliable novelty, or a match-winner with a long-term future at White Hart Lane? Jose Dominguez had Tottenham fans scratching their heads in perplexity during the troubled autumn of 1997.

The tiny Portuguese international flankman had made a sensational instant impact following his unexpected £1.6 million acquisition from Sporting Lisbon in August. Rising from the bench as a substitute for the injured David Ginola in the home clash with Derby, 'Little Joe' gave a mesmerising exhibition of dribbling skills, unhinging the County defence with bewildering changes of direction at breakneck speed and turning the game in Spurs' favour.

Subsequent headlines hailed a new hero but, despite some isolated moments of further delight – notably the brilliant swivel and left-foot projectile which stunned Southampton from 30 yards at The Dell in October -– closer acquaintance revealed distressingly wayward crossing and an infuriating lack of vision and awareness.

Dominguez, who first sampled the English scene with Birmingham City in the mid-1990s, continued to divide opinions among Lane regulars, with the majority perhaps taking the view that he was one of those players who operated most effectively as a substitute.

A groin injury in early 1998 meant that definitive judgement had to be deferred, but his continued absence from the teamsheet over the two and a half seasons before his transfer to Kaiserslautern in November 2001 illustrated graphically where he stood in George Graham's estimation.

**JOSE MANUEL MARTINS DOMINGUEZ**
BORN: Lisbon, Portugal, 16 February 1974.
HONOURS: 3 Portugal caps (95-96).
OTHER CLUBS: Benfica; Sintrense on loan; Fafe on loan, all Portugal; Birmingham City 93/4-94/5 (35, 3); Sporting Lisbon, Portugal, 95/6-96/7 (30, 1); Kaiserslautern, Germany, 00/01-04/05 (22, 3).

GAMES **16 (42)**
GOALS 5

## JOHN SCALES

### 1996/97 → 1999/2000

In theory Spurs had acquired a gem when they paid Liverpool £2.5 million for John Scales in December 1996. Once described by Reds boss Roy Evans as the steadiest defender in the Premiership, the pacy, unflappable Yorkshireman seemed the ideal addition to a rearguard palpably in need of strengthening.

If Scales' desirability was questioned by observers who were a trifle puzzled at Liverpool's willingness to sell the England international, any doubts were dispelled by the interest of Leeds United, for whom he had been about to sign when Gerry Francis stepped in. What followed, however, was something of a nightmare.

No one disputed that Scales was an accomplished performer when he played, but his time at the Lane was devastated by injuries. It came to such a pretty pass that on one almost surreal occasion, at Newcastle in October 1997, he strained his calf running on to the pitch and had to withdraw.

Not surprisingly, the situation appeared to erode Scales' confidence, so that when he did join the action he seemed less secure than expected. Sadly, Spurs were never to see the best of John Scales, who was freed to try his luck with Ipswich Town in July 2000. Alas, despite making a promising start at Portman Road, his battle to regain full fitness proved to be a forlorn one, and in the spring of 2001 he was forced out of the game by his cumulative injuries.

## MOUSSA SAIB

### 1997/98 → 1998/99

In his fleeting handful of appearances for Tottenham, Moussa Saib did enough, and more, to emphasise his immense technical ability. From the moment the vastly experienced Algerian midfielder cantered into the action for the first time, as an 85th-minute substitute at home to Bolton in March 1998, he looked accomplished and at ease.

In short order Saib delivered a sweet pass, got in a shot and revealed effortless control. His every movement suggested strength and assurance, as befitted a man who was captain of his country, and Tottenham's anxious fans gained the impression that a high-class act had been procured.

Four weeks later, after recovering from a back injury, the £2.3 million signing from Valencia confirmed that initial assessment with a stylish full debut at Crystal Palace, displaying an exquisite range of passing and a healthy appetite for the ball. He could score, too, as he showed with a cool finish following a deft flick by Jurgen Klinsmann against Wimbledon.

What went wrong? The answer is simple. He made the fatal mistake of crossing George Graham. The play-maker had joined up with his country's squad for a match against Tunisia even though he had been refused permission by Spurs, and was fined by Graham as a result. Then, after declaring he would do exactly the same again the next time Algeria called on him, Saib was given his marching orders. It seemed a shame. The cultured Algerian just might have proved to be an enormous asset.

| **JOHN ROBERT SCALES** | | |
|---|---|---|
| BORN: Harrogate, Yorkshire, 4 July 1966. | | |
| HONOURS: 3 England caps (95). | | |
| OTHER CLUBS: Bristol Rovers 85/6-86/7 (72, 2); Wimbledon 87/8-94/5 (240, 11); Liverpool 94/5-96/7 (65, 2); Ipswich Town 00/01 (2, 0). | GAMES | **33 (4)** |
| | GOALS | 1 |

| **MOUSSA SAIB** | | |
|---|---|---|
| BORN: Theniet-el-Had, Algeria, 6 March 1969. | | |
| HONOURS: 43 Algeria caps. | | |
| OTHER CLUBS: JS Kabyle, Algeria, 89-92; Auxerre, France, 92/3-96/7 (134, 23); Valencia, Spain, 96/7-97/8 (14, 0); Al Nassr, Saudi Arabia, 99/00-00/01; Monaco, France, 01/02-02/03; Lorient, France, on loan 01/02. | GAMES | **3 (10)** |
| | GOALS | 1 |

# NICOLA BERTI

## 1997/98 → 1998/99

Nicola Berti was an international midfielder of undisputed pedigree, plainly accustomed to a vastly different environment from the one he found himself in at Tottenham during the uneasy second half of the 1997/98 campaign. For a time he performed with the élan which made him a World Cup finalist with Italy in 1994, and enabled him to pocket a clutch of domestic club honours with Inter Milan, leaving Spurs fans to regret that he did not arrive at White Hart Lane several years before his 30th birthday instead of eight months after it.

Usually Berti adopted a defensive brief in front of the back line, also giving notice of his comprehensive all-round ability on occasional leggy forward excursions. There were no apparent flaws in the industrious six-footer's technique and it was clear that he relished a tackle, never shrinking from the responsibility. He settled quickly and showed his quality in an expansive display at Blackburn in February 1998. Shorn of some defensive duties by the dependable presence of David Howells, Berti surged repeatedly into Rovers territory, and stabbed Spurs' opener from six yards.

Time, though, was not on his side, and he seemed leg-weary in his few outings in 1998/99, during which he was freed to join Alaves in Spain. Later he worked with Ian Crook, the former Spur who was coaching in Australia. Tottenham never saw him at his buccaneering best, but it cannot be denied that Nicola Berti had bags of class – a commodity always welcome at the Lane.

**NICOLA BERTI**
**BORN:** Salsomaggiore Terme, Italy, 14 April 1967.
**HONOURS:** 39 Italy caps (88-95).
**OTHER CLUBS:** Parma 84/5 (27, 0); Fiorentina 85/6-87/8 (80, 8); Internazionale 88/9-97/8 (229, 29), all Italy; Alaves, Spain, 98/9; Northern Spirit, Australia.

| GAMES | 23 |
|---|---|
| GOALS | 3 |

# RORY ALLEN

## 1996/97 → 1998/99

Rookie striker Rory Allen appeared to be made of the right stuff. Strong, hard-working and sparkily combative, he ran selflessly and intelligently, used the ball well and finished emphatically. Pressed into action in autumn 1996 during yet another Tottenham injury crisis, the 5ft 11in Kentishman earned lavish praise from both front-line partner Teddy Sheringham, who found him a delight to play alongside, and manager Gerry Francis. Life looked sweet.

A product of the club's youth system, Allen had made his senior entry as a 19-year-old substitute against Wimbledon at Selhurst Park in September 1996, then netted against Newcastle on his home debut three days later. There followed a brace of goals in a League Cup victory over Preston at the Lane and a deft header from a Ramon Vega knockdown when Manchester United were the visitors in January 1997. Unfortunately his momentum was jolted by an ankle injury and he suffered further knocks when he returned to contention late in the year.

Serial fitness difficulties seemed to affect his mood and, with question marks raised over his attitude, his promising Tottenham progress came to an abrupt halt. After a prolific loan spell at Luton, he joined Portsmouth for £1 million in July 1999 before quitting the game at the age of 25, sick of ankle and knee problems which had required eight operations. The finale to Rory's turbulent career proved faintly bizarre, when he found himself in trouble after flying to Australia to watch the Ashes without Pompey's permission. It just wasn't cricket.

**RORY WILLIAM ALLEN**
**BORN:** Beckenham, Kent, 17 October 1977.
**OTHER CLUBS:** Luton Town on loan 97/8 (8, 6); Portsmouth 99/00 (15, 3).

| GAMES | 14 (14) |
|---|---|
| GOALS | 4 |

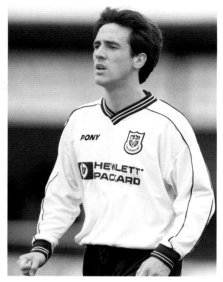

## DANNY HILL

### 1992/93 → 1994/95

Danny Hill's Tottenham career might just have progressed a little fast for its own good in its formative stage. It peaked in only his second outing when the industrious midfielder played a telling part in a splendid 3-1 victory at Arsenal in May 1993. Aged 18, Hill had been asked to fill in for Nicky Barmby in the big Highbury grudge match. For a young man born just a mile from White Hart Lane, the occasion might have proved daunting. But the cool teen repaid his manager's faith with interest, chasing every loose ball and harassing the Gunners' midfield while remaining calm enough to showcase his own sophisticated passing.

It was comic-strip-hero stuff for Danny, who had been on Spurs' books since the age of ten and had made his debut only two weeks before the north London derby. The England under-21 starlet was a creative prompter, adept at manipulating the ball with either foot and with an invaluable instinct for switching the angle of attack. His outlook appeared to be unremittingly bright, but like so many youngsters vying for opportunities in the top flight he spent too long waiting for his chance.

Hill endured five seasons in the reserves before joining Oxford on a free transfer in July 1998. However, the rigours of the lower divisions did not suit his smooth style, and after a stint with Cardiff he moved into non-League circles with Dagenham and Redbridge, then Hornchurch, while training as a plumber.

**DANIEL RONALD HILL**
BORN: Enfield, London, 1 October 1974.
OTHER CLUBS: Birmingham City on loan 95/6 (5, 0); Watford on loan 95/6 (1, 0); Cardiff City on loan 97/8 (7, 0); Oxford United 98/9 (9, 0); Cardiff City 98/9-00/01 (58, 4).

| GAMES | 4 (8) |
|---|---|
| GOALS | 0 |

## NEALE FENN

### 1996/97 → 1997/98

Young marksman Neale Fenn was pleasingly reminiscent of an old-fashioned attacking inside-forward, a skilful support striker rather than an out-and-out target man. He thrived on passes to feet, controlled the ball tidily and distributed it neatly, while boasting both the technique and the strength to retain possession under pressure.

Fenn made his senior debut on the grandest of stages, at Old Trafford in the FA Cup in January 1997, but he refused to be overawed, earning widespread plaudits for his plucky efforts alongside fellow rookie Rory Allen. Then, towards the end of the season, he was called off the bench for a handful of League appearances and continued to look perky. After earning a starting berth for a League Cup clash with Carlisle, Fenn enjoyed his finest moment, pouncing to open the scoring.

Qualifying for the Republic of Ireland because his mother hailed from Cork, London-born Fenn won youth and under-21 honours and was selected for the full international squad. What he needed was top-flight experience but, given the roster of front-runners on the White Hart Lane books, that proved problematic. A popular view in the stands was 'Give the lad a chance', but he was released by Tottenham in the summer of 2001 to join Peterborough. Later he became a popular figure in the League of Ireland.

**NEALE MICHAEL CHARLES FENN**
BORN: Edmonton, London, 18 January 1977.
OTHER CLUBS: Leyton Orient on loan 97/8 (3, 0); Norwich City on loan 97/8 (7, 1); Swindon Town on loan 98/9 (4, 0); Lincoln City on loan 98/9 (4, 0); Peterborough United 01/02-02/03 (50, 7); Cork City, Republic of Ireland, 03/04-06/07; Bohemians, Republic of Ireland, 06/07-.

| GAMES | 2 (8) |
|---|---|
| GOALS | 1 |

## GARRY BRADY

### 1997/98

Brady is an evocative name for any young footballer making his way in north London, especially if he is a midfielder. But while comparisons with Arsenal legend Liam would be farcical, Tottenham's Garry was a performer of promise. From the opening moments of his senior debut in an FA Cup clash with Fulham in January 1998, the 21-year-old Scottish youth international was in his element. There was nothing spectacular, just a series of sensible passes and crisp tackles, spiced here and there by a touch of clever footwork or a perceptive through-ball, and there wasn't the faintest suggestion that he felt tentative or overawed.

After a while chants of 'There's Only One Garry Brady' rose from the stands, and while it was only banter, nevertheless it carried a certain recognition that the lad knew his business. Thereafter Brady impressed on a succession of substitute outings, notably against Leicester at White Hart Lane in February 1998, when he won plenty of important tackles and slotted comfortably into the team plan. Having sprung suddenly into the first-team reckoning, his disappearance was equally swift, however. He was poached by Newcastle when his contract expired, but after a frustrating time on Tyneside, Garry tried his luck north of the border, where he was rewarded at last by the regular first-team football his talent merited.

**GARRY BRADY**
BORN: Glasgow, 7 September 1976.
OTHER CLUBS: Newcastle United 98/9 (9, 0); Norwich City on loan 99/00 (6, 0) and 00/01 (2, 0); Portsmouth 00/01-01/02 (14, 0); Dundee 02/03-05/06 (119, 2); St Mirren 06/07- (47, 2).

| GAMES | 1 (10) |
|---|---|
| GOALS | 0 |

# MARK STIMSON

## 1986/87 → 1988/89

Mark Stimson was courted by six London clubs before choosing Spurs as a teenager in 1984. A quick and enterprising left-back who relished an overlap, he could not dislodge first-choice Mitchell Thomas and joined Newcastle for £150,000 in May 1989.

**MARK NICHOLAS STIMSON**
BORN: Plaistow, London, 27 December 1967.
OTHER CLUBS: Leyton Orient on loan 87/8 (10, 0); Gillingham on loan 88/9 (18, 0); Newcastle United 89/90-92/3 (86, 2); Portsmouth 92/3-95/6 (62, 2); Barnet on loan 95/6 (5, 0); Southend United 95/6-98/9 (56, 0); Leyton Orient 98/9 (2, 0).
MANAGER: Gillingham 07-.

| GAMES | 1 (1) |
| GOALS | 0 |

# PHIL GRAY

## 1986/87 → 1990/91

Ulsterman Phil Gray was a vigorous front-runner who made it to the fringe of Spurs' senior side but was unable to consolidate, partly because of persistent injuries. In August 1991 he was sold to Luton for £275,000 and went on to carve an international niche.

**PHILIP GRAY**
BORN: Belfast, 2 October 1968.
HONOURS: 26 Northern Ireland caps (92-01).
OTHER CLUBS: Barnsley on loan 89/90 (3, 0); Fulham on loan 90/1 (3, 0); Luton Town 91/2-92/3 (59, 22); Sunderland 93/4-95/6 (115, 34); Nancy, France, 96/7 (16, 4); Fortuna Sittard, Holland, 96/7 (12, 1); Luton Town 97/8-99/00 (81, 21); Burnley 00/01 (5, 1); Oxford United 00/01-01/02 (44, 11).

| GAMES | 4 (6) |
| GOALS | 0 |

# MARK ROBSON

## 1988/89 → 1989/90

David Pleat paid £50,000 to recruit pacy 18-year-old flankman Mark Robson from Exeter City in July 1987. After polishing his talents in the reserves, he appeared to have top-level potential but a knee injury jolted his momentum and he was freed to join West Ham in 1992.

**MARK ANDREW ROBSON**
BORN: Newham, London, 22 May 1969.
OTHER CLUBS: Exeter City 86/7 (26, 7); Reading on loan 87/8 (7, 0); Watford on loan 89/90 (1, 0); Plymouth Argyle on loan 89/90 (7, 0); Exeter City on loan 91/2 (8, 1); West Ham United 92/3-93/4 (47, 8); Charlton Athletic 93/4-96/7 (105, 9); Notts County 97/8-99/00 (32, 4); Wycombe Wanderers on loan 98/9 (4, 0).

| GAMES | 4 (5) |
| GOALS | 0 |

# ANDY POLSTON

## 1989/90

When Andy Polston left the bench to line up alongside fellow defender and elder brother John in March 1990, they became the first siblings to see League action together for Spurs since Bobby and Danny Steel in 1912. Injury precluded any more chances for Andy, who was freed in 1992.

**ANDREW ALFRED POLSTON**
BORN: Walthamstow, London, 26 July 1970.
OTHER CLUBS: Cambridge United on loan 89/90 (3, 0); Gillingham on loan 91/2 (2, 0).

| GAMES | 0 (1) |
| GOALS | 0 |

# PETER GARLAND

## 1990/91

Hard-grafting midfielder Peter Garland was an England youth international whose career did not mirror the potential revealed in his teenage days. After his sole senior outing as a Spur he was sold to Newcastle for £35,000, but enjoyed his best run later with Charlton.

**PETER JOHN GARLAND**
BORN: Croydon, Surrey, 20 January 1971.
OTHER CLUBS: Newcastle United 91/2 (2, 0); Charlton Athletic 92/3-95/6 (53, 2); Wycombe Wanderers on loan 94/5 (5, 0); Leyton Orient 96/7 (21, 0).

| GAMES | 0 (1) |
| GOALS | 0 |

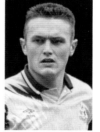

# IAN HENDON

## 1990/91 → 1991/92

Ian Hendon skippered England youth and won under-21 caps, but could not quite embrace the glittering White Hart Lane future which appeared to await him. A classy central defender or full-back who was also comfortable in midfield, he went on to excel at a less exalted level.

**IAN MICHAEL HENDON**
BORN: Ilford, Essex, 5 December 1971.
OTHER CLUBS: Portsmouth on loan 91/2 (4, 0); Leyton Orient on loan 91/2 (6, 0); Barnsley on loan 92/3 (6, 0); Leyton Orient 93/4-96/7 (131, 5); Birmingham City on loan 94/5 (4, 0); Notts County 96/7-98/9 (82, 6); Northampton Town 98/9-00/01 (60, 3); Sheffield Wednesday 00/01-02/03 (49, 2); Peterborough United 02/03 (7, 1).

| GAMES | 1 (6) |
| GOALS | 0 |

# JEFF MINTON

## 1991/92 → 1992/93

Brighton saw the prime of the diminutive Jeff Minton, a sprightly all-purpose midfielder who offered a useful goal threat and was a tenacious marker. Spurs were his first club, but the White Hart Lane competition proved too hot and he was freed to join the Seagulls in 1994.

**JEFFREY SIMON THOMPSON MINTON**
BORN: Hackney, London, 28 December 1973.
OTHER CLUBS: Brighton 94/5-98/9 (174, 31); Port Vale 99/00-00/01 (36, 4); Rotherham United 00/01 (9, 2); Leyton Orient 01/02 (33, 5).

| GAMES | 2 (1) |
| GOALS | 1 |

# JAMIE CLAPHAM

## 1996/97

Jamie Clapham made a promising Spurs debut, deputising for centre-half Colin Calderwood, but was never given another chance and was sold to Ipswich for £300,000 in January 1998. At Portman Road he developed into a cultured, attacking left-back cum midfielder.

**JAMES RICHARD CLAPHAM**
BORN: Lincoln, 7 December 1975.
OTHER CLUBS: Leyton Orient on loan 96/7 (6,0); Bristol Rovers on loan 96/7 (5,0); Ipswich Town 97/8-02/03 (207, 10); Birmingham City 02/03-05/06 (84, 1); Wolverhampton Wanderers 06/07 (26, 0); Leeds United on loan 07/08 (13, 0); Leicester City 07/08- (11, 0).

| GAMES | 0 (1) |
| GOALS | 0 |

# KEVIN DEARDEN

### 1990/91 → 1992/93

Goalkeeper Kevin Dearden played senior football for a dozen clubs, most of them on loan, but never managed a long-term breakthrough with Tottenham, his first employer. A spectacular shot-stopper, he specialised also in accurate and early distribution.

**KEVIN CHARLES DEARDEN**
BORN: Luton, Bedfordshire, 8 March 1970.
OTHER CLUBS: Cambridge United on loan 88/9 (15, 0); Hartlepool United on loan 89/90 (10, 0); Swindon Town on loan 89/90 (1, 0); Peterborough United on loan 90/1 (7, 0); Hull City on loan 90/1 (3, 0); Rochdale on loan 91/2 (2, 0); Birmingham City on loan 91/2 (12, 0); Brentford 93/4-98/9 (205, 0); Barnet on loan 98/9 (1, 0); Wrexham 99/00-00/01 (81, 0); Torquay United 01/02-04/05 (100, 0).

| | |
|---|---|
| GAMES | 1 (1) |
| GOALS | 0 |

# KEVIN WATSON

### 1992/93

Kevin Watson was a classy midfield creator, but possibly he was not physical enough to make a major impact in his Spurs days. After four years without a top-flight outing, he was freed to join Swindon in 1996, going on to help secure promotion four times with lower-division clubs.

**KEVIN EDWARD WATSON**
BORN: Hackney, London, 3 January 1974.
OTHER CLUBS: Brentford on loan 93/4 (3, 0); Bristol City on loan 94/5 (2, 0); Barnet on loan 94/5 (13, 0); Swindon Town 96/7-98/9 (63, 1); Rotherham United 99/00-01/02 (109, 7); Reading 01/02-03/04 (66, 2); Colchester United 04/05- (135, 3).

| | |
|---|---|
| GAMES | 5 (3) |
| GOALS | 2 |

# LEE HODGES

### 1992/93

Lee Hodges was a skilful, industrious left-sided attacker whose senior Spurs career was compressed into 11 days in May 1993, when he rose from the bench during the season's last four games. A year later he was released to join Barnet, and was still playing at Championship level in 2008.

**LEE LESLIE HODGES**
BORN: Epping, Essex, 4 September 1973.
OTHER CLUBS: Plymouth Argyle on loan 92/3 (7, 2); Wycombe Wanderers on loan 93/4 (4, 0); Barnet 94/5-96/7 (105, 26); Reading 97/8-00/01 (79, 10); Plymouth Argyle 01/02- (195, 11).

| | |
|---|---|
| GAMES | 0 (4) |
| GOALS | 0 |

# DAVID McDONALD

### 1992/93

Combative full-back David McDonald earned international honours for the Republic of Ireland at schoolboy, youth, under-21 and 'B' levels but only twice was he offered a senior look-in by Tottenham. Versatile enough to play on either defensive flank, he was a fine long-distance passer.

**DAVID HUGH McDONALD**
BORN: Dublin, 2 January 1971.
OTHER CLUBS: Gillingham on loan 90/1 (10, 0); Bradford City on loan 92/3 (7, 0); Reading on loan 92/3 (11, 0); Peterborough United 93/4 (29, 0); Barnet 93/4-97/8 (96, 0).

| | |
|---|---|
| GAMES | 2 |
| GOALS | 0 |

# PAUL MAHORN

### 1993/94 → 1997/98

Paul Mahorn was a pacy striker whose principal contribution to the Spurs story was scoring the goal which ensured victory in the home first leg of a League Cup clash with Carlisle in September 1997. Soon afterwards he was freed, but made little impact elsewhere before leaving the game.

**PAUL GLADSTONE MAHORN**
BORN: Leytonstone, London, 13 August 1973.
OTHER CLUBS: Fulham on loan 93/4 (3, 0); Burnley on loan 95/6 (8, 1); Port Vale 97/8 (1, 0).

| | |
|---|---|
| GAMES | 3 (2) |
| GOALS | 1 |

# STEVE SLADE

### 1995/96

There were plenty of Spurs fans who reckoned boss Gerry Francis had made a serious mistake when he sold England under-21 striker Steve Slade to QPR for £350,000 in July 1996. However, Slade's career never kicked on and he drifted out of the League in his middle twenties.

**STEVEN ANTHONY SLADE**
BORN: Hackney, London, 6 October 1975.
OTHER CLUBS: Queen's Park Rangers 96/7-99/00 (68, 6); Brentford on loan 96/7 (4, 0); Cambridge United 00/01 (9, 1).

| | |
|---|---|
| GAMES | 1 (7) |
| GOALS | 0 |

# STEVE ROBINSON

### 1993/94

Still in his teens when he was freed by Spurs to join Bournemouth in October 1994, Steve Robinson matured into a potent goal-scoring midfielder with the Cherries, rising to full international status during his lengthy spell at Dean Court. He remained a Championship force in 2008.

**STEPHEN ROBINSON**
BORN: Lisburn, Northern Ireland, 10 December 1974.
HONOURS: 8 Northern Ireland caps (97-).
OTHER CLUBS: Bournemouth 94/5-99/00 (240, 51); Preston North End 00/01-01/02 (24, 1); Bristol City on loan 01/02 (6, 1); Luton Town 02/03- (185, 9).

| | |
|---|---|
| GAMES | 1 (1) |
| GOALS | 0 |

# PAUL McVEIGH

### 1996/97

Paul McVeigh was a clever, nimble little striker who netted on his home debut for Spurs against Coventry. However, having spent several seasons in the reserves, the Northern Ireland international accepted a free transfer to Norwich in March 2000, since when he has prospered for the Canaries both up front and in midfield.

**PAUL FRANCIS McVEIGH**
BORN: Belfast, 6 December 1977.
HONOURS: 20 Northern Ireland caps (99-).
OTHER CLUBS: Norwich City 99/00-06/07 (216, 36); Burnley on loan 06/07 (8, 3); Luton Town 07/08- (25, 0).

| | |
|---|---|
| GAMES | 2 (1) |
| GOALS | 1 |

# PAOLO TRAMEZZANI

## 1998/99

Paolo Tramezzani was sunbathing on the patio of his Italian villa when his phone rang. His agent had received a call from London and wanted to know if he would be interested in joining Tottenham. Having just enjoyed his finest season in *Serie A*, Paolo was not convinced about the prospect of leaving.

The blond, bronzed 28-year-old had established a reputation as a stylish but disciplined defender at Piacenza and a clutch of previous employers. But with a handsome salary in the offing, Tramezzani agreed a £1.3 million transfer and was reunited with former Internazionale team-mate Nicola Berti. Christian Gross, who had identified the left-back berth as a problem, was delighted with his first signing of summer 1998.

The new term, however, would be as harrowing for the Italian as it was for his Swiss manager. Tramezzani made his debut on the opening day against Wimbledon and with the ball at his feet he looked accomplished. But his lack of pace was exposed by Michael Hughes, who skipped past the newcomer to set up goals that secured a shock victory for the bookies' relegation favourites.

Things turned worse for the defender with the abrupt exit of Gross in September. Over the following months Tramezzani was troubled by an Achilles injury and fell out with new boss George Graham, who would not let him seek treatment in Belgium. He threatened Spurs with a law suit as the saga reached boiling point, and soon returned to his homeland, doubtlessly wishing he had never climbed off that sun lounger . . .

**PAOLO TRAMEZZANI**
**BORN:** Reggio-Emilia, Italy, 30 July 1970.
**OTHER CLUBS:** Prato 89/90 (29, 0); Cosenza 90/1 (15, 0); Lucchese 91/2 (30,1); Internazionale 92/3-93/4 (26, 0); Venezia 94/5-95/6 (25, 0); Cesena 95/6 (19, 2); Piacenza 96/7-97/8 (57, 2); Pistoese 99/00, all Italy.

| GAMES | 7 |
|---|---|
| GOALS | 0 |

---

# OYVIND LEONHARDSEN

## 1999/2000 → 2001/02

No one had heard of *eBay* when Oyvind Leonhardsen auctioned his services on the internet. Fed up with quiet Saturday afternoons on Merseyside, Leonhardsen chose the quick route out of Liverpool by posting a message on his own website. 'Midfield player for sale: strong-running, combative,' it said. 'Had enough of reserve-team matches. Looking for better opportunity, hopefully in a warmer place. Price to be discussed.' Whether George Graham had been surfing the web remains unknown, but Tottenham were quickest on the mouse to close a £2.75 million deal in August 1999.

First impressions suggested he was exactly what Spurs needed. The buzzing fetcher and carrier, who combined pace and directness with immense technical skill, scored four goals in eight scintillating outings early in his first campaign. Leonhardsen had been an Anfield misfit but after returning to London he delivered a display that reminded the Premiership why he had been one of its most coveted youngsters during his Wimbledon days. Against Sheffield Wednesday at Hillsborough, Oyvind shone on both flanks, and he netted sublimely from 20 yards. The season had barely begun but the Norwegian's dazzling display had left Spurs top of the table and gleefully optimistic.

Alas, fortunes tumbled quickly. Leonhardsen was hindered by a leg injury which cost him the second half of that campaign, and he never regained his initial sparkle. His travail continued at Aston Villa, whom he was freed to join in August 2002, then he returned to Norway.

**OYVIND LEONHARDSEN**
**BORN:** Kristiansund, Norway, 17 August 1970.
**HONOURS:** 86 Norway caps (90-03).
**OTHER CLUBS:** Molde 89-91 (64, 9); Rosenborg 92-94 (63, 20), both Norway; Wimbledon 94/5-96/7 (76, 13); Liverpool 97/8-98/9 (37, 7); Aston Villa 02/03 (19, 3); Lyn Oslo 04/05-05/06 (37, 2); Stromgodset 05/06-, both Norway.

| GAMES | 59 (13) |
|---|---|
| GOALS | 11 |

# CHRIS PERRY

## 1999/2000 → 2002/03

The signing of Chris Perry was top priority for a man who knew a thing or two about defending. George Graham, who assembled the famous Arsenal rearguard during his trophy-laden years with the old enemy, was scouring Europe for the answer to a back-four crisis at Tottenham Hotspur. 'Twenty years ago you'd walk down the street, shake a tree and centre-halves would fall out,' he said, soon after his arrival at Spurs. 'But now they're nowhere to be seen.' Yet there was a tree, just a few miles down the road from White Hart Lane, whose branches had been left unruffled. Perry, patiently waiting in the shadows of Wimbledon Common, was the Tottenham manager's perfect solution.

He was relatively slight and lacking height for a top-flight stopper, but Perry's almost uncanny sense of anticipation masked his apparent weaknesses well. An incisive tackler, a perceptive reader of the game and a proficient marker, he was, decidedly, Graham's kind of player.

When the Dons agreed a £4 million fee in July 1999, no less an authority than Gary Mabbutt suggested that the 26-year-old could form the Premiership's strongest central-defensive partnership with Sol Campbell. But when Tottenham's captain and linchpin jumped ship in 2001, Chris was left on his own to steer Tottenham's seasick back-line through choppy waters.

Perry's first season as a Spur was also his best. Shoulder to shoulder with a bigger man, he was particularly effective. The slim Londoner was first-choice under Graham and scored with several thumping headers, including a fine goal against Bradford.

Tottenham fans were quietly impressed by the defender's technical ability and scorching pace. He adopted a serious approach to his work and he went quietly about his business as a first-team regular for the best part of four campaigns before his progress was halted by a troublesome back in early in 2003.

Perry was left nursing a slipped disc for several painful months as a clutch of younger centre-backs staked their claim for the vacant berth, and by the time his injury had mended he had fallen behind Ledley King, Gary Doherty and Anthony Gardner in the pecking order.

In August 2003, having recently turned 30, Perry was surprised to be offered to Charlton Athletic, initially on a loan-swap arrangement that took the full-back Paul Konchesky to White Hart Lane, before a cheque for £100,000 made his switch permanent. Though intended originally as cover, he performed so consistently that he made a place his own and enjoyed his time at the Valley, a sojourn which extended to almost three campaigns before he was recruited for West Bromwich Albion's tilt at promotion to the Premiership in 2006/07.

| | |
|---|---|
| **CHRISTOPHER JOHN PERRY** | |
| **BORN:** Carshalton, London, 26 April 1973. | |
| **OTHER CLUBS:** Wimbledon 93/4-98/9 (167, 2); Charlton Athletic 03/04-05/06 (76, 3); West Bromwich Albion 06/07 (23, 0); Luton Town 07/08- (35, 1); Southampton on loan 07/08 (6, 0). | |

| | |
|---|---|
| GAMES | **137 (9)** |
| GOALS | 4 |

# STEFFEN FREUND

## 1998/99 → 2002/03

Like an old Volkswagen Beetle, Steffen Freund was German manufacturing personified. He picked up a few bumps and scratches over the years, yet beneath his rusty bodywork was the most reliable engine in north London. The refined talents of a highly-tuned French racer might have caught the eye more often during the late 1990s, but this high-mileage workhorse was a people's favourite in his own right.

Freund always made an impression – quite literally where opposition shins were concerned. He was a snarling, screaming, fearsome tackler. Other teams loved to hate him and, in truth, a minority of Spurs traditionalists hated to love him. The antithesis of flair, he was the epitome of everything that is often abhorred by the Lilywhite fashionistas. Among his failings, according to his most savage critics, was a serial inclination to pass the ball sideways and an apparent determination never to take a shot on goal, never mind score.

The majority of White Hart Lane regulars felt quite differently, however. Freund changed the concept of defensive midfield play at Tottenham. He was part of a generation of European midfielders who were happy to do the unglamorous work while their more exuberant colleagues took the glory. Like fellow 'hod-carriers' Makelele and Deschamps, Freund patrolled the space in front of defence evidently without feeling the slightest need to sacrifice substance for style.

The German international, an integral part of his country's Euro '96 triumph, was signed by George Graham for £750,000 from Borussia Dortmund in December 1998. A sturdy debut in midfield against Sheffield Wednesday secured his place as a mainstay of the side. Where once the defence was a sieve, Spurs' back-line became well-nigh watertight when Freund was at his best.

That season he played a crucial part in landing the club a long-overdue piece of silverware, namely the League Cup. Thanks to sheer ugly obstinacy, ten-man Tottenham squeezed every last breath out of deeply frustrated Leicester City to hang on to a 1-0 lead in a largely undistinguished final. It was uncharacteristic Tottenham. It was the Steffen Freund effect.

The phenomenon continued until injury diluted his potency in 2002/03, at the end of which he was freed to return to his homeland with Kaiserslautern. 'Steffen Freund is a football genius,' Spurs supporters had chorused in the stands on that victorious afternoon at Wembley. In reality, the German's greatest gift was knowing that he was not.

**STEFFEN FREUND**

| | |
|---|---|
| BORN: | Brandenburg, Germany, 19 January 1970. |
| HONOURS: | League Cup 98/9. 21 Germany caps (95-98). |
| OTHER CLUBS: | Brandenburg 89/90-90/1 (31, 0); Schalke 91/2-92/3 (53, 3); Borussia Dortmund 93/4-98/9 (117, 6); Kaiserslautern 03/04 (7, 0), all Germany; Leicester City 03/04 (14, 0). |

| GAMES | **121 (10)** |
|---|---|
| GOALS | 0 |

# MAURICIO TARICCO

## 1998/99 → 2003/04

Margaret Thatcher, Diego Maradona and David Beckham may have done their utmost to damage Anglo-Argentinian relations – but Tottenham Hotspur, at least, play a crucial diplomacy role. Spurs are the most popular British team among the Latin Americans. That's official, just ask Mauricio Taricco.

Fans at White Hart Lane will need little reminding of their passionate full-back, who was both happy and capable on either defensive flank. His will to win was unmatched in his generation of players, some of whom could be found wanting when it came to muddying their Lilywhite shirts. Certainly the diminutive Taricco wore the Spurs jersey with fearless pride, an emotion born in

his homeland while marvelling at the derring-do of his illustrious countrymen Ossie Ardiles and Ricardo Villa on his flickering black-and-white television.

A host of clubs had been chasing his signature after several exceptional campaigns with promotion-chasing Ipswich Town, but Taricco was holding out for the call from White Hart Lane. When it arrived in December 1998, with George Graham splashing out £1.8 million to secure his services, the Argentinian would have sprinted barefoot across East Anglia to put his signature on the dotted line if his new boss had asked him.

Despite that priceless enthusiasm, however, his first few months at Spurs proved frustrating as he struggled to gain a foothold. For a time he played second fiddle to Justin Edinburgh and was not eligible for a role in the club's encouraging League Cup win after playing in earlier rounds with the Tractor Boys.

Thus it was in the following campaign that Taricco sprang to the fore, an extended run in the side proving that he was a made-to-measure comrade for another long-haired Latin. Indeed, his swashbucklingly physical style was the perfect foil for the more artistic but infinitely less energetic efforts of David Ginola. It was a left-sided match made in heaven. Sighs of anguish would turn regularly to roars of approval as Ginola would surrender the ball limply, then the little warrior from Buenos Aires would win it back with all the tenacious aggression of a flyweight boxer.

Taricco had made more than 150 senior appearances and collected a hatful of bookings before injury, in 2004, gave a newly-arrived deputy a chance to stake his claim. Erik Edman impressed and, sadly for Mauricio, his north London idyll ended that November when Spurs freed him to join West Ham United. Perhaps he lacked some of the subtleties of more refined contemporaries – but no one relished the bargy quite like this Argy.

| | | |
|---|---|---|
| **MAURICIO RICARDO TARICCO** | | **GAMES** **149 (7)** |
| **BORN:** Buenos Aires, Argentina, 10 March 1973. | | **GOALS** **2** |
| **OTHER CLUBS:** Argentinos Juniors 93/4 (21, 0); Ipswich Town 95/6-98/9 (137, 4); West Ham United 04/05 (1, 0). | | |

# LUKE YOUNG

### 1998/99 → 2000/01

While other sports nurture their all-rounders, football is notoriously cruel to its more versatile souls. Luke Young was determined not to become a casualty of his own proficiency – as Tottenham learned to their cost.

The fresh-faced Essex boy was a solution in waiting for George Graham's injury-riddled squad towards the turn of the millennium. Competent in every defensive berth, Young was a glowing advertisement for Spurs' new academy scheme, which had been set up to produce 'total footballers'. Luke, it seemed, could turn his hand to anything. Had the team bus broken down, the manager need not have bothered phoning the AA; he would merely have handed a ratchet and hammer to his teenage protégé.

Shorn of central defenders, Graham first turned to Young soon after taking charge at the club. The rookie had been 'staggered' to see himself on the team-sheet next to Sol Campbell for a Premiership clash with West Ham. The debut proved a resounding success, with Young defending impeccably and even coming close to scoring. He remained in the side for the next seven games.

Over the following two seasons, Young flitted in and out of the side but was always a competent performer, whether deployed at centre-half, at wing-back, in midfield, or in his preferred position of right-back. His reputation, following call-ups to England under-21 squads, was soaring, both on the terraces and among other managers.

Arguably his finest performance in a Spurs shirt came in the unforgettable victory against Manchester United at the Lane in October 1999. Young was a vision of serenity throughout the rainswept clash but his defining moment arrived when Paul Scholes shaped to shoot from ten yards. The prolific midfielder had looked certain to score but Young slid along the wet grass to intercept his shot.

The fans loved him and so did his coaches, but Luke, who felt he was paying the price for being the club's most dependable citizen, was growing frustrated by his 'bit-part' role. Certainly his £4 million departure to Charlton Athletic in the summer of 2001, shortly after Campbell's embittered move to Arsenal, seemed a ludicrous waste to those who had monitored his steady rise to eminence.

Many believed Luke Young had all the qualities of a future Tottenham captain, and they were not surprised by his elevation to full international status in 2005. Unfortunately, at the time of his transfer the young man himself reckoned his likely destiny at White Hart Lane was to become the odd-job man – and he didn't fancy it.

---

**LUKE PAUL YOUNG**

BORN: Harlow, Essex, 19 July 1979.
HONOURS: 7 England caps (05-).
OTHER CLUBS: Charlton Athletic 01/02-06/07 (187, 4); Middlesbrough 07/08- (35, 1).

| | GAMES | 56 (20) |
| --- | --- | --- |
| | GOALS | 0 |

# TIM SHERWOOD

## 1998/99 → 2001/02

Tim Sherwood was so brutally frank it could hurt. But whether on the pitch or in the pressroom, you were sure of one thing – an honest performance. Spurs had been chasing Sherwood, the vastly influential captain of Blackburn's Premier League title-winning side of 1994/95, for two years. However, when they finally landed their man for £3.8 million in February 1999, many feared the club had paid over the odds for an elder statesman who had never won an England cap. The 30-year-old midfielder's response to such speculation was typical. 'You needn't worry about me losing my pace,' he said. 'I never had any in the first place.'

If he wasn't the quickest player, and he wasn't, then certainly he timed his runs expertly. Sherwood settled quickly at Spurs and, for his first two campaigns, became one of the side's most potent attacking threats. It was an unexpected bonus to fans that his eagerness and tenacity in the tackle were matched by a hunger to rampage forward into opposition penalty boxes.

Sherwood boasted a vicious shot with both feet and was brave at heading. His most memorable goal in a Spurs shirt was the club's last of the 20th century during a dour clash with Aston Villa, which burst to life when he belted home a scorching drive from more than 30 yards. His vision and endeavour were always missed when he was not around and it was hugely deserved when he finally won his first full international call-up in 1999.

After enjoying such a successful start to his tenure at the Lane, Tim suffered a slump in fortune following the arrival of Glenn Hoddle as manager. Kindred spirits they were not. Sherwood was infuriated when he was dropped by Hoddle, who claimed the midfielder was not fit at the start of the 2001/02 campaign. Typically and publicly, Tim expressed his dissatisfaction and was frozen out of the side. He refused to give in, however, and having watched from the sidelines for almost six months, eventually he was offered another opportunity when Steffen Freund suffered a knee injury.

Sherwood came into the side with a point to prove and put in a string of combative displays to win a place in the starting line-up for the 2002 League Cup Final against Blackburn. But the veteran, who had been relishing the chance to put one over on his former side, was out of sorts on his big day, one of several lacklustre performers as Rovers overran Spurs' midfield to steal a 2-1 win.

That match marked the beginning of the end of Sherwood's Tottenham adventure. While his desire and work rate were impeccable, he was blighted by minor injuries and his relationship with Hoddle reached an all-time low. In January 2003, it became clear that his future lay elsewhere when he criticised the club's team spirit and Hoddle's man-management skills, and he was freed to join Portsmouth. As Tim Sherwood learned to his cost, sometimes you can be just too honest.

**TIMOTHY ALAN SHERWOOD**
**BORN:** St Albans, Hertfordshire, 6 February 1969.
**HONOURS:** 3 England caps (99).
**OTHER CLUBS:** Watford 87/8-88/9 (32, 2); Norwich City 89/90-91/2 (71, 10); Blackburn Rovers 91/2-98/9 (246, 25); Portsmouth 02/03-03/04 (30, 1); Coventry City 04/05 (11, 0).

| | |
|---|---|
| GAMES | 103 (15) |
| GOALS | 16 |

# MATTHEW ETHERINGTON

## 1999/2000 → 2002/03

Young, gifted and left-sided – Matthew Etherington warranted protected status in English football. Hailed by David Pleat as the club's next David Ginola, Etherington boasted the desirable combination of pace, flair and an enthusiasm to work. But in an era when left feet of quality were rarer than a match-day parking space near White Hart Lane, Tottenham used their precious resource sparingly.

Young Matthew's parents had such faith in his ability that, when he was 12, they sold their family home in Cornwall so he could live nearer the big clubs. England schoolboy caps followed a professional debut at Peterborough at the age of 15. He was already being tipped for stardom and Manchester United cocked a keen eye. But Spurs were dogged in pursuit and the old-fashioned winger arrived at the Lane with Simon Davies, valued at £500,000 in a £1.2 million package in January 2000.

Etherington's progress stuttered initially, however. An energetic debut against Liverpool at Anfield won him some fans but, even following the departure of Ginola, opportunities were sporadic. Coaches felt the wide-man was still some way off the finished article, wayward crossing being the main issue of contention.

A smashing FA Cup goal against Bolton in 2002 and further senior outings suggested the youngster might conquer his doubters. But Etherington had grown tired of the kid-glove treatment. After voicing his disillusionment he was ushered to West Ham for £1 million in August 2003. Good things come to those who wait, but few would blame the under-21 international for fearing that, after 24 starts in four years as a Spur, he was running out of time.

**MATTHEW ETHERINGTON**
BORN: Truro, Cornwall, 14.8.81.
OTHER CLUBS: Peterborough United 96/7-99/00 (51, 6); Bradford City on loan 01/02 (13, 1); West Ham United 03/04- (152, 14).

GAMES **24 (27)**
GOALS **2**

# GARY DOHERTY

## 1999/2000 → 2004/05

Flash cars and million-pound mansions did not appeal to Gary Doherty. He never bothered with driving lessons, and even after breaking into Tottenham's first team and becoming an Ireland international, he still lived with his parents. As his colleagues arrived for training in their Astons and Ferraris, Doherty would turn up in the back of a taxi. His approach to football was equally modest. A lower league background had instilled in him a hard-working approach and an instinct for simplicity.

Doherty, equally adept in his preferred position of centre-half or as a target man, enjoyed a steady rise. After signing from Luton for £1 million in April 2000, he impressed on debut against Manchester United, scored a late winner in an FA Cup tie at Leyton Orient and won man-of-the match champagne for inspiring a 4-2 victory later in the competition at Charlton.

Spurs' policy of buying young, lower-division talent seemed to have unearthed another gem. He was strong in the air and the tackle but also neat with his feet. With a nudge and a wink, fans dubbed him 'The Ginger Pele' and he was voted the club's young player of the season for 2000/01.

His progress was halted during the following autumn, however, by a grisly leg-break in a League Cup encounter with Torquay. Subsequent cameo roles provided scant opportunity to develop and in August 2004 Norwich offered the chance of regular first-team football. Few at Tottenham begrudged Gary a fresh start. If he hadn't quite made the grade at the Lane, it was not through lack of effort.

**GARY MICHAEL THOMAS DOHERTY**
BORN: Camdonagh, Republic of Ireland, 31 January 1980.
HONOURS: 34 Republic of Ireland caps (00-).
OTHER CLUBS: Luton Town 97/8-99/00 (70, 12); Norwich City 04/05- (130, 3).

GAMES **55 (23)**
GOALS **8**

# SIMON DAVIES

## 1999/2000 → 2004/05

If genetically modified footballers exist, then the chances are that Simon Davies was designed by scientists with cockerels emblazoned proudly on their laboratory coats. The extravagantly gifted Welshman was blessed with so many of the attributes that make a cult hero at White Hart Lane. Glenn Hoddle said so – and, let's face it, he should know.

Given Tottenham's glorious history of elegant midfield players who, with just a deft flick or an incisive pass, could ignite the most delicious of moves, it was easy to see why Davies was so welcome in north London, and why he settled in so quickly following his £700,000 arrival in January 2000. The 20-year-old, who had attracted firm interest from Manchester United, had jumped two divisions from his billet with Barry Fry at Peterborough. Unable to contain his glee, David Pleat grinned from ear to ear as he unveiled the new boy, along with his chum Matthew Etherington, to assembled pressmen.

Pleat, the club's director of football, believed he had discovered two rare talents who could, with fine tuning, rejuvenate the club's attacking options with a splash of youthful exuberance. Both were flair players, but it was Davies who really caught the eye with his confidence, vision and explosive shooting power.

In February 2001 he set tongues wagging, lighting up the Lane with two smartly taken goals as Spurs brushed aside Stockport County in the FA Cup. That performance, together with a glut of injuries in the squad, afforded him an extended run in the side.

Never afraid to showcase his thunderous right foot, even from seemingly impossible distances, Davies was alert, quick and could deliver an accurate cross. Particularly when Tottenham were in the ascendancy, he would positively sparkle. Exhilarating displays

for Wales and man-of-the-match contributions in memorable victories over United and Chelsea would prove that, on his day, Davies could be a dynamic and inventive link between midfield and attack.

But it appeared that his fine development was hindered by sensationalism, not of his making. Manager Hoddle talked him up as a £10 million player; press and pundits fuelled the flames with gushing praise. Yet many paying customers believed they were watching a different story unfold. Some reckoned his performance over 90 minutes did not match the glimpses of scintillating brilliance on a highlights reel. Season in and season out, they grew frustrated by a player who would often go missing when the going got tough. He was easily muscled off the ball and appeared reluctant in the tackle.

When he was sold to Everton for £3.5 million in May 2005, there were those who thought the Merseysiders had landed a bargain. But sadly for Simon Davies, time would show that new Spurs manager Martin Jol had been astute. The boffins had got the genes right, but no one can force nature.

| SIMON DAVIES | | | |
|---|---|---|---|
| BORN: | Haverfordwest, Pembrokeshire, 23 October 1979. | GAMES | 119 (28) |
| HONOURS: | 50 Wales caps (01-). | GOALS | 18 |
| OTHER CLUBS: | Peterborough United 97/8-99/00; Everton 05/06-06/07 (45, 1); Fulham 06/07- (51, 7). | | |

# ANDY BOOTH

### 2000/01

Andy Booth was once voted the worst player ever to pull on a Tottenham shirt. The dubious mantle seemed awfully harsh for a man who was given just one month to impress at the club. But, had he heard of the poll, it is safe to say the gap-toothed striker would not have lost much sleep. After all, he was as surprised as anyone at his invitation to become a Spur.

Emergency circumstances brought the hard-working Yorkshireman to White Hart Lane in January 2001. The club's coffers were empty during a boardroom takeover, and with Spurs needing cover for three injured strikers, the tall, awkward target man joined on loan from First Division strugglers Sheffield Wednesday.

He was plunged straight into the heat of a London derby against West Ham, and acquitted himself well with a wholehearted display alongside Sergei Rebrov, the club's only other fit attacker. Remarkably, Booth shrugged off his own shock at the call-up to find the net after only 15 minutes, but his nodded effort was ruled out for offside.

The 27-year-old again featured prominently, but less admirably, in a 2-1 defeat against Derby, Enic's first game as owners. The striker, a hero in his Huddersfield home-town, should have rescued a point but failed with an easy header and a close-range shot. The new money-men were unimpressed and Booth left London almost as quickly as he arrived. He had given it a go – and he had given it his all.

**ANDREW DAVID BOOTH**
**BORN:** Huddersfield, Yorkshire, 6 December 1973.
**OTHER CLUBS:** Huddersfield Town 91/2-95/6 (123, 54); Sheffield Wednesday 96/7-00/01 (133, 28); Huddersfield Town 00/01- (250, 72).

| | |
|---|---|
| GAMES | **3 (1)** |
| GOALS | **0** |

# WILLEM KORSTEN

### 1999/2000 → 2000/01

The architects got it all wrong when they unveiled their plans to rebuild Spurs' training base in the late 1990s. Instead of a treatment room at Chigwell, the general consensus was that an Accident and Emergency wing should have been included in the drawings. Tottenham Hotspur had become the resting place for the walking wounded of world football. But none of the crocked regulars – including Darren 'Sicknote' Anderton and his suffering sidekick Les Ferdinand – endured more wretched luck than Willem Korsten.

The rangy 6ft 3in Dutch under-21 international, who was equally at home on either wing or as a second striker, was signed from Vitesse Arnhem for £1.5 million in July 1999 following a loan stint at Leeds. He was already struggling ominously with the persistent hip complaint which was destined to finish his career prematurely, but he passed his White Hart Lane medical. Korsten's debut against Sheffield Wednesday was delayed for more than six months by injury, though when he did cross the white line he showed encouraging flashes of quality.

Poignantly, his best performance in the Lilywhite shirt was saved for what turned out to be his final match as a Spur – and as a professional footballer. In May 2001, he shone in the 3-1 home victory over Manchester United, terrorising the champions with his pace and vision, and netting twice with rasping efforts from outside the box. But he was never able to play again and he retired at the age of 26.

**WILLEM KORSTEN**
**BORN:** Baxtel, Holland, 21 January 1975.
**OTHER CLUBS:** NEC Breda 92/3 (4, 0); Vitesse Arnhem 93/4-98/9 (71, 12), both Holland; Leeds United on loan 98/9 (7, 2).

| | |
|---|---|
| GAMES | **13 (14)** |
| GOALS | **3** |

# ALTON THELWELL

### 2000/01 → 2001/02

Trailing in the wake of a King is enough to give any man an inferiority complex. But for Alton Thelwell, growing up with Ledley would prove particularly difficult. The two London-born central defenders were brought to the club in their early teens and, when they starred as 20-year-old debutants against Liverpool, both were tipped for greatness. But as Ledley's star soared, Alton's began to wane. He was good, but King was taller, stronger, quicker and ultimately more reliable.

The pair came to the fore when boss George Graham lost Sol Campbell to injury and dropped the defensively vulnerable Ramon Vega against Liverpool in November 2000. Alongside King, Thelwell was calm beyond his years in the 2-1 home victory over the Merseysiders. By February he was a regular England under-21 international.

Alton was powerful, tenacious and quick, but he conceded too many free-kicks and his passes could go astray. In a defeat at Derby in March 2001, he was blamed for giving away a needless penalty. The following month he came under more criticism as Chelsea's Zola and Hasselbaink ran riot. But his confidence reached rock bottom when supporters faulted him in embarrassing defeats against Leicester and then Southampton, when a sloppy back-pass allowed James Beattie to steal in to score.

These were sink-or-swim days at Spurs and new manager Glenn Hoddle had neither the time nor the patience to help his young defender. Thelwell was released after a loan spell in Sweden, then relaunched his career with Hull.

**ALTON ANTHONY THELWELL**
**BORN:** Holloway, London, 5 September 1980.
**OTHER CLUBS:** IFK Hassleholm, Sweden, on loan; Hull City 03/04-06/07 (40, 1); Leyton Orient 06/07- (50, 1).

| | |
|---|---|
| GAMES | **13 (8)** |
| GOALS | **0** |

# SERGEI REBROV

### 2000/01 → 2001/02

Sergei Rebrov was an avid bookworm who polished his English by reading Agatha Christie novels, but he can't have been thrilled by his own whodunit mystery. Unlike the Queen of Crime's indefatigable sleuths – Hercule Poirot and Miss Marple were never defeated – Spurs fans were left hopelessly perplexed by a maddening conundrum at the outset of the new millennium. What killed off the career of one of Europe's finest strikers? No one could crack The Riddle of Rebrov.

It seemed a coup when the Ukrainian left Dynamo Kiev for Tottenham. Rebrov was famed as the man who could unleash the deadly Andriy Shevchenko and had amassed 19 Champions League goals of his own. In fact, Rebrov had outscored Shevchenko for club and country, and was a national hero in the former Soviet state.

Having shown uncharacteristic munificence to part with a club-record £11 million fee in June 2000, boss George Graham was understandably upbeat, declaring his new striker a certainty to become a White Hart Lane icon. 'His control and basic technique are magic,' said the manager.

While small in stature, Rebrov was versatile enough to play in midfield or any forward position, and his intelligence marked

him out as a dream strike partner. Soon stalls around the Lane were selling T-shirts bearing the legend 'Rebrov – gives you wins.' Initially the *Red Bull* reference seemed appropriate as the fans enjoyed their caffeine kick. The newcomer laid on two goals and came desperately close to scoring himself as Tottenham brushed aside Ipswich 3-1 on his home debut. The new number-11 then starred against Everton with two delicately fashioned strikes.

Clearly, in terms of ability, he was unrivalled at the club, but after a lean Christmas period, the boo-boys were in need of a scapegoat. Thus, though he starred with a brace in an entertaining FA Cup quarter-final victory over West Ham, the critics began to turn on the costly acquisition.

The arrival of Glenn Hoddle would pose even more problems, and in the following campaign he found himself competing for a place with Teddy Sheringham, who had returned from Manchester United. Hoddle preferred the elder statesman as his deep-lying forward and Rebrov was discarded to the reserves. He made fleeting appearances as a substitute but it was clear his confidence was shattered. Having been called from the bench against Bolton, he looked sure to score after rounding the 'keeper but – bereft of belief – he sent the shot blazing wide.

The following season his only British outing came in a Ukrainian shirt against Northern Ireland. It was too late now for any rousing tale of vindication. He had fallen into a long-established category of miscast foreigners by the time he was freed to join West Ham in August 2004. Goals in the World Cup and the Champions League in 2006 helped exorcise his ghosts. By then Rebrov was back in the Ukraine, and back to doing what he loved. He was not reading Dame Agatha any more, though – he had moved on to Dostoevsky.

| | |
|---|---|
| **SERGEI REBROV** | |
| BORN: | Gorlovka, Ukraine, 3 June 1974. |
| HONOURS: | 75 Ukraine caps (92-). |
| OTHER CLUBS: | Shakhtyor Donetsk 90/1-91/2; Dynamo Kiev 92/3-99/00 (157, 86), both Ukraine; Fenerbahce, Turkey, on loan 02/03-03/04 (38, 4); West Ham United 04/05 (26, 1); Dynamo Kiev 05/06-07/08 (52, 20); Rubin Kazan, Russia, 08/09-. |

| | |
|---|---|
| GAMES | **48 (27)** |
| GOALS | **16** |

# NEIL SULLIVAN

## 2000/01 → 2001/02

Some footballers change clubs for a pay rise. Others move on for medals. But Neil Sullivan said he signed for Spurs simply because he had grown fed-up with 'pooper-scooping' on Wimbledon Common. In joining Tottenham, Sullivan could forget about scouring the public parks for dog mess before training. Instead he could concentrate on savouring one of the finest seasons of his career – and then enduring arguably the worst.

Having arrived as competition for Ian Walker, Sullivan wasted no time in staking his claim to become the undisputed number-one. Fans had been reluctant to welcome the Wimbledon man who had been infamously lobbed by David Beckham from the half-way line. But Sullivan guarded White Hart Lane's posts so well in his debut term that he ended up as supporters' player of the year.

The club's first signing under the new Bosman ruling was a steady and consistent performer who improved his game through an almost religious devotion to practice. The strapping six-footer was an athletic shot-stopper and after a series of heroic displays, notably against Everton and Arsenal, he established himself as Scotland's first-choice custodian.

But for all that early success, his second year was disastrous. He gained weight, fell out with the new coaching staff and lost form. Two hideous handling errors against Leeds suggested his confidence had been sapped and the following summer he broke a finger and lost his place to Kasey Keller. Not surprisingly, in August 2003 Sullivan was quick to accept a lucrative offer to sit on Chelsea's bench.

# BEN THATCHER

## 2000/01 → 2002/03

It was a conjuring trick to make a bank manager weep. In Spurs' most profligate summer, more than £16 million was spent on two young players who, within 24 months, would be worth very little. Football has no trouble making money disappear – particularly at White Hart Lane.

Much fuss was made about the expensive failure of Sergei Rebrov in north London, but Ben Thatcher also endured a torrid time after joining for an inflated fee. He was acquired from relegated Wimbledon for £5 million in July 2000, following a route mapped by Neil Sullivan and Chris Perry, and footballing director David Pleat hailed the tenacious left-back as a shining prospect. Tenacious and fearless, he was an accurate crosser and his lofted throw-in could pose as many problems as a corner kick.

The former England under-21 skipper made a steady start at Tottenham before an unfortunate sending-off against Sunderland in November. But the sacking of George Graham after the New Year marked the beginning of a downward spiral. Thatcher's combative approach was not to the taste of new boss Glenn Hoddle, who quickly sought a new left-sided defender.

Suspensions and a troublesome hip didn't help, and following the arrival of Christian Ziege, Thatcher was cast into the reserves. In July 2003 he accepted a £300,000 switch to Leicester, where his fortunes were resurrected and he became a Welsh international. Later he joined Manchester City, for whom he promised much before a brush with police over a horrifying challenge on Portsmouth's Pedro Mendes.

**NEIL SULLIVAN**
BORN: Sutton, London, 24 February 1970.
HONOURS: 28 Scotland caps (97-03).
OTHER CLUBS: Wimbledon 90/1-99/00 (181, 0);
Crystal Palace on loan 91/2 (1, 0); Chelsea 03/04
(4, 0); Leeds United 04/05-06/07 (95, 0); Doncaster
Rovers 06/07- (62, 0).

| GAMES | 81 |
|---|---|
| GOALS | 0 |

**BENJAMIN DAVID THATCHER**
BORN: Swindon, Wiltshire, 30 November 1975.
HONOURS: 7 Wales caps (04-).
OTHER CLUBS: Millwall 93/4-95/6 (90, 1);
Wimbledon 96/7-99/00 (86, 0); Leicester City 03/04
(29, 1); Manchester City 04/05-06/07 (47, 0);
Charlton Athletic 06/07- (22,0).

| GAMES | 38 (8) |
|---|---|
| GOALS | 0 |

# CHRISTIAN ZIEGE

## 2001/02 → 2003/04

If Christian Ziege has not yet turned up at your local quiz night, then it is only a matter of time. As the only footballer to have played in the Milan, Munich, Merseyside, Tyne-Tees and north London derbies, he has become trivia fodder for pub questionmasters everywhere. Yet Tottenham fans still scratch their heads over a much tougher question. For a man who, in his own words, was the world's best left wing-back, why did Christian Ziege enjoy such little success in the UK?

The dynamic German walked out on Middlesbrough before falling foul of Gerard Houllier's Liverpool. But his £4 million link-up with Glenn Hoddle at Spurs in August 2001 appeared to be based on a meeting of minds. Certainly Ziege appeared to be enjoying life at the Lane as he scored five thunderous goals in his first nine games. Undeterred by his cumbersome defending, Tottenham's faithful were already hailing a new hero. He was direct, strong and blessed with a brilliant left foot.

After chipping in with a goal in Spurs' League Cup Final defeat by Blackburn in 2002, Ziege indicated that he had found a long-term home for the first time since leaving Munich, but then followed two terms of injury worries.

Ziege did become the only Spur to feature in a World Cup Final, against Brazil in 2002, but in the next campaign he suffered a life-threatening blood clot in his thigh and after only eight starts – which featured two red cards in one week – he moved to Borussia Moenchengladbach.

**CHRISTIAN ZIEGE**
BORN: Berlin, Germany, 1 February 1972.
HONOURS: 72 Germany caps (93-04).
OTHER CLUBS: Bayern Munich, Germany, 90/1-96/7 (172, 41); AC Milan, Italy, 97/8-98/9 (39, 4); Middlesbrough 99/00 (29, 6); Liverpool 00/01 (16, 1); Borussia Moenchengladbach, Germany, 04/05 (13, 0).

GAMES **52 (3)**
GOALS **10**

---

# GORAN BUNJEVCEVIC

## 2001/02 → 2004/05

Goran Bunjevcevic was a born survivor. He may not have lived up to expectations at Tottenham, but that he even made it as a top-class footballer seemed enough of a triumph. The son of a Serbo-Croat, 19-year-old Bunjevcevic believed his family would be killed when gun-wielding Croatian soldiers raided his house in Zagreb. He was forced to flee and became homeless, but the game was his salvation. Goran developed into a calm, sophisticated centre-back, and after captaining Red Star Belgrade to a league and cup double, he was dubbed the Beckenbauer of the Balkans.

In July 2001 'Bunji' became Glenn Hoddle's first signing at Tottenham in a £1.4 million deal, shortly before Sol Campbell's departure. A libero-type who could carry the ball out of defence and use it intelligently, the 28-year-old was deployed initially as a defensive midfielder due to Spurs' crippling injury list. The Serbia and Montenegro international started solidly but then suffered a smashed cheekbone, returning quickly to play in a protective mask but then falling prey to ankle and thigh problems.

His second season was relatively injury-free but Hoddle used him in a bizarre array of positions. After looking reasonably comfortable in central defence and as a midfield anchor, Bunjevcevic struggled at left-back and wing-back, and the fans began to carp. Often he appeared ponderous and slack in possession, and when Hoddle left in 2003, Goran's Lane future looked bleak. But he remained as a mainstay of the reserves, becoming an invaluable mentor to a batch of emerging defenders. From 'Bunji' they learned plenty about football, and even more about real life.

**GORAN PETAR BUNJEVCEVIC**
BORN: Karlovac, Croatia, 17 February 1973.
HONOURS: 16 Serbia and Montenegro caps.
OTHER CLUBS: Rad Belgrade 94/5-96/7 (60, 5), Red Star Belgrade 97/8-00/01 (125, 16), both Yugoslavia; Den Haag, Holland, 06/07 (27, 2).

GAMES **47 (11)**
GOALS **2**

# KASEY KELLER

. . . . . . . . . . . . . . . . . . . . . . . . . . . . . . . . . . .

## 2001/02 → 2004/05

Football was just a job for Kasey Keller. Perhaps while growing up on his family's American poultry farm he was too busy stacking trays of eggs to obsess about the beautiful game. But to state that his trade was never truly his lifeblood is not to criticise a tremendous goalkeeper. Not once in his accomplished tenure at White Hart Lane, even when under the fiercest pressure, did Keller suggest by word or deed that he was treating his occupation with anything other than uncompromising professionalism. Indeed, in an era of marked under-achievement by Spurs managers and players alike, the USA's long-serving net-minder made for a refreshing change.

Initially Keller was signed as cover for first-choice Neil Sullivan in August 2001. The 31-year-old newcomer had been on the verge of joining Turkish side Besiktas, but chose instead to have one last Premiership hurrah, having enjoyed his previous stint in the English top flight, winning the League Cup in his first season at Leicester City.

Now, after impressing on several early Spurs outings, Keller compiled a club-record run of 83 consecutive appearances. It was an amazing feat for a man many saw as an ageing journeyman, but Kasey was always full of surprises. During his time at Tottenham, he

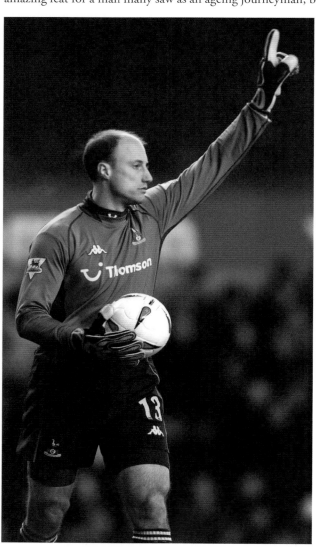

co-hosted a heavy metal rock radio show and was voted football's most avid book reader.

Off the field, Keller did his best to disguise his identity. The balding American, who wore rimless glasses, had an air of detachment from sport. He was a sociology student from Washington State who somehow found himself filling the goal at such disparate locations as Millwall, Leicester and Rayo Vallecano, in Spain. Work and play were kept separate. There were no framed shirts on the walls of his stylish London townhouse.

While Keller was never likely to become 'one of the boys' at Tottenham, he was widely respected. He would prepare methodically for games, adapting his approach according to his opponents' specific qualities. Often he won his duels with opposing strikers, but not always. In one of his first north London derbies, he sprinted from his line to challenge Thierry Henry in what looked like a 50-50 race. But he flattened Arsenal's deadly Frenchman, conceding the penalty from which Robert Pires equalised.

After being ever-present for two years, Keller was unseated by the arrival of Paul Robinson, having let in an average of two goals a game in the second half of 2003/04. Following a loan stint at Southampton, he was freed to join Borussia Moenchengladbach in January 2005, going on to skipper the Germans.

Keller also played in the 2006 World Cup, though none of his displays in Germany would have been as enjoyable as his clean sheet in a historic 1-0 triumph over Brazil in 1998. After that match the great Romario remarked: 'That is the best performance by a goalkeeper I have ever seen.' It was an appropriate tribute from one illustrious international to another.

**KASEY C KELLER**

BORN: Olympia, Washington, USA, 27 November 1969.
HONOURS: 102 USA caps (90-07).
OTHER CLUBS: Portland University, USA; Millwall 91/2-95/6 (176, 0); Leicester City 96/7-98/9 (99, 0); Rayo Vallecano, Spain, 99/00-00/01 (51, 0); Southampton on loan 04/05 (4, 0); Borussia Moenchengladbach, Germany, 04/05-06/07 (43, 0); Fulham 07/08- (13, 0).

| | |
|---|---|
| GAMES | 99 |
| GOALS | 0 |

# GUS POYET

· · · · · · · · · · · · · · · · · · · · · · · · · · · · · · · ·

## 2001/02 → 2003/04

Bulging eyes and grotesque grimaces were part of the White Hart Lane scenery for several seasons early in the new millennium. Gus Poyet could summon facial expressions that might have made the late Les Dawson jealous. Endeavouring to understand his animated features and demonstrative body language was almost as engaging as watching this graceful footballer with the ball at his feet. Win, lose or draw, there was no need to look at the scoreboard when supporters could cast a quick glance at their South American play-maker for the full story.

It was clear Poyet had as much passion for football as he had for life. His exuberance was as vibrant at Tottenham as it had been when he left Montevideo as an ambitious teenager to try his luck in Europe. Quite why he won only 26 Uruguayan caps – and never played for his country in a major tournament – remains a mystery.

The 34-year-old arrived at the Lane from Chelsea for £2.25 million in July 2001, checking in along with fellow senior statesmen Christian Ziege and Teddy Sheringham. At training each morning, the venerable trio would stage art classes for their younger, eager-to-learn protégés. But if there was one knack which Poyet must have found well-nigh impossible to pass on, it would have been his unrivalled ability to skulk unmarked into opposition penalty boxes. That, surely, was down to pure, inspired instinct.

Gus, whose father was an international basketball player, saw red in only his second match for Spurs after a sloppy tackle against Everton. But, following a three-match ban, Poyet soon reasserted himself as one of football's most prolific goal-scoring midfielders. He got off the mark with a glorious 40 yard chip against Derby, then a week later he delivered a trademark goal by drifting beyond his stricken 'shadow' to guide a looping header beyond Newcastle 'keeper Shay Given. In Spurs' next game, against Leeds, a tricky run was capped with a long-range howitzer, and soon afterwards he wrote himself into Tottenham folklore in one of the most vitriolic north London derbies in recent history, the first meeting with Arsenal after Sol Campbell's defection. With Spurs trailing 1-0, the mercurial Poyet volleyed Sergei Rebrov's cross into the bottom left corner, and White Hart Lane erupted.

Yet an even more intense moment of euphoria awaited Spurs fans. The shimmering 5-1 demolition of Chelsea in a League Cup semi-final was a heady triumph for Poyet, who netted smartly and then celebrated by kissing his badge in front of Chelsea fans. The gesture sparked anger but reflected the Uruguayan's hurt at his treatment at Stamford Bridge. Having acted as a translator in the dressing room for Claudio Ranieri, Poyet was irked that, as his appearances became sporadic, his linguistic talents appeared more highly valued than his football skills.

Happily, at Tottenham he rediscovered the joy of the game, and later he coached under former Chelsea team-mate Dennis Wise at both Swindon and Leeds, before returning to the Lane, where he became an active number-two to Juande Ramos. Team talks with Gurning Gus must be a wonder to behold.

| | |
|---|---|
| **GUSTAVO AUGUSTO POYET** | |
| **BORN:** Montevideo, Uruguay, 15 November 1967. | |
| **HONOURS:** 26 Uruguay caps (93-00). | |
| **OTHER CLUBS:** River Plate, Argentina, 89-90; Real Zaragoza, Spain, 90/1-96/7 (239, 63); Chelsea 97/8-00/01 (105, 36). | |

GAMES **80 (18)**
GOALS **23**

# MILENKO ACIMOVIC

### 2002/03

Milenko Acimovic will never forget the date – or, indeed, the exact time – that he joined Tottenham Hotspur. As he signed a lucrative contract over morning coffee with Spurs directors, the midfielder was unaware that his wife had gone into labour with their first child. By the time he switched on his mobile phone, at around 11am on 14 May 2002, daughter Klara had been born. Unfortunately that was by far and away his biggest high at White Hart Lane.

Despite impressing as a goal-scorer for Slovenia at that summer's World Cup, Acimovic would make only five starts for Spurs. Manager Glenn Hoddle had been excited by his stylish attacking play for both club and country and he seemed a natural successor to the ageing Gus Poyet. Accordingly the free signing from Red Star Belgrade was paired initially with Jamie Redknapp, and in contests with Aston Villa and Southampton it appeared to be a promising partnership.

Acimovic's elegant touch and slick passing shone particularly in the home win over the Saints, in which he demanded one marvellous save of 'keeper Paul Jones and curled another imaginative effort narrowly wide. Had he succeeded with either of those attempts, Acimovic's White Hart Lane fate might have been different. But results fell away, Hoddle was sacked and the Slovene was axed, being deemed too lightweight for the hurly-burly of central midfield. In January 2004 he was loaned to Lille, and never played for Spurs again.

**MILENKO ACIMOVIC**
BORN: Ljubljana, Slovenia, 15 February 1977.
HONOURS: 74 Slovenia caps (98-07).
OTHER CLUBS: Olimpija 96/7-97/8 (34, 7); Red Star Belgrade 97/8-01/02 (102, 34), both Yugoslavia; Lille, France, 04/05-06/06 (47, 11); Al Ittihad, Saudi Arabia, 06/07; Austria Vienna 07/08.

| | | |
|---|---|---|
| GAMES | **5 (13)** | |
| GOALS | 0 | |

# HELDER POSTIGA

### 2003/04

The luggage handlers at Heathrow airport may have a lot to answer for. Helder Postiga had bags of talent, but somewhere between holding aloft the UEFA Cup with Porto and landing in London it all went missing. Tottenham endured a host of misfiring strikers in the years preceding the Portuguese marksman's arrival, but in terms of goals per pound, Postiga represented worse value than a Robert Maxwell pension.

'He's got a bit of everything,' was Glenn Hoddle's boast as he attempted to justify the £6.25 million deal. Postiga had arrived at Tottenham barely a month after his Porto team-mates had claimed the European crown, and the 21-year-old was technically proficient. But his tendency to drift out of games would be woefully exposed.

Months passed and managers departed before Postiga scored a League goal. There were lots of horrible misses before finally he struck the winner in a 2-1 home victory over Liverpool in January 2004. Helder savoured the moment, and he was right to do so because that day marked his only memorable performance as a Spur.

In the summer Postiga's name would be stamped on the national consciousness for grabbing a crucial goal for Portugal in their European Championships win over England. Despite that, there were few regretful faces at the Lane when he returned to Porto in exchange for Pedro Mendes the following month. In the costly case of Helder Postiga, the Portuguese sun had left Tottenham with badly burned fingers.

**MANUEL HELDER MARQUES POSTIGA**
BORN: Povoa de Varzim, Portugal, 2 August 1982.
HONOURS: 30 Portugal caps (03-).
OTHER CLUBS: Porto, Portugal, 01/02-02/03 (58, 22) and 04/05-; St Etienne, France, on loan 05/06 (18, 9); Panathinaikos, Greece, on loan 07/08.

| | | |
|---|---|---|
| GAMES | **12 (12)** | |
| GOALS | 2 | |

# BOBBY ZAMORA

### 2003/04

Bobby's dazzling dream looked set to come true the day Spurs came calling. The Londoner's hard graft at Bristol Rovers and Brighton had paid off and now he had the chance to realise his childhood ambition – to score for Tottenham. But, sadly, Zamora endured the worst spell of his career at White Hart Lane. Following his £1.5million arrival in July 2003, he begged, stole and borrowed – but he just could not buy a League goal.

The under-21 international was recruited for his marksmanship and his intelligence off the ball. Glenn Hoddle believed Zamora would prosper through his clever running, drifting deep before using his pace to catch defenders off-guard. It had worked in the lower leagues but his knees would cave under the weight of expectation at Spurs.

When the striker does hang up his boots, however, he will have one set of cuttings from his north London days to savour. Against West Ham, during the extra-time climax of a League Cup clash, Zamora notched his solitary goal in a Tottenham jersey, dispatching a low drive following a Jon Blondel set-up.

However, it was not enough, and in February he was used as a makeweight in the deal which saw Jermain Defoe arrive from West Ham. A season later Zamora's four play-off strikes took the Eastenders back to the Premiership. Glenn Hoddle had said Bobby could score goals in the top flight and, eventually, he did.

**ROBERT LESTER ZAMORA**
BORN: Barking, London, 16 January 1981.
OTHER CLUBS: Bristol Rovers 99/00 (4, 0); Brighton on loan 99/00 (6, 6); Brighton 00/01-02/03 (119, 70); West Ham United 03/04- (130, 30).

| | | |
|---|---|---|
| GAMES | **7 (11)** | |
| GOALS | 1 | |

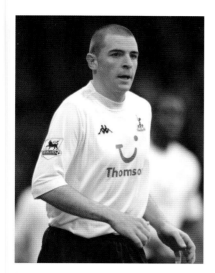

# DEAN MARNEY

2003/04 → 2004/05

For 90 glorious minutes, Dean Marney was Tottenham's best player. It was the day he had waited for since he joined the club as a nine-year-old; the moment he had craved during loan stints in the lower divisions; the hour he feared might never come as, time and again, he was named in Spurs' reserves for dreary outings in front of three men and a dog. Yet in January 2005 the loan stranger of White Hart Lane became the star of a comic-strip plot.

Having earned a surprise call-up to face Everton, Marney outclassed the likes of Keane, King and Carrick to win the man-of-the-match champagne. In the 5-2 drubbing of the Toffees, Dean's contribution was extraordinary. Playing on the right of midfield in his first home start, the 20-year-old struck two goals, the second a roof-raiser. Marney made his first impact with a wild tackle, but his next lunge saw him volley the opening goal. Then, running from half-way, he curved home a delicious effort from 22 yards.

But that was as good as it got. Knee trouble played its part in his failure to rekindle the sparkle of that diamond-bright display before a host of illustrious midfield arrivals at the Lane hastened his departure to Hull in July 2006. But at least Dean Marney had one precious Tottenham memory to savour.

**DEAN EDWARD MARNEY**
BORN: Barking, London, 31 January 1984.
OTHER CLUBS: Swindon Town on loan 02/03 (9, 0); Queen's Park Rangers on loan 03/04 (2, 0); Gillingham on loan 04/05 (3, 0); Norwich City on loan 05/06 (13, 0); Hull City 06/07- (78, 8).

GAMES **4 (7)**
GOALS **2**

# PAUL KONCHESKY

2003/04

Paul Konchesky just wanted to be put in his place. The young Londoner had hoped an early-season loan spell at Spurs would help him break his shackles at Charlton, where he had been condemned to a utility role since he was 14. The tenacious Konchesky could play anywhere along the left flank, but he favoured left-back. Yet having arrived at the Lane with hopes of a permanent move, it was to his immense frustration that not once in a dozen starts did he play in the position he craved.

Konchesky plundered admirably in midfield and on the flank, but he laboured under no delusion that he was the next David Ginola. There were no moments of inspiration, no flashes of brilliance to bring the chairman skipping down the boardroom steps with a permanent contract. His solid displays did help a marked improvement in results, however. Following the departure of Glenn Hoddle, David Pleat reverted to 4-4-2 and the team's goals-against average plummeted. With Konchesky playing in front of the equally ferocious Mauricio Taricco, the opposition's right-midfielders were guaranteed one thing – bruises.

Paul was beginning to win over the fans with his wholehearted approach and it seemed likely that Spurs might extend his stay, but injury-stricken Charlton ordered him home in December. Tottenham and Konchesky were disappointed, but he had not done quite enough to prompt a permanent offer. Had he been tried in his preferred position, the outcome might have been pleasingly different.

**PAUL MARTYN KONCHESKY**
BORN: Barking, London, 15 May 1981.
HONOURS: 2 England caps (03-).
OTHER CLUBS: Charlton Athletic 97/8-04/05 (149, 5); West Ham United 05/06-06/07 (59, 1); Fulham 07/08- (33, 0).

GAMES **12 (3)**
GOALS **0**

# STEPHANE DALMAT

2003/04

As an enigmatic winger of French origin, Stephane Dalmat could rightly expect a warm welcome at White Hart Lane. At a time when David Ginola was still fresh in the memory, the newcomer's pedigree was enough to set any Spurs fan drooling. The 24-year-old could thrill with his repertoire of explosive creativity and yet, sadly, he lived up to his billing only fleetingly after his arrival on loan from Internazionale in September 2003. Two games, two wins and two dazzling performances down Tottenham's right flank.

Dalmat sparkled during a chilly January, first with a man-of-the-match show in the FA Cup against Crystal Palace, then helping to wrench Spurs out of relegation strife with two stunning goals against Birmingham. It was enough to prove this complex individual's remarkable talent, yet his career was always hampered by weight of expectation. His frequent moves involved a total of £23.5 million in transfer fees and his clubs became anxious to see their money's worth. The words stroppy, arrogant and disappointing recurred in analyses of his short-term tenures, and it was his temperament, perhaps, that curtailed his Lane career.

Often caretaker boss David Pleat was bemused by Dalmat's approach to training. Some days he would graft alone after coaching had finished and on others he would complain about hard work. His communication was said to be limited and, at Tottenham's behest, he returned to Milan after only 15 starts.

**STEPHANE DALMAT**
BORN: Joue-les-Tours, France, 16 February 1979.
OTHER CLUBS: Chateauroux 97/8 (29, 1); Lens 98/9 (25, 3); Marseille 99/00 (29, 1); Paris St Germain 00/01 (19, 1), all France; Inter Milan, Italy, 00/01- (33, 3); Toulouse, France, on loan 04/05; Racing Santander, Spain, on loan 05/06; Bordeaux, 06/07 (14, 1); Sochaux 07/08-, both France.

GAMES **15 (13)**
GOALS **3**

# ANTHONY GARDNER

## 2000/01 →

Cardsharps at White Hart Lane might have marvelled at the potential of young Anthony Gardner. If top-trumps could be played with centre-halves, the towering Midlander would surely have been an ace in the pack. All the necessary attributes of a top defender were clearly evident: enviable pace, a certain elegance, imposing presence. Yet, after six years of hovering on the periphery of Tottenham's first team, in 2007/08 Gardner was still waiting to show his winning hand.

His progress, like so many other Spurs of his era, has been severely hampered by confidence-sapping injuries. Riddled with persistent thigh, feet and ankle problems, sometimes he has appeared shorn of belief during his fleeting runs in the senior side. Such was his eagerness to impress that he could appear clumsy, and notoriously hard-to-please supporters would criticise him for being bullied out of games. Accordingly Anthony, despite his undoubted possibilities, has invariably tended to play second fiddle to his rivals for a berth.

Gardner – like Matthew Etherington, Gary Doherty and Simon Davies – was bought as a rookie from the lower leagues and allowed to develop in the reserves. The quartet cost Spurs a total of £3.2 million, with Port Vale receiving £1m for Anthony in January 2000, and soon the investment was looking sound.

Certainly at first, the unassuming giant showed strong evidence that he had the makings of a high-quality centre-half. His most

impressive White Hart Lane campaign was 2003/04, when a string of sterling efforts earned him a full England call-up. International coaches had been impressed particularly by one display against Newcastle, when Gardner won the man-of-the-match award for containing Alan Shearer. At 6ft 5in, he might be expected to win most of his headers but, with the Magpies pushing hard for an equaliser, it was his positioning against Shearer which riveted the attention of seasoned judges. With the ball flashing crazily across the box, he managed to stretch out a long leg more than once to deny his frustrated opponent.

That term, also, he starred in encounters with Arsenal and Liverpool, eradicating the threat of Thierry Henry and Michael Owen. Had Gardner arrived at last? Sadly, no, as niggling ankle and thigh injuries ensured that the next two seasons were virtual write-offs. Then in 2005/06, following a nervy display in Tottenham's FA Cup capitulation against Leicester, there were rumours that he might be heading for the exit, with Portsmouth looking likely suitors.

But then Anthony delivered a timely masterpiece. In the absence of the suspended Michael Dawson, he partnered Ledley King in a heroic defensive display at Highbury. Tottenham came close to pulling off a rare win against the old enemy and Gardner won gushing praise from Martin Jol. It is to be hoped that he listened carefully to his manager's post-match debriefing that day. Time waits for no one – and Anthony Gardner, who spent an injury-wracked interlude on loan at Everton in 2007/08, needs to start believing he is good enough if he is going to make the grade.

| ANTHONY GARDNER | | |
|---|---|---|
| **BORN:** | Stone, Staffordshire, 19 September 1980. | |
| **HONOURS:** | 1 England cap (04). | |
| **OTHER CLUBS:** | Port Vale 98/9-99/00 (41, 4). | |

| | |
|---|---|
| GAMES | **121 (23)** |
| GOALS | 3 |

# DEAN RICHARDS

## 2001/02 → 2003/04

The tale of Dean Richards' all-too-brief Tottenham tenure is a poignant one of emerging excellence being sabotaged by poor health. Having arrived from Southampton in one of the least amicable transfers in Premiership history, the uncompromising Yorkshireman was introduced to Spurs supporters as the defensive linchpin to replace the recently departed Sol Campbell. It was hoped that the big stopper's broad shoulders were wide enough to cope with such heavyweight pressure but, plagued by a string of debilitating injuries and illnesses, he never stood a fair chance of proving himself an accomplished successor to the once-popular Londoner.

Dean began his career in his home-town with Bradford City before joining Wolverhampton Wanderers and flourishing under Glenn Hoddle at Southampton, where he lost little time in forging a reputation as one of England's best uncapped centre-halves. Rugged Richards was aggressive in the tackle and awesome in the air at both ends of the field, so by the time he signed for Spurs in September 2001, he commanded an £8.1 million price tag.

Tottenham's popularity on the south coast plunged to a new low that day. The Saints had already been fuming at the nature of Hoddle's switch to White Hart Lane, and so impressive was Richards in the early months of his north London sojourn that Southampton's bitterness showed little likelihood of abating.

Despite netting with a stooping near-post header to give Spurs an early lead, he endured a somewhat traumatic debut as Hoddle's

men surrendered a three-goal advantage to Manchester United at the Lane, eventually going down 5-3. But soon it became clear that Richards' appealing blend of power, positional awareness and elegance would mesh effectively with the richly promising all-round attributes of the less experienced Ledley King.

Dean's aerial prowess, in particular, is remembered with relish at the Lane, where he settled a dour clash with Blackburn on New Year's Day 2002 by thumping a fierce header beyond Rovers 'keeper Brad Friedel from Darren Anderton's corner. Even more encouraging, that game featured a series of fine defensive performances, with the Tottenham back line looking more orderly than it had done for years. At times Richards was reminiscent of Gary Mabbutt, a reliable bulwark at the back and a natural leader who was always eager to get forward.

High praise indeed, but in subsequent campaigns he became blighted by health problems, suffering periodically from unnatural fatigue, a loss of balance and dizziness. In 2004, he contracted a serious ear infection and went for a brain scan. Results were inconclusive but in March 2005 Richards decided to quit the game at the premature age of 30, when he should have been in his pomp. Later he flirted with the idea of a return to coaching at Bradford City. But after his serious health scare, few would blame Dean Richards for concluding that there might be more important things in life than football.

| DEAN IVOR RICHARDS | | |
|---|---|---|
| **BORN:** Bradford, Yorkshire, 9 June 1974. | GAMES | 81 |
| **OTHER CLUBS:** Bradford City 91/2-94/5 (86, 4); Wolverhampton Wanderers 94/5-98/9 (122, 7); Southampton 99/00-01/02 (73, 4). | GOALS | 4 |

# JAMIE REDKNAPP

## 2002/03 → 2004/05

Jamie Redknapp turned up at White Hart Lane 12 years late. Just ask Terry Venables, the canny observer who, in 1990, spotted a schoolboy with footballing gifts to grace any field. Redknapp was 16 at the time and thrilled by the prospect of learning from his hero Paul Gascoigne. But, when a deal was offered, doubts set in. Would the slightly-built youngster be crushed by the physical demands of the top-flight game? Would he be able to cope with the homesickness which might follow a long-distance move from his Dorset-based family?

For once Venables' celebrated silver tongue failed. Instead of enlisting at the Lane, Redknapp joined his father, Harry, at Bournemouth, and Spurs had lost a midfield general with passing ability to match anyone of his generation.

When Jamie eventually arrived at Tottenham in 2002, he was, by his own admission, damaged goods. At Liverpool, over the past decade, he had endured serial highs and lows. Medals, England caps and garrulous praise had been all too often interrupted by persistent injury problems. Cartilage in his right knee had been removed at the age of 17, and the joint was stripped to the bone by the time he accepted Glenn Hoddle's offer a dozen years on.

Despite the clearly-marked 'fragile' label on his new delivery, Hoddle described his free transfer as 'the steal of the decade', claiming Redknapp could still give David Beckham a contest for his England place. While that prediction would prove somewhat misguided, there was genuine reason for excitement, especially during the newcomer's first few matches in a Lilywhite shirt. The flourishes of magic, sleek skills and vicious shot were still there – even if he relied on only one leg.

Hoddle saw a kindred spirit in Redknapp, paying him due respect by making him club captain. When the man with the matinee looks played, he was the team's linchpin and launchpad, always making space and providing cohesion between midfield and defence.

And his first goal for Tottenham, on his home debut against Aston Villa, furnished a shining example of his resourcefulness and technique. Villa 'keeper Peter Enckelman parried a free-kick before tumbling to the ground; Redknapp, by now 30 yards away from goal, teed the ball up again and dispatched a dipping shot into the far corner. With Poyet and Sheringham purring, Spurs now had three very wise men on whom to rely.

Unfortunately Redknapp's creaky knees were almost finished. With his swollen joints, he was often able to train only once or twice a week, enduring the frustration of endless days on exercise bikes while team-mates enjoyed five-a-sides. The departure of Hoddle and an influx of younger, less injury-prone midfielders would mark the end of Jamie's sojourn.

He relished an opportunity for one last hoorah with dad Harry, who had managed him at Bournemouth as a teenager. But after a handful of games for Southampton, during their doomed relegation fight, he limped away to begin a career as a TV pundit.

**JAMIE FRANK REDKNAPP**

| | |
|---|---|
| BORN: | Barton-on-Sea, Hampshire, 25 June 1973. |
| HONOURS: | 17 England caps (95-99). |
| OTHER CLUBS: | Bournemouth 89/90-90/1 (13, 0); Liverpool 91/2-01/02 (237, 30); Southampton 04/05 (16, 0). |

GAMES **38 (11)**

GOALS 4

# FREDI KANOUTE

## 2003/04 → 2005/06

He had a stubborn streak as wide as the River Seine, but Fredi Kanoute was worth the hassle. Despite countless bust-ups and chin-dropping outbursts during his stay in north London, there was good reason to keep this marvellous Mali marksman happy. When he felt like it, he could destroy oppositions. His intelligence and aerial prowess left defenders flummoxed and his awareness could make his fellow front-runners look like world beaters; Jermain Defoe can pay testament. Speed, vision and a shot of exceptional accuracy marked Kanoute out from the crowd. Here was a performer, admittedly a temperamental one, who did his utmost to make the game look beautiful.

Having started his career with his home-town club, Olympique Lyon, Fredi moved to West Ham, but couldn't settle at Upton Park so in August 2003 he crossed London to White Hart Lane in a £3.5 million-plus deal. His time at Tottenham was peppered with argument and spells of poor form, but he was blessed with a precious capacity for producing sudden shafts of the sublime, often when he had appeared to be at a particularly low ebb.

For instance, in December 2004 Kanoute was lambasted for committing a ludicrous handball, then missing a penalty which handed victory to Liverpool in a League Cup quarter-final. Yet the following week he mustered the confidence to plunder victory out of nothing with a coruscating long-range effort against Manchester City.

That sequence typified Kanoute's stay, as did an unholy row over a trip to represent his country in the African Nations Cup. Tottenham tried to prevent Fredi from playing for Mali on the grounds that he had been capped for France at under-21 level. With the contretemps reaching fever pitch, the stormy petrel seemed certain to be axed from the starting line-up for an FA Cup meeting with Crystal Palace. But he played and, lo and behold, he helped himself to a hat-trick.

Kanoute, the son of a French philosophy teacher, got his way eventually and flew to Africa for the tournament, but the gaping rift between club and player never healed. He failed to turn up for a summer tour in 2005 and, facing an increasingly frustrating battle for his berth with Defoe, Mido and Robbie Keane, he swapped the bench at White Hart Lane for a more active niche in Spain with Sevilla, who paid £4.4 million for his services that August. The 27-year-old thrived with the *Primera Liga* club, top scoring in the following campaign.

For Tottenham fans who still feel sore about the way he abandoned their club for Mali, it might be worth noting that he has since headed an aid project for disadvantaged children in Bamako, the capital, and has recently, in his unamplified way, become a notable champion for West Africans in Andalusia. Undeniably there was an infuriating side to Fredi Kanoute, but he was a man of principle who meant what he said.

**FREDERIC KANOUTE**

| | |
|---|---|
| BORN: | Sainte Foy-les-Lyon, France, 2 September 1977. |
| HONOURS: | 18 Mali caps (04-). |
| OTHER CLUBS: | Olympique Lyon, France, 97/8-99/00 (40, 9); West Ham United 99/00-02/03 (84, 29); Sevilla, Spain, 05/06-. |

| | |
|---|---|
| GAMES | **52 (21)** |
| GOALS | 21 |

# MBULELO MABIZELA

## 2003/04 → 2004/05

If Mbulelo Mabizela had been asked to write the script for his Premiership debut, his wildest fantasy could hardly have improved on the reality. With Spurs trailing 1-0 to Leicester at the Walkers Stadium in October 2003, the South African defender was introduced as a second-half substitute, then scored with virtually his first kick. Latching on to a Bobby Zamora lay-off, Mabizela netted with a ferocious rising strike. Spurs went on to win and Mbulelo was hailed as a star in the making, but this euphoric beginning led to no happy ending. It is said that the glorious moment was the only occasion that the quietly-spoken Mabizela's Tottenham team-mates saw him smile.

Having risen meteorically to become Bafana Bafana's youngest skipper at 21, he was signed by Glenn Hoddle for £1 million after impressing during Tottenham's trip to his homeland. His main strengths were his marking ability, his strength and the versatility which enabled him to double as a midfielder. But, sadly, he suffered acute homesickness in London and, in an era of upheaval at White Hart Lane, he was never given a chance to settle. He started only two games, including one against Manchester United in which, deployed in front of the back four, he was outwitted and outrun by his elusive opponents, impetuously conceding a succession of free-kicks in dangerous areas.

Eventually the unhappy youngster requested a transfer and returned to his home country via a spell in Norway. In 2006, Mabizela was banned for failing a drugs test. His reputation had plunged as quickly as it once soared.

**OLDJOHN MBULELO MABIZELA**
BORN: Pietermaritzburg, South Africa, 16 September 1980.
HONOURS: South Africa caps.
OTHER CLUBS: Mamelodi Sundowns (twice); Maritzburg City; Orlando Pirates 01/02-02/03 (61, 7), all South Africa; Valerenga, Norway.

GAMES **2 (7)**
GOALS 1

# JOHNNIE JACKSON

## 2003/04 → 2005/06

Johnnie Jackson should have played in baggy shorts and a flat cap. He brought to his game an elegant finesse which seemed somewhat out of place in the modern era. The technically accomplished midfielder, who was particularly assured on the left flank, showed vast promise as a teenager and was first choice for a series of games in early 2004. Some onlookers even speculated over his international credentials, but he was never quite able to stamp his authority on matches. Perhaps his sophisticated approach lacked sufficient punch.

Jackson was the brightest prospect in his class of Tottenham academy graduates and he captained England under-20s. Hopes of a senior breakthrough were postponed in 2001/02 through knee trouble, but after successful loan stints at Swindon and Colchester, he got his chance two seasons later.

Johnnie's dead-ball prowess was notable and his pinpoint left-foot crosses set up several goals for team-mates before he made his own headlines with a darting run and fizzing drive which sealed victory at Charlton in February. On that day at the Valley, the Londoner's prospects appeared exceedingly bright, but his hopes were undone by niggling injuries and an influx of new players.

At the end of the 2005/06 campaign he was freed to join Championship new-boys Colchester United, and Spurs fans will be delighted if he prospers with the Essex club. The White Hart Lane cognoscenti have always cherished their more cultured performers.

**JOHN JACKSON**
BORN: Camden, London, 15 August 1982.
OTHER CLUBS: Swindon Town on loan 02/03 (13, 1); Colchester United on loan 02/03 (8, 0); Coventry City on loan 03/04 (5, 2); Watford on loan 04/05 (15, 0); Derby County on loan 05/06 (6, 0); Colchester United 06/07- (78, 9).

GAMES **14 (10)**
GOALS 1

# ROHAN RICKETTS

### 2003/04 → 2004/05

After being thrown out by the neighbours, Rohan Ricketts appeared on Tottenham's doorstep with a big favour to ask. It takes a brave man to take the short bus trip across north London with cap in hand, but the energetic midfielder did more than that; he accomplished a minor miracle. Despite growing up in an Arsenal jersey, he managed to convince Spurs fans that he wanted genuinely to play with a cockerel on his chest.

Ricketts, released by the Gunners in summer 2002, was given a chance by Glenn Hoddle. He had been an FA Youth Cup winner at Highbury and appeared at every schoolboy level for England. Now Hoddle hoped the eager athlete would add energy to Spurs' ageing midfield. After a season of learning on the sidelines, Ricketts was given a run of games at the start of 2003/04 and, operating either on the left or in the centre, he let nobody down.

However, his performances split opinion in the stands. While always enthusiastic and available, Rohan was criticised for failing to spot passing options. Yet he was many pundits' man-of-the-match for a livewire display in a stalemate against Liverpool, while his own fondest memory as a Spur will be an encounter with Aston Villa in which his hyperactive scampering changed the game after he was brought on as a substitute. He rattled Villa's defence before scoring an equaliser and inspiring a stirring victory.

Despite that, he fell out of favour when Spurs opted for a continental management team, being freed to enlist with Wolves, and Hoddle, in March 2005.

# MICHAEL BROWN

### 2003/04 → 2005/06

The arrival of this gung-ho hustler in December 2003 marked a change in direction at White Hart Lane. With the club desperate to ditch its soft-touch image, Michael Brown, a no-nonsense, box-to-box midfielder, was signed from Sheffield United. He lacked the sophisticated touch offered by an Anderton or a Redknapp, instead contributing tenacity, endless energy and an insatiable hunger to get into the opposition's box.

In 2002/03 Brown had netted a remarkable 22 senior goals and been a key man as Neil Warnock's uncompromising Blades had reached the FA Cup semi-finals. David Pleat reckoned a touch of Sheffield steel was just what Spurs needed and two goals on his first outing for the reserves suggested he was a snip at £500,000.

He made a dramatic senior debut in the 2-1 home win over Liverpool in January 2004, slaving inspirationally alongside Anderton to deny the Merseysiders parity between the penalty areas, no mean achievement against Dietmar Hamann and Danny Murphy.

But his most impressive sequence as a Spur came at the end of that year as an eager foot-soldier in the newly-launched Martin Jol revolution. A full-blooded display in an eye-watering 5-4 defeat by Arsenal preceded a 1-0 win against Blackburn which owed much to Brown's enterprise, the highlight being a snaking run past several defenders climaxed by a neat set-up for Robbie Keane to finish comfortably.

However, before long the squad was flooded with new midfielders and Brown slipped out of contention, joining Fulham for £1.5 million in January 2006.

---

**ROHAN ANTHONY RICKETTS**
BORN: Clapham, London, 22 December 1982.
OTHER CLUBS: Coventry City on loan 04/05 (6, 0);
Wolverhampton Wanderers on loan 04/05 (7, 1);
Wolverhampton Wanderers 05/06-06/07 (51, 1);
Queen's Park Rangers on loan 06/07 (2, 0);
Barnsley 07/08- (10, 0).

| | |
|---|---|
| GAMES | 21 (15) |
| GOALS | 2 |

**MICHAEL ROBERT BROWN**
BORN: Hartlepool, County Durham, 25.1.77.
OTHER CLUBS: Manchester City 95/6-98/9 (89, 2);
Hartlepool United on loan 96/7 (6, 1); Portsmouth on
loan 99/00 (4, 0); Sheffield United 99/00-03/04
(151, 27); Fulham 05/06-06/07 (41, 0);
Wigan Athletic 07/08- (31, 0).

| | |
|---|---|
| GAMES | 52 (12) |
| GOALS | 3 |

# ROBBIE KEANE

· · · · · · · · · · · · · · · · · · · · · · · · · · · · · · · · · ·

## 2002/03 →

Robbie Keane is something of an enigma. Away from the game he is softly spoken, engagingly self-effacing with a generous dollop of Irish charm. But when he goes to work, when the Tottenham cockerel crows proudly on his chest, the hitherto decorous Dubliner undergoes an identity change as radical as Clark Kent newly emerged from a telephone box. Now he roars out of the tunnel as a footballing extrovert with passion to burn, a leader by example who has given the Lane's loyal legions more spectacular goals to remember than any contemporary during the 21st century to date.

It had seemed a fanciful prophecy in August 2002 when Glenn Hoddle boldly declared that the energetic Keane, for whose dynamic attacking services he had just paid £7 million to Leeds United, had found his spiritual home at Tottenham. After trying life at four previous clubs, in the process amassing an aggregate of more than £30 million in transfer fees, the 22-year-old marksman appeared to be a confirmed hobo, destined to roam rootlessly, tantalising his latest fans with his capabilities before heading for yet another new horizon.

In the beginning Robbie had turned down Liverpool, whom he idolised, to join Wolves, reasoning that the Black Countrymen offered a better chance of attaining first-team football at an early age. He became an instant star at Molineux, and soon accepted a £6 million move to Coventry City. Again he excelled, but with the Sky Blues failing to satisfy his heady aspirations, he decamped to *Serie A*, a £13 million fee taking him to Internazionale of Milan. The San Siro was the grand stage he craved, but the dream soured when manager Marcello Lippi was sacked, then a £12 million transfer to Leeds proved similarly traumatic. Keane got off to a prolific start at Elland Road, only for his form to plunge almost as fast as the Yorkshire club's fortunes, hence his arrival at White Hart Lane.

Southern media sceptics dubbed him a nomadic outsider, and nobody but Hoddle broached the notion that he might become one of Tottenham's most popular sons. Yet six years on, Keane's cult status at the Lane is unrivalled by any of his peers. Perhaps the doubters should have listened when, from the start of his north London sojourn, the Irish international maintained that he was a man misunderstood, asserting that his serial transfers weren't down to ruthless ambition, rather they indicated his determination to play as much football as possible.

His infectious vitality was vividly apparent as soon as he arrived. Before long he was captivating new admirers by his eagerness to attack from deep positions, usually at high velocity and with a tenacity which tormented weary opponents. His flowing footwork, endless industry and disarming willingness to try wholeheartedly for even the most seemingly impossible of goals were richly appreciated in the stands. At times he demonstrated the enthusiasm of an infant and he could entertain like one, too, with his ungainly cartwheel celebrations striking an affectionate chord with supporters.

Keane responded to the warm welcome with some outstanding displays in his first few months at the club. After a five-match barren spell, any growing anxieties about the wisdom of his purchase were dispelled at Ewood Park when he sprinted through the Blackburn defence to fizz a left-foot drive into the roof of Brad Friedel's net. Even better was in store, for instance his scintillating hat-trick in a 4-3 home victory over Everton, which had an appreciative Hoddle purring about his acquisition's pure quality. Keane's ebullience set a magnificent example and he was more than worthy of his Tottenham player of the year awards as he bagged 13 and 16 goals respectively in his first two campaigns.

There would be tougher times, when his effervescence boiled over into frustration. In his third season as a Spur he grew increasingly angry at playing second fiddle to Jermain Defoe, and the mounting tension culminated in his storming from the dugout towards the end of a game against Birmingham City in April 2005. That gave rise to inevitable speculation about an imminent departure, especially after he was fined £10,000 and forced to train with the reserves.

But Keane knuckled down with characteristic persistence and, given a fresh chance in the following November, he played some of the best football of his career as Tottenham launched a brave assault on a Champions League spot. Typical was a sinew-straining display as he contributed two goals to a thrilling 3-2 home win against Blackburn in March, the highlight being a fabulous solo effort which saw him breeze past a posse of flummoxed defenders before finishing with ferocious certainty. By the end of the season – despite a training ground rift with Edgar Davids which culminated in a fight – his growing stature at the Lane was mirrored by his appointment as vice-captain.

During the summer of 2006 Keane signed a four-year contract and White Hart Lane regulars rejoiced at the prospect of his intuitive partnership with sublimely gifted new arrival Dimitar Berbatov maturing into something even more majestic. Duly, come 2007/08 he prospered like never before, and after playing an integral role in Spurs' Wembley triumph over Chelsea, he broke down in tears of joy as he collected his League Cup winner's medal. A month later he was inflicting more misery on Avram Grant's team, this time with a superlative 20-yard curler which secured a 4-4 home draw in arguably the most enthralling encounter of the entire Premiership season. Robbie Keane had come of age as a Tottenham hero, and he was flying high.

**ROBERT DAVID KEANE**

| | |
|---|---|
| **BORN:** | Dublin, 8 July 1980. |
| **HONOURS:** | League Cup 07/08. 79 Republic of Ireland caps (98-). |
| **OTHER CLUBS:** | Wolverhampton Wanderers 97/8-99/00 (73, 24); Coventry City 99/00 (31, 12); |
| | Internazionale, Italy, 00/01 (6, 0); Leeds United 00/01-02/03 (46, 13). |

| | |
|---|---|
| GAMES | **202 (52)** |
| GOALS | 107 |

# NOUREDDINE NAYBET

## 2004/05 → 2005/06

Noureddine Naybet's arrival at Spurs surprised everyone – even the man who signed him. Sporting director Frank Arnesen had previously declared his reluctance to invest in veterans, and Tottenham had been buying young players by the job lot. But this hulking 34-year-old defender was too good to miss. He was a tad more ponderous in movement than the whippersnappers around him, his weathered looks bearing traces of scrapes and lessons from a trophy-laden career beginning at his home-town club in Casablanca. Yet what Naybet lacked in fleetness of foot he made up for in sound sense. With such a youthful squad, there had to be room for a player Arnesen described as a natural leader.

The Moroccan had played for clubs in five countries, captained his national side for ten years and accumulated more than a century of caps. Come August 2004, after eight hugely successful years in Spain with Deportivo La Coruña, he was keen to play in England and joined Tottenham for £700,000. Making light of his difficulty in speaking English, Naybet proved his worth immediately, emerging as a towering influence in the heart of the defence as Spurs conceded only three goals in the season's first eight games.

That campaign proved so fruitful for Naybet that he was rewarded with another year's contract, but while his brain remained sharp, his legs were beginning to fail and he was unable to disturb the burgeoning partnership of Ledley King and Michael Dawson. After a disappointing 2005/06, he was released, and Spurs bade farewell to a true footballing ambassador.

**NOUREDDINE NAYBET**
BORN: Casablanca, Morocco, 10 February 1970.
HONOURS: 105 Morocco caps (90-06).
OTHER CLUBS: Nantes, France, 93/4 (34, 1); Sporting Lisbon, Portugal, 94/5-95/6 (54, 5); Deportivo La Coruna, Spain, 96/7-03/04 (212, 10).

GAMES 34 (1)
GOALS 1

# ERIK EDMAN

## 2004/05 → 2005/06

Those who remember Erik Edman as an unadventurous left-back may have been missing from the crowd at Anfield on a sunny April afternoon in 2005. It was the day the blond Swedish international cut loose from caution. His moment arrived after an abortive short corner between Robbie Keane and Andy Reid. The ball broke free but Edman seized possession some 35 yards out and, without hesitation, sent a soaring left-footer into the Merseysiders' net.

That sequence of deathless drama apart, supporters and team-mates recall Erik as a zealously enthusiastic servant of the Tottenham cause. An experienced, well-travelled veteran, he was recruited to bring much-needed quality and reliability to the left flank of defence. However, the £1.3 million deal which brought Edman from Heerenveen in August 2004 was mired in controversy and a tribunal decision was necessary to secure his financial deserts.

It was a shame that such wranglings should overshadow much of his time at the Lane as it was clear Edman was a classy performer. Always keen to overlap, he was an expert crosser and an astute defender, although some observers reckoned he lacked aggression.

Early in 2005 he suffered serious concussion, which hampered his progress, while off-field matters also appeared to be taking their toll. Edman recovered to stun the Reds with his wonder goal, but it proved an early parting gift. In August 2005, aged 26, he joined Rennes for an undisclosed amount after it emerged that Spurs were about to sign Lee Young-Pyo.

**ERIK KENNETH EDMAN**
BORN: Huskvarna, Sweden, 11 November 1978.
HONOURS: 53 Sweden caps (01-).
OTHER CLUBS: Helsingborg, Sweden, 97-99 (61, 1); Torino, Italy, 99/00; Karlsruhe, Germany, 99/00 (8, 0); AIK Stockholm, Sweden, 00-01 (21, 0); Heerenveen, Holland, 01/02-02/03 (63, 1); Rennes, France, 05/06-07/08 (56, 0); Wigan Athletic 07/08- (5, 0).

GAMES 33 (1)
GOALS 1

# THIMOTHEE ATOUBA

## 2004/05

Thimothee Atouba brought to mind an old-fashioned football hard-nut who had been taking ballet lessons. Most of the time, the big Cameroonian international utility man exhibited all the subtlety of a rampaging bull, leaving his opponents bruised, battered and confused, while accumulating almost as many bookings as appearances. Yet, during his first few weeks at the Lane, fans were dumbfounded by his occasional daintiness as he danced down the wing.

In August 2004 at Newcastle, making his first Premiership start, Atouba's mazy running left Stephen Carr in a tangle, and the newcomer capped his display with the only goal of the game, a sublime effort from long distance. Earlier he had been wasteful and there had seemed little danger when he accepted a pass from Jamie Redknapp, but he cut inside and curled home an exquisite shot.

But that was an isolated highlight following Atouba's arrival from Basle earlier that month. Sporting director Frank Arnesen had clinched the signing of the 22-year-old after he had shone during the Swiss club's enterprising 2002/03 Champions League campaign. Arnesen believed that Thimothee's strength and versatility would add an extra dimension to Tottenham's left flank, and accordingly he was deployed variously as a southpaw full-back, centre-back and wide midfielder.

But his stock plunged in December when he was charged with violent conduct following a crunching challenge on Paul Dickov at Blackburn, although later he was cleared. There was criticism, too, of his penchant for dwelling on the ball rather than clearing it simply, and in May 2005 Spurs accepted a £1.4million bid from Hamburg.

**THIMOTHEE ESSAMA ATOUBA**
BORN: Douala, Cameroon, 17 February 1982.
HONOURS: 24 Cameroon caps (03-).
OTHER CLUBS: Union Douala, Cameroon; Neuchatel Xamax 00/01-01/02 (45, 2); Basle 01/02-03/04 (69, 3), both Switzerland; Hamburg, Germany, 05/06-.

GAMES **21 (3)**
GOALS **1**

---

# NOE PAMAROT

## 2004/05 → 2005/06

The bigger they come, the harder they fall – and as colossal Noe Pamarot lay apparently lifeless on the St Andrew's turf in April 2005, it was clear that something was seriously wrong. Pamarot had been Tottenham's Mr Indestructible since arriving the previous summer. Confronted by this burliest of right-backs' extreme pace and a physique which would not have shamed a heavyweight boxer, all but the boldest of wingers tended to cower, or at least to keep their distance. But, a few minutes into an end-of-season clash with Birmingham, the Frenchman twisted awkwardly, rupturing a knee ligament. He was back to his robust best within nine months but by then he was a forgotten man in an era of ruthless transition at Tottenham.

As part of a vast summer 2004 shopping spree, sporting director Frank Arnesen had paid £1.7 million to secure 25-year-old Pamarot from Nice. Having featured in French international squads, the defender quadrupled his wages by moving to England, then exuded competitive spirit in an impressive start at White Hart Lane. His strength proved particularly useful in the opposition's box and, choosing to forget a clumsy penalty he conceded against Arsenal, fans fondly remember a fine headed goal which decided a gruelling contest at Everton.

Then came injury, and Pamarot's absence paved the way for Stephen Kelly's emergence. Having returned to fitness, the Frenchman featured in only two more games before joining Portsmouth, in a £7 million package which also took Sean Davis and Pedro Mendes to the south coast, in January 2006. As a teenager he had spent an unsuccessful loan spell at Fratton Park. Now he was eager to prove a point.

**LOUIS NOE PAMAROT**
BORN: Fontenay-sous-Bois, France, 14 April 1979.
OTHER CLUBS: Martigues 97/8-98/9 (25, 2); Nice 99/00-03/04 (122, 6), both France; Portsmouth on loan 99/00 (2, 0); Portsmouth 05/06- (49, 3).

GAMES **28 (2)**
GOALS **2**

# LEDLEY KING

## 1998/99 →

For all the riches invested to satisfy the extravagant aspirations of the White Hart Lane empire builders, Ledley King offers compelling evidence to support those footballing organics who believe local produce is best. Perhaps the men in pinstripe suits should ponder deeply before laying down a landing strip for their exotic imports. The unassuming Eastender, a footballer oozing as much style and elegance as any English defender of his generation, never cost a penny in transfer fees, and he still lives just a few Tube stops from his birthplace.

Ledley, a rap music lover of Antiguan descent, attracts bouquets from way beyond the Paxton Road. Noting his remarkable pace and dexterity in the tackle, Thierry Henry once declared that the Spurs stopper knew few equals in the Premiership; praise, indeed, from the prolific former Gunner and French World Cup winner, who extolled the virtues of few opponents.

Certainly it is easy to appreciate why Martin Jol often described King as his best player, and rebuffed reported approaches for him from both Barcelona and Chelsea. While Tottenham have suffered dire defensive frailties over recent seasons, and have been punished mercilessly for their rearguard's haywire tendencies, it's fair to say that when Ledley has been free of injury he has resembled an island of serenity in a turbulent sea. His unflappable on-field persona has had a calming influence on his colleagues, even tempering the raw and exuberant Michael Dawson so that the promising Yorkshireman has emerged as a genuine international contender. He may not share the blood-and-thunder attributes of some of his predecessors as club captain, but the lean, lanky Londoner has been no less of a leader.

King's defensive instincts and speed of reaction are pretty well unparalleled among centre-halves based in the capital. In Tottenham's unforgettable League victory at home to Chelsea in November 2006, he recovered ten yards in an instant to deny Arjen Robben, his immaculate challenge setting the standard for a rousing team performance which ended an insufferable hoodoo. In previous seasons, momentous last-ditch tackles on Norwich City's Darren Huckerby and Craig Bellamy of Liverpool provided further evidence that Tottenham fans had been wasting their breath bemoaning Sol Campbell's departure to Arsenal quite so vitriolically. It should be noted, too, that King, like Campbell, is more than useful at the attacking end of the pitch, his bullet header to earn Spurs a point against Arsenal at the Lane in October 2005 offering a compelling example.

Ledley's rise to prominence was inexorable, but was not achieved through ruthless ambition or pushy parents. He started playing Sunday football for the highly-rated boys' club, Senrab, after a dinner lady spotted him on a school field impersonating his favourite player, Marco van Basten. Thereafter he graduated to the books of Leyton Orient before switching to Tottenham as a 14-year-old. Initially deployed as a deep-lying midfielder, he made his first-team debut as a half-time substitute in a 3-2 defeat at Liverpool in May 1999, and in December 2000 he made an impact by scoring the quickest goal in Premiership history, only ten seconds into a pulsating 3-3 draw with Bradford City at Valley Parade.

King was always adaptable and managerial upheavals at Tottenham, with different bosses preferring him in different positions, emphasised the extent of his versatility. Whether deployed in his favoured defensive role or handed more attacking duties, invariably he was a polished performer. Soon international recognition became inevitable, and duly it arrived in a 2-1 friendly defeat by Italy in March 2002. His most accomplished display in an England shirt – at least, at the time of writing – came against France during Euro 2004, when he operated as a holding midfielder and stifled the great Zinedine Zidane.

Undeniably Ledley King has been one of Spurs' finest servants of modern times and it is bitterly unfortunate that he has been hampered, almost to the point of career meltdown, by injury. Indeed, 2004/05 has been his only injury-free campaign of recent years. Feet, knees and hips have been broken, twisted, crunched and ripped. Perhaps his cruellest blow came in 2005/06 when, having enjoyed the finest form of his life, he splintered a metatarsal against Everton in April. Not only did it rob Tottenham of a key player who might have been instrumental in their retaining fourth place in the League table, but it also cost him his place in England's World Cup squad. Since then his presence has been intermittent at best. He missed the majority of the following term with a foot injury, only returning to the side for the last month. Jol was so desperate to have him back, he was rushed into a UEFA Cup quarter-final encounter with Sevilla, but to little avail as a ragged team performance saw Spurs crash out.

At least his serial agonies could be forgotten for one memorable day. On 24 February 2008 King led his colleagues on the seemingly interminable climb up the steps to the royal box at new Wembley to collect the League Cup. He was still recovering from knee surgery, yet his newly-formed partnership with Jonathan Woodgate had been faultless against the formidably menacing Chelsea strike-force of Didier Drogba and Nicolas Anelka. Ledley had put his injury-ridden body on the line as only a true leader would, and his admirers were left to pray that their battered King would remain on his throne for a good many more years.

**LEDLEY BRENTON KING**

BORN: Stepney, London, 12 October 1980.
HONOURS: League Cup 07/08. 19 England caps: (02-).

| GAMES | 237 (4) |
| --- | --- |
| GOALS | 11 |

# STEPHEN KELLY

## 2003/04 → 2005/06

Stephen Kelly simply got fed up with waiting at Tottenham Hotspur. The young Dubliner was tipped as an obvious solution to a pressing problem in a squad lacking natural right-backs following the departure of his countryman Stephen Carr to Newcastle United. Like Carr, Kelly was a hard-working, efficient defender who was keen to get forward, but the pair differed in their reaction to being dropped after tasting first-team action.

Martin Jol had promoted the eager rookie in December 2003 after he had performed well during a series of loan stints. His Spurs entrance, just before New Year, had enabled Kelly to join an exclusive coterie, having played in all four divisions during 2003. More importantly, though, he showed himself competent enough to merit a berth in the senior squad for the remainder of the campaign.

Following Carr's exit, Kelly saw his chance to emerge from the shadows, and during 2004/05 he was well received by the White Hart Lane cognoscenti. He lacked a little in physique but, during a settled first-team run from November to season's end, he showed encouraging prowess when supplementing the attack, chipping in with goals against Birmingham and Aston Villa.

However, the arrival of Paul Stalteri in the summer annoyed Kelly, and having publicly voiced his displeasure at being reduced to a bit-part role, in July 2006 he agreed a £750,000 switch to Birmingham, where first-team opportunities would improve. Few could begrudge him that.

**STEPHEN MICHAEL KELLY**
BORN: Dublin, 6 September 1983.
HONOURS: 10 Republic of Ireland caps (06-).
OTHER CLUBS: Southend United on loan 02/03 (10, 0); Queen's Park Rangers on loan 02/03 (7, 0); Watford on loan 03/04 (13, 0); Birmingham City 06/07- (74, 0).

GAMES **36 (8)**
GOALS 2

---

# RETO ZIEGLER

## 2004/05 → 2006/07

Those who voted for Reto Ziegler as Tottenham's finest young footballer of 2004/05 will testify that the future, in football at least, is never certain. The former Grasshopper, with a spring in his step, fully deserved his gong for a sparkling debut season, having slotted seamlessly into a side desperately lacking left-wing options. The 18-year-old was short of experience but Spurs were convinced of his quality.

Indeed, sporting director Frank Arnesen, who had originally arranged to take Ziegler in 2005, renegotiated a deal to secure the blond bombshell ahead of schedule. Thus he was launched into Premiership action against Everton in autumn 2004, and for much of the campaign he excelled.

Coaches and fans alike responded to Ziegler's puppy-like eagerness to chase every loose ball. The Swiss rookie was blessed with quickness in both feet and fine crossing ability with his left, an attribute all too rare at White Hart Lane in recent years. This was put to telling use at home to Arsenal when he delivered an elegant through-ball for Frederic Kanoute to slide home Tottenham's fourth goal in a painfully memorable defeat.

Soon he had impressed sufficiently to earn a first full international call-up, but by the end of that term several ragged performances, during which he repeatedly gave the ball away cheaply, led him to be sent out on loan.

Eventually he returned but four forgettable performances early in 2006/07 convinced Martin Jol that Reto Ziegler was surplus to requirements in a swelling squad. He has since prospered at Sampdoria.

**RETO PIRMIN ZIEGLER**
BORN: Nyon, Switzerland, 16 January 1986.
HONOURS: 5 Switzerland caps (05-).
OTHER CLUBS: Grasshoppers, Switzerland, 02/03-03/04 (38, 0); Hamburg, Germany, on loan 05/06; Wigan Athletic on loan 05/06 (10, 0); Sampdoria, Italy, 06/07-.

GAMES **22 (13)**
GOALS 1

## SEAN DAVIS

### 2004/05 → 2005/06

If Tottenham's insatiable recruitment policy was in any way comparable to Charles Saatchi's penchant for collecting art, Sean Davis was an abandoned canvas left in the shadows gathering dust. The club's gallery of central midfield exhibits was bulging in summer 2004 when the shaven-headed Londoner arrived at White Hart Lane. Yet Frank Arnesen, Spurs' sporting director, insisted that Davis, a fearless enforcer brimming with ambition, was certain of an important role. Wretched fate dictated otherwise.

After he was signed by Jacques Santini from Fulham, the initial signs were positive for Davis, who had recently earned his first England squad call-up. The eager competitor was quickly installed as the midfield fulcrum, performing impressively on his debut at Anfield, guarding his backline with gusto and stifling the rampaging Steven Gerrard. However, Santini soon departed and Martin Jol dissected Tottenham's midfield, sacrificing Davis and calling up Michael Carrick. Without denigrating the north-easterner, many observers were of a mind that Davis's more combative talents could still provide a useful foil for creative colleagues, but then a recurrence of an old knee injury damaged the newcomer's cause. When he did return others had thrived in a resurgent line-up and it seemed that his time was up almost before it had started.

The following campaign he barely featured and it was no surprise in January 2006 when he was released, along with Pedro Mendes and Noe Pamarot, to join Portsmouth in a £7 million package. Thus Tottenham recouped at least some of their outlay of 18 months earlier, but those who remembered Arnesen's ill-advised words were left feeling distinctly short-changed.

## PEDRO MENDES

### 2004/05 → 2005/06

The record books reveal otherwise, but every Spurs fan at Old Trafford on a stormy January evening in 2005 knows Pedro Mendes scored the most bizarre 'goal' that never was. With time ebbing away, he raced to meet a loose ball some three yards short of the halfway line. Improbably he met it with a steepling shot which swirled heavenwards before dipping deceptively. United 'keeper Roy Carroll made a flapping attempt to catch but only succeeded in fumbling the crazily spinning sphere at least a foot over his line. The Portuguese midfielder was in dreamland and pubs across north London erupted. The moment seemed too good to be true. And it was. The referee waved play on and poor Pedro was left to mourn what should have been a perfectly legitimate winning goal.

That almost surreal incident marked a downturn in fortune for Mendes, who had signed for Spurs for £2 million in July 2004, shortly after collecting a Champions League winner's medal with Jose Mourinho's Porto. Unlike Helder Postiga, who had moved in the opposite direction, this long-haired Latino spoke perfect English. He was occasionally played out of position on the wing by Tottenham, but his vision and careful passing game proved a big hit with supporters. However, this was not enough to guarantee him selection.

New boss Martin Jol brought in a clutch of fresh midfielders at season's end and in January 2006 Pedro joined Portsmouth along with fellow misfits Sean Davis and Noe Pamarot. Spurs wished him well. After that night in Manchester, the guy deserved a break.

---

**SEAN DAVIS**
BORN: Clapham, London, 20 September 1979.
OTHER CLUBS: Fulham 96/7-03/04 (155, 14); Portsmouth 05/06- (70, 1).

| GAMES | 12 (5) |
| --- | --- |
| GOALS | 0 |

---

**MIGUEL PEDRO MENDES**
BORN: Guimaraes, Portugal, 26 February 1979.
HONOURS: 2 Portugal caps (02-).
OTHER CLUBS: Felgueiras 98/9 (31, 2); Guimaraes 99/00-02/03 (83, 7); Porto 03/04 (26, 0), all Portugal; Portsmouth 05/06- (58, 5).

| GAMES | 29 (7) |
| --- | --- |
| GOALS | 1 |

# JERMAIN DEFOE

## 2003/04 → 2007/08

Music always played an important part in the life of Jermain Defoe. As a schoolboy with a gap-toothed smile, he won as many trophies for singing and dancing as he did for his precocious footballing skills. Even into adulthood, having forged a reputation as one of England's finest young goalscorers, he continued, at the prompting of his mother, to visit his local Catholic church to belt out the hymns. Should he have been afforded similar extended opportunities to get into his rhythm at Tottenham Hotspur? Might successive managers have exhibited a little more faith in a striker blessed with a precious instinctive talent? The inclination here is to answer both questions with an emphatic affirmative, and to reflect ruefully that no such bounteously gifted marksman would have been denied a major role in any other Spurs side of modern times.

Defoe, an attacking livewire with two deadly feet, made an instant impact after arriving in January 2004 from West Ham in a £7 million transaction which saw Bobby Zamora move in the opposite direction. Despite being only 21, the sparky graduate from Senrab Boys already boasted an impressive history, including a record-breaking scoring spree on loan at Bournemouth and an enviable collection of crucial hits for the Hammers. David Pleat remarked that he could not think of a British striker who had achieved as much in such a short space of time, and it was with those warm words ringing in his ears that Defoe marked his entry at the Lane with a goal in the 4-3 win over Portsmouth in February 2004.

The crowd loved the excitement he injected into the side. Linking fluently with Frederic Kanoute, Jermain was direct, enthusiastic and an endless threat. Some criticised his work off the ball but he was content to let his quicksilver feet do his talking. He could hit a ball with tremendous venom for one so slight, and despite his lack of inches he offered a potent aerial menace.

Everything Defoe did was accomplished at pace and with subtle style. In 2004/05 he became the first player for nine years to score more than 20 goals in a season for Spurs, a quickfire hat-trick in a 5-1 home drubbing of Southampton in December providing a vivid highlight. Now his stock was soaring fast, with Chelsea and Barcelona declaring an interest, but instead of decamping he delighted his Tottenham admirers by extending his stay. He had become a key player under Martin Jol and was featuring regularly for England. Why move on? However, he had not bargained for difficult times that lay ahead.

Though he could not have realised it, the beginning of the end of Defoe's White Hart Lane tenure can be traced back to a chilly night in Bolton in November 2005. Partnering Mido in attack, he endured a frustratingly fruitless evening, and the following week, at home to West Ham, Jol opted for a resurgent Robbie Keane as a foil for the big Egyptian. Thereafter the Londoner never truly regained the tag of first choice.

Keane and Defoe just did not work effectively together and Jol preferred the little Irishman's improvisation and clever touches to Defoe's speed and explosive finishing power. Jermain managed nine goals in 23 League starts that term, but in future his opportunities would be strictly limited.

To rub salt into the wound, as he held a watching brief for his club, his country gradually forgot what a force he once was. Where he had been an automatic second choice to Michael Owen at international level, he began to be dropped from squads, and he was devastated at being omitted from England's World Cup 2006 party.

For a footballer so reliant on pace and sharpness, it is impossible to exaggerate how much Defoe – who expected to be approaching his prime by the time of the German tournament – suffered from not being afforded regular games. Still, he soldiered on manfully and an injury to Keane during the following term enabled Jermain to recover something like his old form, his 18-goal return in all senior competitions being a considerable feat by a striker deemed no better than third choice. The brightest among several jewels in that commendable haul came at home to Wigan in November, when he accepted a sumptuous reverse pass from Dimitar Berbatov, spun like a top to bewilder the posse of markers that surrounded him and dispatched a stinging snap-shot into the roof of 'keeper Chris Kirkland's net.

But if the writing wasn't on the wall on that fulfilling afternoon at the Lane, it was lit up in fluorescent bulbs during the following summer when Darren Bent arrived from Charlton Athletic. Still Defoe insisted that he would stay and fight for his place, but his plight was not lessened by a change in management.

New man Juande Ramos maintained that he had an open mind, but Jermain did not strengthen his case by missing a penalty against West Ham early in the Spaniard's reign. In fairness, he was offered a contract, but having been in no rush to sign it, he was told he could leave. With reported interest from Manchester United cooling, Harry Redknapp, the manager who had first unleashed the young man's talents at West Ham, persuaded Defoe to join him at Portsmouth, clinching a £7 million deal in the January 2008 transfer window. Jermain may have given up on his dancing since leaving school but Redknapp, having secured the prized signature of his former protege, who was still only 25 and with so much more to give, looked ready to kick up his heels in a celebratory jig.

**JERMAIN COLIN DEFOE**

| | | GAMES | 110 (67) |
|---|---|---|---|
| **BORN:** | Beckton, London, 7 October 1982. | | |
| **HONOURS:** | 26 England caps (04-). | GOALS | 64 |
| **OTHER CLUBS:** | West Ham United 00/01-03/04 (93, 29); Bournemouth on loan 00/01 (29, 18); Portsmouth 07/08- (12, 8). | | |

## MARK GOWER

### 1998/99

A Tottenham academy graduate and England semi-professional international, Gower was competent in any midfield position. His versatility earned him a place on the bench as Tottenham lifted the League Cup in 1999. Later he knew his best days as a cultured operator with Southend.

**MARK GOWER**
**BORN:** Edmonton, London, 5 October 1978.
**OTHER CLUBS:** Motherwell on loan 98/9 (9, 1); Barnet 00/01 (14, 1); Southend United 03/04- (203, 35).

| GAMES | 0 (2) |
|---|---|
| GOALS | 0 |

## JOHN PIERCY

### 1999/2000 → 2000/01

Attacking midfielder Piercy was hailed as a future star after signing for Tottenham at 16 and appearing for England at youth level. His most memorable first-team contribution was in earning a last-gasp penalty in a 1-1 League Cup draw at Luton. His career was cut short by illness.

**JOHN WILLIAM PIERCY**
**BORN:** Forest Gate, London, 18 September 1979.
**OTHER CLUBS:** Brighton 02/03-04/05 (30, 4).

| GAMES | 2 (7) |
|---|---|
| GOALS | 0 |

## DAVE McEWEN

### 1999/2000 → 2000/01

Dave McEwen was a hard-working attacker who had gone to university to study business before embarking on his Spurs career. Competing against Rebrov, Iversen, Ferdinand and Armstrong, he did not need his degree to work out he was unlikely to get a look-in.

**DAVID McEWEN**
**BORN:** Westminster, London, 2 November 1977.
**OTHER CLUBS:** Queen's Park Rangers 01/02 (5, 0).

| GAMES | 0 (4) |
|---|---|
| GOALS | 0 |

## JAMIE SLABBER

### 2002/03

Tall striker Jamie Slabber was given 11 minutes to prove he could cut it in the top flight. Thrown on as a late substitute against Liverpool he stood little chance. After a loan spell in Denmark, he proved significantly more successful as a semi-professional.

**JAMIE ANDREW SLABBER**
**BORN:** Enfield, London, 31 December 1984.
**OTHER CLUBS:** AB Copenhagen on loan 03/04; Swindon Town on loan 04/05 (9, 0).

| GAMES | 0 (1) |
|---|---|
| GOALS | 0 |

## HANS SEGERS

### 1998/99

It was hard to tell former Wimbledon stalwart Segers had only reluctantly come out of retirement to provide emergency cover in a 1-1 League draw with Southampton, as he made three reflex saves which belied his 36 years. Now he's a goalkeeping coach.

**JOHANNES SEGERS**
**BORN:** Eindhoven, Holland, 30 October 1961.
Other clubs: PSV Eindhoven, Holland; Nottingham Forest 84/5-87/8 (58, 0); Stoke City on loan 86/7 (1, 0); Sheffield United on loan 87/8 (10, 0); Wimbledon 88/9-95/6 (267, 0); Wolverhampton Wanderers 97/8 (11, 0).

| GAMES | 2 |
|---|---|
| GOALS | 0 |

## ROGER NILSEN

### 1998/99

Nilsen bolstered Tottenham's squad having formed a reputation as a reliable left-back over six campaigns at Sheffield United. The ageing defender performed capably, providing cover in the last few weeks of the 1998/99 season. He went on to coach in Norway.

**ROGER NILSEN**
**BORN:** Tromso, Norway, 8 August 1969.
**HONOURS:** 21 Norway caps.
**OTHER CLUBS:** Viking Stavanger, Norway; Sheffield United 93/4-98/9 (166, 0).

| GAMES | 3 |
|---|---|
| GOALS | 0 |

## JON BLONDEL

### 2002/03 → 2003/04

Big things were expected of the Belgian teenager, who signed from Mouscron after trials at Manchester United. But his cultured passing game was judged unready for the rigours of the Premier League, and he returned to his homeland after just one start.

**JONATHAN BLONDEL**
**BORN:** Ypres, Belgium, 3 April 1984.
**HONOURS:** 3 Belgium caps.
**OTHER CLUBS:** Royal Excelsior Mouscron 01/02 (18, 0); Bruges 03/04-, both Belgium.

| GAMES | 1 (3) |
|---|---|
| GOALS | 0 |

## KAZUYUKI TODA

### 2002/03

Glenn Hoddle swooped for Toda after the midfielder impressed for Japan in the 2002 World Cup finals. The young Japanese was technically adept, but he appeared woefully lightweight and failed to become established during his year-long loan tenure at White Hart Lane.

**KAZUYUKI TODA**
BORN: Tokyo, Japan, 30 December 1977.
HONOURS: 15 Japan caps.
OTHER CLUBS: Shimuzu S-Pulse, Japan; Den Haag, Holland; Tokyo Verdy; Sanfrecce Hiroshima, both Japan.

| GAMES | 2 (2) |
|---|---|
| GOALS | 0 |

## MARK YEATES

### 2003/04 → 2004/05

Left-sided midfielder Yeates, a Republic of Ireland under-21 international, spent most of his Tottenham career playing for other clubs, his most significant senior input as a Spur being the creation of a goal for Robbie Keane against Wolves in 2004. He joined Colchester United in the summer of 2007.

**MARK STEPHEN YEATES**
BORN: Dublin, 11 January 1985.
OTHER CLUBS: Brighton on loan 03/04 (9, 0); Swindon Town on loan 04/05 (4, 0); Colchester United on loan 05/06 (44, 5); Hull City on loan 06/07 (5, 0); Leicester City on loan 06/07 (9, 1); Colchester United 07/08- (29,8).

| GAMES | 1 (3) |
|---|---|
| GOALS | 0 |

## PHILIP IFIL

### 2004/05 → 2006/07

Spurs fans could be excused for rubbing their eyes after seeing the team-sheet on the opening day of 2004/05. At left-back was Philip Ifil, a gutsy 17-year-old who had barely featured in the reserves. The England youth international revealed pace and skill, but could not cement a breakthrough and joined Colchester in 2008.

**PHILIP NATHAN IFIL**
BORN: Willesden, London, 18 November 1986.
OTHER CLUBS: Millwall on loan 05/06 (16, 0); Southampton on loan 07/08 (12, 0); Colchester United 07/08- (20, 0).

| GAMES | 4 (1) |
|---|---|
| GOALS | 0 |

## LEE BARNARD

### 2005/06

Barnard appeared to be on the verge of making his Tottenham dream come true for three years. A prolific scorer for the reserves, he made his Premiership entrance from the bench against Manchester United in spring 2006, but the burly blond's time ran out and he joined Southend in 2008.

**LEE JAMES BARNARD**
BORN: Romford, Essex, 18 July 1984.
OTHER CLUBS: Exeter City on loan 02/03 (3, 0); Leyton Orient on loan 04/05 (8, 0); Northampton Town on loan 04/05 (5, 0); Crewe Alexandra on loan 07/08 (10, 3); Southend United 07/08- (15, 9).

| GAMES | 0 (3) |
|---|---|
| GOALS | 0 |

## DORIAN DERVITE

### 2006/07 →

Spurs hailed Dorian Dervite's huge potential after signing the French under-18 captain from Lille, his home-town club. The 6ft 4ins defender proved a mature and commanding presence for Tottenham reserves before he suffered a serious knee ligament injury in January 2007. Watch this space.

**DORIAN DERVITE**
BORN: Lille, France, 25 July 1988.
OTHER CLUBS: Lille, France.

| GAMES | 1 |
|---|---|
| GOALS | 0 |

## ANDY BARCHAM

### 2006/07 →

Strong and speedy Andy Barcham led the Tottenham line in a League Cup win against Port Vale in November 2006, having shown encouraging form for the reserves. The striker has not featured since for Spurs at senior level and, having overcome injury problems, was weighing up his future in the spring of 2008.

**ANDREW BARCHAM**
BORN: Basildon, Essex, 16 December 1986.
OTHER CLUBS: Leyton Orient on loan 07/08 (25, 1).

| GAMES | 1 |
|---|---|
| GOALS | 0 |

# PAUL ROBINSON

## 2004/05 →

Flat caps at White Hart Lane are a rarity these days, and it's difficult not to agree with the cynics that the notion of the professional game as a working man's entertainment is dead. Footballers are now pampered demi-gods, living in stately homes and watched by prosperous businessmen in their corporate boxes. It's refreshing, then, that Paul Robinson, a fine young goalkeeper of Yorkshire stock, reportedly took a pay cut to join Tottenham Hotspur.

Bearing in mind the assertion of Brian Clough, a man who knew a thing or two about football, that a good goalkeeper saves his team 18 points a season, Spurs had plenty of reason to believe they had struck a bargain when they prised Robinson away from debt-ridden Leeds for £1.5 million in May 2004. After signing from the club he had supported all his life, he gave the impression that he wanted to play for Spurs for all the right reasons, and the amiable family man was loved instantly by the crowd, who delighted in chanting: 'England's Number One'.

Robinson had all the required assets to become an outstanding custodian and immediately became a crucial factor in the stiffening of Tottenham's back line. He enjoyed an encouraging first campaign as a Spur, and no player was more important in achieving the club's highest ever Premiership finish – fifth place – at the end of 2005/06. When he was on top of his game, which he was throughout most of that memorable term, he gave the impression that he was virtually unbeatable.

Fans at Villa Park in September will not forget how his brilliance helped Spurs survive with a point despite his goal being besieged for much of the contest, his succession of terrific reflex saves prompting Villa boss David O'Leary to praise him to the heavens. Quite deservedly, Paul cemented his place in the England side and was quietly impressive during the World Cup in Germany.

But tricky times on the international scene were waiting in ambush. The most unfortunate of incidents during a match in Croatia – a Gary Neville back-pass hit a divot and bounced over Robinson's flailing foot before rolling into the net – irreparably affected his reputation among the fickle masses. Rightly he dismissed that bizarre occurrence as a freak, but chinks were beginning to appear in his solid club form, despite jubilant scenes in March 2007 when he scored at White Hart Lane with a lofted free-kick against Watford.

The absence of Ledley King in front of him – the centre-half was injured, as usual – was a telling handicap, and at a time when Robinson was in dire need of a calming infuence, Spurs' rearguard became ragged and unpredictable. Who was to blame for the serial defensive mishaps? Well, any back four confident in their goalkeeper will defend more soundly than if he is going through a shaky patch, and undeniably there was a desperate interlude when it became painfully apparent that the 6ft 3in net-minder was vulnerable both when facing shots from distance and attempting to deal with crosses.

Like so many 'keepers Robinson would have to reach rock bottom before his fate would improve. Problems continued from the first day of 2007/08 when he was rooted to the spot as Sunderland's Michael Chopra poached a late winner at the Stadium of Light. Then he was substituted by England at half-time after a handling error against Germany, and blunders continued after new boss Juande Ramos arrived.

Now decisive action was taken. The ruthless Spaniard dropped Robinson for the first time in his Tottenham career. Not only was he out of the side, but he missed a League Cup semi-final clash with Arsenal, which Spurs won 5-1, and newspapers declared the following day that Paul had played his last game for the club.

But Ramos would show the courage of his convictions once more, this time to Robinson's advantage. After the Yorkshireman had spent more than a month in exile, the manager reinstated him for a UEFA Cup meeting with Slavia Prague, then stuck with him for the League Cup Final against Chelsea. The necks of both Ramos and Robinson were on the line as the pair walked out at Wembley. Another clanger wouldn't just damage the player, perhaps to the point of no return, but it would call into question Ramos's judgement.

Thus when Didier Drogba stroked home the opener from a free-kick as Paul remained static on his line, the media vultures scented a bloody carcass and began to circle greedily. However, that goal proved the prelude to a dramatic response from both 'keeper and team. Robinson recovered his composure just when he needed it most, and with Tottenham now leading 2-1, he pulled off two crucial saves in the second period of extra time. First he denied Salomon Kalou, jutting out his right boot instinctively to knock the striker's shot to safety, then clung on to a dangerous effort from Joe Cole. Neither stop, in truth, will go down as a classic, but given the occasion, that hardly mattered.

At this most testing of junctures, when his England place had been forfeited following a torrent of criticism, the 28-year-old had played a mammoth part in ensuring that the Ramos revolution got off to a winning start. Paul Robinson had done enough to help secure Spurs' first trophy since 1999, but whether that was enough to save his career at White Hart Lane remained to be seen.

---

**PAUL WILLIAM ROBINSON**

| | |
|---|---|
| **BORN:** | Beverley, Yorkshire, 15 October 1979. |
| **HONOURS:** | League Cup 07/08. 41 England caps (03-). |
| **OTHER CLUBS:** | Leeds United 98/9-03/04 (95, 0). |

| | |
|---|---|
| GAMES | 175 |
| GOALS | 1 |

# GRZEGORZ RASIAK

## 2005/06

Grzegorz Rasiak was inches away from cult status at Tottenham Hotspur. The Polish international striker, whose £2.25 million transfer from Derby County was agreed five minutes before the August 2005 deadline, silenced the Kop on his Spurs debut at Anfield only ten days after arriving in north London. Michael Carrick delivered a raking corner and the 6ft 3in spearhead netted with a powerful header. Instantly he was buried beneath a mound of jubilant Spurs celebrating what they thought was the only goal of the game, only for the referee to rule that Carrick's kick had curled marginally out of play. It was a cruel letdown and, aside from setting up a strike for Robbie Keane against Aston Villa, it proved to be the highlight of Rasiak's brief stay.

Big Grzegorz was a strong, industrious target man, who moved cleverly off the ball and gave manager Martin Jol a contrasting option to the mobile but diminutive front-running partnership of Keane and Jermain Defoe. His 16 League goals for the Rams in the Championship during the previous term augured optimistically for his Tottenham future, but in his nine appearances he looked out of place in a buoyant Spurs team chasing a fourth-place Premiership slot.

Accordingly he joined Southampton on loan in the spring of 2006, and the Saints cemented the arrangement by handing over a £2 million fee the following August. At St Mary's his manager George Burley hailed his outstanding ability. Had Tottenham missed a trick in letting him go? Opinion on the terraces suggested not.

**GRZEGORZ RASIAK**
BORN: Szczecin, Poland, 12 January 1979.
HONOURS: 37 Poland caps (02-).
OTHER CLUBS: Odra, Poland, 00/01 (28, 9); Groclin Dyskobolia, Poland, 01/02-03/04; Derby County 04/05-05/06 (41, 18); Southampton 05/06- (75, 28); Bolton Wanderers on loan 07/08 (7, 0).

| GAMES | 5 (4) |
| GOALS | 0 |

---

# WAYNE ROUTLEDGE

## 2005/06 → 2007/08

With Wayne Routledge earmarked as a future England flankman on his arrival at Tottenham, it appeared that the younger Aaron Lennon, who had completed terms at White Hart Lane that same sunny day in July 2005, would have to bide his time. Fate, however, had different ideas for the would-be star and his understudy.

To Routledge's desperate misfortune, his Spurs career effectively ended the day it began. The lightning-fast right winger had enjoyed an encouraging start to the season's opener at Fratton Park but during the second half he cracked a bone in his foot. There was no doubting he would return from the injury but he had opened a door to Lennon – and the teenaged Yorkshireman raced through it, all the way to the World Cup in Germany.

Routledge had little chance to respond. Having returned to fitness he could barely find a place on the bench, and was loaned to Portsmouth. It had been a crashing fall for the £1.25 million signing who had not put a foot wrong during his formative years with Crystal Palace. He had forged a reputation for his trickery and creativity, and Selhurst Park boss Iain Dowie rated him second only to another Wayne, Rooney, in terms of exciting English talent.

Fast becoming a forgotten man, he accepted an offer to resurrect his career on loan at Fulham in 2006/07, then grabbed a lifeline proffered by Aston Villa, who paid £2 million for his services in January 2008. Will Spurs regret the exit of the young thoroughbred? Only time will tell.

**WAYNE NEVILLE ANTHONY ROUTLEDGE**
BORN: Sidcup, Kent, 7 January 1985.
OTHER CLUBS: Crystal Palace 01/02-04/05 (110, 10); Portsmouth on loan 05/06 (13, 0); Fulham on loan 06/07 (24, 0); Aston Villa 07/08- (1, 0).

| GAMES | 3 (2) |
| GOALS | 0 |

# MIDO

· · · · · · · · · · ·

## 2004/05 → 2005/06 & 2006/07

Bulging with muscles to turn the Incredible Hulk green with envy, Mido was not short on parallels with the tempestuous comic-strip character. The Egyptian was big, powerful and heavy . . . and, boy, was it a bad idea to make him angry! Martin Jol can vouch for that. Yet it is unfair to sum up the enigmatic striker as a one-man wrecking ball. There was subtlety to his game, too, a deftness of touch with the football at his feet and an accuracy with his headwork which matched any of his contemporaries.

Perhaps there were question marks over Mido's attitude when he arrived at Spurs, but certainly there were none regarding his pedigree as a top-flight marksman. The 21-year-old had played in six countries in five years by the time he checked in at White Hart Lane – and from Egypt to Belgium to Italy via spells in Holland, Spain and France, the goals had been plentiful.

He wasted no time making an impact on these shores, either. After agreeing an initial 18-month loan deal from Roma in early 2005, the newcomer netted a brace on his first appearance, at home to Portsmouth, his performance dripping with swagger and self-confidence. Unperturbed by missing with a close-range effort after only three minutes, the debutant opened his account with a typically precise header, then netted with a rasping shot before leaving to a standing ovation as he was replaced by substitute Robbie Keane.

Jol, who had long held reservations about the pairing of Keane and Jermain Defoe, was enamoured with his new recruit who, at 6ft 2in, offered a far more physical option than that relatively diminutive duo. Over the next few months Mido was less than prolific but his power and aerial threat ensured he always required attention from opposing defenders, which often created space in which his colleagues could capitalise.

During 2005/06 the tempestuous target man was integral to Spurs' courageous but ultimately failed attempt to qualify for a Champions League spot, contributing 11 goals, and that despite the interruption of an incident-filled trip to the African Nations Cup. Thereafter Mido returned to Roma before a 'permanent' £4.5 million switch to Tottenham was thrashed out during the autumn of 2006.

Now his north London future seemed redolent with promise and he weighed in with an encouraging sequence of potent displays, the highlight of which was the brilliantly executed volley which secured a home triumph over West Ham in October.

But for all the optimism and his clearly vast potential, frustrations began to get the better of Mido. All too soon poor form and a swelling waistline saw his status plummet among the fans, and the infinitely more refined talents of Dimitar Berbatov ensured that the Egyptian's chances to redeem himself would be limited.

Evidently mortified by his predicament, Mido fell out with Jol following a volatile outburst and it became clear that his future lay elsewhere. Duly he was transferred to Middlesbrough for £6 million in August 2007, and as he departed the Lane he declared that signing for Spurs had been a mistake – a sentiment with which the long-suffering Jol was unlikely to disagree.

**AHMED ABDEL HAMID HOSSAM**
**BORN:** Cairo, 23 February 1983.
**HONOURS:** 44 Egypt caps (01-).
**OTHER CLUBS:** Zamalek, Egypt, 99/00 (4, 3); Gent, Belgium, 00/01 (21,11); Ajax, Holland, 01/02-02/03 (40, 21);
Celta Vigo, Spain, 02/03 (8, 4); Marseille, France, 03/04 (22, 7); Roma, Italy, 04/05 (8, 0); Middlesbrough 07/08- (12, 2).

| GAMES | 41 (20) |
| GOALS | 19 |

# MICHAEL CARRICK

## 2004/05 → 2005/06

Kicking a ball about in the streets near his Wallsend home, a young Michael Carrick imagined he was Paul Gascoigne. Like so many of his age, the nine-year-old allowed himself to fantasise about emulating the exuberant maestro, having watched his fellow Geordie, born not too many miles from his own Northumberland terrace, become the world's most talked-about footballing talent during Italia 90. The boy Michael can hardly have dared to believe how close he would come to living his dream.

In both personality and playing style, the calm, unassuming Carrick bore precious little resemblance to the gregarious Gazza. Yet the pair's impact in north London, during their separate eras, invite an intriguing comparison. For a while, both became the fulcrum of Tottenham's attacking ambition, prompting and inspiring their sides towards yearned-for success; both broke the hearts of their supporters after abandoning promising teams which had been built around them; and both were sold for colossal fees which shattered the club's transfer record. As Terry Venables had drooled over Gascoigne, so Martin Jol was smitten with his own midfield marvel, and to his eternal credit the gruff Dutchman knew how to draw the best from the hitherto underestimated Carrick. Astonishingly, the tall north-easterner's attributes had appeared to go unnoticed by Jol's predecessor, the hapless Jacques Santini, who had initially described him as 'third rate' when chairman Daniel Levy had negotiated a £2.75 million deal to bring him to White Hart Lane from Upton Park in August 2004.

Of all the ill-advised statements during Santini's short-lived sojourn, this was the most outrageous. Clearly the Frenchman hadn't checked the credentials of a play-maker who, during his formative years at West Ham, had been singled out by canny observers as the potential pick of a 'golden generation' of young players which included Joe Cole, Frank Lampard and Rio Ferdinand.

But after Santini's departure, Carrick's understated and pragmatic but endlessly imaginative scheming transformed a pedestrian, distinctly ho-hum Spurs midfield. With Michael installed as his creative general, Jol was rewarded with five straight League wins. For the first time in years, Tottenham appeared genuinely to be on the up, and no player had made a greater difference than Michael Carrick.

The elegance, vision and range of his distribution even moved many among the club's loyal and long-suffering followers to remark on a certain similarity to the work of Glenn Hoddle; and while he was not as explosive a presence as many midfield contemporaries, such was the scope and perception of his passing with either foot that Carrick was compared also to Andrea Pirlo of AC Milan. Like the eminent Italian, he possessed an almost uncanny knack of making time for himself in the most frantic of situations. As Stuart Pearce, his former West Ham team-mate, remarked: 'As a manager or coach I would have Carrick in my side. Brian Clough would have loved him, especially for his consistency and because he still tries to do the right things when the chips are down. He wants the ball, he wants to play, he has a good range of passing and will do what he can with regard to tackling and heading.'

Having established himself as the brains of the team during his first campaign at the Lane, Carrick made even greater strides as Spurs surged to within a whisker of a Champions League spot the following year. If there was a criticism from the stands it was that he scored only two goals – he swept in an angled shot at home to Sunderland in December and there was a powerful close-range effort when Manchester City were the visitors in April.

Overall, though, his contribution as the midfield bedrock was exemplary. He would begin countless attacks with a shrewd interception and a quickly dispatched, raking pass, Jermaine Jenas and Aaron Lennon being the most regular beneficiaries. Never in Premiership history had Spurs' creative department looked so slick and it was truly sickening for the fans that Carrick was one of the worst hit by the stomach bug which disrupted plans to cement fourth place on the final day of the season against his former employers, West Ham.

Inevitably a queue of admirers, all with financial resources way beyond those of Tottenham, began to form, with Manchester United at the head. Carrick declared his ambitions to the Tottenham directors who, having held out for top dollar, were quietly satisfied as the club returned a 500 per-cent profit in sending him to Old Trafford in the summer of 2006 for a fee reportedly rising to £18.6m.

But that contentment was not shared by the manager. Martin Jol was devastated at the loss of his most important footballer; one that, at the age of 25, was still improving. As he put it: 'I think he will continue to get better. He was always one of my best players; he had the legs, the quality and the vision. People would say he is not a complete holding player, but I do not agree. He made so many interceptions – just about every attack started with him."

Like the Spurs side of the early 1990s which struggled without Gascoigne, Tottenham were rudderless again. Still, most supporters, while sorely disappointed to see such a key performer make his exit, did not have it in them to wish the self-effacing 'Carr' anything but success for the future – and certainly it was hoped he would enjoy more luck away from White Hart Lane than did his tragic fellow north-easterner. On that score there were no worries, as Carrick pocketed League title medals in each of his first two campaigns as a Red Devil, topped them off with a European Cup gong.

| | |
|---|---|
| **MICHAEL CARRICK** | |
| **BORN:** | Wallsend, Northumberland, 28 July 1981. |
| **HONOURS:** | 14 England caps (01-). |
| **OTHER CLUBS:** | West Ham United 99/00-04/05 (136, 6); Swindon Town on loan 99/00 (6, 2); Birmingham City on loan 99/00 (2, 0); Manchester United 06/07- (64, 5). |

| GAMES | 70 (5) |
|---|---|
| GOALS | 2 |

# PAUL STALTERI

2005/06 →

Paul Stalteri is an uncomplicated type of defender, quick and strong, athletic and versatile, but maybe lacking the overall class necessary to earn a long-term place in the plans of Juande Ramos.

A Canadian international with more than half a century of caps to his credit, he followed an unorthodox route into the Premiership, spending several campaigns with Werder Bremen and earning a Bundesliga title medal in 2003/04.

In the summer of 2005, still aged only 27, Stalteri joined Spurs on a free transfer under the Bosman ruling, settled into life at the Lane with alacrity and was installed immediately as Martin Jol's first choice at right-back.

During that term he proved generally sound as Spurs battled valiantly but ultimately in vain for a Champions League berth, taking the eye with enterprising sorties along the right touchline, switching to the left defensive flank at need and chipping in with a vital goal in the home win over Manchester City in April. However, a niggling hip injury hampered his progress and as his fitness problems continued, he surrendered his place, first to Young-Pyo Lee and then to Pascal Chimbonda.

Thereafter Stalteri became something of a forgotten man until he rose from the bench to poach the melodramatic winner which capped Spurs' astonishing comeback to beat West Ham 4-3 in March 2007. It was a moment which jolted him back into the collective consciousness with a pleasurable thud, though when he was loaned to Fulham in 2008 his future seemed unclear. Following that Upton Park strike, however, his cult status was guaranteed.

| PAUL STALTERI | | |
|---|---|---|
| BORN: Etobicoke, Ontario, Canada, 18 October 1977. | | |
| HONOURS: 63 Canada caps (97-). | | |
| OTHER CLUBS: Toronto Lynx, Canada, 97-98 (16, 8); Werder Bremen, Germany, 00/01-04/05 (150, 6); Fulham on loan 07/08 (13, 0). | GAMES | 47 (9) |
| | GOALS | 3 |

# CALUM DAVENPORT

2004/05 → 2006/07

The shadow of Ledley King loomed large over Calum Davenport – and it was both a sadness and a frustration that the inevitable opportunities of playing understudy to Tottenham's most regularly stricken star proved as much of a curse to the young stopper as they were a blessing.

Having spent the majority of his first two campaigns as a Spur out on loan following his £1.1 million arrival from Coventry City in August 2004, Davenport addressed the task manfully when first called into regular first-team action during 2006/07. Standing 6ft 4in, the blond centre-half was never lacking in aerial prowess, and neither was he a slouch on the ground, as he demonstrated by latching smoothly on to a Tom Huddlestone free-kick to score in a 2-1 victory at Manchester City.

But where King's judgement was so reliably sound, Davenport could be cumbersome in the tackle and wasteful in possession. In fairness, it had to be remembered that the England under-21 international was working diligently to become attuned to the top flight and, it seemed, Tottenham's coaches were prepared to persevere. But Davenport wasn't.

After learning that West Ham, the club which he had turned down as a schoolboy and since served on loan, were interested in signing him for £3 million in January 2007, he declared his wish to leave the Lane. Playing the King's young pretender had proved too heavy a burden for the slim 24-year-old to shoulder.

| CALUM RAYMOND PAUL DAVENPORT | | |
|---|---|---|
| BORN: Bedford, 1 January 1983. | | |
| OTHER CLUBS: Coventry City 00/01-04/05 (75, 3); West Ham United on loan 04/05 (10, 0); Southampton on loan 04/05 (7, 0); Norwich City on loan 05/06 (15, 1); West Ham United 06/07- (6, 0); Watford on loan 07/08 (1, 0). | GAMES | 13 (7) |
| | GOALS | 1 |

# ANDY REID

## 2004/05 → 2005/06

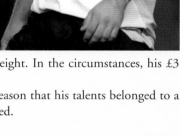

A midfielder inclined to stoutness, but blessed with boundless natural talent – is that reminiscent of anyone? In truth, even Andy Reid would admit that his undoubted abilities did not place him in the same ball park as the mesmerising Paul Gascoigne – but it is easy to understand why Tottenham's sporting director Frank Arnesen was so keen to sign this old-fashioned livewire.

In January 2005, after sealing an £8 million deal with Nottingham Forest which also involved the arrival of Michael Dawson, Arnesen was purring, describing Reid as 'a technical footballer of calibre'. He had acquired a clever left-footer endowed with admirable creative vision and the capacity to operate in central midfield or on either flank. Reid went straight into the side and remained there for the rest of the season, performing effectively enough and distinguishing himself with a rising left-foot rocket in the 5-1 home drubbing of Aston Villa on May Day.

But for all his versatility, the Republic of Ireland international's best position remained a mystery. He was not devastatingly fast as a winger, but neither did he display noticeable appetite for the physical rigours of central midfield. His performances at the outset of 2005/06 were patchy and reportedly he was told to lose weight. In the circumstances, his £3 million switch to Charlton Athletic in August 2006 came as no surprise.

Those supporters disappointed with Reid's lack of success at White Hart Lane could reason that his talents belonged to a bygone era – one in which ketchup-free diets and running machines had not been invented.

**ANDREW MATTHEW REID**
**BORN:** Dublin, 29 July 1982.
**HONOURS:** 27 Republic of Ireland caps (03-).
**OTHER CLUBS:** Nottingham Forest 00/01-04/05 (144, 21); Charlton Athletic 06/07-07/08 (38, 8); Sunderland 07/08- (13, 1).

**GAMES** 21 (6)
**GOALS** 1

---

# DANNY MURPHY

## 2005/06 → 2006/07

Martin Jol needed little convincing of Danny Murphy's ability to win football matches. Not too long before his £2 million arrival at the Lane in January 2006, the chunkily-built Charlton Athletic and former England schemer had done a rather impressive job of humiliating his future colleagues. During the previous spring, having already orchestrated a torrid afternoon for Tottenham's midfield with his beautifully perceptive passing, Murphy stroked home a glorious free-kick with an apparent insouciance that was surely deceptive, thus securing a 2-0 victory at the Valley.

Some nine months later, when Tottenham set about bringing in a player to add guile and experience to a youthful midfield, there could have been few more obvious candidates than the clever Cestrian. Destiny dictated that Danny would have only an intermittent on-field role to play; indeed, in two campaigns at White Hart Lane he made only seven Premiership starts. Yet while there were moments to savour – notably an adroitly flicked goal from a Dimitar Berbatov header at home to Portsmouth in October 2006 – his greatest impact on the club was as a mentor.

Having enjoyed seven largely successful years at Anfield, Murphy, a graduate of Dario Gradi's prolific youth system at Crewe, became a valuable, amiable and sharp-witted source of advice for a Spurs squad bristling with rookies. Understandably, however, he did not see himself as club counsellor and in August 2007, in pursuit of regular action, the 30-year-old joined Fulham, where there awaited a moderate renaissance.

**DANIEL BENJAMIN MURPHY**
**BORN:** Chester, Cheshire, 18 March 1977.
**HONOURS:** 9 England caps (01-03).
**OTHER CLUBS:** Crewe Alexandra 93/4-96/7 (134, 27); Liverpool 97/8-03/04 (170, 25); Crewe Alexandra on loan 98/9 (16, 1); Charlton Athletic 04/05-05/06 (56, 7); Fulham 07/08- (33, 5).

**GAMES** 13 (16)
**GOALS** 1

# MICHAEL DAWSON

· · · · · · · · · · · · · · · · · · · · · · · · · · · · · · · · · · · · · · · · · · · · · · · · · · · · ·

## 2004/05 →

With his cherubic features and customary engaging smile, Michael Dawson hardly resembles a typical footballing hard case. Yet while he may not project the grizzling bad-boy image of a Neil 'Razor' Ruddock or the piratical aspect of a Dave Mackay, this former milkman has already proved he is not short on bottle. Alongside Ledley King, Dawson has done as much as any defender to rid Tottenham of their soft-touch reputation in recent years. A cheery outlook is part of the package with Michael, but opposition strikers need to take the courageous hulk of a defender with the utmost seriousness.

As Martin Jol was delighted to discover, Dawson's ferocious appetite for learning makes him a manager's dream. Professional footballers are often accused of being cocooned from normal life yet the lanky Yorkshireman – whose older brothers, Kevin and Andy, have made their mark in the lower divisions – had already proved he could graft, having been taught the values of hard work from an early age. Even after signing schoolboy terms with Nottingham Forest he continued with his part-time job, getting up at 4am to ride a milk float around the city's quiet streets.

When he arrived at Spurs, on the same day in January 2005 as his Forest colleague Andy Reid, most of the attention was focused on the Irish midfielder. Thus little was expected initially of the 21-year-old stopper, a raw talent regarded by some close observers of the White Hart Lane scene as something of a makeweight in the £8 million package deal. But the rookie made encouraging progress, proving that he had benefited hugely from his days of partnering the veteran Des Walker at the City Ground, and it was fitting that Walker, a Tottenham fan, would become a regular visitor to the Lane to monitor his protégé's progress.

After recovering from a niggling shin problem, Dawson received his first call to senior action as a replacement for the injured Noureddine Naybet at Liverpool in April, and his eager-to-please performance in a hard-fought 2-2 draw won generous praise from Tottenham's travelling fans. True, there were those who questioned whether the impressionable youngster would be an appropriate partner for Ledley King, who was never the most vociferous of leaders. But before long Michael's bravery, strength and aerial power, coupled with a natural defensive instinct which prevented him from being drawn out of position unnecessarily, overwhelmed most of the doubters, who were forced to admit that he was working in pleasing symmetry with Spurs' quietly spoken skipper.

At first he vied for his place with Naybet and Anthony Gardner, but as 2005/06 developed, Dawson emerged as the first-choice foil for King at the core of Jol's rearguard, where he battled like a gladiator as Tottenham strove gallantly, if ultimately in vain, for a Champions League berth.

No arena or opposition daunted the young man, as he showed in the autumn at Old Trafford, with a gloriously timed challenge on Ruud van Nistelrooy shortly before Tottenham grabbed a precious equaliser.

Admittedly, there were moments when the under-21 international's unbridled enthusiasm got the better of him – his red cards proving costly at Craven Cottage and St James' Park – but he had shown enough potential to be named as a standby for England's 2006 World Cup squad.

Though he didn't make the flight to Germany, he continued to flourish in 2006/07 when, with the fragile King a regular absentee, he missed only one of Spurs' 59 matches as the club embarked on an all-too-rare foray into Europe. Both the manager and goalkeeper Paul Robinson – and there could hardly be two individuals better placed to offer an opinion – selected Dawson as the player of the season. The big fellow was often his side's gutsiest performer and, remarkably for one so tender in years, was fast earning a deserved name as Tottenham's Mr Dependable.

From his brilliantly consistent campaign, one game stands out vividly. On a dank November afternoon, not only did he mark one of the world's most predatory strikers, Didier Drogba, out of the game, but also he scored with a thumping header to set Spurs on their way to a historic victory over Chelsea, their first for 16 years. Michael was the outstanding performer on one of the sweetest days at White Hart Lane for many a year, and thus his cult status was cemented. If anyone had ever looked like a future Tottenham captain, it was Michael Dawson on that proud occasion.

However, having made such a blistering start to his career in north London, he was due to experience an unnerving blip. In the autumn of 2007, he appeared uncharacteristically jittery in a team enduring frustrations on the field and uncertainty off it. Jol, under increasing pressure, pointed the finger of blame at Dawson for a string of poor results. It seemed a rash outburst from a manager who knew his days were numbered, although without King alongside him, it could not be gainsaid that Dawson's decision-making had suffered.

Thereafter a sequence of injuries and the arrival of Jonathan Woodgate saw him dislodged as first choice in the centre of defence and he was devastated at missing the League Cup Final triumph over Chelsea. Still, with youth on his side, it seemed certain that there would be ample opportunity to redeem himself under the new regime of Juande Ramos. Sure enough, with poor Ledley King sidelined yet again before season's end, Michael was restored to the team, his characteristic grin was firmly back in place. As for his future, it still bulged with positive possibilities.

| MICHAEL RICHARD DAWSON | | GAMES | 132 (4) |
| --- | --- | --- | --- |
| BORN: | Northallerton, Yorkshire, 18 November 1983. | GOALS | 3 |
| OTHER CLUBS: | Nottingham Forest 01/02-04/05 (83, 7). | | |

# LEE YOUNG-PYO

## 2005/06 →

Martin Jol was all too aware of what the cynics would say when he secured the services of Lee Young-Pyo. There is no Brand Beckham in South Korea; instead a large part of that country's football marketing machine revolves around the Lee Ltd phenomenon. It was clear that Tottenham's profile in the Far East would soar as a result of the signing – the Oriental press pack which follows Lee's every move would see to that.

In fairness, however, his arrival was about so much more than shirts on backs and money in the bank. When Jol claimed Lee was one of the best left-backs in Europe, he meant it. And Spurs fans, who had longed for a swashbuckling raider of a full-back since the days of Chris Hughton, had every reason to believe their wait was over.

PSV Eindhoven could vouch for the fact that Lee was worth the media bandwagon that would ensure a press pass at White Hart Lane was as tough to secure as an interview with Lord Lucan. Having excelled during the 2002 World Cup finals, Lee, who was married to a Korean beauty queen, went on to become a key member of the PSV team that reached a European Cup semi-final and won the Dutch league. But then, having watched his compatriot and former PSV team-mate Park Ji-Sung turn out for Manchester United after signing a lucrative deal, Lee begged his bosses to allow him to join Spurs.

Duly he made his £1.36 million move to White Hart Lane just before the transfer window closed in August 2005, and his adventurous touchline scampers won instant approval at White Hart Lane. Lee played at top speed, every touch, pass and tackle carried out with minimal fuss. His doubters suggested that the lithe but diminutive Korean would not be robust enough to withstand the formidable physical rigours of the Premiership, but while his negligible aerial power was an obvious drawback, his wiry little body was deceptively strong.

Lee proved a fine interceptor of the ball and his blistering pace afforded him time to pickpocket attackers rather than clatter them. He held his place at left-back for the remainder of 2005/06 but, after turning down an offer from Roma, the industrious defender faced an uphill battle to retain his berth during the following campaign. After Spurs had narrowly missed out on a Champions League slot, the full-back positions were identified as an area of weakness, and Jol brought in Benoit Assou-Ekotto and Pascal Chimbonda, believing the pair would add steel.

Still Lee plugged away, though, and after a string of haywire displays fom Assou-Ekotto, he won his place back. However, in subsequent months he was switched occasionally to the right flank and attracted criticism from a vocal minority of supporters, who perceived an unwillingness to cross with his right foot. Following another batch of defensive signings and a change of manager in 2007/08, his days in north London appeared to be numbered. The Lee entourage was ready to move, and a return to PSV looked to be on the cards.

| LEE YOUNG-PYO | | |
|---|---|---|
| **BORN:** | Hongchun, South Korea, 23.4.77. | |
| **HONOURS:** | 90 South Korea caps (99-). | |
| **OTHER CLUBS:** | Anyang Cheetahs, South Korea, 99/00-01/02 (70, 3); PSV Eindhoven, Holland, 02/03-04/05 (82, 1). | |

| GAMES | 91 (2) |
|---|---|
| GOALS | 0 |

# BENOIT ASSOU-EKOTTO

## 2006/07 →

Benoit Assou-Ekotto arrived at Tottenham with a Gallic shrug. When the £3 million capture from Lens was unveiled to the press in July 2006, he curled his lip and declared to reporters he didn't care much for football when he was not playing. He would much rather be shopping or listening to rap music, he reckoned. But there was little sign of this dispassion for the game during his first months in a Tottenham shirt. Assou-Ekotto was a left-back of supreme fitness. And, despite a torrid start to the new season for Tottenham's defenders, he was soon impressing the fans with his eagerness to overlap and ferocity in the tackle.

The 5ft 9in defender had been one of the most highly-rated full-backs in *Le Championnat* before agreeing terms with Spurs. He had been an ever-present in his last season for the French club and had earned his first call-up to the Cameroon squad. Having agreed terms with Lens, Tottenham's sporting director Damien Comolli hailed Benoit's 'extreme talents', and after a performance full of attacking flourish in a friendly encounter with Inter Milan, he was installed as first choice at left-back.

But after a couple of dozen outings in 2006/07, sometimes looking solid and sometimes not, he suffered knee trouble and barely featured for the next 18 months. Initially an eight-week lay-off was predicted but complications ended his season and in the following campaign his progress was halted by swelling and surgery. With the likes of Lee, Gilberto and Bale staking their claim to his left-back berth in 2008, Assou-Ekotto was facing a very tough challenge.

**BENOIT PIERRE DAVID ASSOU-EKOTTO**
**BORN:** Arras, France, 24 March 1984.
**HONOURS:** Cameroon caps.
**OTHER CLUBS:** Lens, France, 03/04-05/06 (66, 0).

| | |
|---|---|
| GAMES | 27 |
| GOALS | 0 |

---

# RADEK CERNY

## 2004/05 → 2007/08

Radek Cerny must have rubbed his eyes sore after seeing the Tottenham Hotspur teamsheet on 9 January 2008. After all, the 33-year-old Czech Republican international goalkeeper had been called up as emergency cover only a handful of times since arriving on an extended loan from Slavia Prague three years earlier. But on a blustery night at the Emirates Stadium, the loyal understudy was given centre stage – and as he performed in that most intimidating of theatres, he didn't fluff his lines.

Cerny got his chance in the first leg of a League Cup semi-final following a string of erratic displays from Paul Robinson, the normally able England number-one. The new manager, Juande Ramos, had justified his reputation for steely ruthlessness in his most important match since taking charge. And while the 6ft 3in Cerny was rarely stretched during a frustrating 1-1 draw, he let no one down, his efficient display demonstrating why Tottenham had taken him from Slavia Prague in January 2005.

After that night at the Arsenal, Radek retained his place for a further nine games, showing himself to be athletic, brave and generally sound in his positional judgement, until an unfortunate gaffe in a UEFA Cup clash with his former employers, Slavia, handed the baton back to Robinson, who could consider himself a very lucky man.

The Czech, an unfussy type of 'keeper with an appealingly self-effacing character to match, could look back with pride on his final season at Spurs, after which he joined Queen's Park Rangers.

**RADEK CERNY**
**BORN:** Prague, Czech Republic, 18 February 1974.
**HONOURS:** 3 Czech Republic caps.
**OTHER CLUBS:** Slavia Prague, Czech Republic 93/4-07/08 (178, 0).

| | |
|---|---|
| GAMES | 27 (1) |
| GOALS | 0 |

# JERMAINE JENAS

## 2005/06 →

The year 2008 had long been pencilled in as the one in which to watch for Jermaine Jenas. As a 16-year-old at Nottingham Forest, his coach Paul Hart took one look at him, noted a physique resembling a coat hanger, and told him he would not reach his potential until the age of 24. With a bit more bulk, Hart insisted, the sublimely talented youngster would have few equals. Eight years on, those lucky enough to be at White Hart Lane on the blessed night of 22 January witnessed the prophecy come true.

On a real Glory Glory Hallelujah occasion, JJ served up a midfield masterpiece to help Tottenham fans feel the chest-swelling pride of flattening their north London neighbours for the first time since 1999. A place in the League Cup Final was the least Jenas deserved for his efforts in the astonishing 5-1 rout. Within three minutes he had taken a smart lay-off from Dimitar Berbatov and rifled Spurs into the lead with a low cross-shot. But even as the visitors tried to rally, Jermaine's focus did not become blurred, and some 20 minutes later he flighted a taxing free-kick into the Gunners' box which induced Nicklas Bendtner to head into his own net for Tottenham's second. After all those years of being tipped as one for the future, Jenas's time had come.

That was the highlight of a hugely satisfying season for a player whose fortunes had fluctuated since David Platt, his first manager at Forest, claimed he would go on to captain England. Jenas, whose father had been a semi-professional, was the pick of an extremely talented crop of youngsters at the City Ground, but the all-action midfielder had not always displayed the lung-bursting box-to-box displays which would become his trademark.

During his subsequent sojourn at Newcastle, with whom he signed as a teenager in a £5 million deal, he won a PFA Young Player of the Year gong, but the St James' Park faithful were never quite convinced about the abundantly gifted Midlander of whom so much was expected. Even after he enlisted with Spurs, at a cost of £7 million in August 2005, it seemed that Lane regulars were equally unsure. The 22-year-old had represented England at every level yet still he was pilloried from the stands for a perceived tendency to drift out of games, and for not contributing enough goals.

The players, however, had an altogether different opinion of their new team-mate. Striker Robbie Keane, who would profit greatly from Jenas's intelligent passing game, was at the front of a long queue of shrewd observers ready to praise the self-effacing young man who had grown up on a working-class Nottingham estate. In noting criticism from fans, Keane said: 'He's got great energy and does a lot for the team, things maybe people can't see. His work rate and break-up play sometimes goes unnoticed. Perhaps the perception is that he's playing well when he's scoring goals, but I think he's underestimated.'

When Jenas was slotted into midfield alongside Michael Carrick, Tottenham swelled with creative ability. After a few quiet games, he came to the fore during a gritty encounter at Old Trafford when, with his team trailing by a goal, he dispatched an arcing free-kick well beyond the reach of Manchester United 'keeper Edwin van der Sar. That secured a draw which sent out a clear message that Spurs were an altogether tougher proposition than in previous years, and it was evident that the gap-toothed smile on Jermaine's face belied a steely determination.

His central combination with Carrick played a colossal part in helping the club launch a serious assault for a Champions League spot, and there seems little doubt that, barring the sickness bug which so weakened the side for their last match of the campaign at Upton Park, Jenas would have been able to measure his worth against the European elite. Spurs finished fifth, however, and he had to console himself with a trip to the World Cup in Germany, albeit as an unused substitute throughout the tournament.

Jenas, who relished the relative anonymity afforded by living in London compared with his previous goldfish-bowl experience in the north-east, was now one of the first names on Martin Jol's teamsheet. As the Dutchman put it: 'I love him. He's always so self-critical, he has such high standards.'

In 2006/07, Jermaine's responsibilities increased following Carrick's departure to Manchester United, and his influence burgeoned as he attained maturity. He prospered from playing behind the inventive strike pair of Berbatov and Keane and despite his season being disrupted cruelly by injury, he weighed in with eight goals in all competitions.

However, his greatest leap in progress became apparent following the appointment of new boss Juande Ramos in October 2007. Thriving under new and physically demanding training routines, Jenas was fitter and – most crucially – stronger than ever. He was scoring for England, there was a brilliant brace at home to Wigan in November and he played a starring role as a rejuvenated Tottenham side roared to League Cup success. Small wonder Jermaine Jenas declared that he was playing the best football of his life. The golden boy had proved himself a man.

**JERMAINE ANTHONY JENAS**
BORN: Nottingham, 18.2.83.
HONOURS: League Cup 07/08. 18 England caps (03-).
OTHER CLUBS: Nottingham Forest 00/01-01/02 (29, 4); Newcastle United 01/02-05/06 (110, 9).

GAMES 108 (3)
GOALS 21

# EDGAR DAVIDS

## 2005/06 → 2006/07

The pit bull regained his bite at White Hart Lane. For a dozen seasons or so, Edgar Davids had been one of the most instantly recognisable icons of the modern game – with his trademark goggles, needed because he suffers from glaucoma, and his distinctive dreadlocks – and he had commanded immense respect everywhere football was played. Yet by the middle of the new millennium's first decade, his top-dog status had begun to slip.

Cast into the international wilderness after losing his place with Internazionale of Milan, the grizzled midfield warrior with a chestful of medals was freed to join Tottenham in August 2005, and when he pulled on the white shirt for the first time he had a point to prove. Opponents – and, indeed, team-mates – knew it would be wise to beware. Now he had found a new pack, Davids was ready to bare his teeth once more.

The familiar pony-tail bounced with renewed life as the tank-like 32-year-old introduced himself to Spurs fans on a sunny afternoon at the Lane, in a 2-0 win against Middlesbrough. After sending Ray Parlour sprawling with a bone-crunching challenge a mere 60 seconds into the encounter, Davids commanded the midfield with a performance bristling with brawn and featuring a succession of lung-bursting runs which would have been beyond the scope of most men ten years his junior.

It had been months since he'd played and yet, over the ensuing weeks, whether deployed in the middle alongside Michael Carrick or out on the left, he played with an eagerness which made nonsense of the numbers on his birth certificate. Having been

recalled to the Dutch national team and having scored a tremendous winning goal against Wigan – a quickfire low finish rounding off a marauding sprint through the middle – Edgar was clearly enjoying himself again.

Martin Jol had brought Davids to Tottenham because his knowhow, garnered at spells with Ajax, AC Milan, Juventus and Barcelona, was unrivalled. The manager reckoned his compatriot would 'lift the team's mentality' and the veteran's early impact on a young squad was tangible.

Aside from a training ground spat with Robbie Keane in December 2005, Davids proved an exemplary role model and, for the first time in more than a decade, Spurs began to exhibit the resilience and determination needed to launch a serious onslaught on a top-four slot.

Perversely though, soon the players around him improved so much that he was struggling to get a game, and while his desire still burned brightly, the stamina needed to carry him through a full 90 minutes of Premiership intensity was fading.

Eventually there was a fall-out with Jol, followed by a return to Ajax midway through 2006/07. Since then Edgar Davids has indicated that he would like eventually to coach at Tottenham – so those dreadlock wigs which became best-sellers outside the Lane might yet come back into fashion.

| | | GAMES | **36 (8)** |
|---|---|---|---|
| **EDGAR STEVEN DAVIDS** | | | |
| **BORN:** | Paramaribo, Surinam, 13.3.73. | | |
| **HONOURS:** | 74 Holland caps (94-05). | | |
| **OTHER CLUBS:** | Ajax, Holland, 91/2-95/6 (106, 20); AC Milan 96/7-97/8 (15, 0); Juventus 97/8-03/04 (142, 8), both Italy; | | |
| | Barcelona, Spain, on loan 03/04 (18, 1); Internazionale, Italy, 04/05 (14, 0); Ajax 06/07-. | GOALS | 1 |

# TEEMU TAINIO

## 2005/06 →

If places in the Tottenham Hotspur starting eleven were awarded for sheer wholehearted fortitude, Teemu Tainio would never miss a game. But then the Terror of Tornio, as the Finlander dubbed himself with tongue firmly in cheek, had already proven himself the most stubbornly determined Scandinavian since Hamlet. As a child in Lapland, one of Tottenham's northernmost fans would study football annuals, reading up on the likes of Paul Gascoigne and Gary Lineker, before wrapping up in countless layers of warm clothes to make his way to a snowy pitch for a kickabout in minus-30C conditions. It wasn't easy getting a game, let alone starting a football career, in a town which never gets light in winter.

Yet Tainio managed it, via military service and a spell at FC Haka Valkeakoski. And in 2005, when his contract at Auxerre expired, his unlikely dream of playing for Spurs came true. Bounteous energy, tenacity and fearlessness have always been the central hallmarks of Tainio's game, and they are traits which endeared him instantly to the White Hart Lane faithful.

After impressing in the pre-season Peace Cup, the stocky blond midfielder, who had signed a long-term deal and expected to play understudy to Edgar Davids, became a regular, largely thanks to his ability to play in all four midfield positions. After a string of heel-snapping displays, 'TT' opened his scoring account at home to Newcastle in December, dancing a jig of sheer delight after rifling Spurs in front and setting them on the way to a 2-0 victory. Subsequent highlights have included an adroitly executed volley from an Aaron Lennon delivery to equalise against West Ham in a pulsating 4-3 win at Upton Park in March 2007, prompting Martin Jol to purr: 'When Teemu plays, we play.'

Even the most carping follower would be hard pushed to find fault with such a plucky workhorse, but there have been times when his enthusiasm has boiled over into self-destruction. All too frequently over-zealous tackles have left him either crocked or entering the referee's notepad, and over his three campaigns at the club to date absences through injury and suspension have seen him slip down the pecking order in a squad crammed with midfielders.

Tainio played a useful role in Tottenham's League Cup triumph at Wembley in 2008 – after rising from the bench he earned a typical booking, having got under the skin of Chelsea's Didier Drogba – but rumours coming out of White Hart Lane in early summer were not in his favour. If they indicate Teemu's early exit, the majority of Tottenham fans will be sad to see him go.

---

**TEEMU TAINIO**
BORN: Tornio, Finland, 27.11.79.
HONOURS: League Cup 07/08. 28 Finland caps (98-).
OTHER CLUBS: FC Haka, Finland, 96/7 (20, 4); Auxerre, France, 97/8-04/05 (148, 14).

| | |
|---|---|
| GAMES | 63 (20) |
| GOALS | 3 |

# AARON LENNON

## 2005/06 →

The life and times of Aaron Lennon have been played in fast-forward mode. A glance at the 21-year-old's event-laden CV is enough to induce the type of gasping fit normally experienced by the stricken defenders he leaves choking on his dust. Having signed a lucrative boot deal at the tender age of 14 and made his Premiership debut at 16, Lennon has never been keen on hanging about. Yet in comparison to his subsequent progress, the 5ft 5in wingman with the quicksilver feet had barely broken sweat before he arrived at N17, where his fortunes truly moved into overdrive.

The boy they call Roadrunner hit the ground sprinting during his first campaign at White Hart Lane. His first task was to establish himself as a first-team contender but in the space of eight months he went much farther than that – he wrote his name across the heavens as one of the most exciting young talents in the land.

Aaron arrived at the Lane as a £1 million purchase from cash-strapped Leeds United on the same July day in 2005 as Wayne Routledge, whose transfer from Crystal Palace cost twice as much, and was told he would need plenty of patience before getting his chance at senior level. As it turned out the warning was superfluous. The unlucky Routledge was injured on the opening day at Portsmouth, and Lennon's moment was not long in coming.

Indeed, August was not spent when he made his Premiership entrance as a substitute at home to Chelsea, and he was selected to start the next game, when Liverpool were the visitors. But it was two weeks later against Fulham that he really announced his arrival, turning heads with a riveting performance, flummoxing defenders on both flanks, his busy little legs seeming to reach full speed in an instant as he burst through on goal on several occasions. That display was enough to earn him an England under-21 call, and he seemed to get better with each successive outing as Spurs climbed to the unfamiliar heights of the division's top four.

With Champions League qualification a possibility, the pressure was mounting on the team, but Lennon continued to play with youthful abandon. Off the pitch the callow Yorkshireman might have been struggling to come to terms with the pace of London life, but on it he appeared delightfully at ease, utterly unafraid of occupying centre stage.

Having netted in a 2-0 victory at Birmingham, supplied the winner in a tight home encounter with Bolton and scintillated in a tense draw at Highbury, he found himself catapulted into the England squad for that summer's World Cup finals. He wasn't the only Spur summoned by Sven-Goran Eriksson, but of all the lions of the Lane who made the trip to Germany, arguably it was Lennon who roared the loudest in the international arena, prompting plenty of canny observers to hail him as the long-term replacement for David Beckham following a clutch of enterprising cameo contributions as a substitute.

Thus 2006 turned out to be the sweetest of years for a footballer who had felt the odds were stacked against him after he was rejected by a dozen Premiership clubs as a youngster. His talent was never questioned but, at every trial, invariably he was the shortest by several inches. In the end it was his home-town club, Leeds, who took a chance on the twinkle-toed winger whose shoulder-dipping sorcery and blistering pace regularly took him past hulking opponents who seemed twice his size.

Alan Hill, a youth coach at Elland Road, said of Lennon: 'There were concerns about his height. He was tiny compared to the other kids. But I always remembered Cloughie's favourite saying: "Can the kid play?" Cloughie would have loved Aaron. He was quick and he had excellent balance, but he stood out because he had a trick. Not many eight-year-olds have a trick that works time after time.'

That trick would still be serving Aaron splendidly more than a decade later with Spurs, whom he joined after being told that Leeds could no longer afford his wages. The early homesickness wasn't pleasant, but rumours of a return north to join Manchester United proved misleading, and during 2006/07 his stock continued to rise at White Hart Lane.

His sensational winner at home to Chelsea in November stands out as Lennon's highlight to date in a Tottenham shirt, but his form began to suffer as he encountered knee problems in mid-season.

There was an exquisitely volleyed flick-on to set up Teemu Tainio in the Upton Park thriller in March, but fans became critical of his crossing, which often was wayward, and it had to be admitted that his finishing was downright awful at times.

Only a few months earlier he had been linked with a £20 million move to Chelsea and been hailed by his manager, Martin Jol, as one of the best wingers to come through in the English game in the last ten years. Realistically, though, it was clear that he remained a work in progress, albeit of the sumptuously promising variety.

Come 2007/08 a combination of niggling injuries and fluctuating form hampered further progress and his new boss, Juande Ramos, warned that he needed to improve his end-product. For all that, springtime speculation that Aaron Lennon might be on his way from the club appeared rash. Clearly, having only just turned 21, the Roadrunner still had a lot of miles left on the clock, and there seemed no good reason why he should not be scorching the grass at White Hart Lane for the foreseeable future.

| AARON JUSTIN LENNON | | |
|---|---|---|
| **BORN:** | Leeds, 16.4.87. | |
| **HONOURS:** | League Cup 07/08. 9 England caps (06-). | |
| **OTHER CLUBS:** | Leeds United 03/04-04/05 (38, 1). | |

| GAMES | **98 (21)** |
|---|---|
| GOALS | 10 |

# DIDIER ZOKORA

## 2006/07 →

Did Tottenham Hotspur cast a voodoo spell to lure Didier Zokora to White Hart Lane? It was a question that supporters could almost take seriously after the in-demand Ivorian, who has admitted to practising a bit of his own black magic, arrived at the club.

After all, Spurs had been at the back of a long queue of extremely well-heeled admirers at the end of the 2005/06 campaign. Zokora, who honed his skills ceaselessly on the streets of his home village throughout his childhood, is known throughout his country as 'The Maestro' and for years he had been high on the list of African footballers who were in demand in Europe.

Certainly, by the time he was starring for St Etienne and causing a stir in the French League, Chelsea, Arsenal, Manchester United and Real Madrid were all taking a keen interest. But the race for his signature was won by Tottenham, who parted with an £8.2 million fee to secure his signature in July 2006. This wasn't a triumph for supernatural powers, however – Didier declared that he had joined Spurs because they were a club on the up and, equally importantly, they could promise him an integral role.

Having shone bightly for the Ivory Coast during that summer's World Cup finals in Germany, Zokora was installed instantly as the central midfield hub of a side bristling with new talent. His debut in a defeat at Bolton suggested there was a lot of work to be

done, but Zokora appeared desperately eager to learn.

The endlessly energetic midfielder took on a deep-lying role, shielding his defence, allowing Jermaine Jenas the opportunity to advance into more attacking positions than previously had seemed prudent. Clearly the newcomer needed to be cured of an alarming tendency to concede free-kicks in dangerous positions, and sometimes he lost possession unnecessarily, but still his first term at the club was regarded widely as a success, although perhaps not a resounding one. Whatever else, his new supporters adored his incessant enthusiasm for covering vast distances in every game and for his willingness to battle for the ball as if his life depended on it.

Didier, who kisses a tattoo of his late brother on his right arm before every kick-off, left the fans in no doubt that he cares passionately about his work. They will never forget the acute apprehension on his face as Dimitar Berbatov stepped up to take a second-half penalty as Tottenham trailed Chelsea 1-0 in the League Cup Final at Wembley. Having turned his back, unable to watch the spot-kick, Zokora waited for the crowd to react before falling to his knees in delight after it was converted.

Several weeks later, the midfielder – by then demonstrating invaluable versatility by performing admirably at full-back and central defence – deserved credit for accepting the responsibility of taking a penalty in the ill-fated shoot-out with PSV Eindhoven, even though he had never scored for the club. While there were some White Hart Lane regulars who still harboured doubts about Didier Zokora's calibre, there were none who questioned his courage.

---

**DIDIER ZOKORA**

BORN: Abidjan, Ivory Coast, 14.12.80.
HONOURS: League Cup 07/08. 46 Ivory Coast caps (00-).
OTHER CLUBS: ASEC Mimosas, Ivory Coast; Genk, Belgium, 00/01-03/04 (126, 1); St Etienne, France, 04/05-05/06 (66, 2).

| | |
|---|---|
| GAMES | **81 (9)** |
| GOALS | 0 |

# HOSSAM GHALY

## 2006/07

The stands at White Hart Lane have never been occupied by the most forgiving of souls. Little surprise, then, that Hossam Ghaly had little hope of redemption following his fit of pique when Blackburn were the visitors in May 2007. Trudging off the pitch, having been substituted only 31 minutes after joining the action from the bench, Ghaly completed an abject performance by ripping off his shirt before launching it at Martin Jol. A spirited chorus of 'You're not fit to wear the shirt' was an inevitable response from the Paxton Road End.

The incident signalled an abrupt and sadly premature finish to a Spurs career that had revealed glimpses of promise. Only rarely was Ghaly afforded the central midfield spot he craved, but certainly the Egyptian international, who had been persuaded to enlist at the Lane by his compatriot, Mido, had been impressive in the intimidating atmosphere of Besiktas, where he rounded off a composed display with a first-half strike to set Spurs on the way to a UEFA Cup victory. Also he shone during several stirring encounters with Chelsea, putting Spurs 3-1 up at Stamford Bridge before the Blues recovered to earn a memorable 3-3 draw in the FA Cup.

But Ghaly, who had arrived from Feyenoord in January 2006 with a view to a permanent £2.5 million transfer if all went well, was undone by his volatile temperament. After the Blackburn business, even a public apology to the fans did not help his plight. Later he signed for Derby on loan after a transfer to Birmingham collapsed amid acrimony.

**HOSSAM EL SAYED GHALY**
BORN: Cairo, Egypt, 15 December 1981.
HONOURS: 21 Egypt caps.
OTHER CLUBS: Al-Ahly, Egypt; Feyenoord, Holland, 03/04-05/06 (43, 3); Derby County on loan 07/08 (15, 0).

| GAMES | 24 (10) |
| GOALS | 3 |

# RICARDO ROCHA

## 2006/07 →

Ricardo Rocha's career at Tottenham Hotspur has not gone according to plan. The experienced defender, who had featured recently in the Champions League with Benfica, was acquired by Martin Jol during the January 2007 transfer window to add much-needed grit to Spurs' flagging rearguard. But life at the Lane proved trickier than expected for the £3.3 million man.

Within a week of arrival, and having been tested only against Southend United in the FA Cup, he was pitchforked into Tottenham's biggest game of the season, the second leg of a League Cup semi-final against Arsenal at the Emirates Stadium. From the moment he left the bench he looked woefully short of sharpness, and duly he played a significant role in handing the tie to the hosts. In the build-up to the Gunners going ahead in extra time, Rocha flung his head at a cross he should have cleared with his foot, and a goal resulted. Then bad turned to worse when he gave the onrushing Tomas Rosicky space to swivel and fire home via a Pascal Chimbonda deflection.

In fairness, the solidity that was supposedly a key characteristic of the Rocha game began to show as he regained confidence in ensuing weeks, and he featured regularly, thanks largely to Ledley King's absence through injury, towards the end of the season. But just as Ricardo was proving himself as a valuable squad member, an ankle problem sidelined him for vast chunks of 2007/08. Under the new and demanding regime of Juande Ramos, a fellow fast reaching his 31st year was in urgent need of a change of luck.

**RICARDO SERGIO ROCHA**
BORN: Santo Torso, Portugal, 3 October 1978.
HONOURS: 5 Portugal caps (02-).
OTHER CLUBS: Braga 00/01-01/02 (44, 2); Benfica 02/03-06/07 (115, 3), both Portugal.

| GAMES | 16 (2) |
| GOALS | 0 |

# YOUNES KABOUL

## 2007/08 →

Younes Kaboul's imposing physical presence has come in useful at White Hart Lane, though he has needed all the strength he could muster to handle the weight of expectation deposited on his sizeable shoulders. Having been unveiled by Spurs in the summer of 2007, France's under-21 captain was lauded as one of the brightest defensive prospects in the game. Yet Kaboul, who spurned offers from Lyon and several Italian sides to fulfil his Premiership dream, was soon cast unfairly as a scapegoat as early-season jitters beset the Tottenham rearguard.

After agreeing an £8 million switch from Auxerre, Kaboul was instantly installed in the side, only to suffer with his new comrades as injury-ridden Spurs slipped to a last-gasp defeat on the opening day of the season at Sunderland.

With Ledley King and Michael Dawson absent, Younes was handed the tallest of orders over the ensuing weeks. But he battled manfully and after several error-strewn displays he redeemed himself by equalising with a left-foot rocket in a 4-4 draw at home to Aston Villa, thus completing a remarkable comeback from 4-1 down and contributing his third goal in only his seventh outing.

The subsequent arrival of Juande Ramos posed more challenges for the young Frenchman. A string of shaky performances in December prompted the Spanish supremo to leave Kaboul out of the squad for a UEFA Cup meeting with Anderlecht, despite having only one other fit stopper in his ranks. And, with Didier Zokora and Tom Huddlestone often being used as makeshift centre-backs under the new regime, the signing of Jonathan Woodgate made Kaboul's future appear more than a tad uncertain.

**YOUNES KABOUL**
BORN: Saint-Julien-en-Genevois, France, 4 January 1986.
HONOURS: League Cup 07/08.
OTHER CLUBS: Auxerre, France, 04/05-06/07 (52, 3).

| GAMES | 26 (3) |
| GOALS | 4 |

# PASCAL CHIMBONDA

## 2006/07 →

Pascal Chimbonda's stubborn streak became starkly apparent in a Spurs jersey. Whether he was battling for possession, climbing to win a seemingly impossible header or just generally making a nuisance of himself, no one could match the doughty warrior for downright obstinacy. Even Mother Nature, unable to dissuade the French international defender from running out in leggings and gloves for matches played in warm sunshine, has proved unequal to swaying him from his singular habits.

As a boy Pascal demonstrated his determination by single-handedly building his youth team a set of goals and still, when the bit is firmly between his teeth, nothing gets in his way. Not even injury. He proved that during Tottenham's hoodoo-ending victory against Chelsea at White Hart Lane in November 2006. Despite being left in considerable pain by a bone-juddering challenge from Frank Lampard, Chimbonda turned in one of his finest displays since signing for the club. Only later would it emerge that he had damaged knee ligaments. Manager Martin Jol, who had been so patient in securing his services from Wigan Athletic, didn't know whether to laugh or cry.

During his tenure at the JJB, Chimbonda, who was an unused substitute for France in the 2006 World Cup Final, was named in the Premierhip team of the season by his fellow professionals and it became inevitable that bigger clubs than Wigan would come calling. There followed a tedious, sometimes acrimonious transfer saga, but finally he joined Spurs for £5 million on the last day of the January 2006 window.

Chimbonda began repaying Tottenham's faith virtually as soon as he arrived, revealing himself as a magnificent athlete with the technical accomplishment to play anywhere across the back four. Though right-back was his specialist position, his fabulous heading ability – his spring from a standing start was truly startling – enabled him to thrive in the centre, often dominating opponents who towered above him. He had a certain presence about him, too, and the supporters came to relish his character-crammed displays, so demonstrative and full of life. With Pascal Chimbonda, it seemed, there was never a dull moment.

However, his second season as a Spur would not be remembered so fondly. After the club reportedly snubbed a bid from Chelsea for the man from Guadeloupe, suddenly it seemed the power brokers were making preparations for his departure. Juande Ramos signed two new right-backs – Alan Hutton and Chris Gunter – and the sight of Chimbonda trudging off the Wembley turf in a sulk after being replaced by substitute Tom Huddlestone when Tottenham were a goal down in the League Cup Final lost him many an ally. A few weeks later he missed the shoot-out penalty which saw his team knocked out of the UEFA Cup by PSV Eindhoven, although nobody blamed him for that.

The feeling persisted that Pascal Chimbonda had the capacity to succeed in any arena, but that his perceived eccentricity might stand in his way. In the summer of 2008, his future remained unclear.

---

**PASCAL CHIMBONDA**

BORN: Les Abymes, Guadeloupe, 21 February 1979.
HONOURS: League Cup 07/08. 1 France cap (06).
OTHER CLUBS: Le Havre 99/00-02/03 (85, 5); Bastia 03/04-04/05 (67, 4), both France; Wigan Athletic 05/06-06/07 (38, 2).

GAMES 97 (1)
GOALS 4

# GARETH BALE

· · · · · · · · · · · · · · · · · · · · · · · · · · · · · · · · · · · ·

## 2007/08 →

Tottenham fans can rest assured that Gareth Bale will remain blissfully unaffected by his really rather daft billing as 'Welsh football's next Ryan Giggs'. In the autumn of 2007, there appeared to be a welcome maturity about the precociously gifted 18-year-old which not only belied his own tender years, but also – and this is remarkable – exceeded that of certain of his new colleagues.

Thrust into a Tottenham side enduring an early-season wobble, Bale revealed himself to possess an admirably cool head, exactly what it took to help guide a club away from crisis. A barnstorming debut at Old Trafford was followed by stunning goals against Fulham and Arsenal and although injury restricted the rookie to only eight League outings in his first Premiership campaign, the Spurs fans had seen enough. Clearly, equating his ultimate impact to that of the distinguished veteran Giggs was fanciful at such an early stage, but there was every reason to conclude that Bale, barring further troubles with his fitness, possessed the potential to become one of the finest attacking full-backs or wide midfielders the club has known for many a year.

Tottenham Hotspur triumphed in recruiting Bale, a natural athlete endowed with the skills and instincts of a born footballer. Among the front-runners for his signature was Sir Alex Ferguson, who had been monitoring the leggy youngster since he made his debut as a 16-year-old for Southampton.

Yet not too many months before that Gareth had been unsure of his future in the game. The part-timer with Southampton's academy was commuting from Cardiff, and doubts were expressed over his physique. It seemed that all the excitement was focused on his room-mate Theo Walcott, already earmarked as England's next bright young thing. Yet while Walcott would embrace the bright lights of the Premiership with Arsenal at the first opportunity, Bale bided his time and bulked up with the Saints before eventually agreeing his switch to Tottenham in May 2007 for a fee likely to reach £10 million when all the add-on conditions are met.

Soon the callow newcomer was suggesting that he could become the answer to Tottenham's long-standing deficiencies on their left flank. The Welshman, who became his country's youngest full international debutant as a 16-year-old, sparkled as he played in a more advanced role than the left-back position he had usually been assigned at St Mary's.

Nothing seemed to faze him as, in only his second Spurs appearance, he latched on to a flick from Robbie Keane, charged in from the left touchline and coolly slotted his shot beyond Fulham 'keeper Antti Niemi at Craven Cottage. His strike in the north London derby will linger even longer in the memory, though. It was a perfectly placed free-kick which flashed inside the near post of Arsenal custodian Manuel Almunia, and represented just about the surest way imaginable to cement his place in the affections of his new admirers.

Unfortunately Gareth Bale's first season as a Spur came to a premature end after he fell awkwardly and severely damaged ankle ligaments in a tackle at home to Birmingham in December. Supporters, coaches and colleagues alike awaited his return with unrestrained eagerness.

**GARETH BALE**

| | |
|---|---|
| BORN: | Cardiff, 16 July 1989. |
| HONOURS: | 11 Wales caps (06-). |
| OTHER CLUBS: | Southampton 05/06-06/07 (40, 5). |

| | |
|---|---|
| GAMES | **10 (2)** |
| GOALS | 3 |

# DIMITAR BERBATOV

## 2006/07 →

He may not welcome the comparison with an occasionally controversial politician of Romanian descent. But when Michael Howard's fellow Tory Ann Widdecombe said famously of the former Home Secretary that 'there's something of the night about him' she could easily have been talking about Dimitar Berbatov.

After all, with his jet-black hair scraped back, faintly disconcertingly, in the style of a vampire, and his long shirtsleeves tugged over his hands as if they were bat wings, Tottenham's slender Bulgarian centre-forward plays as though ice runs through his veins, gliding around White Hart Lane with the shuddering menace of a Mafioso killer. Yet the marksman who rarely grins has brought nothing but joy to the serried ranks of the faithful Tottenham legions since his arrival in the summer of 2006.

It had not been too long since another bounteously gifted striker from Eastern Europe had arrived at N17 following a hefty transfer fee and carrying weighty expectations. But where Sergei Rebrov floundered, Berbatov has flourished. Before his £11 million recruitment from Bayer Leverkusen, there were rumours that his languid skills might be undermined by a liking for nightclubs and a distaste for training. But he proved to be a master of improvisation whose contribution could not be measured in buckets of sweat; indeed, though he can sprint and forage at need, he tended to let his brain do most of the hard work for him.

The gulf in class between Berbatov and most of his Premier League peers reminds fans of a certain age of an earlier thoroughbred Spurs striker, the stylishly graceful Alan Gilzean, who also tended to employ guile rather than guts to outwit his opponents. As with 'Gilly' in the second half of the 1960s and the early 1970s, Dimitar's superior touch affords him extra time and space in which to work his spell, while his heading, passing and shooting are all elegantly exquisite in their execution. Berbatov would never try to burst a ball's stitching when a deft caress would do the job. Minimal effort and maximum effect would soon become the vividly apparent hallmarks of his game.

The Bulgarian, whose parents were both successful athletes, endured a quiet opening few weeks in London, summoning only one goal in his first eight outings. But travelling fans were granted a telling glimpse of his genius during a UEFA Cup encounter with Besiktas in Turkey, when he climaxed an exhibition of mesmeric forward play with a conversion of sublime quality. Nursing the ball as if it were a newborn babe, Berbatov twice feigned to shoot, leaving a brace of markers in a tangle as he rounded the 'keeper before planting the leather into an empty net.

In the ensuing months he proved to be the most versatile of performers, a play-maker or a poacher at need, combining equally effectively with Jermain Defoe or Robbie Keane. He excelled on his own, too, as he demonstrated graphically in a 4-1 home victory over Bolton in February 2007, his input lauded by Martin Jol as the best display he had ever witnessed by a solitary striker.

Bulgaria's international skipper had come an awful long way since he started out at CSKA Sofia, where he was once subjected to merciless flak and made a scapegoat for fluffing several scoring chances as his team missed out on a league title. Inevitably his talents shone through eventually, however, and, having won his homeland fans over, he joined Bayer Leverkusen as a 20-year-old, going on to establish himself over the next six seasons as one of the Bundesliga's most creative attackers.

By the end of his first Premiership campaign, the brilliance of Berbatov had made a similar impression in England. After a glorious free-kick at Upton Park and /several exceptional efforts against Chelsea, he was fast emerging as one of the most prized strikers in the game.

After he received the club's player of the season award and been named by his fellow professionals in the Premiership's best eleven, murmurs of a switch to Manchester United were getting louder by the day. Yet, despite voicing his displeasure over uncertainties concerning both his own future and the club's managerial situation, he remained at the Lane and the sumptuous displays continued to come thick and fast during 2007/08.

One highlight was a four-goal haul at home to Reading in December, which preceded his crucial role in ensuring that Spurs secured their first silverware since 1999. Not even the pressure of taking a penalty in the League Cup Final at Wembley could melt Tottenham's Mr Cool. Juande Ramos's men were trailing 1-0 and Chelsea were doing their unattractive best to kill the game in the second half when Wayne Bridge handled inside the area. Ignoring a chorus of boos and catcalls from the fans in blue, Berbatov strode up to dispatch the spot-kick as nonchalantly as if he were enjoying a game with his mates in the park.

That set Spurs up for a memorable comeback and, as he celebrated victory with Keane, the iceman at last cracked into a smile. Silver usually repels vampires, but the medal in Berbatov's palm might, just might, be enough to keep the footballing aristocrat at White Hart Lane for a few more seasons.

---

**DIMITAR BERBATOV**

| | |
|---|---|
| **BORN:** | Blagoevgrad, Bulgaria, 30.1.81. |
| **HONOURS:** | League Cup 07/08. 65 Bulgaria caps (99-). |
| **OTHER CLUBS:** | Pirin; CSKA Sofia 98/9-00/01 (50, 25), both Bulgaria; Bayer Leverkusen, Germany, 00/01-05/06 (154, 69). |

| | |
|---|---|
| GAMES | **91 (10)** |
| GOALS | 46 |

# TOM HUDDLESTONE

## 2005/06 →

Tom Huddlestone makes football pitches look small. He towers over most of his colleagues and opponents like a heavyweight boxer wandering in a playground, but this midfield schemer is no bruiser. Huddlestone is 6ft 3in of footballing elegance, drifting around White Hart Lane with all the lofty poise of a giraffe lolloping across the African plains.

Crucially, he is of the stock Tottenham fans have always relished. Whether deployed as the creative hub of the side or at the heart of the rearguard, the Midlander is unflappable on the ball and capable of picking out team-mates with sumptuous dispatches both long and short. On rare forays forward he has also shown a keen eye for goal, witness the exquisite execution of his volley against Manchester City at Eastlands in December 2006.

Understandably expectations have been high since Huddlestone arrived at Tottenham in the summer of 2005 in a £2.5 million deal. After being released as a 12-year-old by Nottingham Forest he had enjoyed nothing but success at Derby County, representing England at every youth level. And having played an integral role in helping the Rams to the Championship play-offs in 2004/05 he became one of the most in-demand youngsters outside the top-flight.

Following Tom's arrival in north London, Martin Jol lost little time in predicting that the teenager would become a long-term partner for Jermaine Jenas in the centre of midfield, and soon enough his prospects of fulfilling that prophecy were boosted by the departure to Manchester United of Michael Carrick, a performer with similar ball-playing instincts.

But for many months it remained baffling that Huddlestone, who spent part of his first term as a Spur on loan with Wolves, had been unable to fully impose his intimidating figure on the Premiership scene. During 2006/07, his second campaign at the Lane, he was rarely afforded a full 90 minutes of senior action by Jol, who grew to worry that his friendly giant lacked both the aggression and fitness levels demanded by the rigours of his midfield berth.

But fears that he would be one of the first names facing the axe under the new regime of Juande Ramos, a self-proclaimed fitness freak who took over as Tottenham manager in October 2007, were to prove unwarranted. Huddlestone gave up tomato ketchup and sugary drinks to slim down considerably, and he featured prominently in the midfield or as a makeshift centre-back for the remainder of the season. Boring food, it seemed, had hauled his Spurs career back on track.

| | |
|---|---|
| **THOMAS ANDREW HUDDLESTONE** | |
| **BORN:** | Nottingham, 28 December 1986. |
| **HONOURS:** | League Cup 07/08. |
| **OTHER CLUBS:** | Derby County 03/04-04/05 (88, 0); Wolverhampton Wanderers on loan 05/06 (13, 1). |

| | |
|---|---|
| GAMES | **52 (30)** |
| GOALS | 7 |

# STEED MALBRANQUE

## 2006/07 →

Tony Blair became well accustomed to provoking passionate protest during his tenure at Number 10, yet his assertion in 2005 that Steed Malbranque, then of Fulham, could become a major Premiership force hardly prompted a whisper of objection.

It was an interesting claim from a football fan of fairly slight credentials about an admittedly dynamic player, yet one who lacked the raw talent of the league's more cultured performers. But clearly it was a point of view shared by Spurs boss Martin Jol, who was delighted when the industrious midfielder joined his White Hart Lane revolution, and duly the Dutchman was fully vindicated as the trusty Steed became one of the side's most useful members during his first two campaigns at White Hart Lane.

Spurs pulled off something of a coup in securing the Frenchman, who was born in Belgium but, with his sallow complexion and distinctively aquiline features, could hardly look more Gallic if you stuck him on a bicycle and draped a string of onions round his neck.

Malbranque was Fulham's most prized possession, and he had resisted transfer approaches from Newcastle and a gaggle of enthusiastic rivals in favour of a virtual guarantee of regular first-team football if he remained at Craven Cottage. But where others had failed, Tottenham succeeded on the last day of the August 2006 transfer window, eventually sealing a £2.5 million switch after protracted negotiations.

However, Lane regulars faced a lengthy wait before they saw the best of their new signing, whom Jol had predicted would invigorate the left flank of his team. Already injured at the time of his arrival, he held a watching brief from the stands for several months, finally making an encouraging entrance in a 3-1 home victory over Port Vale in November. Thereafter Steed featured regularly during the remainder of the season. He was a relentlessly industrious and sometimes creative contributor who was ready to run any opponent off his feet in the interests of pursuing the merest whiff of a half-chance at goal for his side, his irrepressible on-pitch demeanour contrasting vividly with a perceived diffidence away from the game.

After rifling home his first goal in a 5-1 White Hart Lane trouncing of Charlton, Malbranque grew in assurance. Like most of his colleagues, though, he suffered an end-of-season dip in form and his predicament was not helped when he rashly slashed a header from Sevilla's Christian Poulsen into his own net to effectively end Spurs' hopes of progressing to the UEFA Cup semi-final.

Come the following term, invigorated by a brace at home to Derby in August, he seemed a brighter prospect than ever. The new manager, Juande Ramos, was a clear admirer of the Frenchman, and rather than restricting him to a berth wide on the left, he was now afforded the freedom to drift inside.

Malbranque revelled in his new job and played no small part in helping Spurs to lift the League Cup. A coolly dispatched goal in the glorious 5-1 semi-final victory over Arsenal preceded a confident Wembley display against Chelsea. Now there seemed little doubt that the former prime minister had voted for the right man.

**STEED MALBRANQUE**

BORN: Mouscron, Belgium, 6 January 1980.
HONOURS: League Cup 07/08.
OTHER CLUBS: Lyon, France, 97/8-00/01 (77, 5); Fulham 01/02-05/06 (172, 32).

| | |
|---|---|
| GAMES | 82 (14) |
| GOALS | 12 |

# DARREN BENT

## 2007/08 →

One of Darren Bent's first mentors dared to predict that his impressionable young rookie could have as much impact on the English game as Gary Lineker. Overlook their obvious differences in appearance, Ipswich boss Joe Royle insisted, and they were strikers from the same footballing womb. Two players who were born to take chances, born to run and, most importantly, he said, born to score goals.

But compare the pair's debut campaigns at Tottenham Hotspur and the likeness is shot down in flames. While Lineker was instantly welcomed as the lion king of White Hart Lane after his arrival in 1989, Bent has resembled a caged tiger, a £16.5 million big cat long overdue a feed since prowling across London from the Valley in the summer of 2007.

It must be stressed that if Bent's Tottenham career continues to falter as it did during his first testing 12 months, then certainly it won't be for want of trying. From the day he arrived from Charlton Athletic the pacy, athletic marksman has remained unfailingly positive in even the most difficult of circumstances.

In 2006/07 Darren had enjoyed the best season of his career to date, his prolific efforts for the Addicks deservedly earning him a regular England squad berth. But at Tottenham, where four front-runners of international pedigree – Berbatov, Keane, Defoe and the soon-to-depart Mido – were already vying for position, the club's record signing faced an almighty task to become

established, and the circumstance that he had been recruited through a deal engineered principally by the club's directors, rather than manager Martin Jol, was not exactly a help.

Bent, a former Portman Road trainee who quietly admits his boyhood idol was the old Highbury hero Ian Wright, enjoyed a prolific pre-season but was omitted from the starting line-up when the Premiership campaign kicked off. Thereafter his fortunes, despite netting against Derby in only his second start, descended from disappointing to downright dreadful as he missed a succession of gilt-edged chances in a sobering defeat at the Emirates.

Times were leaner than they had ever been for the England striker as Jol's tenure in charge teetered on the brink of extinction. Then, under new manager Juande Ramos, Bent's future looked decidedly precarious, but instead it was Jermain Defoe, a player with whom he had forged a close relationship, who was sold.

Now five experienced strikers had become three and suddenly Bent's chances improved. A cameo appearance at home to Portsmouth in March, when he rose from the bench to join a contest which had been deadlocked at 0-0, then scored one goal and set up another, offered genuine cause for optimism and must have done wonders for his confidence. It was still early days for the 24-year-old, but here at least was a suggestion, however faint, that Joe Royle's Lineker comparison might ultimately prove to be not quite so hysterical after all.

| | DARREN ASHLEY BENT | | | |
|---|---|---|---|---|
| BORN: | Wandsworth, London, 6 February 1984. | | | |
| HONOURS: | 3 England caps (06-). | | GAMES | 15 (21) |
| OTHER CLUBS: | Ipswich Town 01/02-04/05 (122, 49); Charlton Athletic 05/06-06/07 (68, 31). | | GOALS | 8 |

# KEVIN-PRINCE BOATENG

## 2007/08 →

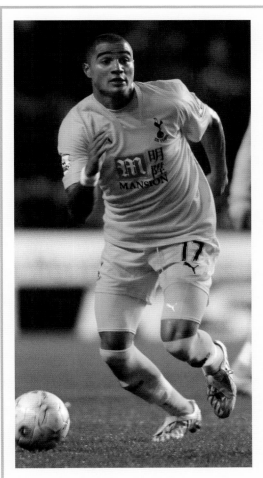

There was only one possible dissenting voice on the day Tottenham acquired steely midfielder Kevin-Prince Boateng – that of his lovely bride. Boateng, a former young player of the year in Germany, was so intent on proving he could make a big impact in England that he agreed to fly to White Hart Lane on the day after his wedding in July 2007.

For their £6 million investment, the north Londoners had signed a 20-year-old with a burgeoning reputation. The 6ft 1in midfielder's athleticism, and enthusiasm to try the spectacular, had already attracted offers from Newcastle and Sevilla. But Boateng, a confident character who called himself 'The Ghetto Kid' because of his upbringing in one of Berlin's poorest areas, chose Tottenham, having seen the success enjoyed by fellow Bundesliga graduate Dimitar Berbatov.

Yet the German under-21 international, who was offered a chance to play in the African Nations with Ghana but declined it, was not to enjoy the same instant success as the Bulgarian maestro. The start of Boateng's campaign was hindered by injury and even after breaking into the first team – via a stunning individual strike for the reserves – he found himself identified as an understudy for Jermaine Jenas. However, there were enough lively, if not spectacular, displays in front of new manager Juande Ramos to suggest that the Boat's future is buoyant.

| **KEVIN-PRINCE BOATENG** | | |
|---|---|---|
| **BORN:** | Berlin, Germany, 6 March 1987. | **GAMES** 10 (11) |
| **OTHER CLUBS:** | Hertha Berlin, Germany, 05/06-06/07 (42, 4). | **GOALS** 0 |

# ADEL TAARABT

## 2006/07 →

Martin Jol compared him to Zinedine Zidane; Robbie Keane calls him 'Zizou Junior'. The consensus of opinion at White Hart Lane is that this boy's a bit special.

Tottenham snatched Adel Taarabt from under the noses of European football's superpowers, and if the exuberantly talented youngster fulfils his awesome promise, he will prove the steal of the century.

Taarabt, a French youth international of Moroccan descent, has never, at the time of writing, played a full 90 minutes in his senior career. Yet Jol put his neck on the line by declaring his belief that on the ball Adel had no equal in England. Tricky, unpredictable and capable of playing on either flank, Taarabt was destined, according to the enthusiastic Dutchman, to become the next David Ginola.

Certainly Spurs fans lucky enough to have been at Upton Park when he was called from the bench to make his Tottenham debut in March 2007 have been practically salivating over his prospects ever since. On a magical evening on which the visitors recovered from a 3-1 deficit to triumph 4-3, the rookie sliced through the West Ham defence to earn a free-kick which resulted in a goal for Dimitar Berbatov.

Still, since his recruitment in January 2007, initially on loan before a £2.5 million fee was agreed with Lens, one or two flaws have emerged, notably a tendency towards self-indulgence and an apparent distaste for a midfielder's defensive duties, but they are traits likely to be eradicated by maturity and careful coaching. Meanwhile, as 2007/08 drew to a close, his enthusiastic admirers in the White Hart Lane stands were yearning to see Adel Taarabt start a game.

| **ADEL TAARABT** | | |
|---|---|---|
| **BORN:** | Berre-l'Etang, France, 24 May 1989. | **GAMES** 0 (12) |
| **OTHER CLUBS:** | Lens, France, 06/07 (1, 0). | **GOALS** 0 |

# CHRIS GUNTER

## 2007/08 →

The prospect of a prized Welshman on either Tottenham flank will not seem unfamiliar to gnarled denizens of White Hart Lane old enough to recall the thrilling exploits of Terry Medwin and Cliff Jones during the middle years of the last century. That gilded pair set formidable standards of bold, adventurous wing-play, but optimism was high in the late summer of 2008 that Gareth Bale and Chris Gunter – combined ages a mere 38 – may be up to the task of reprising that golden era of derring-do.

At the time of writing, Gunter is the lesser known of the two teenage hot-shots, who were born within five days of each other. But already he is held in high regard at his new workplace, where he arrived at a cost of £3 million from Cardiff City to become one of new boss Juande Ramos' first signings in January 2008.

The Bluebirds were desperately sorry to lose their reliable youngster, who had rarely missed a game since making his debut shortly after his 17th birthday, but they needed the cash and were reluctant to stand in his way.

Already a full international, Chris wasted no time in making a positive impact as a Spur, enlivening his debut in an FA Cup replay at Reading with a series of attacking forays, one of which climaxed in a penetrating cross which almost produced a goal for Jermain Defoe. The subsequent arrival of the more experienced Alan Hutton reduced his immediate opportunities but, having made such rapid progress while still in his teens, there is little doubt that the precocious Gunter will be back.

| | | | |
|---|---|---|---|
| **CHRISTOPHER ROSS GUNTER** | | | |
| BORN: | Newport, Gwent, 21 July 1989. | GAMES | **2 (2)** |
| HONOURS: | 4 Wales caps (07-). | GOALS | 0 |
| OTHER CLUBS: | Cardiff City 06/07-07/08 (28, 0). | | |

# JAMIE O'HARA

## 2007/08 →

Jamie O'Hara never shirks a challenge. Indeed, since boldly swapping life with Arsenal's academy for a career at Spurs in 2003, the shaven-headed rookie has dealt admirably with every obstacle thrown his way. Many a youngster might have felt disheartened at spending extended loan spells in the lower reaches of the Football League. But Jamie soaked up every ounce of experience he could get during stints with Chesterfield and Millwall – and what a breath of fresh air he proved to be when Tottenham finally rewarded him for his persistence in December 2007.

The energetic midfielder is a left-footed workhorse with no shortage of skill, as he proved on his debut against Portsmouth. Just a few weeks after his final game at The Den, he helped to set up Dimitar Berbatov's winner at Fratton Park, then three days later he won plaudits for a sublime pass which sent in Steed Malbranque for Spurs' second goal in a League Cup victory over Manchester City at Eastlands. His proudest moment to date was still to come, however, when he made the starting line-up against the Gunners.

As if from nowhere, suddenly O'Hara seemed to be an indispensable member of a new-look Spurs squad. Amiable, enthusiastic and able to play anywhere across midfield as well as in both full-back slots, he became an overnight hero in the stands, and he revealed how his dad had cried with emotion after hearing fans sing his name.

Jamie went on contribute a couple of goals and by season's end he was firmly entrenched as a crowd-pleaser, his future redolent with promise.

| | | | |
|---|---|---|---|
| **JAMIE DARRELL O'HARA** | | | |
| BORN: | Dartford, Kent, 25 September 1986. | GAMES | **12 (13)** |
| OTHER CLUBS: | Chesterfield on loan 05/06 (19, 5); Millwall on loan 07/08 (14, 2). | GOALS | 2 |

# JONATHAN WOODGATE

## 2007/08 →

Jonathan Woodgate won the race for Tottenham's Wembley champagne – by a nose. The central defender's winning goal in the League Cup Final, which involved the ball cannoning into Chelsea's net via the tip of his snout, may have had a generous dollop of good fortune about it. But if anyone deserved a helping of jam it was Woody, who had endured a career of injury-ravaged under-achievement before signing for Spurs.

Now Woodgate's eyes, set deep in their somewhat cavernous sockets, were twinkling with the reflection of silverware within a mere month of his arrival at White Hart Lane in a £7 million move from Middlesbrough towards the end of the January 2008 transfer window.

Such an outcome bordered on the incredible. Indeed, the majority of media pundits and most bookies had written off the prospect of the former Champions League semi-finalist (in his Leeds days) being declared fit to figure alongside Ledley King in the showdown with Avram Grant's men. But England's two perennially absent stoppers were wholly present come the big day. And, for 120 minutes at least, Tottenham had a central defensive partnership that would be the envy of any side.

Both men were commanding, decisive and completely unflappable, and it seemed that the most demanding struggle they would face on that glorious afternoon would be over who picked up the man of the match award. It turned out to be Woodgate who reigned supreme, for his imperious handling of the dangerous Didier Drogba. After all his years at Elland Road, St James' Park, the Bernabeu and the Riverside without a medal, suddenly he had a gong in each hand.

In Jonathan Woodgate, Tottenham have a player with virtually all the characteristics traditionally demanded of a dominant central defender. Seemingly as strong as a shire-horse and almost frighteningly competitive, he rarely gives away free-kicks, thanks to his impeccable timing; he is a titan in the tackle and in aerial combat, and having won the ball he distributes it simply, sensibly, invariably safely.

As 2008/09 approached, the Lilywhite half of north London could only hope that the 28-year-old – who surely would have quadrupled his meagre handful of England caps by this stage of his career but for the serial injuries which have plagued him so mercilessly – can cast off his grisly luck at last. Before arriving at Spurs he had completed 30 games in a season only twice in his nine Premier League campaigns. His fortune was even worse at Real Madrid, for whom he was unable to play a single minute of 2004/05. Happily, at the time of writing, since enlisting at the Lane Woodgate has been virtually ever-present in Juande Ramos' side, although perhaps it would be unwise to tempt fate by dwelling on the poor fellow's fitness record.

After an unsavoury, potentially destabilising courtroom saga just after the turn of the century, an horrendously cruel succession of injuries, and being sold for fees totalling more than £28 million, it seemed that the rugged north-easterner might finally get the chance to concentrate on what he does best.

| | |
|---|---|
| **JONATHAN SIMON WOODGATE** | |
| BORN: | Middlesbrough, 22 January 1980. |
| HONOURS: | League Cup 07/08. 6 England caps (99-). |
| OTHER CLUBS: | Leeds United 98/9-02/03 (104, 4); Newcastle United 02/03-03/04 (28, 0); Real Madrid, Spain, 04/05-05/06 (9, 0); Middlesbrough 06/07-07/08 (46, 0). |

| | |
|---|---|
| GAMES | 17 |
| GOALS | 2 |

# ALAN HUTTON

## 2007/08 →

That barnstorming full-back Alan Hutton is regarded at Tottenham Hotspur as one of the fittest young athletes in the game is something of a miracle to those who were at Ibrox on a chilly afternoon in February 2005. Those who saw the Rangers man writhing in agony, his leg dangling at an unnatural angle, doubted whether he would be walking within three years, let alone be embarking on a £9 million transfer south of the border. Yet Hutton, whose tibia and fubula were both shattered in the horrendous collision with a Kilmarnock player, was destined to become the bionic man of White Hart Lane.

Spurs supporters breathed a heartfelt sigh of relief after the young defender arrived at the club with the clock ticking fast towards the January 2008 transfer deadline. Shortly before the transaction was secured Sir Alex Ferguson had been singing the praises of his fellow Glaswegian. Speaking after Hutton's typically marauding display for his country against Italy, the Manchester United manager declared that the galloping overlapper would become a superstar with a little more experience.

Polished performances in the Champions League against Stuttgart, Lyon and Barcelona saw his stock rise even further. Yet despite rumours of interest from Old Trafford and reports of offers from *Serie A*, the main obstacle in Tottenham completing the deal was Hutton himself. The Scot was devoutly loyal to his boyhood club, had only recently signed a new contract and claimed he was looking forward to featuring in the forthcoming Scottish League Cup Final.

Fortunately Tottenham had an enticing bargaining tool – they were in a final, too. The carrot at the end of the stick duly worked, and in only his third outing in a Spurs shirt, Hutton ran out at Wembley to play a major role in stifling Chelsea's rapacious attack. From that happy afternoon onwards, he demonstrated to Spurs fans why his tackling was held in such regard and, in the ensuing weeks as his confidence grew, there were also signs that he could attack with menace.

Standing 6ft 1in and as lean as a rake, Alan appeared to be exactly the type of athletic, accomplished all-round footballer craved by the new White Hart Lane boss, Juande Ramos. Graham Roberts, another renowned performer for both Rangers and Spurs, insisted that Hutton would eventually go down in legend in north London.

He was still only 23 in the summer of 2008, and the lengthy lay-off following his Kilmarnock accident had deprived him of considerable experience, so it was understandable that his game was in need of fine-tuning. But as with the new healthy menu which caused such a stir at Spurs' training ground canteen following the arrival of the diet-conscious Spanish manager, the ingredients were in place for long-lasting success.

**ALAN HUTTON**
**BORN:** Glasgow, 30 November 1984.
**HONOURS:** League Cup 07/08. 7 Scotland caps (07-).
**OTHER CLUBS:** Rangers 02/03-07/08 (94, 2).

| | |
|---|---|
| GAMES | 15 |
| GOALS | 0 |

# GILBERTO

## 2007/08 →

After a teeth-gratingly hapless debut in a Spurs jersey, things could only get better for Gilberto. Indeed, they could hardly get worse.

The seasoned Brazilian international was heralded as accomplished cover for long-term absentees Gareth Bale and Benoit Assou-Ekotto when he arrived in a £2 million deal from Hertha Berlin in the middle of the 2007/08 campaign.

Expectations were high of the solidly built, immensely gifted utility defender whose rarefied experience included appearances in the 2006 World Cup finals. Yet the 31-year-old got off to a disastrous start. His first senior outing was delayed by several weeks because he was hampered by a niggling shin complaint, and when he finally took to the field, in early March as a left-back at home to PSV Eindhoven in the UEFA Cup, he looked woefully short of match sharpness. After gifting the Dutch side a goal which would eventually prove decisive in the tie, he was taken off at half-time.

Gilberto's redemption began as he scored after coming off the bench against West Ham at White Hart Lane the following week, but during the remainder of the season he was granted only a handful of senior games after being told to lose weight. Apparently it was muscular bulk rather than fat which was causing the Tottenham coaches concern but he was left in no doubt that a few pounds would have to be shed if he wanted to nurture his Spurs career.

| | GILBERTO DA SILVA MELO | | |
|---|---|---|---|
| BORN: | Rio de Janeiro, Brazil, 25 April 1976. | | |
| HONOURS: | 24 Brazil caps (03-). | GAMES | 4 (3) |
| OTHER CLUBS: | America 93-95; Flamengo 96-98; Cruzeiro 98-99, all Brazil; Internazionale, Italy, 99/00 (2, 0); Vasco de Gama 00-01; | GOALS | 1 |
| | Gremio 02-03; San Caetano 03-04, all Brazil; Hertha Berlin, Germany, 04/05-07/08 (86, 13). | | |

# PLAYERS' STATISTICS

## AUGUST 1958 → MAY 2008

Dates shown indicate the first year of each season. Thus 64–66 means 1964/65 to 1966/67. A single entry means one season only, eg 2002 refers to 2002/03.

| Player | Season | League App | (Sub) | Gl | FA Cup App | (Sub) | Gl | League Cup App | (Sub) | Gl | Europe App | (Sub) | Gl | Others App | (Sub) | Gl | Total App | (Sub) | Gl |
|---|---|---|---|---|---|---|---|---|---|---|---|---|---|---|---|---|---|---|---|
| Acimovic M | 2002 | 4 | (13) | 0 | 0 | (0) | 0 | 1 | (0) | 0 | 0 | (0) | 0 | 0 | (0) | 0 | 5 | (13) | 0 |
| Aleksic M | 78–81 | 25 | (0) | 0 | 7 | (0) | 0 | 0 | (0) | 0 | 0 | (0) | 0 | 0 | (0) | 0 | 32 | (0) | 0 |
| Allen C | 84–87 | 97 | (8) | 60 | 11 | (1) | 9 | 13 | (1) | 13 | 3 | (1) | 2 | 0 | (0) | 0 | 124 | (11) | 84 |
| Allen L | 59–64 | 119 | (0) | 47 | 15 | (0) | 13 | 0 | (0) | 0 | 3 | (0) | 1 | 1 | (0) | 2 | 138 | (0) | 63 |
| Allen P | 85–93 | 276 | (16) | 23 | 26 | (1) | 1 | 42 | (2) | 4 | 6 | (1) | 0 | 1 | (0) | 0 | 351 | (20) | 28 |
| Allen R | 96–98 | 10 | (11) | 2 | 1 | (0) | 0 | 3 | (3) | 2 | 0 | (0) | 0 | 0 | (0) | 0 | 14 | (14) | 4 |
| Anderton D | 92–03 | 273 | (26) | 34 | 26 | (2) | 6 | 30 | (1) | 8 | 0 | (0) | 0 | 0 | (0) | 0 | 329 | (29) | 48 |
| Archibald S | 80–83 | 128 | (3) | 58 | 17 | (1) | 5 | 18 | (0) | 7 | 22 | (0) | 8 | 2 | (0) | 0 | 187 | (4) | 78 |
| Ardiles O | 78–87 | 222 | (16) | 16 | 32 | (0) | 4 | 31 | (1) | 3 | 8 | (1) | 2 | 1 | (0) | 0 | 294 | (18) | 25 |
| Armstrong C | 95–00 | 117 | (24) | 48 | 9 | (5) | 4 | 15 | (0) | 10 | 3 | (0) | 0 | 0 | (0) | 0 | 144 | (29) | 62 |
| Armstrong G | 76–80 | 65 | (19) | 10 | 6 | (4} | 3 | 3 | (1) | 3 | 0 | (0) | 0 | 0 | (0) | 0 | 74 | (24) | 16 |
| Assou-Ekotto B | 06– | 17 | (0) | 0 | 1 | (0) | 0 | 3 | (0) | 0 | 6 | (0) | 0 | 0 | (0) | 0 | 27 | (0) | 0 |
| Atouba T | 2004 | 15 | (3) | 1 | 5 | (0) | 0 | 1 | (0) | 0 | 0 | (0) | 0 | 0 | (0) | 0 | 21 | (3) | 1 |
| Austin D | 92–96 | 117 | (7) | 0 | 16 | (1) | 0 | 7 | (2) | 0 | 0 | (0) | 0 | 0 | (0) | 0 | 140 | (10) | 0 |
| Baardsen E | 96–98 | 22 | (1) | 0 | 2 | (1) | 0 | 3 | (0) | 0 | 0 | (0) | 0 | 0 | (0) | 0 | 27 | (2) | 0 |
| Baker P | 52–64 | 299 | (0) | 3 | 27 | (0) | 0 | 0 | (0) | 0 | 16 | (0) | 0 | 2 | (0) | 0 | 344 | (0) | 3 |
| Bale G | 07– | 8 | (0) | 2 | 0 | (0) | 0 | 1 | (0) | 1 | 1 | (2) | 0 | 0 | (0) | 0 | 10 | (2) | 3 |
| Barcham A | 06– | 0 | (0) | 0 | 0 | (0) | 0 | 1 | (0) | 0 | 0 | (0) | 0 | 0 | (0) | 0 | 1 | (0) | 0 |
| Barmby N | 92–94 | 81 | (6) | 20 | 12 | (1) | 5 | 7 | (1) | 2 | 0 | (0) | 0 | 0 | (0) | 0 | 100 | (8) | 27 |
| Barnard L | 2005 | 0 | (3) | 0 | 0 | (0) | 0 | 0 | (0) | 0 | 0 | (0) | 0 | 0 | (0) | 0 | 0 | (3) | 0 |
| Barton K | 60–63 | 4 | (0) | 0 | 0 | (0) | 0 | 0 | (0) | 0 | 0 | (0) | 0 | 0 | (0) | 0 | 4 | (0) | 0 |
| Beal P | 63–74 | 330 | (3) | 1 | 30 | (0) | 0 | 27 | (0) | 0 | 30 | (0) | 0 | 0 | (0) | 0 | 417 | (3) | 1 |
| Beavon S | 78–79 | 3 | (1) | 0 | 0 | (1) | 0 | 0 | (0) | 0 | 0 | (0) | 0 | 0 | (0) | 0 | 3 | (2) | 0 |
| Bent D | 07– | 11 | (16) | 6 | 0 | (0) | 0 | 0 | (1) | 0 | 4 | (4) | 2 | 0 | (0) | 0 | 15 | (21) | 8 |
| Berbatov D | 06– | 63 | (6) | 27 | 6 | (1) | 5 | 7 | (2) | 2 | 15 | (1) | 12 | 0 | (0) | 0 | 91 | (10) | 46 |
| Bergsson G | 88–92 | 51 | (2) | 2 | 2 | (2) | 0 | 4 | (2) | 0 | 5 | (1) | 0 | 0 | (0) | 0 | 62 | (25) | 2 |
| Berti N | 97–98 | 21 | (0) | 3 | 2 | (0) | 0 | 0 | (0) | 0 | 0 | (0) | 0 | 0 | (0) | 0 | 23 | (0) | 3 |
| Blanchflower D | 54–63 | 337 | (0) | 15 | 33 | (0) | 4 | 0 | (0) | 0 | 12 | (0) | 2 | 2 | (0) | 0 | 384 | (0) | 21 |
| Blondel J | 02–03 | 0 | (2) | 0 | 0 | (0) | 0 | 1 | (1) | 0 | 0 | (0) | 0 | 0 | (0) | 0 | 1 | (3) | 0 |
| Boateng K-P | 07– | 7 | (6) | 0 | 1 | (1) | 0 | 1 | (2) | 0 | 1 | (2) | 0 | 0 | (0) | 0 | 10 | (11) | 0 |
| Bond D | 66–70 | 20 | (3) | 1 | 0 | (0) | 0 | 2 | (1) | 0 | 1 | (0) | 0 | 0 | (0) | 0 | 23 | (4) | 1 |
| Booth A | 2000 | 3 | (1) | 0 | 0 | (0) | 0 | 0 | (0) | 0 | 0 | (0) | 0 | 0 | (0) | 0 | 3 | (1) | 0 |
| Bowen M | 83–86 | 14 | (3) | 2 | 3 | (0) | 0 | 0 | (0) | 0 | 0 | (0) | 0 | 0 | (0) | 0 | 17 | (3) | 2 |
| Brace R | 1983 | 0 | (1) | 0 | 0 | (0) | 0 | 0 | (0) | 0 | 0 | (0) | 0 | 0 | (0) | 0 | 0 | (1) | 0 |
| Brady G | 1997 | 0 | (9) | 0 | 1 | (1) | 0 | 0 | (0) | 0 | 0 | (0) | 0 | 0 | (0) | 0 | 1 | (10) | 0 |
| Brazil A | 82–83 | 29 | (2) | 9 | 1 | (0) | 0 | 0 | (1) | 0 | 3 | (2) | 4 | 0 | (0) | 0 | 33 | (5) | 13 |
| Brooke G | 80–84 | 49 | (24) | 15 | 4 | (8) | 1 | 4 | (1) | 1 | 6 | (5) | 1 | 0 | (0) | 0 | 63 | (38) | 18 |
| Brooks J | 52–59 | 166 | (0) | 46 | 13 | (0) | 5 | 0 | (0) | 0 | 0 | (0) | 0 | 0 | (0) | 0 | 179 | (0) | 51 |
| Brotherston N | 1975 | 1 | (0) | 0 | 0 | (0) | 0 | 0 | (0) | 0 | 0 | (0) | 0 | 0 | (0) | 0 | 1 | (0) | 0 |
| Brown L | 63–65 | 62 | (0) | 3 | 3 | (0) | 0 | 0 | (0) | 0 | 0 | (0) | 0 | 0 | (0) | 0 | 65 | (0) | 3 |
| Brown M | 03–05 | 39 | (11) | 2 | 9 | (0) | 0 | 4 | (1) | 1 | 0 | (0) | 0 | 0 | (0) | 0 | 52 | (12) | 3 |
| Brown R | 1966 | 1 | (0) | 0 | 0 | (0) | 0 | 0 | (0) | 0 | 0 | (0) | 0 | 0 | (0) | 0 | 1 | (0) | 0 |
| Brown W | 59–65 | 222 | (0) | 0 | 23 | (0) | 0 | 0 | (0) | 0 | 17 | (0) | 0 | 2 | (0) | 0 | 264 | (0) | 0 |
| Bunjevcevic G | 01–04 | 41 | (10) | 0 | 0 | (0) | 0 | 6 | (1) | 2 | 0 | (0) | 0 | 0 | (0) | 0 | 47 | (11) | 2 |
| Butters G | 88–89 | 34 | (1) | 1 | 1 | (0) | 0 | 2 | (1) | 0 | 0 | (0) | 0 | 0 | (0) | 0 | 37 | (2) | 1 |
| Calderwood C | 93–98 | 152 | (11) | 7 | 15 | (1) | 1 | 19 | (1) | 0 | 0 | (0) | 0 | 0 | (0) | 0 | 186 | (13) | 8 |
| Campbell S | 92–00 | 246 | (9) | 10 | 28 | (2) | 1 | 28 | (0) | 4 | 2 | (0) | 0 | 0 | (0) | 0 | 304 | (11) | 15 |
| Carr S | 93–03 | 222 | (4) | 7 | 16 | (1) | 0 | 23 | (0) | 1 | 4 | (0) | 0 | 0 | (0) | 0 | 265 | (5) | 8 |
| Carrick M | 04–05 | 61 | (3) | 2 | 6 | (0) | 0 | 3 | (1) | 0 | 0 | (0) | 0 | 0 | (0) | 0 | 70 | (5) | 2 |
| Caskey D | 93–95 | 20 | (12) | 4 | 5 | (1) | 0 | 3 | (1) | 1 | 0 | (0) | 0 | 0 | (0) | 0 | 29 | (14) | 5 |
| Cerny R | 04–07 | 15 | (1) | 0 | 4 | (0) | 0 | 4 | (0) | 0 | 4 | (0) | 0 | 0 | (0) | 0 | 27 | (1) | 0 |
| Chiedozie J | 84–86 | 45 | (8) | 12 | 5 | (3) | 2 | 7 | (0) | 0 | 7 | (0) | 0 | 0 | (0) | 0 | 64 | (11) | 14 |
| Chimbonda P | 06– | 64 | (1) | 3 | 6 | (0) | 0 | 8 | (0) | 1 | 19 | (0) | 0 | 0 | (0) | 0 | 97 | (1) | 4 |
| Chivers M | 67–75 | 268 | (10) | 118 | 22 | (2) | 11 | 33 | (0) | 23 | 32 | (0) | 22 | 0 | (0) | 0 | 355 | (12) | 174 |
| Claesen N | 86–87 | 37 | (13) | 18 | 1 | (5) | 2 | 7 | (0) | 3 | 0 | (0) | 0 | 0 | (0) | 0 | 45 | (18) | 23 |
| Clapham J | 1996 | 0 | (1) | 0 | 0 | (0) | 0 | 0 | (0) | 0 | 0 | (0) | 0 | 0 | (0) | 0 | 0 | (1) | 0 |
| Clarke R | 1972 | 0 | (1) | 0 | 0 | (0) | 0 | 0 | (0) | 0 | 0 | (0) | 0 | 0 | (0) | 0 | 0 | (1) | 0 |
| Clayton E | 57–67 | 88 | (4) | 20 | 9 | (0) | 0 | 1 | (0) | 0 | 1 | (0) | 0 | 0 | (0) | 0 | 99 | (4) | 20 |

| Player | Season | League App | (Sub) | Gl | FA Cup App | (Sub) | Gl | League Cup App | (Sub) | Gl | Europe App | (Sub) | Gl | Others App | (Sub) | Gl | Total App | (Sub) | Gl |
|---|---|---|---|---|---|---|---|---|---|---|---|---|---|---|---|---|---|---|---|
| Clemence R | 81–87 | 240 | (0) | 0 | 25 | (0) | 0 | 38 | (0) | 0 | 27 | (0) | 0 | 2 | (0) | 0 | 332 | (0) | 0 |
| Clemence S | 97–02 | 68 | (22) | 2 | 7 | (1) | 1 | 7 | (1) | 0 | 2 | (1) | 0 | 0 | (0) | 0 | 84 | (25) | 3 |
| Close S | 86–87 | 3 | (6) | 0 | 0 | (0) | 0 | 3 | (0) | 2 | 0 | (0) | 0 | 0 | (0) | 0 | 6 | (6) | 2 |
| Coates R | 71–77 | 173 | (15) | 14 | 11 | (1) | 0 | 19 | (3) | 1 | 26 | (0) | 9 | 0 | (0) | 0 | 229 | (19) | 24 |
| Cockram A | 1983 | 2 | (0) | 0 | 0 | (0) | 0 | 0 | (0) | 0 | 0 | (0) | 0 | 0 | (0) | 0 | 2 | (0) | 0 |
| Collins Jimmy | 1961 | 2 | (0) | 0 | 0 | (0) | 0 | 0 | (0) | 0 | 0 | (0) | 0 | 0 | (0) | 0 | 2 | (0) | 0 |
| Collins John | 65–67 | 2 | (0) | 0 | 0 | (0) | 0 | 0 | (0) | 0 | 0 | (0) | 0 | 0 | (0) | 0 | 2 | (0) | 0 |
| Collins P | 68–72 | 77 | (6) | 4 | 8 | (1) | 0 | 5 | (2) | 1 | 1 | (1) | 0 | 0 | (0) | 0 | 91 | (10) | 5 |
| Conn A | 74–76 | 35 | (3) | 6 | 2 | (0) | 0 | 1 | (2) | 1 | 0 | (0) | 0 | 0 | (0) | 0 | 38 | (5) | 7 |
| Cooke R | 82–85 | 9 | (2) | 2 | 1 | (0) | 0 | 1 | (1) | 0 | 1 | (2) | 0 | 0 | (0) | 0 | 12 | (5) | 2 |
| Corbett P | 81–82 | 3 | (2) | 1 | 0 | (0) | 0 | 0 | (0) | 0 | 0 | (0) | 0 | 0 | (0) | 0 | 3 | (2) | 1 |
| Crook I | 81–85 | 10 | (10) | 1 | 0 | (1) | 0 | 1 | (0) | 0 | 0 | (2) | 0 | 0 | (0) | 0 | 11 | (13) | 1 |
| Crooks G | 80–84 | 121 | (4) | 48 | 21 | (0) | 9 | 19 | (1) | 9 | 15 | (1) | 9 | 1 | (0) | 0 | 177 | (6) | 75 |
| Culverhouse I | 1983 | 1 | (1) | 0 | 0 | (0) | 0 | 0 | (0) | 0 | 0 | (0) | 0 | 0 | (0) | 0 | 1 | (1) | 0 |
| Cundy J | 91–95 | 23 | (3) | 1 | 0 | (0) | 0 | 2 | (0) | 0 | 0 | (0) | 0 | 0 | (0) | 0 | 25 | (3) | 1 |
| Daines B | 71–80 | 146 | (0) | 0 | 11 | (0) | 0 | 14 | (0) | 0 | 2 | (0) | 0 | 0 | (0) | 0 | 173 | (0) | 0 |
| Dalmat S | 2003 | 12 | (10) | 3 | 2 | (1) | 0 | 1 | (2) | 0 | 0 | (0) | 0 | 0 | (0) | 0 | 15 | (13) | 3 |
| Davenport C | 04–06 | 9 | (6) | 1 | 1 | (0) | 0 | 2 | (0) | 0 | 1 | (1) | 0 | 0 | (0) | 0 | 13 | (7) | 1 |
| Davids E | 05–06 | 34 | (6) | 1 | 0 | (0) | 0 | 2 | (1) | 0 | 0 | (1) | 0 | 0 | (0) | 0 | 36 | (8) | 1 |
| Davies S | 99–04 | 99 | (22) | 13 | 10 | (3) | 2 | 10 | (3) | 3 | 0 | (0) | 0 | 0 | (0) | 0 | 119 | (28) | 18 |
| Davis S | 04–05 | 11 | (4) | 0 | 0 | (0) | 0 | 1 | (1) | 0 | 0 | (0) | 0 | 0 | (0) | 0 | 12 | (5) | 0 |
| Dawson M | 04– | 99 | (2) | 2 | 10 | (0) | 0 | 8 | (1) | 0 | 15 | (1) | 1 | 0 | (0) | 0 | 132 | (4) | 3 |
| Dearden K | 90–92 | 0 | (1) | 0 | 0 | (0) | 0 | 1 | (0) | 0 | 0 | (0) | 0 | 0 | (0) | 0 | 1 | (1) | 0 |
| Defoe J | 03–07 | 88 | (51) | 43 | 8 | (5) | 5 | 10 | (5) | 10 | 4 | (6) | 6 | 0 | (0) | 0 | 110 | (67) | 64 |
| Dervite D | 06– | 0 | (0) | 0 | 0 | (0) | 0 | 1 | (0) | 0 | 0 | (0) | 0 | 0 | (0) | 0 | 1 | (0) | 0 |
| Dick A | 81–85 | 16 | (1) | 2 | 2 | (0) | 0 | 0 | (0) | 0 | 3 | (3) | 0 | 0 | (0) | 0 | 21 | (4) | 2 |
| Dillon M | 72–73 | 21 | (3) | 1 | 1 | (0) | 0 | 1 | (0) | 0 | 2 | (1) | 0 | 0 | (0) | 0 | 25 | (4) | 1 |
| Ditchburn E | 46–58 | 418 | (0) | 0 | 34 | (0) | 0 | 0 | (0) | 0 | 0 | (0) | 0 | 1 | (0) | 0 | 453 | (0) | 0 |
| Dodge W | 58–59 | 6 | (0) | 0 | 4 | (0) | 0 | 0 | (0) | 0 | 0 | (0) | 0 | 0 | (0) | 0 | 10 | (0) | 0 |
| Doherty G | 99–04 | 45 | (19) | 4 | 7 | (1) | 4 | 3 | (3) | 0 | 0 | (0) | 0 | 0 | (0) | 0 | 55 | (23) | 8 |
| Dominguez J | 97–00 | 12 | (33) | 4 | 2 | (1) | 0 | 2 | (6) | 1 | 0 | (2) | 0 | 0 | (0) | 0 | 16 | (42) | 5 |
| Dozzell J | 93–96 | 68 | (16) | 13 | 5 | (1) | 1 | 8 | (2) | 0 | 0 | (0) | 0 | 0 | (0) | 0 | 81 | (19) | 14 |
| Dumitrescu I | 94–95 | 16 | (2) | 4 | 0 | (0) | 0 | 2 | (0) | 1 | 0 | (0) | 0 | 0 | (0) | 0 | 18 | (2) | 5 |
| Duncan J | 74–78 | 101 | (2) | 53 | 7 | (0) | 2 | 10 | (0) | 7 | 0 | (0) | 0 | 0 | (0) | 0 | 118 | (2) | 62 |
| Dunmore D | 53–59 | 75 | (0) | 23 | 6 | (0) | 3 | 0 | (0) | 0 | 0 | (0) | 0 | 0 | (0) | 0 | 81 | (0) | 26 |
| Durie G | 91–93 | 58 | (0) | 11 | 2 | (0) | 0 | 10 | (0) | 3 | 8 | (0) | 3 | 0 | (0) | 0 | 78 | (0) | 17 |
| Dyson T | 54–64 | 184 | (0) | 41 | 16 | (0) | 6 | 0 | (0) | 0 | 9 | (0) | 8 | 1 | (0) | 0 | 210 | (0) | 55 |
| Edinburgh J | 90–99 | 190 | (23) | 1 | 27 | (1) | 0 | 25 | (4) | 0 | 4 | (2) | 0 | 0 | (0) | 0 | 246 | (30) | 1 |
| Edman E | 04–05 | 31 | (0) | 1 | 2 | (1) | 0 | 0 | (0) | 0 | 0 | (0) | 0 | 0 | (0) | 0 | 33 | (1) | 1 |
| England M | 66–74 | 300 | (0) | 14 | 32 | (0) | 2 | 30 | (0) | 0 | 35 | (0) | 3 | 1 | (0) | 0 | 398 | (0) | 19 |
| Etherington M | 99–02 | 20 | (25) | 1 | 1 | (1) | 1 | 3 | (1) | 0 | 0 | (0) | 0 | 0 | (0) | 0 | 24 | (27) | 2 |
| Evans R | 68–74 | 132 | (4) | 2 | 7 | (0) | 0 | 13 | (0) | 0 | 22 | (3) | 2 | 0 | (0) | 0 | 174 | (7) | 4 |
| Fairclough C | 87–88 | 60 | (0) | 5 | 3 | (0) | 0 | 7 | (0) | 0 | 0 | (0) | 0 | 0 | (0) | 0 | 70 | (0) | 5 |
| Falco M | 78–86 | 162 | (12) | 68 | 15 | (0) | 5 | 19 | (3) | 3 | 21 | (4) | 14 | 1 | (1) | 2 | 218 | (20) | 92 |
| Fenn N | 96–97 | 0 | (8) | 0 | 1 | (0) | 0 | 1 | (0) | 1 | 0 | (0) | 0 | 0 | (0) | 0 | 2 | (8) | 1 |
| Fenwick T | 87–92 | 90 | (3) | 8 | 7 | (0) | 0 | 14 | (0) | 2 | 4 | (0) | 0 | 1 | (0) | 0 | 116 | (3) | 10 |
| Ferdinand L | 97–02 | 97 | (21) | 33 | 15 | (1) | 1 | 11 | (4) | 5 | 0 | (0) | 0 | 0 | (0) | 0 | 123 | (26) | 39 |
| Fox R | 95–99 | 95 | (11) | 13 | 11 | (1) | 1 | 7 | (3) | 1 | 1 | (0) | 0 | 0 | (0) | 0 | 114 | (15) | 15 |
| Freund S | 98–02 | 92 | (10) | 0 | 11 | (0) | 0 | 14 | (0) | 0 | 4 | (0) | 0 | 0 | (0) | 0 | 121 | (10) | 0 |
| Galvin A | 78–86 | 194 | (7) | 20 | 23 | (1) | 2 | 20 | (3) | 3 | 25 | (0) | 6 | 2 | (0) | 0 | 264 | (11) | 31 |
| Gardner A | 00– | 94 | (20) | 2 | 11 | (3) | 0 | 13 | (0) | 1 | 3 | (0) | 0 | 0 | (0) | 0 | 121 | (23) | 3 |
| Garland P | 1990 | 0 | (1) | 0 | 0 | (0) | 0 | 0 | (0) | 0 | 0 | (0) | 0 | 0 | (0) | 0 | 0 | (1) | 0 |
| Gascoigne P | 88–90 | 91 | (1) | 19 | 6 | (0) | 6 | 13 | (1) | 8 | 0 | (0) | 0 | 0 | (0) | 0 | 110 | (2) | 33 |
| Ghaly H | 06– | 17 | (4) | 1 | 2 | (2) | 1 | 2 | (1) | 0 | 3 | (3) | 1 | 0 | (0) | 0 | 24 | (10) | 3 |
| Gibson T | 79–82 | 16 | (2) | 4 | 5 | (0) | 1 | 1 | (0) | 1 | 0 | (2) | 1 | 0 | (0) | 0 | 22 | (4) | 7 |
| Gilberto | 07– | 3 | (3) | 1 | 0 | (0) | 0 | 0 | (0) | 0 | 1 | (0) | 0 | 0 | (0) | 0 | 4 | (3) | 1 |
| Gilzean A | 64–73 | 335 | (8) | 93 | 40 | (0) | 21 | 27 | (1) | 6 | 27 | (1) | 13 | 1 | (0) | 0 | 430 | (10) | 133 |
| Ginola D | 97–99 | 100 | (0) | 12 | 11 | (0) | 5 | 13 | (0) | 4 | 2 | (1) | 0 | 0 | (0) | 0 | 126 | (1) | 21 |
| Gorman J | 76–78 | 30 | (0) | 0 | 2 | (0) | 0 | 0 | (0) | 0 | 0 | (0) | 0 | 0 | (0) | 0 | 32 | (0) | 0 |
| Gough R | 86–87 | 49 | (0) | 2 | 6 | (0) | 0 | 10 | (0) | 0 | 0 | (0) | 0 | 0 | (0) | 0 | 65 | (0) | 2 |
| Gower M | 1998 | 0 | (0) | 0 | 0 | (0) | 0 | 0 | (2) | 0 | 0 | (0) | 0 | 0 | (0) | 0 | 0 | (2) | 0 |
| Gray A | 91–93 | 23 | (10) | 3 | 0 | (0) | 0 | 0 | (0) | 0 | 0 | (0) | 0 | 0 | (0) | 0 | 23 | (10) | 3 |
| Gray P | 86–90 | 4 | (5) | 0 | 0 | (1) | 0 | 0 | (0) | 0 | 0 | (0) | 0 | 0 | (0) | 0 | 4 | (6) | 0 |
| Greaves J | 61–69 | 321 | (0) | 220 | 36 | (0) | 32 | 8 | (0) | 5 | 14 | (0) | 9 | 2 | (0) | 2 | 381 | (0) | 268 |
| Gunter C | 07– | 1 | (1) | 0 | 1 | (1) | 0 | 0 | (0) | 0 | 0 | (0) | 0 | 0 | (0) | 0 | 2 | (2) | 0 |

| Player | Season | League | | | FA Cup | | | League Cup | | | Europe | | | Others | | | Total | | |
|---|---|---|---|---|---|---|---|---|---|---|---|---|---|---|---|---|---|---|---|
| | | App | (Sub) | Gl | App | (Sub) | Gl | App | (Sub) | Gl | App | (Sub) | Gl | App | (Sub) | Gl | App | (Sub) | Gl |
| Hancock K | 69–70 | 3 | (0) | 0 | 0 | (0) | 0 | 1 | (0) | 0 | 0 | (0) | 0 | 0 | (0) | 0 | 4 | (0) | 0 |
| Harmer T | 51–59 | 205 | (0) | 47 | 17 | (0) | 4 | 0 | (0) | 0 | 0 | (0) | 0 | 0 | (0) | 0 | 222 | (0) | 51 |
| Hazard M | 79-85 & 93-94 | 88 | (31) | 15 | 9 | (3) | 2 | 12 | (4) | 5 | 22 | (1) | 3 | 1 | (0) | 0 | 132 | (39) | 25 |
| Hendon I | 90–91 | 0 | (4) | 0 | 0 | (0) | 0 | 1 | (0) | 0 | 0 | (2) | 0 | 0 | (0) | 0 | 1 | (6) | 0 |
| Hendry J | 90–93 | 5 | (12) | 5 | 0 | (1) | 0 | 0 | (2) | 0 | 0 | (0) | 0 | 0 | (0) | 0 | 5 | (15) | 5 |
| Henry R | 54–65 | 247 | (0) | 1 | 23 | (0) | 0 | 0 | (0) | 0 | 17 | (0) | 0 | 2 | (0) | 0 | 289 | (0) | 1 |
| Hill D | 92–94 | 4 | (6) | 0 | 0 | (0) | 0 | 0 | (2) | 0 | 0 | (0) | 0 | 0 | (0) | 0 | 4 | (8) | 0 |
| Hills J | 57–59 | 29 | (0) | 0 | 3 | (0) | 0 | 0 | (0) | 0 | 0 | (0) | 0 | 0 | (0) | 0 | 32 | (0) | 0 |
| Hoddle G | 75–86 | 370 | (7) | 88 | 47 | (1) | 11 | 44 | (0) | 10 | 17 | (4) | 1 | 2 | (0) | 0 | 480 | (12) | 110 |
| Hodge S | 86–87 | 44 | (1) | 7 | 7 | (0) | 2 | 2 | (0) | 0 | 0 | (0) | 0 | 0 | (0) | 0 | 53 | (1) | 9 |
| Hodges L | 1992 | 0 | (4) | 0 | 0 | (0) | 0 | 0 | (0) | 0 | 0 | (0) | 0 | 0 | (0) | 0 | 0 | (4) | 0 |
| Holder P | 71–73 | 9 | (4) | 1 | 0 | (0) | 0 | 0 | (0) | 0 | 0 | (6) | 1 | 0 | (0) | 0 | 9 | (10) | 2 |
| Hollowbread J | 58–63 | 67 | (0) | 0 | 6 | (0) | 0 | 0 | (0) | 0 | 0 | (0) | 0 | 0 | (0) | 0 | 73 | (0) | 0 |
| Holmes J | 76–78 | 81 | (0) | 2 | 9 | (0) | 0 | 2 | (0) | 0 | 0 | (0) | 0 | 0 | (0) | 0 | 92 | (0) | 2 |
| Hopkins M | 52–63 | 219 | (0) | 0 | 20 | (0) | 0 | 0 | (0) | 0 | 1 | (0) | 0 | 0 | (0) | 0 | 240 | (0) | 0 |
| Houghton S | 1991 | 0 | (10) | 2 | 0 | (0) | 0 | 0 | (2) | 0 | 0 | (2) | 0 | 0 | (0) | 0 | 0 | (14) | 2 |
| Howells D | 85–97 | 238 | (39) | 22 | 18 | (4) | 1 | 26 | (5) | 4 | 6 | (0) | 0 | 1 | (0) | 0 | 289 | (48) | 27 |
| Hoy R | 65–67 | 10 | (0) | 0 | 0 | (0) | 0 | 0 | (0) | 0 | 2 | (0) | 0 | 0 | (0) | 0 | 12 | (0) | 0 |
| Huddlestone T | 05– | 33 | (20) | 4 | 3 | (2) | 0 | 5 | (4) | 3 | 11 | (4) | 0 | 0 | (0) | 0 | 52 | (30) | 7 |
| Hughton C | 79–89 | 293 | (4) | 12 | 34 | (2) | 1 | 33 | (2) | 2 | 29 | (1) | 4 | 2 | (0) | 0 | 391 | (9) | 19 |
| Hutton A | 07– | 14 | (0) | 0 | 0 | (0) | 0 | 1 | (0) | 0 | 0 | (0) | 0 | 0 | (0) | 0 | 15 | (0) | 0 |
| Ifil P | 04–06 | 3 | (0) | 0 | 0 | (0) | 0 | 1 | (1) | 0 | 0 | (0) | 0 | 0 | (0) | 0 | 4 | (1) | 0 |
| Iley J | 57–58 | 53 | (0) | 1 | 4 | (0) | 0 | 0 | (0) | 0 | 0 | (0) | 0 | 0 | (0) | 0 | 57 | (0) | 1 |
| Ireland J | 57–58 | 3 | (0) | 0 | 0 | (0) | 0 | 0 | (0) | 0 | 0 | (0) | 0 | 0 | (0) | 0 | 3 | (0) | 0 |
| Iversen S | 96–02 | 112 | (31) | 36 | 10 | (5) | 4 | 11 | (4) | 6 | 4 | (0) | 1 | 0 | (0) | 0 | 137 | (40) | 47 |
| Jackson J | 03–05 | 12 | (8) | 1 | 1 | (2) | 0 | 1 | (0) | 0 | 0 | (0) | 0 | 0 | (0) | 0 | 14 | (10) | 1 |
| Jenas J | 05– | 82 | (2) | 16 | 6 | (0) | 2 | 8 | (0) | 2 | 12 | (1) | 1 | 0 | (0) | 0 | 108 | (3) | 21 |
| Jenkins D | 68–69 | 11 | (3) | 2 | 2 | (1) | 0 | 0 | (0) | 0 | 0 | (0) | 0 | 0 | (0) | 0 | 13 | (4) | 2 |
| Jennings P | 64–76 | 472 | (0) | 0 | 43 | (0) | 0 | 39 | (0) | 0 | 36 | (0) | 0 | 1 | (0) | 1 | 591 | (0) | 1 |
| Johnson N | 65–70 | 27 | (7) | 5 | 4 | (0) | 1 | 0 | (0) | 0 | 0 | (0) | 0 | 0 | (0) | 0 | 31 | (7) | 6 |
| Jones Chris | 74–81 | 149 | (15) | 37 | 10 | (2) | 4 | 7 | (1) | 1 | 0 | (1) | 0 | 0 | (0) | 0 | 166 | (19) | 42 |
| Jones Cliff | 57–68 | 314 | (4) | 135 | 35 | (4) | 16 | 2 | (0) | 1 | 19 | (0) | 7 | 2 | (0) | 0 | 372 | (8) | 159 |
| Kaboul Y | 07– | 19 | (2) | 3 | 1 | (0) | 0 | 3 | (1) | 0 | 3 | (0) | 1 | 0 | (0) | 0 | 26 | (3) | 4 |
| Kanoute F | 03–05 | 41 | (19) | 14 | 6 | (0) | 3 | 5 | (2) | 4 | 0 | (0) | 0 | 0 | (0) | 0 | 52 | (21) | 21 |
| Keane R | 02– | 158 | (39) | 80 | 15 | (4) | 11 | 14 | (5) | 7 | 15 | (4) | 9 | 0 | (0) | 0 | 202 | (52) | 107 |
| Keeley A | 1976 | 5 | (1) | 0 | 0 | (0) | 0 | 0 | (0) | 0 | 0 | (0) | 0 | 0 | (0) | 0 | 5 | (1) | 0 |
| Keller K | 01–04 | 85 | (0) | 0 | 4 | (0) | 0 | 10 | (0) | 0 | 0 | (0) | 0 | 0 | (0) | 0 | 99 | (0) | 0 |
| Kelly S | 03–05 | 29 | (8) | 2 | 6 | (0) | 0 | 1 | (0) | 0 | 0 | (0) | 0 | 0 | (0) | 0 | 36 | (8) | 2 |
| Kendall M | 78–80 | 29 | (0) | 0 | 6 | (0) | 0 | 1 | (0) | 0 | 0 | (0) | 0 | 0 | (0) | 0 | 36 | (0) | 0 |
| Kerslake D | 93–95 | 34 | (3) | 0 | 1 | (1) | 0 | 5 | (0) | 0 | 0 | (0) | 0 | 0 | (0) | 0 | 40 | (4) | 0 |
| King L | 98– | 194 | (3) | 7 | 17 | (1) | 3 | 18 | (0) | 1 | 8 | (0) | 0 | 0 | (0) | 0 | 237 | (4) | 11 |
| Kinnear J | 65–75 | 189 | (7) | 2 | 24 | (0) | 0 | 20 | (0) | 0 | 18 | (0) | 0 | 1 | (0) | 0 | 252 | (7) | 2 |
| Klinsmann J | 1994 & 1997 | 56 | (0) | 29 | 9 | (0) | 5 | 3 | (0) | 4 | 0 | (0) | 0 | 0 | (0) | 0 | 68 | (0) | 38 |
| Knowles C | 64–75 | 400 | (1) | 15 | 42 | (0) | 1 | 32 | (1) | 0 | 30 | (0) | 1 | 1 | (0) | 0 | 505 | (2) | 17 |
| Konchesky P | 2003 | 10 | (2) | 0 | 0 | (0) | 0 | 2 | (1) | 0 | 0 | (0) | 0 | 0 | (0) | 0 | 12 | (3) | 0 |
| Korsten W | 99–00 | 12 | (11) | 3 | 0 | (3) | 0 | 1 | (0) | 0 | 0 | (0) | 0 | 0 | (0) | 0 | 13 | (14) | 3 |
| Lacy J | 78–82 | 99 | (5) | 2 | 12 | (0) | 0 | 11 | (0) | 1 | 4 | (1) | 0 | 1 | (0) | 0 | 127 | (6) | 3 |
| Lee C | 77–79 | 57 | (5) | 18 | 6 | (1) | 3 | 2 | (0) | 0 | 0 | (0) | 0 | 0 | (0) | 0 | 65 | (6) | 21 |
| Lee T | 1973 | 1 | (0) | 0 | 0 | (0) | 0 | 0 | (0) | 0 | 0 | (0) | 0 | 0 | (0) | 0 | 1 | (0) | 0 |
| Lee Y-P | 05– | 68 | (2) | 0 | 7 | (0) | 0 | 6 | (0) | 0 | 10 | (0) | 0 | 0 | (0) | 0 | 91 | (2) | 0 |
| Leonhardsen O | 99–01 | 46 | (8) | 7 | 3 | (3) | 1 | 6 | (2) | 2 | 4 | (0) | 1 | 0 | (0) | 0 | 59 | (13) | 11 |
| Lennon A | 05– | 68 | (14) | 7 | 8 | (2) | 1 | 7 | (3) | 1 | 15 | (2) | 1 | 0 | (0) | 0 | 98 | (21) | 10 |
| Leworthy D | 84–85 | 8 | (3) | 3 | 0 | (0) | 0 | 0 | (1) | 1 | 0 | (0) | 0 | 0 | (0) | 0 | 8 | (4) | 4 |
| Lineker G | 89–91 | 105 | (0) | 67 | 9 | (0) | 3 | 16 | (0) | 8 | 8 | (0) | 2 | 1 | (0) | 0 | 139 | (0) | 80 |
| Low R | 64–66 | 6 | (2) | 1 | 0 | (0) | 0 | 0 | (0) | 0 | 0 | (0) | 0 | 0 | (0) | 0 | 6 | (2) | 1 |
| Mabbutt G | 82–97 | 458 | (19) | 27 | 45 | (2) | 5 | 60 | (2) | 2 | 22 | (3) | 4 | 2 | (0) | 0 | 587 | (26) | 38 |
| Mabizela M | 03–04 | 1 | (6) | 1 | 0 | (0) | 0 | 1 | (1) | 0 | 0 | (0) | 0 | 0 | (0) | 0 | 2 | (7) | 1 |
| McAllister D | 74–80 | 168 | (4) | 9 | 16 | (1) | 0 | 13 | (0) | 1 | 0 | (0) | 0 | 0 | (0) | 0 | 197 | (5) | 10 |
| McDonald D | 1992 | 2 | (0) | 0 | 0 | (0) | 0 | 0 | (0) | 0 | 0 | (0) | 0 | 0 | (0) | 0 | 2 | (0) | 0 |
| McEwen D | 99–00 | 0 | (4) | 0 | 0 | (0) | 0 | 0 | (0) | 0 | 0 | (0) | 0 | 0 | (0) | 0 | 0 | (4) | 0 |
| McGrath C | 73–75 | 30 | (8) | 5 | 0 | (0) | 0 | 1 | (0) | 0 | 7 | (1) | 5 | 0 | (0) | 0 | 38 | (9) | 10 |
| Mackay D | 58–67 | 268 | (0) | 42 | 33 | (0) | 4 | 0 | (0) | 0 | 7 | (0) | 5 | 3 | (0) | 0 | 321 | (0) | 51 |
| McMahon G | 94–95 | 9 | (7) | 0 | 0 | (1) | 0 | 3 | (0) | 0 | 0 | (0) | 0 | 0 | (0) | 0 | 12 | (8) | 0 |
| McNab N | 73–78 | 63 | (9) | 3 | 2 | (0) | 0 | 5 | (1) | 0 | 0 | (0) | 0 | 0 | (0) | 0 | 70 | (10) | 3 |
| McVeigh P | 1996 | 2 | (1) | 1 | 0 | (0) | 0 | 0 | (0) | 0 | 0 | (0) | 0 | 0 | (0) | 0 | 2 | (1) | 1 |

| Player | Season | League App | (Sub) | Gl | FA Cup App | (Sub) | Gl | League Cup App | (Sub) | Gl | Europe App | (Sub) | Gl | Others App | (Sub) | Gl | Total App | (Sub) | Gl |
|---|---|---|---|---|---|---|---|---|---|---|---|---|---|---|---|---|---|---|---|
| Mahorn P | 93–97 | 3 | (0) | 0 | 0 | (1) | 0 | 0 | (1) | 1 | 0 | (0) | 0 | 0 | (0) | 0 | 3 | (2) | 1 |
| Malbranque S | 06– | 53 | (9) | 6 | 7 | (2) | 1 | 9 | (0) | 2 | 13 | (3) | 3 | 0 | (0) | 0 | 82 | (14) | 12 |
| Marchi A | 49-56 & 59-64 | 232 | (0) | 7 | 16 | (0) | 0 | 0 | (0) | 0 | 12 | (0) | 0 | 0 | (0) | 0 | 260 | (0) | 7 |
| Marney D | 03–04 | 4 | (4) | 2 | 0 | (3) | 0 | 0 | (0) | 0 | 0 | (0) | 0 | 0 | (0) | 0 | 4 | (7) | 2 |
| Mazzon G | 80–82 | 3 | (1) | 0 | 1 | (0) | 0 | 0 | (2) | 0 | 0 | (0) | 0 | 0 | (0) | 0 | 4 | (3) | 0 |
| Medwin T | 56–62 | 197 | (0) | 65 | 13 | (0) | 7 | 0 | (0) | 0 | 5 | (0) | 0 | 1 | (0) | 1 | 216 | (0) | 73 |
| Mendes P | 04–05 | 25 | (5) | 1 | 2 | (0) | 0 | 2 | (2) | 0 | 0 | (0) | 0 | 0 | (0) | 0 | 29 | (7) | 1 |
| Metgod J | 1987 | 5 | (7) | 0 | 0 | (0) | 0 | 2 | (0) | 0 | 0 | (0) | 0 | 0 | (0) | 0 | 7 | (7) | 0 |
| Mido | 04–05 & 2006 | 35 | (13) | 14 | 2 | (3) | 2 | 2 | (2) | 3 | 2 | (2) | 0 | 0 | (0) | 0 | 41 | (20) | 19 |
| Miller P | 78–86 | 206 | (2) | 7 | 30 | (1) | 1 | 22 | (1) | 0 | 23 | (0) | 2 | 2 | (0) | 0 | 283 | (4) | 10 |
| Mimms R | 87–89 | 37 | (0) | 0 | 2 | (0) | 0 | 5 | (0) | 0 | 0 | (0) | 0 | 0 | (0) | 0 | 44 | (0) | 0 |
| Minton J | 91–92 | 2 | (0) | 1 | 0 | (0) | 0 | 0 | (1) | 0 | 0 | (0) | 0 | 0 | (0) | 0 | 2 | (1) | 1 |
| Moncur J | 86–91 | 10 | (11) | 1 | 0 | (0) | 0 | 1 | (2) | 0 | 0 | (0) | 0 | 0 | (0) | 0 | 11 | (13) | 1 |
| Moores I | 76–78 | 25 | (4) | 6 | 0 | (0) | 0 | 3 | (0) | 2 | 0 | (0) | 0 | 0 | (0) | 0 | 28 | (4) | 8 |
| Moran P | 86–93 | 14 | (22) | 2 | 3 | (1) | 0 | 1 | (6) | 0 | 0 | (1) | 0 | 0 | (0) | 0 | 18 | (30) | 2 |
| Morgan R | 68–71 | 66 | (2) | 8 | 6 | (0) | 2 | 3 | (0) | 1 | 2 | (1) | 1 | 0 | (0) | 0 | 77 | (3) | 12 |
| Mullery A | 63–71 | 312 | (0) | 25 | 33 | (0) | 1 | 18 | (0) | 0 | 10 | (0) | 4 | 1 | (0) | 0 | 374 | (0) | 30 |
| Murphy D | 05–06 | 7 | (15) | 1 | 1 | (0) | 0 | 3 | (0) | 0 | 2 | (1) | 0 | 0 | (0) | 0 | 13 | (16) | 1 |
| Naybet N | 04–05 | 29 | (1) | 1 | 2 | (0) | 0 | 3 | (0) | 0 | 0 | (0) | 0 | 0 | (0) | 0 | 34 | (1) | 1 |
| Nayim | 88–92 | 95 | (17) | 11 | 6 | (3) | 4 | 11 | (6) | 3 | 6 | (0) | 0 | 1 | (0) | 0 | 119 | (26) | 18 |
| Naylor T | 69–79 | 237 | (6) | 0 | 17 | (1) | 0 | 23 | (1) | 1 | 13 | (6) | 0 | 0 | (0) | 0 | 290 | (14) | 1 |
| Neighbour J | 70–76 | 104 | (15) | 8 | 10 | (1) | 1 | 14 | (3) | 1 | 6 | (3) | 1 | 0 | (0) | 0 | 134 | (22) | 11 |
| Nethercott S | 92–96 | 31 | (23) | 0 | 5 | (3) | 1 | 0 | (0) | 0 | 0 | (0) | 0 | 0 | (0) | 0 | 36 | (26) | 1 |
| Nielsen A | 96–99 | 78 | (18) | 12 | 5 | (2) | 3 | 10 | (1) | 3 | 1 | (0) | 0 | 0 | (0) | 0 | 94 | (21) | 18 |
| Nilsen R | 1998 | 3 | (0) | 0 | 0 | (0) | 0 | 0 | (0) | 0 | 0 | (0) | 0 | 0 | (0) | 0 | 3 | (0) | 0 |
| Norman M | 55–65 | 357 | (0) | 16 | 37 | (0) | 2 | 0 | (0) | 0 | 17 | (0) | 1 | 2 | (0) | 0 | 413 | (0) | 19 |
| O'Hara J | 07– | 9 | (8) | 1 | 1 | (1) | 0 | 1 | (1) | 0 | 1 | (3) | 1 | 0 | (0) | 0 | 12 | (13) | 2 |
| O'Reilly G | 80–83 | 39 | (6) | 0 | 2 | (0) | 0 | 4 | (0) | 0 | 2 | (2) | 0 | 1 | (0) | 0 | 48 | (8) | 0 |
| Osgood K | 73–77 | 112 | (1) | 13 | 3 | (0) | 0 | 11 | (0) | 1 | 0 | (0) | 0 | 0 | (0) | 0 | 126 | (1) | 14 |
| O'Shea T | 86–87 | 1 | (2) | 0 | 0 | (0) | 0 | 0 | (0) | 0 | 0 | (0) | 0 | 0 | (0) | 0 | 1 | (2) | 0 |
| Pamarot N | 04–05 | 23 | (2) | 1 | 2 | (0) | 1 | 3 | (0) | 0 | 0 | (0) | 0 | 0 | (0) | 0 | 28 | (2) | 2 |
| Parks R | 81–87 | 37 | (0) | 0 | 5 | (0) | 0 | 1 | (0) | 0 | 5 | (1) | 0 | 0 | (0) | 0 | 48 | (1) | 0 |
| Pearce J | 68–72 | 108 | (33) | 21 | 4 | (6) | 3 | 21 | (6) | 7 | 8 | (7) | 4 | 0 | (0) | 0 | 141 | (52) | 35 |
| Perry C | 99–02 | 111 | (9) | 3 | 9 | (0) | 0 | 13 | (0) | 0 | 4 | (0) | 1 | 0 | (0) | 0 | 137 | (9) | 4 |
| Perryman S | 69–85 | 653 | (2) | 31 | 69 | (0) | 2 | 66 | (0) | 3 | 63 | (1) | 3 | 1 | (1) | 0 | 852 | (4) | 39 |
| Peters M | 69–74 | 189 | (0) | 46 | 16 | (0) | 5 | 23 | (0) | 12 | 32 | (0) | 13 | 0 | (0) | 0 | 260 | (0) | 76 |
| Piercy J | 99–00 | 1 | (7) | 0 | 0 | (0) | 0 | 1 | (0) | 0 | 0 | (0) | 0 | 0 | (0) | 0 | 2 | (7) | 0 |
| Piper R | 1962 | 1 | (0) | 0 | 0 | (0) | 0 | 0 | (0) | 0 | 0 | (0) | 0 | 0 | (0) | 0 | 1 | (0) | 0 |
| Pitt S | 1965 | 1 | (0) | 0 | 0 | (0) | 0 | 0 | (0) | 0 | 0 | (0) | 0 | 0 | (0) | 0 | 1 | (0) | 0 |
| Polston A | 1989 | 0 | (1) | 0 | 0 | (0) | 0 | 0 | (0) | 0 | 0 | (0) | 0 | 0 | (0) | 0 | 0 | (1) | 0 |
| Polston J | 86–89 | 17 | (7) | 1 | 0 | (0) | 0 | 3 | (1) | 0 | 0 | (0) | 0 | 0 | (0) | 0 | 20 | (8) | 1 |
| Popescu G | 1994 | 23 | (0) | 3 | 3 | (0) | 0 | 2 | (0) | 0 | 0 | (0) | 0 | 0 | (0) | 0 | 28 | (0) | 3 |
| Possee D | 63–65 | 19 | (0) | 4 | 0 | (0) | 0 | 0 | (0) | 0 | 0 | (0) | 0 | 0 | (0) | 0 | 19 | (0) | 4 |
| Postiga H | 2003 | 9 | (10) | 1 | 2 | (0) | 0 | 1 | (2) | 1 | 0 | (0) | 0 | 0 | (0) | 0 | 12 | (12) | 2 |
| Poyet G | 01–03 | 66 | (16) | 18 | 6 | (1) | 3 | 8 | (1) | 2 | 0 | (0) | 0 | 0 | (0) | 0 | 80 | (18) | 23 |
| Pratt J | 68–79 | 307 | (24) | 39 | 23 | (5) | 2 | 27 | (4) | 7 | 24 | (1) | 1 | 0 | (0) | 0 | 381 | (34) | 49 |
| Price P | 81–83 | 35 | (4) | 0 | 6 | (0) | 0 | 7 | (0) | 0 | 10 | (0) | 0 | 0 | (0) | 0 | 58 | (4) | 0 |
| Rasiak G | 2005 | 4 | (4) | 0 | 1 | (0) | 0 | 0 | (0) | 0 | 0 | (0) | 0 | 0 | (0) | 0 | 5 | (4) | 0 |
| Rebrov S | 00–01 | 37 | (22) | 10 | 7 | (1) | 3 | 4 | (4) | 3 | 0 | (0) | 0 | 0 | (0) | 0 | 48 | (27) | 16 |
| Redknapp J | 02–04 | 37 | (11) | 4 | 0 | (0) | 0 | 1 | (0) | 0 | 0 | (0) | 0 | 0 | (0) | 0 | 38 | (11) | 4 |
| Reid A | 04–05 | 20 | (6) | 1 | 0 | (0) | 0 | 1 | (0) | 0 | 0 | (0) | 0 | 0 | (0) | 0 | 21 | (6) | 1 |
| Richards D | 01–03 | 73 | (0) | 4 | 5 | (0) | 0 | 3 | (0) | 0 | 0 | (0) | 0 | 0 | (0) | 0 | 81 | (0) | 4 |
| Ricketts R | 03–04 | 17 | (13) | 1 | 0 | (0) | 0 | 4 | (2) | 1 | 0 | (0) | 0 | 0 | (0) | 0 | 21 | (15) | 2 |
| Robb G | 51–58 | 182 | (0) | 53 | 18 | (0) | 5 | 0 | (0) | 0 | 0 | (0) | 0 | 0 | (0) | 0 | 200 | (0) | 58 |
| Roberts G | 80–86 | 200 | (9) | 23 | 27 | (0) | 2 | 24 | (1) | 5 | 25 | (1) | 6 | 1 | (0) | 0 | 277 | (11) | 36 |
| Robertson J | 63–68 | 153 | (4) | 25 | 18 | (0) | 3 | 2 | (0) | 0 | 4 | (0) | 3 | 1 | (0) | 1 | 178 | (4) | 32 |
| Robinson M | 75–77 | 5 | (1) | 2 | 0 | (0) | 0 | 0 | (0) | 0 | 0 | (0) | 0 | 0 | (0) | 0 | 5 | (1) | 2 |
| Robinson P | 04– | 137 | (0) | 1 | 12 | (0) | 0 | 10 | (0) | 0 | 16 | (0) | 0 | 0 | (0) | 0 | 175 | (0) | 1 |
| Robinson S | 1993 | 1 | (1) | 0 | 0 | (0) | 0 | 0 | (0) | 0 | 0 | (0) | 0 | 0 | (0) | 0 | 1 | (1) | 0 |
| Robson M | 88–89 | 3 | (5) | 0 | 0 | (0) | 0 | 1 | (0) | 0 | 0 | (0) | 0 | 0 | (0) | 0 | 4 | (5) | 0 |
| Rocha R | 06– | 13 | (1) | 0 | 3 | (0) | 0 | 0 | (1) | 0 | 0 | (0) | 0 | 0 | (0) | 0 | 16 | (2) | 0 |
| Rosenthal R | 93–96 | 55 | (33) | 4 | 7 | (2) | 6 | 3 | (0) | 1 | 0 | (0) | 0 | 0 | (0) | 0 | 65 | (35) | 11 |
| Routledge W | 05–07 | 3 | (2) | 0 | 0 | (0) | 0 | 0 | (0) | 0 | 0 | (0) | 0 | 0 | (0) | 0 | 3 | (2) | 0 |
| Ruddock N | 86–87 & 1992 | 45 | (2) | 3 | 6 | (1) | 1 | 4 | (0) | 0 | 0 | (0) | 0 | 0 | (0) | 0 | 55 | (3) | 4 |
| Ryden J | 55–58 | 63 | (0) | 2 | 5 | (0) | 0 | 0 | (0) | 0 | 0 | (0) | 0 | 0 | (0) | 0 | 68 | (0) | 2 |

| Player | Season | League | | | FA Cup | | | League Cup | | | Europe | | | Others | | | Total | | |
|---|---|---|---|---|---|---|---|---|---|---|---|---|---|---|---|---|---|---|---|
| | | App | (Sub) | Gl | App | (Sub) | Gl | App | (Sub) | Gl | App | (Sub) | Gl | App | (Sub) | Gl | App | (Sub) | Gl |
| Saib M | 97–98 | 3 | (10) | 1 | 0 | (0) | 0 | 0 | (0) | 0 | 0 | (0) | 0 | 0 | (0) | 0 | 3 | (10) | 1 |
| Samways V | 86–93 | 165 | (28) | 11 | 14 | (1) | 2 | 27 | (4) | 4 | 6 | (0) | 1 | 1 | (0) | 0 | 213 | (33) | 18 |
| Saul F | 60–67 | 112 | (4) | 37 | 7 | (0) | 6 | 1 | (0) | 0 | 5 | (0) | 2 | 1 | (0) | 1 | 126 | (4) | 46 |
| Scales J | 96–99 | 29 | (4) | 0 | 0 | (0) | 0 | 4 | (0) | 1 | 0 | (0) | 0 | 0 | (0) | 0 | 33 | (4) | 1 |
| Scott K | 93–95 | 16 | (2) | 1 | 0 | (0) | 0 | 0 | (1) | 0 | 0 | (0) | 0 | 0 | (0) | 0 | 16 | (3) | 1 |
| Sedgley S | 89–93 | 147 | (17) | 8 | 11 | (1) | 1 | 24 | (3) | 1 | 4 | (3) | 0 | 1 | (0) | 0 | 187 | (24) | 10 |
| Segers H | 1998 | 1 | (0) | 0 | 0 | (0) | 0 | 1 | (0) | 0 | 0 | (0) | 0 | 0 | (0) | 0 | 2 | (0) | 0 |
| Sharpe F | 1958 | 2 | (0) | 1 | 0 | (0) | 0 | 0 | (0) | 0 | 0 | (0) | 0 | 0 | (0) | 0 | 2 | (0) | 1 |
| Sheringham E | 92–96 & 01–02 | 230 | (6) | 98 | 20 | (0) | 14 | 20 | (1) | 13 | 0 | (0) | 0 | 0 | (0) | 0 | 270 | (7) | 125 |
| Sherwood T | 98–01 | 81 | (12) | 12 | 13 | (0) | 1 | 6 | (3) | 2 | 3 | (0) | 1 | 0 | (0) | 0 | 103 | (15) | 16 |
| Sinton A | 95–98 | 66 | (17) | 6 | 4 | (4) | 1 | 6 | (3) | 0 | 0 | (0) | 0 | 0 | (0) | 0 | 76 | (24) | 7 |
| Slabber J | 2002 | 0 | (1) | 0 | 0 | (0) | 0 | 0 | (0) | 0 | 0 | (0) | 0 | 0 | (0) | 0 | 0 | (1) | 0 |
| Slade S | 1995 | 1 | (4) | 0 | 0 | (2) | 0 | 0 | (1) | 0 | 0 | (0) | 0 | 0 | (0) | 0 | 1 | (7) | 0 |
| Smith G | 78–81 | 34 | (4) | 1 | 0 | (0) | 0 | 6 | (0) | 0 | 0 | (1) | 0 | 0 | (0) | 0 | 40 | (5) | 1 |
| Smith I | 1975 | 2 | (0) | 0 | 0 | (0) | 0 | 0 | (0) | 0 | 0 | (0) | 0 | 0 | (0) | 0 | 2 | (0) | 0 |
| Smith J | 59–63 | 21 | (0) | 1 | 2 | (0) | 0 | 0 | (0) | 0 | 1 | (0) | 0 | 0 | (0) | 0 | 24 | (0) | 1 |
| Smith R | 55–63 | 271 | (0) | 176 | 32 | (0) | 22 | 0 | (0) | 0 | 14 | (0) | 10 | 2 | (0) | 2 | 319 | (0) | 210 |
| Souness G | 1971 | 0 | (0) | 0 | 0 | (0) | 0 | 0 | (0) | 0 | 0 | (1) | 0 | 0 | (0) | 0 | 0 | (1) | 0 |
| Southey P | 1979 | 1 | (0) | 0 | 0 | (0) | 0 | 0 | (0) | 0 | 0 | (0) | 0 | 0 | (0) | 0 | 1 | (0) | 0 |
| Stalteri P | 05– | 37 | (5) | 2 | 3 | (2) | 1 | 3 | (0) | 0 | 4 | (2) | 0 | 0 | (0) | 0 | 47 | (9) | 3 |
| Statham B | 87–88 | 20 | (4) | 0 | 0 | (1) | 0 | 2 | (0) | 0 | 0 | (0) | 0 | 0 | (0) | 0 | 22 | (5) | 0 |
| Stead M | 75–77 | 14 | (1) | 0 | 0 | (0) | 0 | 0 | (0) | 0 | 0 | (0) | 0 | 0 | (0) | 0 | 14 | (1) | 0 |
| Stevens G | 83–89 | 140 | (7) | 6 | 13 | (4) | 0 | 19 | (2) | 0 | 15 | (0) | 3 | 0 | (0) | 0 | 187 | (13) | 9 |
| Stewart P | 88–91 | 126 | (5) | 28 | 9 | (0) | 2 | 23 | (0) | 7 | 8 | (0) | 0 | 1 | (0) | 0 | 167 | (5) | 37 |
| Stimson M | 86–88 | 1 | (1) | 0 | 0 | (0) | 0 | 0 | (0) | 0 | 0 | (0) | 0 | 0 | (0) | 0 | 1 | (1) | 0 |
| Stokes A | 52–58 | 65 | (0) | 40 | 4 | (0) | 2 | 0 | (0) | 0 | 0 | (0) | 0 | 0 | (0) | 0 | 69 | (0) | 42 |
| Sullivan N | 00–01 | 64 | (0) | 0 | 9 | (0) | 0 | 8 | (0) | 0 | 0 | (0) | 0 | 0 | (0) | 0 | 81 | (0) | 0 |
| Taarabt A | 06– | 0 | (8) | 0 | 0 | (1) | 0 | 0 | (0) | 0 | 0 | (3) | 0 | 0 | (0) | 0 | 0 | (12) | 0 |
| Tainio T | 05– | 48 | (13) | 3 | 5 | (2) | 0 | 3 | (3) | 0 | 7 | (2) | 0 | 0 | (0) | 0 | 63 | (20) | 3 |
| Taricco M | 98–03 | 125 | (5) | 2 | 9 | (2) | 0 | 12 | (0) | 0 | 3 | (0) | 0 | 0 | (0) | 0 | 149 | (7) | 2 |
| Taylor P | 76–80 | 116 | (7) | 31 | 8 | (3) | 2 | 4 | (2) | 0 | 0 | (0) | 0 | 0 | (0) | 0 | 128 | (12) | 33 |
| Thatcher B | 00–02 | 29 | (7) | 0 | 3 | (0) | 0 | 6 | (1) | 0 | 0 | (0) | 0 | 0 | (0) | 0 | 38 | (8) | 0 |
| Thelwell A | 00–01 | 13 | (5) | 0 | 0 | (3) | 0 | 0 | (0) | 0 | 0 | (0) | 0 | 0 | (0) | 0 | 13 | (8) | 0 |
| Thomas D | 83–86 | 80 | (7) | 1 | 4 | (0) | 0 | 11 | (2) | 0 | 8 | (4) | 0 | 0 | (0) | 0 | 103 | (13) | 1 |
| Thomas M | 86–90 | 136 | (21) | 6 | 12 | (0) | 1 | 28 | (1) | 1 | 0 | (0) | 0 | 0 | (0) | 0 | 176 | (22) | 8 |
| Thorstvedt E | 88–94 | 171 | (2) | 0 | 14 | (0) | 0 | 25 | (0) | 0 | 6 | (0) | 0 | 1 | (0) | 0 | 217 | (2) | 0 |
| Toda K | 2002 | 2 | (2) | 0 | 0 | (0) | 0 | 0 | (0) | 0 | 0 | (0) | 0 | 0 | (0) | 0 | 2 | (2) | 0 |
| Tramezzani P | 1998 | 6 | (0) | 0 | 0 | (0) | 0 | 1 | (0) | 0 | 0 | (0) | 0 | 0 | (0) | 0 | 7 | (0) | 0 |
| Turner A | 92–94 | 8 | (12) | 3 | 0 | (1) | 0 | 0 | (2) | 1 | 0 | (0) | 0 | 0 | (0) | 0 | 8 | (15) | 4 |
| Tuttle D | 90–92 | 10 | (3) | 0 | 0 | (0) | 0 | 3 | (1) | 0 | 1 | (0) | 1 | 0 | (0) | 0 | 14 | (4) | 1 |
| Van den Hauwe P | 89–92 | 110 | (6) | 0 | 7 | (0) | 0 | 16 | (0) | 0 | 6 | (0) | 0 | 1 | (0) | 0 | 140 | (6) | 0 |
| Vega R | 96–00 | 53 | (11) | 7 | 8 | (1) | 0 | 9 | (2) | 1 | 0 | (0) | 0 | 0 | (0) | 0 | 70 | (14) | 8 |
| Venables T | 65–68 | 114 | (1) | 5 | 15 | (1) | 2 | 6 | (0) | 1 | 4 | (0) | 1 | 1 | (0) | 0 | 140 | (2) | 9 |
| Villa R | 78–82 | 124 | (9) | 18 | 21 | (0) | 3 | 15 | (1) | 3 | 8 | (1) | 1 | 1 | (0) | 0 | 169 | (11) | 25 |
| Waddle C | 85–88 | 137 | (1) | 33 | 14 | (0) | 5 | 21 | (0) | 4 | 0 | (0) | 0 | 0 | (0) | 0 | 172 | (1) | 42 |
| Walford S | 1975 | 1 | (1) | 0 | 0 | (0) | 0 | 0 | (0) | 0 | 0 | (0) | 0 | 0 | (0) | 0 | 1 | (1) | 0 |
| Walker I | 90–00 | 257 | (2) | 0 | 25 | (0) | 0 | 22 | (1) | 0 | 4 | (0) | 0 | 0 | (0) | 0 | 308 | (3) | 0 |
| Walsh P | 87–91 | 84 | (44) | 19 | 4 | (4) | 0 | 9 | (7) | 2 | 1 | (3) | 1 | 0 | (0) | 0 | 98 | (58) | 21 |
| Want A | 67–71 | 46 | (4) | 0 | 3 | (0) | 0 | 3 | (0) | 0 | 0 | (0) | 0 | 0 | (0) | 0 | 52 | (4) | 0 |
| Watson K | 1992 | 4 | (1) | 1 | 0 | (1) | 0 | 1 | (1) | 1 | 0 | (0) | 0 | 0 | (0) | 0 | 5 | (3) | 2 |
| Webster S | 82–83 | 2 | (1) | 0 | 0 | (0) | 0 | 0 | (0) | 0 | 0 | (0) | 0 | 0 | (0) | 0 | 2 | (1) | 0 |
| Weller K | 64–66 | 19 | (2) | 1 | 0 | (0) | 0 | 0 | (0) | 0 | 0 | (0) | 0 | 0 | (0) | 0 | 19 | (2) | 1 |
| White J | 59–63 | 183 | (0) | 40 | 19 | (0) | 1 | 0 | (0) | 0 | 17 | (0) | 6 | 2 | (0) | 1 | 221 | (0) | 48 |
| Wilson C | 95–97 | 67 | (3) | 1 | 7 | (1) | 1 | 4 | (0) | 0 | 0 | (0) | 0 | 0 | (0) | 0 | 78 | (4) | 2 |
| Woodgate J | 07– | 12 | (0) | 1 | 0 | (0) | 0 | 1 | (0) | 1 | 4 | (0) | 0 | 0 | (0) | 0 | 17 | (0) | 2 |
| Woolcott R | 1969 | 1 | (0) | 0 | 0 | (0) | 0 | 0 | (0) | 0 | 0 | (0) | 0 | 0 | (0) | 0 | 1 | (0) | 0 |
| Worley L | 1959 | 1 | (0) | 0 | 0 | (0) | 0 | 0 | (0) | 0 | 0 | (0) | 0 | 0 | (0) | 0 | 1 | (0) | 0 |
| Yeates M | 03–04 | 1 | (2) | 0 | 0 | (1) | 0 | 0 | (0) | 0 | 0 | (0) | 0 | 0 | (0) | 0 | 1 | (3) | 0 |
| Yorath T | 79–80 | 44 | (4) | 1 | 7 | (0) | 0 | 7 | (0) | 0 | 0 | (0) | 0 | 0 | (0) | 0 | 58 | (4) | 1 |
| Young L | 98–00 | 44 | (14) | 0 | 9 | (2) | 0 | 1 | (3) | 0 | 2 | (1) | 0 | 0 | (0) | 0 | 56 | (20) | 0 |
| Young W | 75–76 | 54 | (0) | 3 | 2 | (0) | 0 | 8 | (0) | 1 | 0 | (0) | 0 | 0 | (0) | 0 | 64 | (0) | 4 |
| Zamora R | 2003 | 6 | (10) | 0 | 0 | (1) | 0 | 1 | (0) | 1 | 0 | (0) | 0 | 0 | (0) | 0 | 7 | (11) | 1 |
| Ziege C | 01–03 | 44 | (3) | 7 | 3 | (0) | 2 | 5 | (0) | 1 | 0 | (0) | 0 | 0 | (0) | 0 | 52 | (3) | 10 |
| Ziegler R | 04–06 | 12 | (12) | 1 | 5 | (0) | 0 | 4 | (0) | 0 | 1 | (1) | 0 | 0 | (0) | 0 | 22 | (13) | 1 |
| Zokora D | 06– | 51 | (8) | 0 | 6 | (0) | 0 | 5 | (1) | 0 | 19 | (0) | 0 | 0 | (0) | 0 | 81 | (9) | 0 |